Institutional Economics
Volume III

Schools of Thought in Economics

Series Editor: Mark Blaug
Emeritus Professor of the Economics of Education,
University of London and Consultant Professor of
Economics, University of Buckingham

For greater convenience, a cumulative index to all titles in this series will be published in a separate volume number 12.

Institutional Economics
Volume III

Edited by

Warren J. Samuels

Professor of Economics
Michigan State University

EDWARD ELGAR

Published by
Edward Elgar Publishing Limited
Gower House
Croft Road
Aldershot
Hants GU11 3HR
England

Gower Publishing Company
Old Post Road
Brookfield
Vermont 05036
USA

British Library Cataloguing in Publication Data

Institutional economics. — (Schools of
    thought in economics; 5).
    1. Institutional economics
    I. Samuels, Warren J. (Warren Joseph),
    1933– II. Series
    330.15′5

Library of Congress Cataloging-in-Publication Data

Institutional economics/edited by Warren J. Samuels.
    p. cm. — (Schools of thought in economics; 5)
    Includes indexes.
    1. Institutional economics. I. Samuels, Warren J., 1933–
II. Series.
HB99.5.I56   1988
330—dc19

ISBN 1 85278 069 X (vol. III)   88–16347
    1 85278 116 5 (3 volume set)   CIP
Printed and bound in Great Britain at
The Camelot Press Ltd, Southampton

Contents

Acknowledgements

The editor and publishers wish to thank the following who have kindly given permission for the use of copyright material.

Association for Evolutionary Economics for articles from the *Journal of Economic Issues*: Malcolm Rutherford (1981), 'Clarence Ayres and the Instrumental Theory of Value', 15 (3), September, pp. 657–73; Marc Tool (1977), 'A Social Value Theory in Neoinstitutional Economics', 11 (4), December, pp. 823–46; Thomas R. DeGregori (1977), 'Technology and Ceremonial Behavior: Aspects of Institutionalism', 11 (4), December, pp. 861–70; Thomas R. DeGregori (1980), 'Instrumental Criteria for Assessing Technology: An Affirmation by Way of a Reply', 14 (1), March pp. 219–225; Warren J. Samuels (1977), 'Technology *vis-a-vis* Institutions in the JEI: A Suggested Interpretation', 11 (4), December, pp. 871–95; Philip A. Klein (1974), 'Economics: Allocation or Valuation?', 8 (4), December, pp. 785–811; W. Paul Strassmann (1974), 'Technology: A Culture Trait, a Logical Category, or Virtue Itself?', 8 (4), December, pp. 671–87; Karl de Schweinitz Jr, (1974), 'Technology, Idealogy, and the State in Economic Development', 8 (4), December, pp. 841–58; Wendell Gordon (1983), 'Welfare Maxima in Economics', 17 (1), March, pp. 1–16; Seymour Melman (1975), 'The Impact of Economics on Technology', 9 (1), March, pp. 59–72; James H. Street (1967), 'The Latin American "Structuralists" and the Institutionalists: Convergence in Development Theory', 1 (1), June, pp. 44–62; James H. Street and Dilmus D. James (1982), 'Institutionalism, Structuralism, and Dependency in Latin America', 16 (3), September, pp. 673–89; Daniel R. Fusfeld (1977), 'The Development of Economic Institutions', 11 (4), December, pp. 743–84; Philip A. Klein (1977), 'An Institutionalist View of Development Economics', 11 (4), December, pp. 784–807; Wendell Gordon (1973), 'Institutionalized Consumption Patterns in Underdeveloped Countries', 7 (2), June, pp. 267–87; David Dale Martin (1974), 'Beyond Capitalism: A Role for Markets?', 8 (4), December, pp. 771–84; Andrew K. Dragun (1983), 'Externalities, Property Rights, and Power', 17 (3), September, pp. 667–80; Alan Randall (1978), 'Property Institutions and Economic Behavior', 12 (1), March, pp. 1–21; Don Kanel (1974), 'Property and Economic Power as Issues in Institutional Economics,' 8 (4), December, pp. 827–40.

Every effort has been made to trace all the copyright holders but if any have been inadvertently overlooked the publishers will be pleased to make the necessary arrangement at the first opportunity.

In addition the publishers wish to thank the Library of the London School of Economics and Political Science and the British Library Document Supply Centre for their assistance in obtaining these documents.

Introduction

Institutional economists attempt to comprehend the economy as a whole and as an evolutionary process. They conceive of the economy as comprising more than the market, to include the institutions which form the market and the power structure which both controls and emanates from institutions and which therefore also both forms and operates through the market. They also conceive of the economy as possessing meaning not only at a point in time, the context of the static allocation of resources, but as a process continually undergoing transformation both from without and, especially, from within; that is, as having attributes of both being and becoming. Institutional economists are thus interested in the factors and forces which govern the evolution of the economy as a whole. These factors and forces they often specify in terms reducible to the three facets of power, knowledge and psychology.

Institutional economists also comprehend the economy as comprising a valuational process which far transcends the market and its process of commodity pricing. They understand the valuational process bearing on, indeed governing, economic perform-ance to include the entire array of cultural complexes: political, sociological, religious, and so on, including of course the narrowly or technically economic. They see the total economic valuational process encompassing the on-going identification, juxta-position, conflict, clarification, and selection of values. Most fundamentally, these values pertain not, or not so much, to the pricing of goods and services, but to the determination of whose/which interests count in the formation and operations-enforcement of the working rules of law, morals and custom. It is these values which operate to help form the self-identities and private and social preferences of economic actors. It is these values which both govern and are governed by the institutional-power structure of society and economy. Institutional economists are also prone to identify the ultimate level of values as those pertaining to the dynamic life process of the species as a whole, although they often, not unexpectedly, differ as to what values are ensconced in that process.

Institutional economists thus see collective action as a principal mode of responding to and overcoming scarcity, or poverty. They emphasize the behaviour of individuals within the institutional arrangements of the larger society which help govern, for example, the range of individual discretion allocated to each actor. They also emphasize the methodologically collectivist nature of the market and of all other institutions which channel individual behaviour.

If the core of economic life to institutionalists is the legal–economic nexus, articles explorative of which are contained in the second volume of this three-volume collection, then most economists also stress the impact on individual and organized economic activity or two processes which they deem historically dominant in the Western economies and increasingly so in the less developed ones: the pecuniary mode of life and the process or logic of industrialization. They insist that the increasing pecuniary and industrial nature of economic life has transformed the entire life of mankind; that it is, in some sense more or less deterministic, the driving forces behind socio-economic change; and that it has been so in the developed economies and is becoming more so in the developing countries. Indeed, they often seem to be saying that development to no small extent in fact consists of the growth of the pecuniary and industrial logics of life.

Institutional economists, for all their emphasis, however, on the progressive, modernizing nature and impacts of the pecuniary and industrial logics of life, also often call attention to the limits of those two forces. The pecuniary is in fact, they aver, but one aspect of the total valuational process; and technology, while it is the major source of overcoming both scarcity and the problems generated by technology itself, continues to generate problems of a widespread, and perhaps increasingly serious, externality type.

The first group of articles, in this third volume of the three-volume collection on Institutional Economics, examines the complex issues of technology, industrialization and valuation. Most of the articles deal directly with the institutions-technology dichotomy so central to the Veblenian tradition within institutionalism. Two articles, those by Malcolm Rutherford and Marc Tool, treat the larger aspects of the theory of value so manifest in institutional economics. These also recognize that there are considerations which go beyond the institutions-technology dichotomy. That dichotomy is specifically explored in the articles by Thomas DeGregori, Paul Strassmann and Warren Samuels. In another article, DeGregori examines deep questions concerning technology assessment. Seymour Melman, in his article, takes issue with the idea that technology encompasses or constitutes an imperative force, insisting that technology actually comprises an array of alternatives from which choices are made on the basis of other, power-weighted considerations. The articles by Philip Klein and Wendell Gordon explore aspects of allocation usually treated by neoclassical economics but here within an institutionalist rubric. The article by Karl de Schweinitz expands the discussion of technology to include considerations of ideology and the state. Considered together, these ten articles illustrate the centrality and subtleties of the institutions-technology dichotomy.

A great deal of institutionalist work has been done in such fields as labour economics, industrial organization, law and economics, comparative economic systems, public choice, agricultural economics, macroeconomics, and, *inter alia*, public utility regulation. Still another field has been chosen to exemplify institutionalist work: economic development. The second group of four articles is representative of an enormous literature in the institutionalist tradition which brings the insights and models of the school to bear on the terribly important problem of development. Not surprisingly, given the general emphasis by institutionalists on the problem of organization and control and thereby the structure of power, two of the articles, by James Street and by Street and Dilmus James, explore the structural facet of development. Two other articles, by Daniel Fusfeld and Philip Klein, treat both structural and other dimensions of the subject.

The two traditions comprising institutional economics have, as has been seen, somewhat different attitudes towards institutions: the Veblen tradition denigrates them, at least insofar as they represent efforts to reproduce invidious and hierarchical power structures, through their juxtaposition to the (generally) progressive force of technology; whereas the Commons tradition treats them as an important determinant of economic performance, only afterward, as it were, introducing normative distinctions. But that difference notwithstanding, the research by institutional economists tends to be focused on the origins, development, operation and performance consequences of specific institutions or specific institutional complexes. Many of these studies have dealt with legal institutions, for example, various aspects of the institution of private property, and with the institutions, including the legal, involved in economic development.

Three of the articles in the final group in this volume deal with the institution of property – and intimately relate to the materials on the economic role of government in the second volume of this collection. Don Kanel examines the general relation of property and economic power. Alan Randall examines the relation of property institutions to economic behaviour. And Andrew Dragun presents a summary of the institutionalist application of welfare economics to the subject of externalities, in terms of property rights and power. In addition, in an article which clearly could have been included in the preceding group on economic development, Wendell Gordon examines the nature and significance of institutionalized consumption patterns in the less developed countries; in effect reminding us that, according to the institutionalists, consumer demand even in the developed countries is profoundly influenced by institutionalized consumption forces. And David Dale Martin, reminding us that the central institution of economic study is the market, examines, in an analysis which necessarily is simultaneously both positive and normative, the prospective role of markets 'beyond capitalism'.

The three groups of articles in this volume are indicative of all the articles in this three-volume collection, especially in their demonstration of the vitality and on-going research tradition of institutional economics as an important component of both heterodox economics and of the larger discipline of economics properly and fully understood.

Warren J. Samuels

Part I
Technology, Industrialization and Valuation

[1]

Jei JOURNAL OF ECONOMIC ISSUES
Vol. XV No. 3 September 1981

Clarence Ayres and the
Instrumental Theory of Value

Malcolm Rutherford

Having rejected the individualism usually associated with orthodox economics, institutionalists have always faced a problem in finding some alternative criterion of value, and one consistent with their reformist leanings. A variety of value theories can be found in the institutionalist literature, but the one of most interest involves the use of an instrumentalist philosophy, based on the work of John Dewey, combined with a study of the nature of the evolutionary process. Examples of this approach can be found in the work of W. H. Hamilton [1953] and John R. Commons [1932], but it is in the writings of C. E. Ayres that it is most fully developed. Ayres, however, was not simply a Deweyan but significantly extended and modified Dewey's ideas [Breit and Culbertson 1976, p. 14]. Ayres's version of instrumentalism has had a considerable influence on the current generation of institutionalist writers and appears to have become closely associated with the term "neo-institutionalism" [Junker 1968; Tool 1977]. The purpose of this article is to outline the Ayresian approach to questions of social value and evaluate its strengths and weaknesses. In addition, it will be argued that the least satisfactory aspects of Ayres's views are to be found in precisely those areas where he departed from Dewey's lead.

The author is Assistant Professor of Economics, University of Victoria, British Columbia, Canada. He is indebted to several referees for helpful criticisms of earlier drafts.

657

Ayres's Instrumentalism

The key to a thorough understanding of Ayres's value theory involves coming to terms with his instrumentalism. For Ayres, values are not to be thought of as "ultimate" ends. Following Dewey, he rejects the traditional dichotomy between means and ends and bases his theory of value on the continuity of human experience: "Day to day experience reveals no generic difference between 'ends' and 'means.' Every . . . item of our experience is both an end and a means. There is no difference of 'substance' or 'essence' by which, in the continuum of day to day experience, 'means' and 'ends' can be distinguished" [Ayres 1949a, p. 19].

Values have significance only in terms of this continuum of experience. Indeed, Ayres goes so far as to argue that "value" is "a synonym for continuity" [Ayres 1962, p. 221]; the continuity in human affairs is to be found in what he calls the "life process," conceived of in cultural terms as the "continuous, developmental process from which all the achievements of mankind have flowed" [Ayres 1949a, p. 19], that is, man's progression from prehistory to the present "industrial way of life." Ayres's instrumentalism is not directed toward obtaining "immediate, and perhaps temporary, operational success" but toward "our continued—perhaps indefinitely continued—operation" [Ayres 1952, p. 310].

In determining "whether anything is good or bad, or whether any act is right or wrong," what is being sought is "clear and certain knowledge of its causal bearing on the life process of mankind" [Ayres 1961, p. 122]. Questions of value, therefore, are not essentially different from "the mechanic's choice of the right tool" [Ayres 1962, p. 219], and, as everyone "knows what *better* and *worse* mean with reference to tools" [Ayres 1961, p. 8], values can be established in an objective manner provided the requisite scientific knowledge is available.

In order to apply this value theory, the nature of the "life process" must be known. Ayres, consistent in his instrumentalism, argues that the life process itself is instrumental; a process of "doing and knowing" which is continuous, cumulative, and developmental [Ayres 1961, p. 111]. The foundation of this process is the use of tools. Knowing is a function of doing; the use of tools is a process "which imposes the necessity for knowing something of materials and their properties" and involves the development of skills [Ayres 1961, pp. 105, 111]. Ayres extends this line of thought to the claim that "all that man has done and thought and felt has been achieved by the use of tools. The continuity of civilization is the continuity of tools. All the arts, all the sciences, and the whole elaboration of organized activity . . . together owe their existence and derive their substance from the continuity which links the surrealist's pigments to the clays with which the Aurignacian caves were daubed, and in terms of which the cyclotron is but a continuation of Neanderthal experiments in chipping flint" [Ayres 1962, p. 222].

Attention should be given to the cultural nature of this process. It is cumulative and developmental because of the objective existence of tools and the fact that skill and knowledge do not perish with individuals but become embedded in culture. This allows for the accumulation of tools, skills, and knowledge, but accumlation is not the "major premise" to development. Innovation and the developmental nature of the process rest on the combining of previously existing tools, knowledge, or culture traits in new ways. As the number of tools or devices grows, so the number of potential combinations increases. "Technology" is therefore "inherently progressive" and contains a tendency to accelerating advance inherent in the nature of tools and independent of individual genius [Ayres 1962, pp. 112–17; 1961, pp. 111–12].

Despite the emphasis on "machines" to be found in some of Ayres's work [1953; 1962, p. 223], it is vital to understand that the instrumental process or, as Ayres calls it, the "technological continuum," contains much more than "mere gadgets." It is the source of all true human achievement. "All creative intelligence, all systematic inquiry—the good and the beautiful, no less than the true—derive from it" [Ayres 1949a, p. 19]. Perhaps the most important aspect of the technological continuum is its connection with the growth of factual knowledge and rationalism. For Ayres, what is "true" is what is based on such factual knowledge, and all "true" achievements thus depend on and are contained within the technological continuum.

Questions of value, as noted above, are instrumental in nature. What is valuable is what aids or continues the technical process. True values are those based on knowledge of their beneficial consequences for the technical continuum [Ayres 1961, p. 113]; since such knowledge is itself a function of the technical process, the technical continuum is the locus of all true values [Ayres 1962, pp. 220–21].

Ayres applies these arguments to every community, and on that basis he claims to have found in the technological continuum a criterion of value that is transcultural, the "same for all ages, all peoples, and all cultures" [Ayres 1957, p. 125]. True values are not a matter of individual taste or institutional conditioning, but a matter of demonstrable efficiency in the maintenance and promotion of the technical continuum and the life process. In terms of economics, Ayres argues as follows: "Throughout the ages every community has owed its existence to its heritage of tools and apparatus. . . . It is by carrying on this instrumentally organized activity that every community—and each separate individual—'makes a living.' Whatever contributes to carrying on this activity is economically valuable, and whatever arrests or even hinders this activity is therefore economically deleterious" [Ayres 1962, pp. 222–23]. He goes on to maintain that every economic choice "involves a judgment as to which of the alternatives presented will in fact contribute most to the continued efficient working of the technological system upon which all life depends" [Ayres 1962, p. 223].

The difficulty that comes to the fore here is that if all human activity is of the instrumental nature outlined above, then, except to the extent that knowledge is incomplete, questions of value could hardly be in dispute. Ayres's point, however, is that the instrumental or technological process is not the whole of culture. Culture also contains what Ayres calls "ceremonialism," which consists of myths, mores, arbitrary distinctions of status and rank, and conventional rules. Ayres suggests that the ceremonial aspects of culture arise from a search for operational success in the absence of knowledge of "true" cause and effect relationships. The " 'ceremonial adequacy' of mores and mystic rites is always thought to be attested by actual physical consequences"; the difference between technological and ceremonial functions is that the latter "rests on a foundation of falsehood" [Ayres 1961, pp. 124–26]. This would not be much of a difficulty except that such ceremonialism becomes deeply embedded in the institutional structure of society and may resist the instrumental promptings of the technological continuum. This is not to say that institutions, as usually understood, exist neatly separated from technology [Ayres 1961, pp. 76–77]. Ayres is not always consistent in his use of the term *institution*, but his most common usage is to denote "segments of social behaviour predominantly ceremonial in character" [Ayres 1962, p. 184]. Organizational forms that are predominantly instrumental are, therefore, not to be classed as institutions [Ayres 1966b, p. 8].

Institutions, thus defined, tend to be backward-looking and inhibitory of change. The ceremonial system may carry values with it, but these are false. Institutions do change, but only slowly and in response to the dynamism of the technical continuum [Ayres 1962, pp. 186–87]. Thus, the life process can be hindered or endangered by ceremonial forces, but only continued or enhanced by instrumental ones. The problem of value is to identify, distinguish, and disentangle true values from false.

True Values

Ayres is not always easy to interpret, but his position appears to be that human life and history consist of a developmental sequence that rests upon the cumulative growth of ability and technique. Value can properly be found only within and through this process, and hence the technological continuum becomes both the criterion and locus of value.

Ayres has sometimes been accused of placing machines above people, but he went to considerable lengths to combat such views, arguing that technology is "*not* something to be considered *instead of* the values of human life and personality," and that the technological continuum "does in fact contain and embody the judgment of all mankind and of all ages as to what is most valuable in life and what makes life worth while" [Ayres 1945, p. 939].

Ayres takes this line of argument farthest in *Toward a Reasonable Society*, in which he attempts to show that freedom, equality, security, abundance, excellence, and democracy are all true values contained in and implied by the technological process. Despite some contrary statements, Ayres does not intend these values to be taken as ultimates or ends in themselves, nor does he mean that they are valuable only because they are products of the technological continuum [Ayres 1961, p. 246, compare p. 196]. His point is that the technological process and such values as freedom, equality, and the rest, are quite inseparable. True values have instrumental significance; they are a part of and necessary for technological and instrumental progress. If, for example, democracy were not an effective tool, it would be a "sad mistake," a false rather than a true value [Ayres 1961, pp. 8–9, 171, 225–27; 1943b, p. 480].

Freedom

Ayres finds the usual definition of *freedom*—the absence of coercion—mired in "metaphysical individualism." While he sees the doctrines of natural rights and individualism as the outcome of the growth of industrial society and the need to provide an alternative to the doctrinal underpinnings of the feudal system, he argues that such a conception of freedom is not adequate for modern purposes. For Ayres, "there is no such thing as an individual"; individuality is a social product, and the principle of freedom cannot therefore be based on the ultimacy of the individual [Ayres 1961, pp. 171–75].

Freedom is the result of the technological process and is "virtually synonymous with the fullness of life as it has been realized by industrial society" [Ayres 1961, p. 177]. Freedom of choice is equated with the range of actual or potential alternatives; freedom of movement and communication is linked to the existing means of transport and communication; freedom from ignorance is a product of technical and scientific progress, as is freedom from want. In this way the extension of freedoms is presented as a result of the technical process [Ayres 1961, pp. 177–84].

Ayres comes closer to an orthodox position in his instrumental justification of freedom of thought and inquiry. He points out that such freedom is required for scientific and technical advance, and he agrees with J. S. Mill's views that dissident opinion should not be suppressed in case the dissident is correct. Yet he disagrees with Mill's argument that dissident opinion should be tolerated even if it is known to be incorrect. Ayres deems this "intellectual nonsense" because "it is enough that freedom is the condition *sine qua non* of intellectual, scientific, and technological development" [Ayres 1961, pp. 183–84].

Equality

Equality is "the absence of artificial and arbitrary barriers." Inequality, therefore, is discrimination on grounds that are not concerned with instrumental efficiency. Building on his distinction between the ceremonial and the instrumental aspects of culture, Ayres can easily locate those forces leading to greater equality in the instrumental/technological continuum, while inequality is seen as a result of the power of tradition, superstition, and myth. As technical advance occurs in conjunction with the growth of scientific and technical competence, which is in opposition to notions of "mythical group differences," technical progress tends to lead to a lessening of arbitrary inequality. Technical progress also requires that decisions be made on the basis of instrumental considerations of efficiency. Choices made on ceremonial grounds will not aid the technological process [Ayres 1961, pp. 187–206].

Security

Ayres's treatment of security begins with a critique of the view that some myths are necessary to provide emotional security, social cohesion, and direction. Security based on myth is imaginary, while actual security comes from the use of tools and efficient organization [Ayres 1961, pp. 208–10]. Ayres directs particular attention to security from disease, famine, poverty, and war.

The connection between scientific knowledge and medical progress is obvious, as is the link between agricultural knowledge and technique and reduced potential for famine. On poverty, Ayres argues that the industrial wage system tends to lead to financial insecurities, but it also leads to the development of social security and redistributional schemes. Technological advance increases productivity and output and comes to require, as an instrumental necessity, a large volume of aggregate purchasing power. "The wage system fails to keep pace with burgeoning production," and social security systems are the result. Ayres championed the use of a guaranteed income plan for exactly this reason: "The citizens of industrial society must consume more abundantly ... because if they do not industrial society will collapse" [Ayres 1943b, p. 480].

Ayres's arguments on war are particularly interesting. He does not deny that modern technology has resulted in weapons that could destroy civilization and most of its works, but he maintains that history shows that "no great civilization has ever disappeared," and that such an event is therefore unlikely [Ayres 1961, p. 214]. According to Ayres, the hazards of war are not clearly greater now than before: "It is at least an open question whether the total amount of suffering inflicted by earlier wars— say the Thirty Years War or the American Civil War—was not considerably greater for the areas affected than that of World War II" [Ayres 1961, p. 214]. True to his principles, Ayres takes the view that knowledge of atomic fission is a good thing, despite its use in war, for the same reason that the invention of the "stone ax was a good thing notwithstanding its use also as a weapon" [Ayres 1966a, p. 88].

Ayres also relates warfare to the ceremonial aspects of civilization. He uses this basis to argue that, with the growth of rationalism and the expanding scale of organization, the sentiments of "tribal separatism" underlying international conflict will decline [Ayres 1961, pp. 213–19].

Abundance

Technical advance is capable of producing abundance in the sense of "a substantial degree of comfort to all members of the community" [Ayres 1961, p. 229]. According to Ayres, the barriers to achieving it are institutional, not natural or technical. The market institution means that production ceases when it is no longer profitable, and "overproduction" can result in crises. Rather than rationally reorganizing economic institutions, resort has been made to international dumping of surplus output, colonial control of markets, wasteful military expenditures, and other types of "systematic ceremonial waste." In Ayres's view, economic growth depends on technical progress and not on economizing or on abstinence or saving. He suggests not only that it is possible to have high levels of con-

664   Malcolm Rutherford

sumption together with high rates of growth, but also that high rates of growth depend on high levels of consumption [Ayres 1961, pp. 229–39].

This argument links abundance with the issue of security dealt with above, but Ayres also links abundance to freedom and equality. Abundance leads to equality, for example, when all members of a community have gained access to certain goods their possession can no longer be used as a mark of distinction. Since Ayres defines freedom partly in terms of the available goods and services, abundance also leads to greater freedom [Ayres 1961, pp. 240–41].

Excellence

Ayres asks whether industrial society has "sacrificed quality for quantity." His answer is that each development in arts and crafts has occurred "solely because it represented an improvement on what was being done before." Anything that "earlier people ever did can be done much better and more easily today," and much more can be done besides. Some criticisms of the quality of modern life Ayres classifies as "tribal fictions," resting on standards of taste based on the past, a kind of "ancestor worship" [Ayres 1961, pp. 247–52]. He does recognize that modern techniques and materials have sometimes been used inappropriately, but such "absurdities" are the result of attempts to imitate styles from the days of handicrafts. Some skills may no longer be in use, but technological advance has not brought about a reduction in skill, only new and different skills. Pride in one's work is just as possible now as before [Ayres 1961, pp. 248–52].

Mass production and mass communication are not only compatible with excellence but also help to promote it. Advances in arts, crafts, and knowledge are inseparable from the technological process. With mass production and mass communication, access to works of merit is increased, and appreciation is no longer confined to an elite. Mass communication contains great educational potential and "unquestionably constitutes a powerful stimulus to the highest achievement." The cultural conformity stemming from mass communication Ayres does not see as a problem. Local dialects and customs may die, but if this is bad, then the "whole course of modern civilization has been bad" [Ayres 1961, pp. 255–56].

Democracy

Democracy is an "operational concept" that stands for "the procedure by which alone all the other values can be achieved" [Ayres 1961, p. 282]. Democracy is not "merely" majority rule; its "essence" is the "process by which majorities are formed." Ayres regards this process as one involving the freedom from prejudice and ignorance resulting from "industrial-scientific culture." Democratic self-government is "a possibility only because it is possible for large numbers of people—in effect, whole communities—to arrive at common conclusions" [Ayres 1961, pp. 282–83]. Ayres does allow that confusion may exist as conditions change, and it is temporarily unclear "in what direction operational efficiency lies" [Ayres 1961, pp. 284–85], but "in all such cases the democratic process is a process of learning the truth and operating accordingly, and the unanimity towards which the process aims is that of the universality of science and technology" [Ayres 1961, p. 285].

The Unity of Value

Ayres's attempt to demonstrate the indissoluble nature of the links between freedom, equality, security, abundance, excellence, democracy, and technological process is prefaced and concluded with an exposition of what he calls the "unity of value." All true values increase together; there are not genuine conflicts.

Freedom is a necessary condition to the attainment of abundance, and abundance is a necessary condition to the attainment of freedom. Freedom is possible only among equals, and equality is possible only when men are free from arbitrary social distinctions. These values are attainable only when men have achieved a measure of security; and real security is possible only when men have achieved a measure of abundance. . . . But it is also possible only for those who enjoy freedom among equals; for any other condition implies a threat of insecurity. . . . Only free men can know excellence, and only affluent societies can afford to indulge in such pursuits. But only through excellence can societies become affluent. Such is the industrial way of life. It is a way of life to which modern man has dedicated himself because it is the epitome of the real values that take their meaning from the life process of mankind [Ayres 1961, pp. 293–94].

A Critique

Ayres's value theory pervades all his work. His support of measures to increase consumer demand, particularly guaranteed income schemes; his criticism of orthodox value theory with its assumption that consumption is the "end" of economic activity; his theory of economic growth, which emphasizes the role of technical change; and his attacks on vested interests and the "power system" of Western society [Ayres 1952; 1962, pp. 3–85] are all firmly linked to his theory of value. A recent comment to the effect that Ayres's value theory is disjointed and incoherent [Walker 1979, p. 533] indicates a neglect of the instrumentalist premise that is consistently applied throughout. Nevertheless, Ayres's views are open to criticism on a number of grounds.

Ayres's view of the process of technical change, his categorization of markets and private property as ceremonial, his tendency to ignore problems of the allocation of resources among competing uses, the difficulties of clearly distinguishing the instrumental from the ceremonial, and his deemphasis of the individual have all formed the basis of critiques of Ayres's work. These points are important, but as they have been discussed at length elsewhere [Coats 1976; Knight 1935b; Lerner 1945; Miller 1944; Samuels 1977a; Walker 1979, 1980; Wolfe 1944], they will not be dealt with here except as they touch on the fundamentals of Ayres's instrumentalism.

The foundation of Ayres's approach consists of two propositions: All true human achievements and values stem from or are part of an instrumental tool-using process, and all true values can be objectively defined by scientific investigation. On the first point, Ayres claims a secure scientific foundation and tends to dismiss opposition as ceremonialism. Of course, it is impossible to deny that some degree of technical ability (including language skills) was necessary to distinguish man from other animals, or that scientific and technical advances have brought benefits to mankind and weakened traditional beliefs. But to admit as much does not imply either that the continued accumulation of instruments is necessarily desirable or that all human progress, achievements, and values are instrumental in nature.

The first question concerns the possible adverse consequence of technical change and development. Ayres does admit that, in a given cultural setting, technical change may be a mixed blessing [Ayres 1961, pp. 169, 227], and that no amount of historical illustration can guarantee that man will not destroy himself with the tools he has developed [Ayres 1961, p. 214]. Against this he argues that the advance of the technological continuum brings with it the growth of science and a more rational approach to human affairs, which tends to preclude destructive acts. In other words, the tool-using process generates a rational habit of mind that can have a pervasive cultural effect. It is for this reason that Ayres displays a relative lack of concern for the uses to which instruments are put. The growth of technology is closely linked to the growth of a scientific rationality, based on a full realization of consequences, and to the decline of ceremonial, nonrational, or emotional forces. This is a highly optimistic argument, and it depends on the existence of a strong and dependable connection between technological advance and habits of mind, an idea reminiscent of Thorstein Veblen's work on the "cultural incidence of the machine process" [Veblen 1904].

It is worth comparing Ayres with Dewey on this point. Dewey seems less deterministic and more concerned about possible adverse consequences from technical advance: "We know that the earlier optimism which thought that the advance of natural science was to dispel superstition, ignorance, and oppression, by placing reason on the throne, was unjustified. Some superstitutions have given way, but the mechanical devices due to science have made it possible to spread new kinds of error and delusion among a larger multitude. . . . In truth science is impersonal; a method and a body of knowledge. It owes its operation and its consequences to the human beings who use it" [Dewey 1931, p. 319].

In other words, Dewey is aware that a *choice* must be made to apply scientific and technical abilities in a way that enhances human life rather than the opposite, while Ayres frequently seems to suggest that, given technical advance, the rest will tend to follow. This element of optimistic determinism is very evident in the links Ayres makes between economic and technical advance and greater freedom, equality, security, excellence, abundance, and democracy. But if the deterministic element is dropped, and if the use of instruments for human benefit is seen as depending on the exercise of a will to do so independent of the process of instrumental advance itself, then it is not clear how the technological continuum can still be regarded as the only source, basis, or locus of human progress. Rather, the technical continuum becomes value neutral and takes on value only when directed in ways that add to the life experience, that is, when instruments are directed to achieving purposes with some prior value attached to them.

Criticism can also be directed at Ayres's version of the instrumental view of scientific knowledge, the idea that knowing is a function of doing and that tool-using activities bring about "the acquisition of clear and certain knowledge along with technical skills or as an aspect of those skills" [Ayres 1961, pp. 92–93]. In other words, science is the "thinking part of the tool using process" [Ayres 1973, p. vi]. This implies that operational success is the criterion of "truth," and that it is the search for such success that gives rise to scientific theorizing. Against this idea it can be argued that science stems from the attempt to understand the world and may be promoted as much by idle curiosity as by a search for instrumentalities. At times, Ayres puts considerable emphasis on the *source* of scientific knowledge in the technical continuum, but what is important is testability (there is no authoritative source). If we are interested in truth or falsity, testing must consist of more than the search for operational success. Instrumentalism cannot account for the scientist's interest in the critical testing of theories or for scientific progress, as "it is only in searching for refutations that science can hope to learn and advance" [Popper 1968, p. 113]. Practical application can only indicate what does or does not work under certain conditions, not what is false. If scientific progress is seen as the gradual elimination of falsity, then instrumentalism is inadequate for the task.

In doubt is not only the connection between tool-using activity and science, but also the connection between the technical continuum and artistic achievement. Ayres argues that artistic development is similar to technical development: The "art (or technique) of using symbols to evoke emotion . . . is in a continuous process of development" on the basis of the combination and recombination of tools, just as with any other technology [Ayres 1961, pp. 149–51]. However, it is hard to believe that art is such a purely technical affair and that individual creative genius does not play a role far in excess of that which Ayres is willing to allow. There is, in addition, a problem in applying an instrumental criterion to aesthetic judgment. The function of art is to "evoke emotion," a personal and subjective matter, and in this sense it is quite different from the process of appraising the relative efficiency of tractors. Ayres's response is to argue that among those with knowledge of the art in question there is much agreement over aesthetic matters, and he dismisses criticism of the notion of "progress" in art as "ancestor worship" [Ayres 1961, pp. 152–53]. This idea of objectivity as the consensus of informed individuals will be dealt with below.

On the instrumental nature of true values, similar difficulties arise. Ayres asserts that true values are part and parcel of the search for operational success: those that arise from and forward the technological continuum. Of course, if the instrumental nature of scientific or artistic achievement is doubted, or if it is agreed that technological development may impose social costs, the technological continuum, or the "maximal growth of technology" [Ayres 1949a, p. 19], may not be a sensible guide to what will enhance the life process. Moreover, even if Ayres's arguments on these points are granted, it is not obvious why values may not arise from sources other than the instrumental, or why what is important to the life process should not legitimately be thought of as consisting of things other than continued instrumental advance.

Ayres clearly regards true values as in some sense "objective," and his position has similarities with Dewey's: To say that something is desirable means that it has been so judged after an "impartial review of the relevant facts" [Rachels 1977, p. 158]. However, Ayres seems to go beyond the Deweyan stance. Dewey argues simply that value judgments should be informed, a quite unobjectionable position. Ayres, in contrast, emphasizes the unanimity imposed by science; true values are good because they have demonstrable functional significance in terms of the life process, and to endorse other values is to fall into ceremonialism. Ayres's treatment of democracy as a process of generating unanimity on the basis of a rational assessment, the absence of any treatment of conflicts either between or over true values, and his lengthy analogy between value judgments and the mechanic's choice of a tool, are all based on the idea that science can determine the nature of the life process and provide "clear and certain knowledge" of the instrumentally best set of actions or principles. In this there is "no room" for differences in taste [Ayres 1962, pp. 212–19; 1961, p. 122].

It could be argued that it should not be *assumed* that differences of opinion are not amenable to rational discussion and investigation, but Ayres does not demonstrate that differences in outlook are necessarily due only to prejudice, dogma, or a lack of rationality or information. To sustain the Ayresian position, one would have to argue that science can be conclusive in matters of value judgment. While emotionalism and dogma most certainly do become involved in debates about desirability, it is not clear that calm rationality and scientific appraisal would lead to agreement unless a consensus had already been reached on what weight or interpretation to give certain facts; in other words, on values.

Ayres is attempting to demonstrate through science what ought to be valued, an example of the naturalistic fallacy that statements of obligation can be derived from statements of fact. Ayres's work is based on the necessarily metaphysical premise that the continued growth of human abilities is the central "true" value. This premise may be thought reasonable or unreasonable, but in either case it is not entirely a matter of science or of fact. It may be that many people would agree with Ayres, but it is equally possible that many would not. There is a role for science in debates over values; it can elucidate consequences and prevent disagreements that arise from misinformation or ignorance; but there is no basis in science or fact for claiming that certain values are true or false, or that all fully rational and informed individuals will tend to value the same things. Yet, without the idea that science is capable of making the "truth" of certain values manifest and of fostering agreement among reasonable men, Ayres's value theory loses its claimed objectivity.

It must be said that Ayres is much less a pluralist than Dewey. Although Dewey also stresses the continuity of human experience, the importance of science and investigation, and democracy as a process of creating a value consensus, he also pays explicit attention to the need for "amicable co-operation," toleration, and respect for those with opposing views [Gouinlock 1972, pp. 206–32, 348–55]. Dewey is concerned that, as far as possible, value judgments be made on the basis of full information about consequences and discussions of differences in outlook, that is, with a rational *approach* to the making of value judgments. He goes less far than Ayres toward the idea that scientific investigation can itself be decisive. Other institutionalists, too, are closer to Dewey than to Ayres. Commons certainly believes that scientific knowledge is important in the resolution of conflict, but he does not brand certain values or interests as "false" or only ceremonial in character. Commons emphasizes the creation of consensus in the light of the best information, but this also involves bargaining, accommodation of opposing views, and "reasonable adjustment" to a "workable mutuality" [Commons 1925; 1932; 1935]. Commons's use of the term *reasonable* includes moderation and accommodation, while Ayres's "reasonable society" is based on scientific rationality and the unanimity implied by the "universality of science."

The weaknesses in Ayres's position stem largely, although not entirely, from the modifications he made to Dewey. Yet, despite these weaknesses, there is much in Ayres which is valuable. His emphasis on the importance of instrumental advance is a useful counterweight to those who see no good in modern technical achievements, but Ayres's optimism needs to be tempered by an understanding that technical or instrumental progress is not, by itself, a sufficient condition for the betterment of life. Also, if we ignore the overstatements in his position, we are left with a very Deweyan message: Values should not be thought of as entirely beyond rational discussion. To say that something is good is not to state a personal belief beyond all criticism or investigation. This is not an unimportant point. As Frank Knight has put it: "There are no rules for judging values, and it is the worst of errors to attempt to make rules—beyond the rule to 'use good judgement'; but it is also most false to assert that one opinion is as good as another, that *de gustibus non disputandum est*" [Knight 1935a, p. 40]. Ayres, at least, attempts to justify his views on the basis of what he thinks is important for continued human achievement. He forcefully reminds us not to be content with conventional wisdom and to pursue, wherever possible, a reasoned approach to human affairs.

References

Ayres, Clarence E. 1917–1918. "The New Era of Fruitfulness in Ethical Thinking." *International Journal of Ethics* 28 (April): 373–92.

_____. 1934. "Values: Ethical and Economic." *International Journal of Ethics* 45 (July3: 452–54.

_____. 1935a. "Moral Confusion in Economics." *International Journal of Ethics* 45 (January): 170–99.

_____. 1935b. "Confusion Thrice Confounded." *International Journal of Ethics* 45 (April): 356–58.

_____. 1942. "Economic Value and Scientific Synthesis." *American Journal of Economics and Sociology* 1 (July): 341–60.

_____. 1943a. "The Path of Progress." *Southwest Review* 28 (Spring): 229–44.

_____. 1943b. "The Significance of Economic Planning." In *Development of Collective Enterprise*, edited by Seba Eldridge et al. Lawrence, Kansas: University of Kansas Press.

_____. 1943c. "Technology and Progress." *Antioch Review* 3 (Spring): 6–20.

_____. 1945. "Addendum to *The Theory of Economic Progress*." *American Economic Review* 35 (December): 937–40.

_____. 1949a. "Instrumental Economics." *New Republic* 121 (October): 18–20.

_____. 1949b. "The Value Economy." In *Value: A Co-operative Inquiry*, edited by Ray Lepley. New York: Columbia University Press.

_____. 1950. "The Values of Social Scientists." *Journal of Social Issues* 6, no. 4: 17–20.

_____. 1951. "The Co-ordinates of Institutionalism." *American Economic Review* 41 (May): 47–55.

_____. 1952. *The Industrial Economy*. Boston: Houghton Mifflin.

_____. 1953. "The Role of Technology in Economic Theory." *American Economic Review* 43 (May): 279–87.

_____. 1957. "The Pestilence of Moral Agnosticism." *Southwest Review* 42 (Spring): 116–25.

_____. 1959. "Excellence in an Industrial Society." *Southwest Review* 44 (Spring): 139–49.

_____. 1961. *Toward a Reasonable Society*. Austin: University of Texas Press.

_____. 1962. *The Theory of Economic Progress*. 2d ed. New York: Schocken.

_____. 1966a. "The Nature and Significance of Institutionalism." *Antioch Review* 26 (Spring): 70–90.

_____. 1966b. "The Theory of Institutional Adjustment." *Texas Quarterly* 9 (Spring): 125–36.

_____. 1967. "Ideological Responsibility." *Journal of Economic Issues* 1 (June): 3–11.

_____. 1970. "Beyond the Market Economy: Building Institutions that Work." *Social Science Quarterly* 50 (March): 1053–57.

_____. 1973. "Prolegomenon to Institutionalism." Preface to *The False*

672   Malcolm Rutherford

Messiah and Holier Than Thou: The Way to the Righteous. New York: Augustus M. Kelley.

Breit, William. 1973. "The Development of Clarence Ayres's Theoretical Institutionalism." *Social Science Quarterly* 54 (September): 244–57.

Breit, William, and William Patton Culbertson Jr. 1976. "Clarence Edwin Ayres: An Intellectual's Portrait." In *Science and Ceremony: The Institutional Economics of C. E. Ayres,* edited by William Breit and William Patton Culbertson. Austin: University of Texas Press.

Coats, A. W. 1976. "Clarence Ayres's Place in the History of American Economics: An Interim Assessment." In *Science and Ceremony: The Institutional Economics of C. E. Ayres,* edited by William Breit and William Patton Culbertson. Austin: University of Texas Press.

Commons, J. R. 1925. "Law and Economics." *Yale Law Journal* 34 (February): 371–82.

————. 1932. "The Problem of Correlating Law, Economics and Ethics." *Wisconsin Law Review* 8 (December): 3–26.

————. 1935. "The Place of Economics in Social Philosophy." *Journal of Social Philosophy* 1 (October): 7–22.

Dewey, John. 1929. *The Quest for Certainty.* New York. Minton, Balch.

————. 1931. *Philosophy and Civilization.* New York: Minton, Balch.

Frankel, Charles. 1977. "John Dewey's Social Philosophy." In *New Studies in the Philosophy of John Dewey,* edited by Steven M. Cahn. Hanover, N.H.: University Press of New England.

Gouinlock, James. 1972. *John Dewey's Philosophy of Value.* New York: Humanities Press.

Hamilton, Walton H. 1953. "The Law, the Economy, and Moral Values." In *Goals of Economic Life,* edited by A. D. Ward. New York: Harper.

Homan, Paul T. 1963. "Review of *Toward a Reasonable Society.*" *American Economic Review* 53 (March): 147–51.

Junker, Louis J. 1968. "Theoretical Foundations of Neo-Institutionalism." *American Journal of Economics and Sociology* 27 (April): 197–213.

Kadish, Mortimer R. 1977. "John Dewey and the Theory of Aesthetic Practice." In *New Studies in the Philosophy of John Dewey,* edited by Steven M. Cahn. Hanover, N.H.: University Press of New England.

Knight, Frank H. 1935a. *The Ethics of Competition.* Chicago: University of Chicago Press.

————. 1935b. "Intellectual Confusion on Morals and Economics." *International Journal of Ethics* 45 (January): 200–20.

Lerner, Abba P. 1945. "Review of *The Theory of Economic Progress.*" *American Economic Review* 35 (March): 160–64.

Margolis, Joseph. 1977. "The Relevance of Dewey's Epistemology." In *New Studies in the Philosophy of John Dewey,* edited by Steven M. Cahn. Hanover, N.H.: University Press of New England.

Miller, D. L. 1944. "The Theory of Economic Progress." *Southwestern Social Science Quarterly* 25 (December): 1949–77.

Nagel, Ernest. 1961. *The Structure of Science.* London: Harcourt, Brace and World.

Popper, Karl C. 1968. *Conjectures and Refutations: The Growth of Scientific Knowledge.* New York: Harper and Row.

Rachels, James. 1977. "John Dewey and the Truth about Ethics." In *New Studies in the Philosophy of John Dewey,* edited by Steven M. Cahn. Hanover, N.H.: University Press of New England.

Samuels, Warren J. 1977a. "Technology *vis-à-vis* Institutions in the JEI." *Journal of Economic Issues* 11 (December): 871–74.

————. 1977b. "The Knight-Ayres Correspondence: The Grounds of Knowledge and Social Action." *Journal of Economic Issues* 11 (September): 485–524.

Seckler, David. 1980. "Individualism, Collectivism and the Latter-Day Institutionalists." *American Journal of Economics and Sociology* 39 (January): 105–106.

Tilman, Rick. 1974. "Value Theory, Planning, and Reform: Ayres as Incrementalist and Utopian." *Journal of Economic Issues* 8 (December): 689–706.

Tool, Marc R. 1977. "A Social Value Theory in Neoinstitutional Economics." *Journal of Economic Issues* 11 (December): 823–45.

————. 1979. *The Discretionary Economy.* Santa Monica: Goodyear Publishing.

Veblen, Thorstein. 1904. *The Theory of Business Enterprise.* New York: Charles Scribner's.

Walker, Donald A. 1979. "The Institutionalist Economic Theories of Clarence Ayres." *Economic Inquiry* 17 (October): 519–38.

————. 1980. "Clarence Ayres's Critique of Economic Theory." *Journal of Economic Issues* 14 (September): 649–80.

Wolfe, A. B. 1944. "Review of *The Theory of Economic Progress.*" *Political Science Quarterly* 59 (December): 622–24.

[2]

Jei *JOURNAL OF ECONOMIC ISSUES*
Vol. XI   No. 4   December 1977

A Social Value Theory in
Neoinstitutional Economics

Marc R. Tool

As the economics of allocation is gradually replaced or succeeded by the economics of valuation, to employ Philip Klein's useful distinction between neoclassical orthodoxy and neoinstitutional heterodoxy,[1] the necessity of formalizing and extending concepts of social value (criteria of choice) in neoinstitutional thought becomes more and more important. The shift from critique to reconstruction is mandated by the pressure of economic problems unresolved and by demands for relevant counsel.

Many, if not most, neoinstitutionalists recognize that there is no way to avoid value judgments in economic analysis. If inquiry is purposive, it is value laden. Purposive social inquiry is directed to problem solving. To perceive a problem is to distinguish between is and ought, to apply value theory. Value premises focus and direct inquiry; they define significance and relevance. Neoinstitutionalists are not, presumably, normally among those "in the unhappy position of seeming to believe that reason and evidence have persuasive roles in scientific inquiry but are somehow either absent, or radically different in their efficacy in evaluation. Since it is through evaluation that we determine what is important, it comes perilously close to saying of the important we have nothing important to say."[2]

They appear likely to agree with John H. Schaar that "a rigorous ad-

The author is Professor of Economics, California State University, Sacramento.

herence to the 'fact-value dichotomy' renders intelligence cautious just where it must be bold, dumb where it should be articulate."[3] They would probably concur with Joan Robinson that "to eliminate value judgments from the subject-matter of social science is to eliminate the subject itself,"[4] and with Kenneth Arrow that "a public or social value system is essentially a logical necessity."[5]

Reason and evidence—these must be the key. Neoinstitutionalists seek value theory that is a product of reasoned, logically credible inquiry into the evidences of human experience.

Most neoinstitutionalists evidently have long since refused to be impaled on either horn of the positive-normative dilemma, have recognized the sterility and inapplicability of ethical relativism, and have rejected the exclusivity and certitude of ethical absolutism. Most seem intellectually unwilling and unable to have recourse to the positivist and relativist utility value theory of capitalists,[6] to the normativist and absolutist "fulfill-the-historical-design" value theory of the Marxists, or to the differently formulated normativist and absolutist coercive power value theory of the fascists.

Gunnar Myrdal has for many years called for the inclusion and rational examination of value theory in social and economic analysis.[7] Robert Heilbroner and Ben Seligman,[8] among others, have called for the articulation of a neoinstitutional paradigm as an alternative to orthodoxy. Prominent in such a paradigm must be a theory of social value.[9]

But neoinstitutionalists must continue to move beyond the underbrush clearing, beyond the pointing to infirmities in orthodoxy, beyond the calling for new paradigms, to the formulation of integrated, coherent, and relevant statements of their own basic position. Many have been and are now, of course, engaged in that effort.[10] This compendium is also directed to that end.

The purpose of this article is to provide a synthetic and integrative identification of a neoinstitutional theory of social value. Specifically, the contributions of Thorstein Veblen, John Dewey, Clarence Ayres, and J. Fagg Foster are examined. While the views on social value of these men obviously do not include all contributions, they appear to constitute an intelligible core around which others have built and/or are now building. Some particulars will doubtless already be familiar; a synthesis perhaps not yet so.

Thorstein Veblen

Nowhere, ironically, in the writings of Veblen will one find an explicitly formulated theory of social value. Indeed, in his failure to address directly the initiation of institutions as an act of choice and thus confront the problem of criteria of choice, Veblen seems actually to have been blocked by the value problem as such. There are repeated disclaimers of an interest in evaluation.

About tastes, we are told, "there is no disputing."[11] "In making use of the term 'invidious,' it may perhaps be unnecessary to remark, that there is no intention to extol or deprecate, or to commend or deplore any of the phenomena which the word is used to characterize."[12] In the discussion of the institution of the leisure class, we are informed that " 'right' and 'wrong' are of course here used without conveying any reflection as to what ought or ought not to be."[13]

Whether or not Veblen expected these comments to be taken literally or seriously is interesting but of no consequence here. What is obvious is that Veblen, despite his blockage, was extensively and consistently engaged in evaluation. He was applying value theory in distinguishing between institutions which exhibit "compatibility or incompatibility with the effective evolutionary process."[14] He distinguishes between institutions which are "imbecile" and those which are not—hardly a morally colorless term.[15] In point of fact, as is well known, much if not most of his scholarly work was directed to a fundamental critique of prevailing social customs and business practices and the theory that gave each its credibility. Veblen's inquiry is purposive; it is value laden. His value theory can be identified.

Veblen's main contributions to a theory of social value are found primarily in his theory of instincts and in the familiar fundamental Veblenian distinction or dichotomy. Let us consider each briefly.

Observing the fact of social change from his anthropological reading, Veblen, as did Karl Marx before him, sought inclusive and continuously applicable theory to explain that change. The evolutionary development of institutional forms appeared to him to parallel the Darwinian account of the evolutionary development of life forms. Veblen sought to identify those modes of thought and behavior which promote or provide for the continuity of culture and those that tend to impair or obstruct developmental cultural continuity. These supportive and inhibitive modes of thought and behavior are for Veblen reflective of "innate and persistent propensities of human nature."[16] The term *instinct* is used to designate these most basic human propensities. More modern usage would probably characterize them as basic urges or drives.

Veblen does not use *instinct* to mean that people inherit predispositions to choose or act in particular ways. He understood cultural conditioning, habitual behavior, and the mores principle. *Instincts* are not the hereditary

transmission of choice behavior; they are "native proclivities" which consciousness and intellect channel into culturally acknowledged modes of
behavior.[17] "Men take thought," but the "instinctual proclivities decide
what they shall take thought of and how and to what effect."[18]

The constructive or supportive proclivities for Veblen are "the instinct
of workmanship," "parental bent," and "idle curiosity." The instinct of
workmanship "occupies the interest with practical expedients, ways and
means, devices and contrivances of efficiency and economy, proficiency,
creative work and technological mastery of facts. Much of the functional
content of the instinct of workmanship is a proclivity for taking pains . . .
a disposition to do the next thing and do it as well as may be."[19]

The parental bent "appears to be an unselfish solicitude for the well-
being of the incoming generation—a bias for the highest efficiency and
fullest volume of life in the group, with particular drift to the future."[20]
The instinct of workmanship may be viewed as a "propensity to work out
the ends which the parental bent makes worth while."[21]

Idle curiosity suggests that "men instinctively seek knowledge, and
value it. The fact of this proclivity is well summed up in saying that men
are by native gift actuated with an idle curiosity—'idle' in the sense that
a knowledge of things is sought apart from any ulterior use of the knowledge so gained."[22] But Veblen does not mean that knowledge so obtained
will not be put to practical use. "The instinct of workmanship will un-
avoidably incline men to turn to account, in a system of ways and means,
whatever knowledge so becomes available."[23] The outcome sought in such
endeavor "is a theoretical organization, a logical articulation of things
known, the lines of which must not be deflected by any consideration of
expediency or convenience."[24] Thus, the derivation of knowledge and the
disposition to give it effective use in the pursuit of cultural continuity com-
bine as propensities to initiate and guide social change along constructive
channels.

Juxtaposed as "contaminants" are equally omnipresent propensities
which operate to thwart or obstruct the constructive propensities. These
parallel and inhibitive proclivities are impulses to predaciousness and to
emulation and invidious self-regard. The former are reflected in practices
of exploit, prowess or mastery (warfare), ownership (material acquisition), and in pecuniary control of industry. The latter are apparent in the
anthropomorphism of primitive societies, in practices of conspicuous display and conspicuous waste, and in leisure class elitism.[25]

Evident in the distinction between the constructive and contaminating
instincts is an embryonic value principle. The former account for the continuity of culture, contribute a net gain in comfort or in the fullness of life,

and should be encouraged. The latter sabotage that quest and should be discouraged.

But Veblen's implicit value theory is apparent even more obviously in what has come to be called the Veblenian distinction or the fundamental Veblenian dichotomy. While it is formally offered as a descriptive or classifying principle, it is obviously and continuously used as an evaluative principle.

In *Leisure Class* we are offered this descriptive statement: "Institutions —the economic structure—may be roughly distinguished into two classes or categories, according as they serve one or the other of two divergent purposes of economic life . . . they are institutions of acquisition or of production . . . they are pecuniary or industrial institutions . . . they are institutions serving either the invidious or the non-invidious economic interest."[26] Veblen uses the term *invidious* to describe a "comparison of persons with a view to rating and grading them in respect of relative worth or value."[27]

But the forms or versions of the distinction extend well beyond the three mentioned above. Indeed, the distinction appears in all of Veblen's published works in one form or another; it was for him a *general* principle. Note the following diverse additional examples:

salesmanship	workmanship[28]
business	industry[29]
ceremonial	technological[30]
ownership	production[31]
free income	tangible performance[32]
vested interests	common man[33]
sabotage	community serviceability[34]
pecuniary employment	industrial employment[35]
invidious emulation	technological efficiency[36]
conscientious withdrawal of	inordinately productive
efficiency	enterprise[37]
competitive advertising	valuable information & guidance[38]
business prosperity	industrial efficiency[39]

And the foregoing does not exhaust the list. Entries in the left-hand column refer to individuals, behaviors, or institutions which are different in kind from those in the right-hand column; the distinction is a dichotomy.

The normative use of this set of distinctions can hardly be in doubt. "The interest of the community at large demands industrial efficiency and serviceability of the product, while the business interest of the concern as such demands vendibility of the product."[40] It is scarcely morally colorless to contend that "all business sagacity" in the final analysis "reduces itself . . . to a judicious use of sabotage." "Captains of industry" through owners' discretion give "authoritative permission" and "authoritative limitation" to the industrial process. It is Veblen's lament that such authority is not used with "an eye single" to produce the "largest and most serviceable output of goods and services, or to the most economical use of the country's material resources and man-power, regardless of pecuniary consequences." "The volume and serviceability of the output must wait unreservedly on the very particular pecuniary question of what quantity and what degree of serviceability will yield the largest net return in terms of price."[41]

Veblen characterizes a "vested interest" as a "prescriptive right to get something for nothing."[42] He sees the objective of competitive advertising as the establishment of "differential monopolies resting on popular conviction" which are of "slight if any immediate service to the community."[43] Can these observations be considered devoid of normative content? Obviously not.

In sum, Veblen's fundamental concern is to further the "life process taken impersonally," to enhance "human life on the whole," to achieve "the largest and most serviceable output of goods and services." His theory of instincts indicates which sorts of basic impulses are contributive to or inhibitive of that quest. His fundamental "distinction" identifies institutions and behaviors which are supportive of or destructive of that quest. Veblen applies value theory; his concept of what ought to be is evident.

John Dewey

Dewey addresses the social value problem directly and, contrary to Veblen, finds that "instead of there being no disputing about tastes, they are the one thing worth disputing about, if by 'dispute' is signified discussion involving reflective inquiry."[44] Dewey's distinctive contribution is his formulation of an instrumental logic as the core of scientific social inquiry and of its application to the realm of social value. We here sample that contribution.[45]

Dewey sets the context for his own value theory by attempting to remove two conventional blockages to value inquiry. The first contention to be refuted is the idea that judgmental matters have no evidential or empirical content. They are alleged to be expressions of emotions or feelings states and not amenable to inquiry. Dewey contends, on the contrary, that "valuations exist in fact and are capable of empirical observation so that propositions about them are empirically verifiable. What individuals and groups hold dear or prize and the grounds upon which they prize them are capable, in principle, of ascertainment."[46] Since all social choices require the application of criteria, and since choices produce consequences, one may reflect upon the *character* of conseqences emerging from the use of a criterion and thus upon the propriety of the criterion itself. Value judgments are brought within social inquiry.

The second and related contention to be refuted is the alleged necessary acceptance of the positive-normative dichotomy.[47] This formulation presumes a fundamental divorcement between questions of "is" and questions of "ought," between means and ends, between that which is observable in a descriptive sense and that which is evaluational and judgmental. Positivistic analysis employs an epistemology of scientific cause-effect reasoning and evidential demonstration. Normative analysis employs an epistemology of metaphysical or subjectivistic reasoning; it is noncausally knowable. Positive and normative have no common content; they are mutually exclusive, it is argued.

Dewey rejects this dichotomy on several grounds, the principle one of which perhaps concerns the logic of inquiry.[48] Inquiry for Dewey is a search for observable regularities in a continuum of evidently knowable phenomena. By whatever caption—cause-effect connections, means-consequence connections, or means-ends connections—it is clear that causes or means are determinant of effects, consequences, or ends in the continuum of inquiry. Moreover, "effects are also causes. . . . Nothing happens which is *final* in the sense that it is not part of an ongoing stream of events."[49] Thus, ends attained *function* as means for the attainment of *further* ends or ends-in-view. The designation by the inquirer of means and ends within the process of inquiry itself is a necessary condition of their serving as operational hypotheses, as instrumentalities in the inquiry process. Ends which are conceived *a priori,* through nonevidential or extraexperiential epistemologies, cannot function instrumentally. A social value principle must be found that is internal to or consistent with the instrumental logic of social inquiry. We suggest, without elaboration, that Dewey rejects evaluation employing tradition, desires, given tastes, utility, metaphysical essences, mystic power, and the like, because they cannot function as instrumentalities.

Finally, what is (are) Dewey's principle(s) of social value? What does he offer in lieu of deference to utility and/or tradition?

One response which is directly tied to the means-ends analysis is the following: "The generalized ideal and standard of economy-efficiency which operates in every advanced art and technology is equivalent, upon analysis, to the conception of means that are constituents of ends attained and of ends that are usuable as means to further ends."[50]

Economy-efficiency for Dewey is a criterion the significance of which is established in its problem-solving role:

> In all inquiry, even the most completely scientific, what is proposed as a conclusion (the end-in-view in that inquiry) is evaluated as to its worth on the ground of its ability to resolve the *problem* presented by the conditions under investigation. There is no a priori standard for determining the value of a proposed solution in concrete cases.[51]

> Ends-in-view are appraised or valued as *good* or *bad* on the ground of their serviceability in the direction of behavior dealing with states of affairs found to be objectionable because of some lack or conflict in them. They are appraised as fit or unfit, proper or improper, *right* or *wrong*, on the ground of their *requiredness* in accomplishing this end.[52]

But the foregoing does not suffice. Admittedly, a criterion must arise from within inquiry, and procedurally it must function to resolve the problematic situation, but the substantive character of the criterion itself is so far largely undisclosed. Some substantive content may be suggested.

In its logical form, Dewey's criterion may be identified as to act so as to "increase the meaning of present experience."[53] To increase the meaning of present experience is to understand the way in which present experience connects and relates to past experience and will relate and connect with future experience. To attain meaning is to place in appropriate context. Increased knowledge of origins of experience and increased perception of consequences inform judgment and convey meaning. To expand such comprehensions of connections, to increase meaning, is to multiply the possibilities for effective action and participation. Such participation takes on meaning when the way in which that participation relates to the social whole is understood. "Morality is a continuing process, not a fixed achievement. Morals means growth of conduct in meaning; at least it means that kind of expansion in meaning which is consequent upon observations of the conditions and outcome of conduct. It is all one with growing."[54] Moreover, "in the largest sense of the word, morals is education. It is learning the meaning of what we are about and employing that meaning in action. The good, satisfaction, 'end,' of growth of present action in shades and scope of meaning is the only good within our control, and the only one, accordingly, for which responsibility exists. The rest is luck, fortune."[55]

If "present meaning in action" is an identifiable "good," and if the enhancement of the attainment of such meaning is a function of education, of "learning the meaning of what we are about and employing that meaning in action," it follows that judgment among alternative modes of social behavior may be made in terms of the extent to which they facilitate or retard the achievement of meaning by the community at large. Thus, anything obstructive of the continuity of the inquiry process as that process is utilized to enhance the achievement of meaning would be "bad." To impair opportunities for the attainment of increments in meaning is to produce consequences of a *kind* which make resolution of problems more difficult: To impair meaning is to impair comprehension, which impairs problem resolution.

Closely allied with the foregoing criterion is another formulation that perhaps is more expressly and obviously a social value premise. This variant may fairly be captioned the "common welfare" criterion.

That which furthers the common welfare is what ought to be in Dewey's view. But no doubt hundreds of scolars have advocated that judgments be based on some notion of welfare; indeed, a version appears in the U.S. Constitution. Dewey's position can be differentiated from other seemingly similar views. The substance of his conception of the "common welfare" is approximated in the following:

> The conception of the common good, of general well-being is a criterion which demands the full development of individuals in their distinctive individuality, not a sacrifice of them to some alleged vague larger good under the plea that it is "social." Only when individuals have initiative, independence of judgment, flexibility, fullness of experience, can they act so as to enrich the lives of others and only in this way can a truly common welfare be built up. The other side of this statement, of the moral criterion, is that individuals are free to develop, to contribute and to share, only as social conditions break down walls of privilege and of monopolistic possession.[56]

The denial of social and economic participation on grounds of status, "privilege," or "monopolistic possession" is an unwarranted judgment, according to Dewey.

The corollary political criterion for the common welfare is the "democratic ideal."

> For democracy signifies, on one side, that every individual is to share in the duties and rights belonging to control of social affairs, and, on the other side, that social arrangements are to eliminate those external arrangements of status, birth, wealth, sex, etc., which restrict the opportunity of each individual for full development of himself. On the individual side, it takes as the criterion of social organization and of law and government release of the potentialities of individuals. On the social side,

it demands cooperation in place of coercion, voluntary sharing in a process of mutual give and take, instead of authority imposed from above. . . . It serves . . . as ·[a] basis for criticism of institutions as they exist and of plans of betterment.[57]

The concept of democracy itself, when conceived as the noninvidious determination of social policy, serves for Dewey as a criterion of judgment in choosing social policy. The commonality of the above with elements of Veblen's fundamental distinction is apparent. Dewey's "walls of privilege and monopolistic possession" or "arrangements of status, birth, wealth, sex, etc.," presumably would exemplify what Veblen calls ceremonial or invidious behavior and attitudes. It is the position of Veblen and Dewey (the former implicitly, the latter explicitly) that judgments based upon these sorts of grounds are evidently demonstrable as erroneous. And whether the obverse of these obstructive judgments be viewed as "industrial efficiency" or as the "release of human potentialities," each is offered as a criterion with which to choose adjustments in institutional structure to resolve problems.

Finally, how do we distill from these expressions of "economy-efficiency," increasing "the meaning of experience," pursuit of the "common welfare," and the "democratic ideal" a common and intelligible referent for Dewey's value principle? Perhaps the following will serve as a satisfactory approximation: Maximize opportunities for instrumentally effective social and individual noninvidious development.

Although, as has been evident, the value theory of Veblen and Dewey correlates well in many respects, it remains for Clarence Ayres to provide a comprehensive integration.

Clarence Ayres

Ayres's singular achievement of imaginatively combining Dewey's instrumental logic and instrumental value theory with Veblen's evolutionary analysis of the economic process provides a stellar theoretical monument to his own thesis that new knowledge derives from fresh combinations of prior knowledge. If Veblen in his day "compelled a whole generation of economists to search their hearts lest the truth be not in them,"[58] and if Dewey was partially successful in persuading "his fellow philosophers to have done with the building of sand piles on the shores of life" and to "come inland to help build habitations fit for men,"[59] surely Ayres and his fellow institutionalists are, in these days, playing the David to the Goliath of the conventional wisdom. Ayres well understood the power of ideas to affect the course of events.[60]

Others have recently commented on Ayres's remarkable breadth of vision and scholarship, his recourse to many disciplines for insight and evidence.[61] Here, we focus solely and briefly upon his social value theory —its underpinnings and context and its fundamental differences with more conventional views.

Consider first his differences with conventional views as a *general* case. Ayres decries the "pestilence of moral agnosticism" and the ethical relativism which undergirds it.[62] This value avoidance, says Ayres, arises from three cultural aspects.[63] (1) "Scientific separatism" has compartmentalized knowledge and experience and delimited the impact of new knowledge on cultural convention. Old customary value beliefs often remain unchallenged. (2) "Economic individualism" extolled the primacy and efficiency of the self-regulating market system and deferred to the hedonistic, utilitarian value reflected in commercial and consumer behavior. (3) "Cultural relativism" asserted the absence of any "general or transcultural criterion by which cultural patterns can be judged." The traditions of the culture itself provide the only warrant or sanction for behavior—what is, is right. "To each his own," and then no one "can say naught agin' him." In combination, says Ayres, these theories "destroy all genuine moral leadership."[64]

Ayres also cannot abide ethical absolutists' position on value, whether rooted in metaphysical or supernatural sources, or in materialistic certitudes of race, class, and the like. But we cannot pursue this matter here.

Ayres's value theory also represents a fundamental rejection of the specific value assumptions of orthodox economics as a *specific* case of "moral agnosticism." Building on Veblen's essays in the *Place of Science* which cut away at the roots of orthodoxy—essays which explain the taxonomic, teleological, tautological, and hedonistic qualities of neoclassical analysis —Ayres directly attacks the value assumptions of price theory.

In price theory, price (value in exchange) is a measure of and an evidential surrogate for utility (value in use). Utility is the ability of goods to satisfy hedonistic wants. The maximization of utility is the inclusive goal of economic activity. The real worth and hence significance of the market process is therewith identified.[65]

But the attribution of real worth and hence significance to the maximization of utility through market phenomena is for Ayres wholly conjectural. There is no communicable referential content, for

> the concept of utility is peculiarly open to criticism on the ground of tautology. Indeed, it was for years the chief focus of such criticism. It is all very well to say that utility is the want-satisfying quality, whatever wants may be. But if we have no way of knowing, let alone measuring,

wants, how can we know utility—let alone measure it? It is all very well
to say that price is the measure of utility. But if we have no independent
measure of utility, (and we have none), that only means that we have
equated price and utility by definition. Such being the case, nothing can
be inferred from the correspondence.[66]

Accordingly, Ayres is unable to find meaning or significance in the orthodox use of utility as a value principle. He urges that we look elsewhere.

Some underpinnings for Ayres's value theory may now be noted. From
Dewey, Ayres incorporates and utilizes extensively the means-ends-means
continuum and rejects the means-ends dichotomy.[67] In addition, he insists
on the abandonment of "sand piles on the shores of life," that is, of views
of value grounded in nonexperiential or nonevidential sources. With
Dewey, he insists that philosophical value must be derived from and be
relevant to the factual and demonstrable experience of human life.[68]

The locus of social value for Ayres is the social process, more particularly, the "technological continuum" of that process. Ayres's alternative
to mores nihilism or ethical relativism and ethical absolutism is to be found
in the existential facts of human experience. "We know that social development is a continuous process, and it is in terms of this continuity . . . that
value and welfare can be quite objectively defined and understood. For
not only is the social process a continuous one in the chronological sense;
on the technological side it is a logical continuum, a true progression each
item of which implies succeeding items by the same process by which each
has been itself derived from preceding items in the series. It is this technological continuum which is the locus of truth and value."[69]

By "technological continuum" Ayres means substantially what Dewey
meant by the "continuum of inquiry."[70] Its significance as the locus of
social and economic value derives from "the logical significance of the
instrumental continuum."[71] "Truth . . . derives from the use of instruments, tools, and instrumentally manipulated materials. The very word,
'truth,' is in effect a synonym for continuity and the continuity it postulates
is that of instruments and tools—that is to say, technology. . . . Such is
also the meaning of value. In the same sense the word value is a synonym
for continuity, and the continuity of which it is a synonym is technological
continuity. 'Value' means continuity literally; and that is its sole meaning."[72] In Ayres's last major work, he reaffirms that in his view "it is the
dissociation of truth and value that defines the moral crisis of the twentieth
century."[73]

As has been implicit in the foregoing, Ayres's value principle may now
be identified as the furtherance of the "life process" of mankind. "When
we judge a thing to be good or bad, or an action to be right or wrong, what

we mean is that, in our opinion, the thing or act in question will, or will not, serve to advance the life process insofar as we can invision it."[74]

Referential content is provided for this value principle by Ayres's use of Veblen's fundamental distinction. For Ayres, the distinction usually takes one of the following forms: technology versus institutions, instrumental versus invidious, or science versus ceremony. Perhaps the most meaningful and frequent version poses technological (instrumental) versus ceremonial (invidious) behavior.[75] For Ayres, these are "humanity's two aspects."[76]

But as his students are well aware, Ayres provides a somewhat more particularistic, if not reductionistic, interpretation of technology than did Veblen or Dewey. Ayres's classic statement in *The Theory of Economic Progress* defines technology as "organized skill."[77] "All acts of skill involve the use of tools"; "all technology . . . is progressive"; "the developmental character of technology . . . is in the character of tools"; "inventions are combinations of previously existing devices"; "these combinations are physical not less than ideational"; "the more tools there are the greater the number of combinations"; "the tool combination principle is indeed a law of progress."[78] Almost two decades later this position remains substantially unchanged.[79]

Ceremonial patterns of behavior for Ayres (the second of humanity's two aspects) are distinguished by two universal traits. One is that "distinctions of rank and status ape differences of technological competence." Rank is presumed to coincide with "technological reality."[80] "Ceremonial adequacy" means attribution of competence by ritual not by technological demonstration. The second trait of ceremonial behavior is its mores base; it is defined by and given sanction in the mores.[81] The mores define status patterns and functions, and these differ depending on people's rank, age, sex, and the like. Cultures prescribe what is right and what is wrong. Persons gain "mystic potency" by "scrupulous observance" of the mores. Status systems stipulate difference in mystic potency and order or array persons based on these alleged differences.

In contrast with technological activity, which is inherently developmental, ceremonial activity is "static, resistant to and inhibitive of change"; it is "past-preserving."[82]

In a sweeping summation, Ayres contends that "the history of the human race is that of a perpetual opposition of these forces, the dynamic force of technology continually making for change, and the static force of ceremony—status, mores, and legendary belief—opposing change.[83]

Ayres seems to have retained this interpretation through his more recent work. Technological patterns "are predominantly working, operational, tool-skill relationships."[84] Ceremonial patterns are still seen as "predominantly status relationships of power and subservience, arbitrarily established by 'legitimate' birth, authentically performed ceremonies, and the like."[85]

It follows, obviously, that for Ayres, technological (instrumental) behavior furthers the life process of mankind; ceremonial (invidious) behavior retards or obstructs the life process of mankind. Here is a value principle grounded in evidence and instrumental logic.

J. Fagg Foster

One of Ayres's intellectual progeny, Fagg Foster,[86] was recently described as "one of the last great practitioners of the oral tradition in economic scholarship."[87] That characterization is appropriate. Foster has spent his professional life seeking to reformulate the fundamental principles of economics on the Veblen-Dewey-Ayres base and to communicate that reformulation to successive groups of students through lectures, addresses, and monographs. Although there is not available a definitive publication of Foster's position,[88] his profound and substantial impact on his students and on scholarship on the "American contribution" is routinely acknowledged in professional circles of institutional economists.

Comments here will be confined to his formulation of the theory of social value and the theory of institutional adjustment which incorporates his value theory. Hopefully, this presentation will reflect Foster's quest for coherence, pattern, and precision in neoinstitutional thought. The presentation which follows is an ordered sequence of propositions. Space constraints preclude elaboration, but the foregoing commentary on Veblen, Dewey, and Ayres provides much of the needed background.

Consider Foster's formulation of the theory of social value.[89]

(1) Economics is "concerned with the process of providing the means of life and experience." This process is coextensive with human life; it is an omnipresent functional category of human activity.

(2) The inclusive economic function (provision of real income) and all subsidiary functions (for example, production of food and fiber, education of the young) are organized and given effect through structural institutions. *Institutions* are defined as "prescribed patterns of correlated activity and attitudes among groups of persons." The functions are continuous and developmental; the institutional structures are discontinuous and displacemental.

(3) The purpose of economic inquiry is "to explain the institutional determination of the level and character [and distribution] of real income,"

to conduct "rational inquiry into the institutions through which man provides himself with the means of life and experience."

(4) The reason for such inquiry, its claim to significance, derives from its relevance or applicability to real problems facing real people, to economic problems such as unemployment, inflation, poverty, and discrimination. Social and economic inquiry is purposive; it is directed to problem solving.

(5) The mode of economic inquiry must be scientific in the instrumental logic sense. Sought are causal explanations of phenomena under review. Inquiry is a continuum in the means-consequence-means sense and in the means-determine-ends sense. It utilizes the interdependencies of deductive and inductive modes, of rationalist *and* empiricist models.

(6) The outcome of inquiry is reliable knowledge—increments to the stock and flow of causally comprehended regularities in existential physical and social phenomena. Applied to the productive process as technology, such knowledge-technology is at once the basic source of the perceptions of differences between what is and what ought to be and is the basic resource on which scholars and the community must draw creatively to adjust institutions to resolve problems.

(7) Economic problems are instances of breakdown, termination, impairment, disorder, discrimination, or obsolescence in the performance of economic functions by economic institutions. Problems are perceived as the difference between what is and what ought to be. Problem solutions must take the form of institutional adjustment, of modification of those institutions (or parts thereof) which are causally responsible for the impairment in the production and distribution of real income. "The economic general theory must be the theory of institutional adjustment."

(8) All institutions perform two different kinds of functions. One is an instrumental function which provides for the full and continuous application of knowledge-technology in pursuit of the primary purpose or activity for which the institution exists (for example, generating energy, providing transport, communicating word and image). The other is a ceremonial function, which provides for the creation or maintenance of status, power, rank, privilege, and/or tradition, or of invidious differentiation on grounds of race, creed, color, sex, and the like. The resolution of a problem *consists* of the reduction or removal of ceremonial behavior and attitudes and the creation or extension of instrumental behavior and attitudes.

(9) Since problems consist of institutional malfunctioning, impairment, or breakdown, and since the restoration of effectual functioning requires the choice among institutional options, the criterion of choice

must be "independent of any particular institution." Structural givens (public *or* private ownership of property, for example) cannot be used as criteria of choice without committing tautological error. "Institutions are constituted of habits but they are not determined by habits." People create institutions which become habitual. In creating structure, a principle of choice, a criterion of judgment, must be employed. "What is" cannot be "what is right," or there would be no problem. The mores encapsule value judgments; they cannot constitute a principle of values for problem solving.

(10) Having located social value, following Ayres, in the social and technological processes and the continuity thereof, the specific identification of the value principle becomes both necessary and possible. The only value principle which conforms to the continuity and substance of instrumental logic, which itself possesses processional characteristics, which is noninstitutional in form, which is consistent with the evidence of problem solving, and which is continuously applicable to problem solving is "the continuity and instrumental efficiency of the social process."

(11) The instrumental efficiency criterion does not specify *direction*; it does not point toward some utopian state or ideological recipe of institutional structure. The principle does not lead an economy "down the road" to an ism. The test is not conformity with or movement toward a preconceived set of institutions—as with capitalism, socialism, or communism. This suggests why isms do not apply and why all economies are always mixed economies.

(12) The instrumental efficiency criterion is a value principle which does specify *condition*. But it does not validate a condition of invidious differentiation—of efficiency in preserving privilege or according status. It is not a matter of efficiency in the exercise of power over others, denigration of persons, or the preservation of tradition. On the contrary, it validates a condition of efficiency in the use of warrantable knowledge in the carrying on of the instrumental, noninvidious functions of institutions.

(13) The instrumental efficiency criterion has a constancy of meaning over time. It will apply to the whole or any part of the social and economic processes. It displays real and unimpaired continuity. It satisfies all requirements for truth. It is the only criterion which has produced or can produce solutions for real problems in the only sense in which "solution" can have a credible meaning, that is, structural change (validated by this criterion) has removed the human incidences of the breakdown or disruptions in the production and distribution of real income.

Consider, finally, Foster's theory of institutional adjustment. His reformulation of the fundamental principles of economics prominently in-

corporates "the most obtrusive of the continuing and inclusive factors in
the process of solving problems."[90] These "factors" are the three principles
of institutional adjustment. These set the terms of and limitations upon
the adjustment of institutions to resolve problems. They incorporate the
value theory described above.

(1) The Principle of Technological Determination. Instrumentally
efficient problem solving requires a sufficient availability of reliable knowledge. While full knowledge in any sense is never in hand, it is still tha
data, institutional and noninstitutional, are required sufficient to perceiv
a difference between is and ought, to grasp the determinants of a problem
and to permit the formulation of institutional alternatives. Once sucl
knowledge becomes available and is widely known, however, a communit
cannot "unknow" it, cannot disclaim its understanding. That understand
ing provides a continuing pressure or prod for the pursuit of instrumentally more efficient arrangements of institutional structure so long as the
understood problems remain. The availability of reliable knowledge will
permit the determination of whatever level of instrumentally efficient performance of instrumental functions is considered tolerable or desirable by
those affected.

(2) The Principle of Recognized Interdependence. The ability of a
people to understand and accept the contemplated institutional adjustment is also a limiting condition on social and economic change. Institutions are constituted of social habits. Change in structure obviously must
be initiated as a choice or judgment to change habits. Those affected by
the change must comprehend and themselves choose or agree to in-
voke altered behavior or attitudes—modify habitual modes—or nothing
changes substantively. In choosing, people must be able to see themselves
functioning normally and effectively after the adjustment in their interdependencies with other people and other institutions. The recognition of
such interdependencies permits recorrelation and new coordination of
instrumental activity. This principle "specifies the pattern of understanding which must be accomplished in order to solve any particular social
problem."

The foregoing suggests why revolutions from above typically fail effectively to rewrite living and working rules. According to this principle, only
evolutions from below are likely to succeed. Those whose behavior is to be
revised must themselves understand the need for it, concur with it, and
participate in it if the change is actually to occur. This is a substantial part
of the argument for democratic participation in social and economic policy
making.

(3) The Principle of Minimal Dislocation. "All institutional modifica-

tions must be capable of being incorporated into the remainder of the institutional structure." This principle sets limits of adjustment with reference to scope, area, or extent of adjustment and with regard to timing and rate of introduction.

All structural change is dislocative. Contemplated change could be invoked with reference to rate and extent so as to intrude upon or disrupt as little as possible other instrumental functioning in nonproblematic but interrelated and affected institutions. If adjustments are more extensive than people think is needed or necessary (given the first two principles), and if nonproblematic areas are adversely affected in the instrumental efficiency sense, the change will be resisted and may be aborted. Effective change must then await a more adequate recognition of the constraints and a revision of proposed changes in observance of this principle.

This principle explains in part why proposals for comprehensive reordering of entire political economies usually fail in the achievement of their aims. No people can stop and start over; none can wholly or even mostly reorder the interdependent patterns of belief and behavior which correlate their relations with others. Change must proceed piecemeal. On the other hand, *if* the other two principles are observed, institutional adjustment may be surprisingly rapid. Especially is this so if the problems are extensive and severe.

For Foster, the instrumental efficiency theory of social value and the principles of institutional adjustment together provide the core of an alternative to orthodoxy and the core, then, of a restatement of the fundamental principles of economics. Foster, like his precursers, finds neoclassical price theory devoid of a *general* theory of the economic process. Foster and his mentors have attempted to provide the "theoretical formulation" of "the economic life process" for which Veblen called.

Summary and Synthesis

Veblen, although blocked by value analysis itself as an inquiry problem, nevertheless provides rudimentary value constructs and makes extensive application of them throughout his writing.

Dewey moves the value problem back into the area of social inquiry and ties value identification to that of truth seeking. He addresses the value problem directly and clears away obstructions to its consideration, but his identification of a value principle is not sufficiently precise or applicable.

Ayres ties the Veblenian distinction and instrumental logic together, identifies the locus of value in the social process and the technological continuum, and mounts an assault on the particulars of price theory from this base.

Foster, building on all three, provides a more specific identification of the value, the criterion of judgment; in the theory of institutional adjustment he reformulates, on this value base, fundamental principles of economics. These set the terms and define the constraints for the application of value theory to real economic problems.

The following synthetic statements inevitably represent a selection of elements, both explicit and implicit, from the four contributors discussed.[91] Others would, of course, distill a different residue, but the significance of this synthesis is to provide constructs which are manageable and useful for inquiry and conduct. That is the test.

A criterion of social value is "the continuity and instrumental effectiveness of recreating community non-invidiously." This is a criterion with which to choose among alternative economic and social policies formed as institutional options. It is general in its relevance to the social process, to the functional components of that process (economy, polity), and to choices among institutional forms which organize that process. The resolution of problems compels the employment of this principle of value.

In this value principle, "continuity" is grounded in the fact that there is no human history except that of evolutionary development of human organisms and of the culture such persons create and preserve. The principle asserts the obvious as an "ought"—that the continuance of human life is the first and primary charge to any community. Providing for continuity implies, beyond the obvious, an awareness of conditions which positively foster human life and exhibit a solicitous concern for human life. Recall Veblen's parental bent. Especially included is a deference to human potential and developmental capabilities. The social process is the locus of value.

"Instrumental effectiveness" incorporates the idea that reliable knowledge is instrumental to an understanding of social reality and should be employed efficiently to relevant areas of human problems and experience. Reliable knowledge includes science and technology. It includes the whole fund or stock of evidentially grounded, logically evolved recognitions of means-consequence connections emerging incrementally as a knowledge continuum. It is the aggregative product of tool and idea contributions and combinations running back beyond written records. New knowledge is derived from recast or reconstituted old knowledge. This value principle encompasses the use of such knowledge in the identification and resolution of real economic problems.

Reference to *instrumental* effectiveness conditions and constrains the use of reliable knowledge to that which is pertinent and compatible with the remainder of the principle. At issue is the appropriateness of means chosen to serve ends-in-view, recognizing that means determine ends-in-view. One does not repair a watch with a sledge hammer, create a depression to cope with inflation, or enhance political democracy with campaign sabotage.

"Re-creating community" makes clear that human life is feasible only in a context of culture. Individuals are born into communities as going concerns with language, custom, and order already affirmed. Institutions pattern lives. Re-creating community means reconstituting the structural fabric of that social order by utilizing effectively the stock of human wisdom. Since all already reside in community, the task is to re-create.

Finally, "noninvidiously" speaks to the *character* of community just mentioned. Veblen's usage of "invidious" obtains. Human differences of race, sex, ethnicity, color, wealth, ownership, rank, age, status, power, and the like, have been and are being used as invidious indices of relative worth of individuals. In this value principle, the invidious use of any distinction is, so far as is possible, to be avoided in the application of reliable knowledge to the re-creation of community to assure continuity. This principle affirms the inherent potential and ultimate worth of human beings.

Noninvidiousness as a value component permits qualitative judgments to be made. Does a proposed structural change enhance the dignity and sense of self-worth which arises from having discretion in one's own life? Does it foster the ability to think critically and coherently? Does it extend meaningful and popular participation? Or does it erode or destroy by denigration, discrimination, and disenfranchisement? Where the latter occurs, continuity and community suffer. As Ayres often remarked, to cripple a part is to cripple the whole of a community to that degree. "We are members one of another" in fact. Participatory democracy is a corollary of the instrumental effectiveness theory of value. It may offer surcease from "the pestilence of moral agnosticism" and other judgmental ills.

Notes

1. Philip A. Klein, "Economics: Allocation or Valuation?" *Journal of Economic Issues* 8 (December 1974): 785–811 (hereafter, *JEI*).
2. Eugene J. Meehan, *Value Judgment and Social Science* (New York: Dorsey Press, 1969), p. v.
3. John H. Schaar, "Some Ways of Thinking about Equality," *Journal of Politics* 26 (1964): 868.

4. Joan Robinson, *Freedom and Necessity* (New York: Random House/ Vintage Books, 1971), p. 122.
5. Kenneth J. Arrow, "Public and Private Values," in *Human Values and Economic Policy*, edited by Sidney Hook (New York: New York University Press, 1967), p. 107.
6. Melville J. Ulmer, "Human Values and Economic Science," *JEI* 8 (June 1974): 255–66.
7. Gunnar Myrdal, *An International Economy* (New York: Harper & Bros., 1956), *Value in Social Theory* (London: Routledge & Kegan Paul, 1958), and *Asian Drama* (New York: Random House/Pantheon Books, 1968).
8. Robert L. Heilbroner, "On the Possibility of a Political Economics," *JEI* 4 (December 1970): 1–22; and Ben B. Seligman, "Philosophic Perspectives in Economic Thought," *JEI* 5 (March 1971): 1–24.
9. See also E. Ray Canterbery, *The Making of Economics* (Belmont, Calif.: Wadsworth Publishing Co., 1976), pp. 255ff.
10. Surely John Kenneth Galbraith's *Economics and the Public Purpose* (Boston: Houghton Mifflin, 1973) is such an undertaking.
11. Thorstein Veblen, *The Place of Science in Modern Civilization* (1919; New York: Russell & Russell, 1961), p. 29.
12. Thorstein Veblen, *The Theory of the Leisure Class* (1899; New York: Random House/Modern Library, 1934), p. 34.
13. Ibid., p. 207.
14. Ibid.
15. Thorstein Veblen, *The Instinct of Workmanship* (1914; New York: Viking Press, 1946), p. 25.
16. Ibid., p. 2.
17. Ibid., pp. 3–4.
18. Ibid., p. 6.
19. Ibid., pp. 33–34.
20. Ibid., pp. 46–47.
21. Ibid., p. 48.
22. Thorstein Veblen, *The Higher Learning in America* (1918; New York: Augustus M. Kelley, 1965), p. 5.
23. Ibid.
24. Ibid., p. 8.
25. The following of Veblen's works provide numerous examples: *Leisure Class, Instinct of Workmanship,* and *Imperial Germany and the Industrial Revolution* (1915; New York: Augustus M. Kelley, 1964), passim.
26. Veblen, *Leisure Class,* p. 208.
27. Ibid., p. 34.
28. Veblen, *Instinct of Workmanship,* pp. 216ff, and Thorstein Veblen, *Absentee Ownership and Business Enterprise in Recent Times: The Case of America* (1923; New York: Augustus M. Kelley, 1964), pp. 284ff.
29. Veblen, *The Theory of Business Enterprise* (New York: Charles Scribner's Sons, 1904), pp. 20ff, and *Absentee Ownership,* pp. 82ff.
30. Veblen, *Imperial Germany,* pp. 26ff.
21. Veblen, *Absentee Ownership,* pp. 65ff.
32. Veblen, *The Vested Interests and the Common Man* (1919; New York: Viking Press, 1946), pp. 63ff.

844   Marc R. Tool

33. Ibid., pp. 85ff and 159ff.
34. Thorstein Veblen, *An Inquiry into the Nature of Peace and the Terms of Its Perpetuation* (1917; New York: Viking Press, 1945), pp. 167ff, and *The Engineers and the Price System* (1921; New York: Augustus M. Kelley, 1965), pp. 3ff.
35. Veblen, *Business Enterprise*, pp. 314ff.
36. Veblen, *Leisure Class*, passim, and *Instinct of Workmanship*, pp. 217ff.
37. Veblen, *Engineers and the Price System*, chapters 1 and 2.
38. Veblen, *Business Enterprise*, pp. 57ff.
39. Ibid., pp. 178ff.
40. Ibid., pp. 157–58.
41. Veblen, *Nature of Peace*, pp. 168–69.
42. Veblen, *Vested Interests*, p. 162.
43. Veblen, *Business Enterprise*, pp. 57–58.
44. John Dewey, *The Quest for Certainty: A Study of the Relation of Knowledge and Action* (New York: Minton, Balch & Co., 1929), p. 262.
45. Dewey's most important books in this area are *Logic: The Theory of Inquiry* (New York: Henry Holt and Co., 1938) and *Theory of Valuation* (Chicago: University of Chicago Press, 1939).
46. Dewey, *Theory of Valuation*, p. 58.
47. T. W. Hutchison provides a historical commentary on this dichotomy in economic thought in his *'Positive' Economics and Policy Objectives* (London: George Allen & Unwin, 1964).
48. Dewey, *Theory of Valuation*, chapters 4, 5, and 6.
49. Ibid., p. 43.
50. Ibid., p. 50.
51. Ibid., pp. 46–47.
52. Ibid., p. 47.
53. John Dewey, *Human Nature and Conduct* (New York: Random House/ Modern Library, 1930), p. 283.
54. Ibid., p. 280.
55. Ibid., pp. 280–81.
56. John Dewey and James H. Tufts, *Ethics* (rev. ed.) (New York: Henry Holt and Company, 1932), pp. 387–88.
57. Ibid.
58. P. T. Homan, *Contemporary Economic Thought* (New York: Harper and Brothers, 1928), p. 107.
59. Joseph Ratner, ed., *Intelligence in the Modern World: John Dewey's Philosophy* (New York: Random House/Modern Library, 1939), from the Introduction, p. 8.
60. Clarence E. Ayres, *The Theory of Economic Progress* (Chapel Hill: University of North Carolina Press, 1944), chapter 13.
61. For example, William Breit and William Patton Culbertson, Jr., "Clarence Edwin Ayres: An Intellectual's Portrait," in *Science and Ceremony: The Institutional Economics of C. E. Ayres*, edited by Breit and Culbertson (Austin & London: The University of Texas Press, 1976), pp. 3–22.
62. Clarence E. Ayres, *Toward a Reasonable Society: The Values of Industrial Civilization* (Austin: The University of Texas Press, 1961), p. 42.

63. This section draws on ibid., pp. 42–49. See also Rick Tilman, "Value Theory, Planning, and Reform: Ayres as Incrementalist and Utopian," *JEI* 8 (December 1974): 689–706.

64. Ibid., p. 49.

65. Clarence E. Ayres, *The Industrial Economy: Its Technological Basis and Institutional Destiny* (Boston: Houghton Mifflin Co., 1952), p. 335.

66. Ibid., pp. 337–38.

67. See Alfred F. Chalk, "Ayres's Views on Moral Relativism," in *Science and Ceremony*, Breit and Culbertson, eds., p. 151.

68. Ibid., pp. 147–61.

69. Clarence E. Ayres, "The Significance of Economic Planning," in *Development of Collective Enterprise,* edited by Seba Eldridge (Lawrence: University of Kansas Press, 1943), p. 477.

70. Ayres, *Economic Progress*, p. 220.

71. Ibid.

72. Ibid., p. 221.

73. Ayres, *Reasonable Society*, p. 49.

74. Ibid., p. 113.

75. In Ayres's early work, institutions as such are often regarded as wholly or substantially ceremonial (*Economic Progress,* chapter 9, *Industrial Economy,* pp. 42–50). In later work, Ayres recognizes (or redefines "institutions" to acknowledge) that institutions perform both technological and ceremonial functions (*Reasonable Society,* pp. 77–78). These and related matters are the subject of an excellent paper by Paul D. Bush, "A Veblen-Ayres Model of Institutional Change," presented at the Western Economic Association Meeting, Anaheim, California, 21 June 1977.

76. Ayres, *Reasonable Society,* chapter 5.

77. Ayres, *Economic Progress,* p. 105.

78. Ibid., pp. 107, 111, 112, 115, and 119.

79. Ayres, *Reasonable Society,* p. 80.

80. Ayres, *Economic Progress,* p. 159.

81. Ibid., p. 162.

82. Ibid., p. 174.

83. Ibid., p. 176.

84. Ayres, *Reasonable Society,* p. 77.

85. Ibid.

86. Professor Emeritus of Economics, University of Denver. Foster was for several years my mentor and colleague. I am deeply indebted to him for an introduction to and insights into the perspective of which this article is an expression.

87. Bush, "A Veblen-Ayres Model," p. 89.

88. My forthcoming book, "The Discretionary Economy: A Normative Theory of Political Economy" (Santa Monica: Goodyear Publishing Co., 1978), is in part an interpretive presentation of some of Foster's ideas.

89. These ordered propositions, including quotations, are drawn from two unpublished essays by J. Fagg Foster and from lecture notes. The essays are "The Relation between Value Theory and Economic Analysis," 1949, and "Current Structure and Future Prospects of Institutional Economics," 1975.

846   Marc R. Tool

90. This commentary and quotations are drawn primarily from two unpublished essays of J. Fagg Foster and from lecture notes. The essays are "The Theory of Institutional Adjustment," 1949, and "The Fundamental Principles of Economics," 1972. In this connection also see Bush, "A Veblen-Ayres Model."

91. Adapted from my forthcoming book, "The Discretionary Economy," chapter 15.

[3]

Jei *JOURNAL OF ECONOMIC ISSUES*
Vol. XI No. 4 December 1977

Technology and Ceremonial Behavior: Aspects of Institutionalism

Thomas R. De Gregori

The social and economic implications of technology are the subject of considerable debate and inquiry. Technology is alternately seen as the culprit or as the salvation for the current environmental or energy "crisis" in the world's industrial countries. Technology is increasingly receiving emphasis as a prime factor in the transformation of underdeveloped countries. For centuries, romantics have attacked the technology of their time as the cause for social ills. Comparison was made to earlier, more idyllic times, when man and tools were closer to nature. Ironically, although technology receives praise and blame, it is rarely defined. It is readily assumed that technology is like a camel or an elephant: We all know what it is, so who needs a definition?

Even when technology is not explicitly defined, the context in which the term is used gives rise to some implicit conceptions. Generally, a reductionist mentality prevails; technology is implicitly conceived of as a succession of devices. Even Clarence Ayres, one of the major theoreticians of the subject, thought of technology primarily in terms of "physical objects" until well into the mature years of his writing on the subject.[1]

From Thorstein Veblen through Ayres, institutionalists have sought to overcome the limitations of the Newtonian-based science of mainstream

The author is Professor of Economics, University of Houston, Houston, Texas.

economics. They have tried to replace it with a process-oriented theory of change consistent with nineteenth- and twentieth-century science. We will argue that some elements of Ayres carry vestigial traces of Newtonianism. In part, Ayres's conception of technology is one of a problem-solving process, but in his presentation he commits the Newtonian sin of begging the question as to the nature of reality. Ayres virtually assumes that the specification of the problem to be solved is essentially self-evident.

As the quotations from Ayres will indicate, his conception of technology and problem solving is rooted in the idea of tool using. There is clearly a definable process by which reasonable, knowledgeable human beings select the correct tool to solve a mechanical problem. Questions of taste hardly matter in the determination of the size of the wrench that one uses. Ayres sees this method of thought successfully penetrating other realms of human endeavor. As Veblen said: "Hence men have learned to think in the terms in which the technological processes act."[2]

It is the major contention of this article that the Ayresian technological scheme is useful for interpreting large-scale historical change. In the application of the theory to particular historic or contemporary issues, however, the theory's lack of specificity in delineating and defining problems renders it virtually inoperable. Problem specification is the core normative issue. A theory of value in economics that does not guide us in the definition of problems fails the first fundamental test in problem solving. We propose a modified theory of technology as a problem-solving process and as habits of mind with some effort at establishing the context in which the nature of the problem is to be defined.

Central to the institutional economics of Clarence E. Ayres was the dichotomy between the technological and the ceremonial realms of behavior. Ayres was always careful to note that the technology-ceremony distinction was a dichotomy and not a duality. This distinction in Ayresian institutional economics refers primarily to different aspects of human behavior and as such is clearly a dichotomy and not a duality in the traditional sense of that term. The technological and the ceremonial are interactive elements of the same process. Consequently, although they may be definitely distinct, in that technological and ceremonial behavior are essentially the antithesis of one another, they are also very closely interrelated, and cognition of one element of the dichotomy depends upon proper understanding of the other. This is particularly vital in the application of the Ayresian dichotomy to historical processes, where the technological element is the *élan vital* of progressive transformation, and ceremonial behavior becomes the explanatory condition of institutional resistance to change. Ceremonial behavior relates to certain kinds of change, and therefore any misspecification or misunderstanding of the nature or content of technological change can greatly exaggerate or understate the extent of institutional resistance, that is, ceremonial behavior.

The study of the history of technology has grown rapidly in the last two decades, generating a vast quantity of empirical data and theoretical insight. Institutional economics can put these gains to good account to refine the theory of technological change and institutional resistance and/or adaptation. A careful articulation of such a theory can contribute to an understanding of problems that are of current concern. In some instances definitional clarity can almost transform problems into nonproblems.

Clarence Ayres was a prolific writer, but one work, *The Theory of Economic Progress*,[3] stands out as being the best statement of his ideas in several important areas. The book contains the fullest statements of Ayres's concepts of technological change and institutional inhibition. The formulation remains essentially unchanged down through Ayres's last book, *Toward a Reasonable Society,* in which it is more succinctly restated.[4] To Ayres, technology was based upon tool using, it involved human skills, and it was inherently developmental.[5] "All tool using is social," and all human societies are tool using.[6] Technological change, that is, invention, proceeds by the combination and recombination of already existing technologies.[7] Art and science are also inherently developmental and similarly advance by the combination and recombination of existing techniques.[8] This process of tool combination is continuous, cumulative, ongoing, and dynamic, and is in essence the law of progress.[9] Given that invention is part of a process of the combination of existing elements, it follows that when circumstances are ripe for certain inventions, they in a sense are almost "bound" to occur.[10] Furthermore, technology is cumulative. This leads to a constant acceleration of the process; the more tools there are, the greater the number of possibilities for combination and recombination. This dynamic development process, operating independently of any change in human skill, works in terms of its own laws and therefore seems to evolve *almost* independent of human motive. Ayres very clearly states:

> No one supposes that technological progress is the whole of culture. . . . On the contrary . . . it is but one aspect of culture. . . . There is no community whose history does not reveal periods in which technology has been virtually stationary for long periods of time. But these facts do not deny the existence of technological development in terms of a continuous, cumulative progressive process. . . . It means that other forces also are at work, not that technological progress is an illusion.[11]

The other forces at work are those of ceremonial behavior. There is, in Ayres, a perpetual opposition between technology and institutions which are based on ceremony.[12] Behind all ceremonial practices is the specter of hierarchy and status.[13] Ceremonial behavior is nonexperimental; its legitimacy is derived from investiture, and normative judgments are made in terms of "ceremonial adequacy" (Veblen's term), not in terms of operational efficacy.[14] Ceremonial practices or institutions are inherited from the past (that is, they are past binding), which serves to hallow and legitimize them.[15] Ceremonies, by their very nature and mode of sanctification, are static, are resistant to, and inhibitors of, change.

The dichotomous nature of human behavior is derived from several factors. First, the same object or activity can have both technological and ceremonial attributes. Thus, an automobile is a piece of technology that allows people to move with greater facility than did previous technologies. At the same time, built into the automobile are status elements that are a vital aspect of the use of the car for ceremonial purposes. Second, the ceremonial beliefs, according to Ayres, simulate technology in that they purport to some instrumental efficacy, although they do not derive their sanctions from a testing of this efficacy.[16]

Making Ayres's technology-ceremony conceptualization operational to contemporary problems requires further refinement. Ayres applied his theory to the interpretations of Western European history from the Middle Ages through industrialization.[17] He provides insight and understanding as he argues that medieval Europe was technologically linked with the classical civilizations of the Mediterranean, yet at the same time was a frontier with relatively weak institutional ties to older cultures. Consequently, there was a fertile field for technological and scientific advancements with far fewer of the institutional restraints that characterized other great civilizations of that time. For these reasons, Ayres argued, the industrial and scientific revolutions took place where they did, in Western Europe.

When the realm of discourse is shifted from the level of generalization of large civilizations undergoing long-term change to the level of seeking to understand specific transformations over shorter periods, greater specificity is needed for the concept of invention or scientific discovery than is found in Ayres. It is one thing to argue that the heliocentric theories of astronomy developing in the 1500s were a movement in the right direction away from the more prevailing geocentric notions; it is another to understand at what point navigation practices predicated upon heliocentric theory were in fact operationally superior to those in practice that were derived from a Ptolemaic conception of the universe. As Thomas Kuhn has noted, after the emergence of a new paradigm, it takes some time for "normal science" to work out the practical implications of the discovery.[18] If our theory is to be useful we must make precisely the distinction between resistance to an idea or tool that is warranted on the grounds that it is not yet operationally superior to existing practice, and resistance which is primarily and fundamentally institutional. We must also recognize shades and variations of conditions between these two polar conditions.

The question remains, what is an invention or scientific discovery? Abbot Payson Usher, writing on the invention of printing, argues:

> It is fairly clear that we have to deal with a process of development which involves a number of technological changes, any one of which must properly be classed as an invention though none of them could in propriety be described in such a general phrase as the "invention of printing" nor even in a more restricted sense as the "invention of printing from movable type." The inconclusiveness of the long-drawn-out controversy is due in large measure to the inaccuracy of the statement of the problem and to the naive disposition to assume that only one invention was involved.[19]

Usher speaks of the "strategic" invention. After many earlier forms of the invention had been developed, printing by movable type was still inferior to other forms of reproduction.[20] According to Usher, a part of printing was for the luxury trade, for which it took some time for the new process to be an improvement, although its real contribution was to be mass printing.[21] Yet, there was considerable resistance to printing, and many still preferred hand-copied texts.[22] It is unclear, however, to what extent opposition to the newer processes was based on tradition or on conservation.

From Usher, again, we learn that "strictly speaking, printing from movable type begins with the use of sand-cast type, but this was not the strategic invention in the series because the results were imperfect and the process was incapable of any large development. With such technique, accomplishment would be restricted to small school texts and devotional books."[23] The question becomes: At what point is resistance to an invention operationally legitimate (even though institutional factors may have influenced this assessment) and at what point is continued opposition to an invention or scientific idea no longer operationally justifiable? Obviously, each stage in the evolutionary development of a technique or idea is necessary for subsequent developments. These steps must be understood as integral parts of the technological and scientific processes.

This situation poses a dilemma for a theory of technology-ceremony dichotomy. Resistance to a new improved technology can be labeled ceremonial. Was that resistance any less ceremonial at the time when that invention was demonstrably inferior to the technology currently in use? Similarly, how does one handle ritualistic commitment to current technology prior to the time that it has been superseded? To respond by saying that the technology-ceremony dichotomy is a functional analysis that looks at aspects of behavior sounds plausible until we attempt to apply it to specific cases. For, as we have noted above, Ayres argued that ceremonies simulate technology in that the beliefs upon which they are based purport to some causal efficacy. We test them only by the consequence. The problem with the manner in which Ayres presents his theory of technology is that he seems to assume that all new technology is in some way better than existing technology. Ayres continually reiterates that he is talking about behavior and even argues that "the value of a tool is not a function of its materiality," but of its instrumental character.[24] Despite the strongly avowed intellectual position of Ayres, tools as physical objects play an important role in Ayres's theorizing.

The way out of these dilemmas would seem to be to focus upon and refine Ayres's concept of technology as being a process. Technology, skills, and science can be conceived as the sum of human problem-solving capabilities. Progressive technological change, then, is any invention of a tool or combination of tools or new ways to improve existing tools that expand our problem-solving capability. We could also include any organizational innovation that facilitates use of tools (whether new or old) superior to those in use. Equally important, particularly to development economists, is the modification or adaptation of existing tools to fit the circumstances of a specific cultural or physical environment.[25] Included also are the motor skills necessary to use certain tools and the closely related habits of mind necessary to operate complex technologies.[26] Finally, and most important, are the other nonmaterial aspects of technology. The habits of mind necessary to operate a specific array of technologies are subsets of the larger mental processes, that is, technological ways of looking at problems.[27] These patterns of thought are essentially synonymous with what most of us learned in a simplified form in school as the scientific method, that is, defining a problem, establishing a hypothesis, testing it, and so forth. All tools are the material embodiment of ideas; all skills, no matter how seemingly rote, imply the practical use of ideas; all problem solving therefore involves ideas and cannot be understood apart from the ways of thought involved in the effective use of technology.

Viewing technology as problem solving makes the definition of the problem a vital element in the specification of any tool as being technological for a specific objective. What we are doing is stressing what Ayres called the "instrumental nature of technology." Thus, a hammer is a tool; a lock is a tool. If one has a lock and no key, a hammer (or similar instrument of force) would be the appropriate tool (technology) for the purpose of opening it. If the objective is to reuse the lock, then a hammer might not be the technology for this circumstance, while a key would. This is obvious, and virtually everyone would assent to it. To define it as technology, we look at the instrumental function of a tool in terms of the use to which it is put. This is so elementary that it should not have to be stated.

Technology as problem solving is consistent with the Ayresian concept of resources. In his lectures Ayres was fond of quoting Erich Zimmermann to the effect that resources are not "static and fixed"; "resources become."[28] Zimmermann speaks of a "resource process." The universe contains "neutral stuff." "Human wants and human capabilities" convert the "neutral stuff" of the universe into resources.[29] Human wants or needs are defined in problem specification and problem solving, and technology as problem solving defines "human capability." Raw materials become resources when humans acquire the technology to use them. Many materials have lost some or all of their resource character as technology has created processes using other raw materials that are more efficient at solving particular problems. Technology creates resources; technology uses resources. The two are aspects of one process; you cannot use resources that you have not created. Whether we will run out of any particular resources, that is, use resources faster than technology can create them, depends in part on whether we define our short- and long-term problems and how we order our priorities.[30] Thus, paradoxically, if technology is "destroying" resources, the solution is more technology, properly defined and understood.

Technology is a problem-solving process; ceremonies seek to simulate technology. Ayres believed that the differences between the two were *inherent* in the process. We argue the contrary, that the nature of the process of sciences or technologies does not vary over the time in which they become superior to existing science and technology. It is not their nature that has changed, but their operational capabilities. And whether theory or technique is operationally superior can only be determined by testing.[31] Simply stated, we are arguing that technology is technologizing. The analogy to mind and minding is helpful. We have a physical object, the brain. We cannot observe mind, but we can see human (or other animals) behave, that is, mind-in-use or minding.[32] If we find patterns in behavior, we can infer a mind in the sense that there are commonalities in the mind-in-use or minding that we have observed. Similarly, we have physical objects that we call tools. The use of tools by humans in the act of problem solving is technologizing. Technology is the inference from the observation of repeated acts of technologizing. And technologizing cannot be fully de-

868   Thomas R. De Gregori

fined without specification of the problems to be solved. The changes that we propose in Ayres's theory of technology and in institutional economics are minor; the practical consequences of these modifications for problem solving are, in our judgment, significant.

Notes

1. See W. Paul Strassmann, "Technology: A Cultural Trait, a Logical Category, or Virtue Itself?" *Journal of Economic Issues* 8 (December 1974): 674–75.
2. Thorstein Veblen, "The Place of Science in Modern Civilization," *American Journal of Sociology* 11 (March 1906), reprinted in Thorstein Veblen, *The Place of Science in Modern Civilization, and Other Essays* (New York: Russell & Russell, 1961), p. 17.
3. Clarence E. Ayres, *The Theory of Economic Progress* (Chapel Hill: University of North Carolina Press, 1944).
4. Clarence E. Ayres, *Toward a Reasonable Society; The Values of Industrial Civilization* (Austin: University of Texas Press, 1961), pp. 71–86, 123–38.
5. Ayres, *Theory of Economic Progress*, pp. 108, 11, and *Toward a Reasonable Society*, p. 77.
6. Ayres, *Toward a Reasonable Society*, p. 77.
7. Ayres, *Theory of Economic Progress*, p. 112, and *Toward a Reasonable Society*, p. 80.
8. Ayres, *Theory of Economic Progress*, p. 112, and *Toward a Reasonable Society*, pp. 113–14.
9. Ayres, *Theory of Economic Progress*, pp. 123, 119, 120.
10. Ibid., p. 121. For example, the camera obscura and discoveries in chemistry made the development of photography so likely that a leading historian of that subject has argued that "in 1685 the camera was absolutely ready and waiting for photography," and "the circumstance that photography was not invented earlier [than the nineteenth century] remains the greatest mystery in its history." Helmut Gernsheim, *The History of Photography* (New York: McGraw-Hill, 1969), pp. 27 and 13.
11. Ayres, *Theory of Economic Progress*, p. 121.
12. Ibid., p. 176.
13. Ibid., p. 157.
14. Ibid., p. 160, and *Toward a Reasonable Society*, pp. 137 and 31. Ayres attributes the term "ceremonial adequacy" to Veblen without citing a specific source.
15. Ayres, *Theory of Economic Progress*, p. 166, and *Toward a Reasonable Society*, p. 137.
16. Ayres, *Theory of Economic Progress*, pp. 168–69 and pp. 158–59.
17. Ibid., chapter 7, pp. 125–54, and *Toward a Reasonable Society*, pp. 178–80.
18. Thomas S. Kuhn, *The Structure of Scientific Revolutions*, 2nd ed., enlarged (Chicago: University of Chicago Press, International Encyclope-

dia of Unified Sciences, vol. I and II: Foundations of the Unity of Science, 1970), volume II, no. 2. See also A. Rupert Hall, *The Scientific Revolution, 1500–1800: The Formation of Modern Scientific Attitude,* 2nd ed. (Boston: Beacon Press, 1967).

19. Abbott Payson Usher, *A History of Mechanical Inventions* (Boston: Beacon Press, 1959), p. 247. See also pp. 254–55.

20. Ibid., p. 254.

21. Ibid.

22. J. B. Priestly, *Literature and Western Man* (New York: Harper and Brothers, 1960), p. 4. For similar resistance to printing in Japan, see Donald Keene, *World within Walls: Japanese Literature of the Pre-Modern Era, 1600–1867* (New York: Holt, Rinehart and Winston, 1976), pp. 2–4.

23. Usher, *Mechanical Inventions,* p. 254.

24. Ayres, *Toward a Reasonable Society,* p. 80. See also Strassmann, "Technology," pp. 674–75.

25. On this point see Thomas R. De Gregori, *Technology and the Economic Development of the Tropical African Frontier* (Cleveland: Case Western Reserve University Press, 1969), chapters 2 and 4, pp. 35–60, 83–182.

26. Ibid., chapter 5, pp. 183–230, for the concept of industrial habits of mind.

27. Thomas R. De Gregori, *Technology and Economic Change: Essays and Inquiries,* Notes and Papers on Development No. 9. (Comox, British Columbia: McLoughlin Associates, Ltd., 1974), chapter 4, pp. 30–34.

28. See Ayres, *Theory of Economic Progress,* pp. 84–85, 113; and Erich W. Zimmermann, *World Resources and Industries,* rev. ed. (New York: Harper & Bros., 1951), chapter 1, particularly pp. 11–12.

29. Zimmermann, *World Resources,* p. 10; and De Gregori, *Tropical African Frontier,* pp. 4–5.

30. The resource creation process of technology involves not only discovery of means of using iron, copper, uranium, and so forth, making them resources in a generic sense, but also the technical means by which certain grades and kinds of these materials become more readily usable. For example, in the last century, almost continuous technological change has facilitated the use of copper of vastly lower quality.

31. The philosophical basis for any theory of problem stating and problem solving would probably still draw heavily on the work of John Dewey. Ayres gave ample credit to Dewey for his influence on Ayres's theory of technology. Dewey, however, gave heavier and in our judgment appropriate emphasis to problem stating, while Ayres tended to pass over this issue in his theory of technology. For three of the more important of the many books and articles by Dewey on this subject, see John Dewey, *Logic: The Theory of Inquiry* (New York: Henry Holt and Co., 1938), *Essays in Experimental Logic* (Chicago: University of Chicago Press, 1916), and *Theory of Valuation* (Chicago: University of Chicago Press, International Encyclopedia of Unified Science, 1939), vol. II, no. 4.

32. Our terminology here in influenced by Leslie White's "Science Is Sciencing and Mind Is Minding." See Leslie White, *The Science of Culture: A Study of Man and Civilization* (New York: Grove Press, 1949), pp. 3–21, 49–54. In 1960, as a student, I submitted a paper to Ayres, "Technology

870   Thomas R. De Gregori

Is Technologizing." He thought that the idea was original and worth an A
but fundamentally misconceived. He argued that one could tell the difference between a shaman and an agronomist before the crop was in.

References

Ayres, Clarence E. *The Theory of Economic Progress.* Chapel Hill: University
of North Carolina Press, 1944.
Ayres, Clarence E. *Toward a Reasonable Society: The Values of Industrial
Civilization.* Austin: University of Texas Press, 1961.
De Gregori, Thomas R. *Technology and Economic Change: Essays and In-
quiries.* Notes and Papers in Development No. 9. Comox, British Columbia:
McLoughlin Associates, Ltd., 1974.
De Gregori, Thomas R. *Technology and the Economic Development of the
Tropical African Frontier.* Cleveland, Ohio: Case Western Reserve Univer-
sity Press, 1969.
Dewey, John. *Essays in Experimental Logic.* Chicago: University of Chicago
Press, 1916.
Dewey, John. *Logic: The Theory of Inquiry.* New York: Henry Holt & Com-
pany, 1938.
Dewey, John. *Theory of Valuation.* Chicago: University of Chicago Press,
International Encyclopedia of Unified Science, Foundations of the Unity of
Science, 1939. Vol. II, No. 4.
Gernsheim, Helmut (in collaboration with Alison Gernsheim). *The History
of Photography: From the Camera Obscura to the Beginning of the Modern
Era.* New York: McGraw-Hill, 1969.
Hall, A. Rupert. *The Scientific Revolution 1500–1800: The Formation of
Modern Scientific Attitude.* 2nd ed. Boston: Beacon Press, 1967.
Kuhn, Thomas S. *The Structure of Scientific Revolutions.* 2nd ed., enlarged.
Chicago: University of Chicago Press, International Encyclopedia of Uni-
fied Sciences, Volumes I and II: Foundations of the Unity of Science, 1970.
Vol. II, No. 2.
Keene, Donald. *World within Walls: Japanese Literature of the Pre-Modern
Era, 1600–1867.* New York: Holt, Rinehart and Winston, 1976.
Strassmann, W. Paul. "Technology: A Cultural Trait, a Logical Category, or
Virtue Itself?" *Journal of Economic Issues* 8 (December 1974): 671–87.
Usher, Abbot Payson. *A History of Mechanical Inventions.* Boston: Beacon
Press, 1959.
Veblen, Thorstein. "The Place of Science in Modern Civilization." Reprinted
in Thorstein Veblen, *The Place of Science in Modern Civilization: And
Other Essays.* New York: Russell & Russell, 1961. Pp. 1–31.
White, Leslie A. *The Science of Culture: A Study of Man and Civilization.* New
York: Grove Press, 1949.
Zimmermann, Erich W. *World Resources and Industries: A Functional Ap-
praisal of the Availability of Agricultural and Industrial Materials.* Rev. ed.
New York: Harper & Brothers, 1951.

[4]

Instrumental Criteria for Assessing Technology: An Affirmation by Way of a Reply

The teleological tautology (whatever that may be) is purely a figment of Gregory Hayden's imagination. He quotes me: "Technology understood as problem solving carries its own concept of appropriateness."[1] The technology of a tool lies in its ability to solve a problem. This is not a "privileged status"; in the same sentence from which the above quotation was taken, I argue for the importance of problem definition. "Viewing technology as problem solving makes the definition of the problem a vital element in the specification of any tool as being technological for a specific objective."[2] Need we add that specification is an individual and societal task. I trust that this also addresses Hayden's concern about a supposed technological determinism in my article.

The "thinly veiled tautology" of technology-development-technology is referenced to page 468 (and page 473), on which the reasons for technological borrowing were given, that is, to improve levels of living, survival, and so forth.[3] Hayden may not agree with these, but he cannot deny that they are there in the text, while the alleged completion of the circular reasoning is not. Similarly, I am not entirely uncomfortable with his interpretation that "technology is universal because everyone uses it in his milieu," although I would have worded it differently. But nowhere do I say that people use technology *because* it is universal. People use technology because it solves problems as they define them.

Hayden delivers the coup de grace by saying that I justified a concept of interdependent technologies by using Ayres's Institutional Theory. "He did not say *all communities are interdependent*" (italics are Hayden's). Since Ayres's basic concept of knowledge was dynamic and developmental, normally it would be pointless to argue whether an idea fits the exact letter of his theories or whether it was an evolutionary outgrowth of the spirit of them. Presumably, Ayres would wish us to use his writing to open inquiry rather than close it by appeal to doctrinal purity. However, Hayden has made a claim that must be answered. I mention Clarence Ayres once in reference to "Veblen, Clarence Ayres, and other institutionalists," and that is in a sentence concerned solely with the advance of technology "by the combination and recombination of existing tools and technology." The point being made was that appropriate technology, by the small-scale local criterion I noted and by Hayden's criteria, can cut a people off from the benefits of technological progress that occurs worldwide in a combinational process. Thus, an institutional theory of technology is useful because it points out the potential gains and losses that are

Notes and Communications

involved in the choice of a technology. This is one of the things that theory is supposed to do. It gives us operational questions to ask. The combinational aspect of technology is one that Hayden attests to as being Ayresian. Nowhere else do I refer to Ayres, although I speak of institutional theory. Never mind; Hayden is incorrect on both counts. I did not say Ayres said 220 it, but I could have, because he did. In a work cited by Hayden, Ayres refers to the state as a "jurisdictional subdivision of a technologically integrated world."[4] For that matter, I was speaking primarily of interdependence between countries and not communities. Hayden should finish a book before he states categorically and unequivocally what is not in it or in the entirety of an author's work.

It is unfortunate that the character of Hayden's critique might obscure the fundamental issue that separates us, a division that reflects a similar schism among those who have thoughts on the subject. Namely, it concerns our attitude toward modern technology (or whatever Hayden chooses to call it—I will not quibble). There have always been people who distrusted the latest technology in their time, but I find it strange that a group calling itself Ayresian and institutionalist takes this position. Each to his own, and let a thousand flowers bloom! If a few simple statements about urban concentration in industrial countries, or about conceivable agricultural schemes having large dams as a component, trigger a polemic against agriculture as it is practiced in industrial countries, and if advocacy of any facet of industrial technology makes one guilty of all the sins that Hayden catalogs, then we can only reasonably conclude that Hayden himself rejects this technology. For if he accepts any part of it, by his own reasoning processes, he would be the legitimate subject of a critique comparable to his own. Similarly, the élan of appropriate technology (or intermediate technology) as an all-encompassing system is predicated upon some supposed failure in existing technologies to come to grips with problems of poor countries and of industrial countries.

Amory Lovins, one of the two appropriate technology advocates cited by Hayden (along with an annotated bibliography), contends that there are two kinds of technology, soft (that is, appropriate, and so forth) and hard, and that we must choose one path of technological development or the other.[5] Similarly, from Schumacher we learn that in "the subtle system of nature, technology, and in particular the super-technology of the modern world, acts like a foreign body, and there are now numerous signs of rejection."[6] One does not need to "misrepresent" Schumacher to those who have not read his work in order to make him appear not entirely modern or scientific in his perspective on issues. He thinks that a woman's place should be in the home.[7] He thinks that unemployment is not a problem in countries such as the United States if it is viewed and attacked from the perspective of the local community or neighborhood.[8] Hayden has placed himself solidly in this camp. In my article (including one section quoted by Hayden), I advocated the use of all kinds of technologies, in-

221   cluding appropriate technology. I even conceded that "it might well be that for some countries under present circumstances, the bulk of their effort should be directed toward a basic needs strategy employing small-scale technology." What I argued for was "empirical investigation" and testing, not for *a priori* assumptions.[9] But this is not good enough for Hayden. He tell us: "It is impossible even to consider providing nutrition to the world population with current technology."

Has "current technology" failed us so badly? If we cannot trust our local supermarket, who can we trust? Hayden's documentation is impressive. Impressive though Hayden's documentation may be, the question is, where is the aggregate evidence? Since Hayden thinks that reference to Ayres's value base is important to our debate, let us note his observation on this point. "Industrial society is the most successful way of life mankind has ever known. Quite literally, we have never had it so good. People eat better, sleep better, live in more comfortable dwellings, get around more and in far better comfort, keep in better repair, and notwithstanding all the manifold dangers of the industrial way of life—live longer than men have ever done before."[10]

We can raise the same issue of aggregate implications of the technology that has been used for development in poorer countries. David Morawetz sums up the actual circumstances of development in the last few decades.

> In average per capita income the developing countries grew more rapidly between 1950 and 1975—3.4 percent a year—than either they or the developed countries had done in any comparable period in the past. They thereby exceeded both official goals and private expectations. That this growth was real and not simply statistical artifact may be seen in the progress that occurred simultaneously in various indexes of basic needs. Increases in life expectancy that required a century of economic development in the industrialized countries have been achieved in the developing world in two or three decades. Progress has been made in the world in the eradication of communicable diseases. And the proportion of adults in developing countries who are literate has increased substantially.[11]

This development is not cause for euphoria, despite the fact that it is unprecedented in magnitude. For some, the levels of living are so low that even high rates of per capita growth will leave them in poverty for too long. And there are major problems of distribution. But, as Morawetz and Irma Adelman have noted, distribution is largely a problem of ownership

Notes and Communications

of productive assets (including education), not of the rate of growth, the type of economic system, or of the technology used.[12] These difficulties and others are hardly grounds for condemning modern technology, or for abandoning it for one that, according to Schumacher, does not yet exist (although the knowledge for it does).[13] And on the question of distribu- 222
tion raised by critics of the use of modern technology in economic develop- ment, when we wish to compare countries to models of more equitable distribution, which ones do we use but Sweden or Holland?

Hayden and the appropriate technology people have a strange habit of reversing the truth. Three times Hayden speaks of vulnerability, including a country's being "vulnerable to modern technology." Which countries of the world are most vulnerable to small changes in rainfall or climatic varia- bles? Which countries are most vulnerable to pestilence or disease? The rich or the poor? And when these areas suffer some disaster, which coun- tries have the means to help—the industrial or the nonindustrial? These rhetorical questions are so obvious that they answer themselves. And it is quite clear that Third World countries would like to be "vulnerable" to modern technology. The call for a New International Economic Order is a recognition of the necessity to try to achieve genuine interdependence (difficult as that may be), since complete self-sufficiency is not a viable alternative.

If Hayden is charging me with believing that, with all its faults, the in- dustrial way of life is the best that humans have ever created, then I plead guilty as charged. However, I would argue that we can use our technology and develop new technology to improve the quality of life even further in developed and underdeveloped countries, including solving some of the ills referred to by Hayden. Modern sophisticated science and technology, from satellites to plant genetics, offer great potential for continuing and accelerating development. That does not mean that I advocate sophisti- cated technology exclusively (and my article is clear on that point). The more the technologies that are available, the greater the range of choices. What the sections on appropriate technology in my article argued against were *a priori* theories of technology that beg the question by giving answers to all questions before they are asked, and that seek to eliminate totally other forms of technology from consideration for problem solving. An earlier draft of this comment contained specific arguments in response to Hayden. These are issues that need to be debated in detail in the *JEI* and other journals or forums.

My article opposes economic and technological dependency, naïve free market beliefs, and autarchic theories of small-scale technologies. It ad- vocates that democracy and education, institutional economic theory, and

Notes and Communications

empirical investigation (meaning the scientific method) be used in the process of choosing technologies. After trying to cut through Hayden's jargon about teleological tautologies, and so forth, I am still at a loss to see what his fuss is about, unless he does actually believe that peoples of 223 the world can do without modern science and technology (not only in the sense of what exists but also what is continually coming into being). If that is the case, then I would have to say, respectfully, that he is wrong and that it is unfortunate that space does not permit us to have a detailed empirical debate (with "substantiating evidence," as he calls it), because the issues involved here are at the heart of the development process. I am grateful to Hayden for the opportunity of joining some of them here.

Thomas R. De Gregori

The author is Professor of Economics, University of Houston, Houston, Texas.

Notes

1. Thomas R. De Gregori, "Technology and Economic Dependency," *Journal of Economic Issues* 12 (June 1978): 474.
2. Thomas R. De Gregori, "Technology and Ceremonial Behavior: Aspects of Institutionalism," *Journal of Economic Issues* 11 (December 1977): 866. This article also deals with the question of technology and the creation of resources to which Hayden alludes.
3. De Gregori, "Technology and Economic Dependency," p. 478.
4. C. E. Ayres, *The Theory of Economic Progress* (Chapel Hill: University of North Carolina Press, 1944), p. 290.
5. Amory B. Lovins, "Energy Strategy—The Road Not Taken," *Foreign Affairs* 55 (October 1976): 65–96.
6. E. F. Schumacher, *Small Is Beautiful: Economics as If People Mattered* (New York: Harper & Row, 1973), p. 139.
7. Ibid., pp. 53–54.
8. E. F. Schumacher, "Taking the Scare Out of Scarcity," *Psychology Today* 11 (September 1976): 16. E. F. Schumacher, *A Guide for the Perplexed* (New York: Harper & Row, 1977), is chock full of the occult.
9. De Gregori, "Technology and Economic Dependency," p. 474.
10. C. E. Ayres, *Toward a Reasonable Society: The Values of Industrial Civilization* (Austin: Uuniversity of Texas Press, 1961), p. 13. The purpose in writing the book was to argue and justify that industrial society was not at a "dead end" and that science was not "spiritually sterile" (p. 5).
11. David Morawetz, *Twenty-five Years of Economic Development 1950–1975* (Washington, D.C.: World Bank, 1977), p. 67. See also his article, same title, in *Finance and Development* 14 (September 1977): 10–13.

Notes and Communications

On population, see also Rati Ram and Theodore W. Schultz, "Life Span, Health, Savings, and Productivity," *Economic Development and Cultural Change* 27 (April 1979): 399–421; and the entire issue of *Population Reports*, Series M., no. 3 (July 1979).

12. Morawetz, *Twenty-five Years*, pp. 71–72; and Irma Adelman, "A Theory of Development Strategy for Equitable Growth in Developing Countries," in *Research in Economic Anthropology, A Research Annual*, edited by   224

George Dalton (Greenwich, Ct.: JAI Press, 1979), vol. 2, pp. 247–67. It is, after all, Irma Adelman's statistical work(along with that of Cynthia Taft Morris) that is probably the most frequently cited research on the problem of inequality in developing areas. See, for example, Irma Adelman and Cynthia Taft Morris, *Economic Growth and Social Equity in Developing Countries* (Stanford, Calif.: Stanford University Press, 1973).

13. Schumacher, *Small Is Beautiful*, p. 146.   225

JƏi *JOURNAL OF ECONOMIC ISSUES*
Vol. XI   No. 4   December 1977

Technology *Vis-à-Vis* Institutions in the *JEI*: A Suggested Interpretation

Warren J. Samuels

The conflict of technology and institutions has been a distinguishing theme and an important issue in institutional economics, especially in the Thorstein Veblen and Clarence Ayres tradition, with contemporary counterparts in John Kenneth Galbraith, Robert Solo, and others who deliberately use the Veblen-Ayres dichotomy as a framework of research and policy analysis. The *JEI* has published considerable and diverse materials bearing on the relation of technology to institutions. The purpose of this article is to present a systematic interpretation and integration of those materials.[1]

I recognize that the dichotomy can be so formulated as to be absolute and irreconcilable. The aim here, in part, is to indicate the unrealism of such a formulation. Material has been published in the *JEI*, not to mention elsewhere, which contributes to a searching reexamination and amplification of the technology-institutions dichotomy and which can be integrated into a comprehensive and meaningful body of analysis, understandably and predictably with unresolved conflicts and open questions. The continued reliance on rather narrow formulations of the dichotomy and related themes itself may evidence the ceremonial hold of past thought patterns, whereas the larger picture appears to be far more complex. The journal thus also represents the inevitable reinterpretation of past ideas.[2] Needless to say, this article cannot do justice to the depth and elaborateness of

---

The author is Professor of Economics, Michigan State University, East Lansing.

the many materials cited or to the subjects themselves. Hopefully, the article will present a rounded interpretation. The later work of Clarence Ayres indicates that the interpretation given here is inconsistent only with a simplistic formulation of his views, but that is a different story.

The Problem of Definition

There are advantages in using the terms *technology* and *institutions* as primitive, that is, undefined, terms so as not to foreclose analysis or channel conclusions tautologically, which necessarily creates considerable ambiguity, to put it mildly. But to define them one way or another for greater precision raises problems of comparability and channeling. The terms, for example, can be defined so as to be mutually exclusive or somewhat partially overlapping. Also, each word can be narrowly or broadly defined. The safest alternative is to juggle several definitions simultaneously, but that creates problems of ambiguity and does not eliminate the problem of channeling. To avoid becoming mired in terminological discussion, and since I do not propose to touch base with definitions at every point, I leave it to the reader to do so. The problem is endemic to the relevant literature.

Technology can be defined quite narrowly as tools, less narrowly as the material arts, and much more broadly as knowledge about how to do things, especially with respect to activity characterized by means-ends relationships appropriate to intended purposes.[3] In this article I tend generally to use *technology* in the broadest sense.

Institutions can be defined as collective action in control and liberation of the individual, or as modes of thought, action, and organization of relations. As a synonym, *ceremony* can be defined as emotional, as opposed to rational (means-end consonance), beliefs and practices, that is, as widely prevalent habits of thinking, feeling, and acting which are largely customary or traditional in character.[4]

The many and subtle nuances must be largely forgone here, but we may suggest the difficulty of clear-cut distinctions. May not technology be considered as a widely prevalent habit of thought, feeling, and action? (Matter-of-fact thinking, *vis-à-vis* ceremonial, may be substituted for *technology* in that question.) May not institutions serve intended purposes through consonant means-end relationships, that is, cannot an organizational technology exist? In response to the anticipated objection that such queries involve a change of definitions or play on words, I urge that we proceed cautiously with the terms. The reader, at the end, can conclude whether the analysis renders any terminological abuse, and if so in what way.

The Received Doctrine

The received doctrine of the Veblen-Ayres tradition of institutionalism maintains, first, that progressive technology may be juxtaposed to passive and inhibitive institutions (the instrumental to the ceremonial point of view) and, second, that technology is the primary, if not the imperative, force in economic and social evolution.

According to the first theme, economic development is a function of the pressure of technological change against the inertia of traditional modes of organized behavior (institutions or power structure and orientation of economic and social policy). Economic growth is a product of the conflict of the instrumental logic of technology *vis-à-vis* resisting forces. Technology represents new modes of organization and a distinctive way of thinking and acting, with emphasis upon operational efficiency. Economic development requires a revolution in patterns of life and the relative power of groups and interests.[5] The accumulation of technological knowledge is regulated by the resistance of the institutional order; its assimilation is a function of its adoption and use, with institutional change or adaptation being a byproduct.

> The basic pattern, as suggested by institutional theory, is that the accumulation of technical knowledge (an inherently dynamic process in which the unearthing of one bit of new knowledge naturally leads to the unearthing of another) occurs with a speed regulated by the effectiveness with which the institutional order resists the assimilation of the new knowledge. The assimilation of the new knowledge or technology is a rational act as people (and institutions) become aware of the implications and usefulness of it. The institutional changes needed then will happen more or less as an automatic by-product of the assimilation process—no fuss, no feathers. People eat food that contains the protein supplement because they have come to understand that is the best thing to do. Through their understanding of the implications of the technology they have played a role in development.[6]

The process may yield a dual economy, with one sector maintained by institutional and cultural forces inhibiting adjustment to superior technology.[7] In one case study or application, an early period of growth was attributed to a fusion of propitious conditions: technological, engineering, managerial, and educational innovations in an area well endowed with natural resources and institutionally and demographically receptive. Later stagnation was attributed to a lapse into institutionalized cultural predispositions inconsistent with the functional requirements of an industrial society, specifically, an inability to domesticate and propagate a technological process earlier derived from abroad and a resumption of cultural

874   Warren J. Samuels

attitudes and habits (institutions) inhibiting the formation of an ongoing diversified economy.[8]

According to this view, institutional adjustment is called for when superior production capabilities are available.[9] Thus, economic development is seen primarily as a problem of technological development or transfer and institutional adaptation.[10] One role of the institutional framework is to adjust so as to permit technological utilization and to minimize the socioeconomic dislocations arising from technological change and economic growth.[11] Two implications are, first, that wastefulness is a function of practices not furthering the technological life process (for example, status oriented uses of goods or resources[12]) and, second, that no technological reason exists for poverty in modern industrial society.[13] In the latter regard, imputations of productivity in society represent a habit of thought reinforcing and justifying existing institutions.[14] Massive institutional change is required to eliminate poverty but is inhibited by the circular justification of income distribution by productivity attributions developed in terms of existing institutions.[15] The theme thus asserts the social value of instrumental efficiency, the necessity to remove institutional constraints on industrial efficiency, the necessity for social leadership by those least contaminated by ceremonial adherence to established ways, and the conception of freedom as both an end in itself and a means to the realization of the growth potential of the tool continuum (technology),[16] which is typically viewed as promoting the welfare of all people rather than an established elite. Instrumental efficiency is thus the criterion of selection for institutional adjustment.[17]

The second theme is an extension of the first: Technological advancement is the driving force of economic and social change.[18] Thus, "technological determinism . . . is the core of institutionalism,"[19] according to one interpreter. Scientific and technological progress can be inhibited by cultural lag;[20] although institutions are retardational, technology is the dynamic force.[21] Technology is the primary, if not the imperative, force in economic and social evolution.[22]

Some Initial Comments

Several preliminary comments are in order. First, it is clear that the technology-institutions dichotomy has been used in the interpretation and policy analysis of experiences in economic development or nondevelopment.

Second, several distinct but interrelated themes concerning technology must be distinguished from one another: technology as a critical but neglected force in economic development; technology as the dynamic, if

not imperative, force in economic development; technology as an exogenous, or determining, variable; technology as possessed of an objective
character (say, once traditional modes of thought are transcended); technology as a valuational basis, in juxtaposition to and conflict with ceremonial beliefs and practices; and technology as central to a theory of the
modern industrial system (constituting an emphasis upon the process or
logic of industrialization).

Third, it must be understood that reliance upon technology as an evaluative basis constitutes an exercise in conditional normativism.[23] The
analyst first assumes certain normative premises or preconceptions (as at
least implicit antecedent normative assumptions) and then considers the
most effective mode(s) of their achievement or realization. (For example,
the analyst may assume the desirability of the fact, structure, and rate of
economic growth and development and from preconceptions concerning
the technological bases thereof.) The normative element is the subjectively
chosen and valued goal; the positive element is the use of instrumental or
scientific method in the achievement of the goal.

Fourth, both primary themes raise a question of the role of choice in
human society concerning, for example, resource allocation, income distribution, and institutional organization, that is, the question of the *purposes* (or social goals) for which technology is to be used. Consideration
of the role of human social choice leads to the further question of the role
of *power* in economy and society.

The importance of the points raised in these comments will emerge in
the subsequent discussion.

Some Critiques and Rival Themes

The elevation of technology above institutions as the dynamic force and
perhaps above all else in the explanation and evaluation of economic
organization and evolution has not gone unchallenged within institutional
economics, not to mention orthodox economics. Also, the *JEI,* from its
inception, has published materials which more or less severely qualify the
probative value of the technology-institutions dichotomy (even if both
parts are given parity) and which assert other themes, all of which taken
together may lead to a more rounded treatment.

Critique of the
Technology-Institutions Dichotomy

Whatever else may be said of the matter, the Veblen-Ayres emphasis
on technology served to remedy its neglected treatment as a factor in ex-

plaining economic evolution and the neglect of economic evolution itself, especially in an industrial economy. In so doing, it performed the function of indicating the relativity (and cultural diversity) of institutions, thereby offering both an explanation for systematic change and a foundation for critiquing extant habits of thought, practice, and organization. At the least, it diagnosed the myopia of continuing the institutions-as-given assumption of static social and economic theory when analysis and policy were confronted with deeper questions. But the fundamental technology-institutions dichotomy itself has been subject to serious questioning in the *JEI*.

It has been argued that technology is not readily systematized as a research tool. A narrow conception of technology raises problems of exclusion; a broad conception, problems of the meaningfulness of the dichotomy itself. For example, technology can include the instrumental role and value of symbols and organizations, as a result of an understanding that institutions (ceremonial thought and behavior) are not always irrational but may function instrumentally to organize behavior.[24] One writer, Paul Strassmann, seems to transcend a simplistic dichotomy by suggesting that Clarence Ayres's broad conception of technology was ahead of both his and our generation.[25]

It is understandable, then, that technology may be perceived as intangible and ambiguous and may be specified and interpreted differently by different analysts.[26]

At least equally important is the argument that the technology-institutions dichotomy involves a complex blend of positive and normative elements. There is, for example, a normative element or role in the use of technology as both an analytic and evaluative category in reaching such characterizations as "economic stagnation," "waste," and "technological advance." The use of the technology category as a valuational basis gives effect to implicit antecedent normative premises, nowhere more importantly than in the selective identification of one set of arrangements as technological (and thus progressive) and another as institutional (and thus repressive or inhibitive).

Closely related to the above is the status of organizational technology, namely, the question whether organizational knowledge is technology within the confines of the dichotomy and, therefore, the problems of the possibility and mode of separation of that dimension of institutions from those normally denigrated by the analysis. This line of reasoning also raises questions of the status of the designer role and of the place of choice in institutional design and assessment.[27]

A number of other points have been made. One of them questions the probative value of the dichotomy (and the imperative role of technology) in light of the great institutional diversity evident among capitalist countries.[28] A second underscores the complex array of factors which seem to produce institutional change and the specific character (or absence) of economic development. A third suggests that the conceptualization of technology itself may be a function of deep socialization forces within an industrial economy.[29]

Rejection of Untenable
Technological Determinism

In light of the above, it is not surprising that considerable criticism has been directed at the idea of technology as the primary, if not imperative, force in economic evolution. Technological determinism has been held narrow and inflexible,[30] indeed untenable.[31] It is a single-factor explanation at variance with the institutionalist critique of neoclassical economics which rejects narrow mechanism and urges multifactor cumulative causation. It is at variance, too, with institutionalist conceptions of systemic and institutional and evolutionary diversity. Technological determinism involves reification, hypostatization, misplaced concreteness, and the subtle intrusion of ideological or normative premises into the process channeling the role of choice in society. Its role in institutional economics seems akin to that of the theology of an industrial economy in neoclassical economics.[32] The sense in which technology may be understood as the primary, if not imperative, force in economic evolution and as the critical evaluative criterion is thus severely constrained.

Technology as a Determined Variable

The idea of technology as an imperative force is countered, or at least supplemented, by a number of themes whose collective thrust is that the development and impact of technology are a function of institutions or power structure. Technology is understood to consist of an array of possible alternatives, and the realized or actualized technological alternative is projected as a dependent variable.

Among the themes which contribute to that understanding is the modified neoclassical proposition that the course of technological change is a partial function of relative prices.[33]

The main theme, however, is that technology is an array of alternatives subject to choice, and that choice is a function of criteria which are themselves a function of the power structure and attitudes. According to this view, society *is* deeply affected by technology, but technology is neither autonomous nor all-determining. On the contrary, technology is man-made and changeable; especially, it is given varying characteristics by machine designers and builders. The production of capital, among other things, is influenced by technology, which is itself influenced by design criteria which reflect social structure and working rules, especially of those who decide on technology. Social and economic relations are reflected in technology, which therefore is a function of and reflects the structure of human choice. Technology builds upon the preferred economic criteria of those with the capacity to decide. Once created and used, technology has an important bearing on man's life, but the location and direction of decision making with regard to technology derive from power relations and the values prevailing in the social structure. Technology is a function of design criteria, which are a function of power structure.[34] A key role, then, is attributed to power structure or institutions in the evolution of technology itself.

Contributing to and/or expanding upon that theme are others. The introduction of technology is a partial function of power structure. A role of hierarchical power structures is to govern the distribution of technological opportunities.[35] Both the origins and consequences of technology are a partial function of institutions.[36] Technology assessment is a function of values or attitudes; a change in power structure likely will lead to a change in technology assessment. Institutions govern the choice of technology and thereby give effect to the power structure as to whose choices and interests will count. Thus, there is legal-economic power play over technology and its consequences. There is power play within and among all relevant extant institutions (for example, the state, corporations) selectively to capture profit opportunities, for example. through newly defined property rights. Technology is both channeled and exploited, but along one line rather than another, by those seeking larger gains than possible under already existing institutions through their efforts to revise institutions to permit them rather than others to take advantage of technological opportunities. In this process institutional adjustment follows upon technology, but not in any simple one-to-one relation or predetermined direction. The specific adjustment(s) forthcoming depends upon which strategies and calculations of advantage are successful. This result, in part, depends upon differential access to legal institutions, and differential alertness to conditional economic prospects, and thereby opportunity to seek and gain revision of rights to permit capture of gain from technology.[37] In whatever sense or to whatever degree technology is an imperative force, it is also true that choice remains necessary and is exercised over institutions, technology, and the allocative and distributional consequences of both.

Whether More or Less Is Better

An area of ambiguity or, more likely, disagreement in the argument over economic growth concerns the general impression that an emphasis on technology seems to maintain that more is better than less. The issue is complicated, especially because Ayres's analysis was developed before the contemporary attention to the limits to growth. Thus, we find both Ayres's emphasis upon a technology of plenty and the more recent suggestion that Ayres favored abundance,[38] but in ways consistent with limits to growth, for example, through elimination of conspicuous waste.[39] A further theme of long standing in institutionalist thought has been that welfare is not to be reckoned in material terms alone. However, this line of reasoning raises the kind of problem noted above with the technological-institutional dichotomy, for example, when an institutional-ceremonial practice or belief is promotive or inhibitive of welfare. One instance of the problem involves the trade-off between growth of production and correction of maldistribution.[40] Finally, one finds the generalized notion that there are conditions under which an increase in total output would decrease, or not increase, welfare.[41]

The Question of Adverse Technology

Institutionalists generally believe that technology can be and has been an instrument of liberation:[42] from reactionary modes of thought, from drudgery, from established concentrations of power, and from poverty. The *JEI,* however, also has published materials which discuss the adverse consequences of technology. (There is apparently no direct and certainly no extended joining of the issue as to whether the adversity is due to the technology, the relevant institutions, or both.) Among the important themes are the possibility that technology may destroy the institutional basis required by technology itself;[43] that technology produces adverse effects on human beings, for example, alienation and the loss of meaningful situations,[44] dehumanization,[45] displacement costs,[46] and social conflict;[47] that advanced technology is especially vulnerable in the context of contemporary trends in social conflict; and that modern technology endangers the planetary life support system.[48] It would appear, then, that technology requires evaluation before it can be meaningfully juxtaposed to inhibitive institutions.

Technology, Antitrust, and Social Control

The emphasis in received doctrine upon technology, in part as an imperative force, raises the question of the social control of business through such institutions as antitrust. Indeed, it has been argued that the social control of business is the capitalist system's version of the problem of the control of technology.[49] Thus, the status of antitrust is approached differently by those who stress a technological imperative (and perhaps are not concerned about the distribution of power) and those who urge the social control of business (in, say, both structural and behavioral respects).[50] A prevalent theme is that the corporate state system is not a result of technology but of business efforts to shape economic and social structure for its own purposes through the use of both government and technology.[51] On the international level, whereas it has been argued that the multinational corporation and international investment and production patterns are a result of technological improvements in communications, transportation, the computer, and business management techniques,[52] others have insisted that these phenomena are due to an institutional regulatory lag which has left the power play of multinational businesses substantially devoid of effective social control.[53]

Some Tentative Statements

It is obvious that the above doctrines and themes involve difficult if not intractable conceptual and empirical considerations. The following attempt at synthesis is on the level of paradigm construction and seeks to foreclose neither more careful conceptual specification nor more elaborate and detailed substantive empirical amplification. However preliminary and equivocal, the following outline of conclusions is offered as the basis for further research and discussion.

Within this outline there is one unifying thread: the role of choice and valuation in regard to both sides of the technology-institutions dichotomy. Technology, as I read the relevant materials, is not independent of human choice and valuation, and institutions perform a role, among other things, in structuring decision making. (See also the postscript.)

General Observations

The actual performance and evolution of the economy are a function of technology, institutions, and their interactions.[54] Technology is a partial function of institutions, and vice versa, which is to say the system is a process of cumulative causation,[55] permitting, among other things, both systematic diversity and interpretive flexibility and fecundity.[56] Institutional economics is descriptive but, especially, explanatory and interpretive of institutions, technology, and their interrelations. Technology and institutions are not given or exogenous but emerge and operate in a process of becoming.

Institutional economics, among other things, is concerned with the factors and forces governing the course of "development," and the problems thereof are both technological and social-institutional.[57] Socioeconomic reality includes tensions between innovative and resistant forces, for example, the variables governing the transfer and reception of technology, and the force of marketization *vis-à-vis* the resistance of the indigenous cultural system and institutionalized relations.

Socioeconomic reality includes the processes of human decision making and valuation, that is, the processes of choice and the exercise of volition.[58] What is distinctively human is the normative. The technology-institutions dichotomy is valuational as to attribution of content. Technology is normative or valuational in its specification and in its operation and consequences. Technology has its relatively objective aspects, but the critical ones are laden with subjectivity. The specification of "gaps," "lags," and "necessary" institutional adjustments is a valuational exercise. "Enhancement of the life process" through technology is normative. As a valuational basis, technology involves antecedent normative or valuational premises and/or specifications-identifications. The Ayresian rejection of the value-fact dichotomy itself means that there is a valuational aspect to "objective" technology.[59] Institutions are relevant and important because they help govern who decides and evaluates.[60] Institutions are normative and function in the larger valuational process,[61] for example, in regard to distribution.[62] The designation "ceremonial" may be a name for the rejected and may be dependent upon the acceptance of whatever is perceived as impeded thereby. The determination of dysfunctional or outdated institutions, for example, particular property rights, unions, the welfare state, or of inadequate or overly rapid institutional change is in each case a function of valuation. Similarly, the concepts *growth* and *development*, the definition of *output*, and the specific evaluations of institutions are all imbued with a more or less evident normativism.

We must differentiate technology as a developmental force from the attribution of specific content and status to technology by individual participant-interpreters.

Deliberative and nondeliberative social choice inevitably requires power and therefore some organization of decision making.[63] The central prob-

lem which the Veblen-Ayres analysis addresses is the positive versus
normative treatment of the conflict of continuity and change over the
status quo structure of power. The key is the tension between old and new
ways of doing things and between old and new things to do, but especially
as to who is able to do what, that is, between conflicting interests. To the
extent that the function of knowledge is control and that the truth or
validity thereof is a function of efficiency in problem solving, both knowledge and control are a function of whose perspective is used in defining
and evaluating problem solving. This tension may and often does take the
form of conflict between established interests and new interests seeking
realization or legitimacy. Each has its own rationalization process.[64] It
seems impossible to eliminate all ceremonial factors. Order requires
legitimation, even of technology and of the interests promoted by technology. Institutionalists have their own (varying) conceptions as to whose
interests should count and of the proper mode of their effectuation, that
is, the proper organization and distribution of power. Some of these conceptions enter into their identification of phenomena as technology *vis-à-
vis* institutions.

"Efficiency" is a function of power and the valuational process (governing whose interests count) which operates through the power structure.
The technology-institutions dichotomy is subject to the same limit as
neoclassical welfare economics: "Optimal" solutions in neoclassical economics are power structure specific and require a specification of rights
and interests being given effect. Similarly, determinations of efficient technology (say, as the basis for removing institutional constraints) also require a specification of rights and interests, with policy and effective valuation a function of power structure. In all cases, the specification of the
rights and interests which are to count is a function of institutions, power
structure, and power play. One cannot use "efficiency" to determine
rights, since "efficiency" is a function of rights, without giving effect to
some implicit antecedent presumption as to whose interests, or rights, are
to count.[65] The same is true with regard to all institutions, whether or not
they are defined explicitly in terms of rights.

This means that the technology-institutions dichotomy is a surrogate
for (or a way to regard) conflict between power structures.[66] Moreover,
both technology and institutions can be power diffusing or concentrating,
even at the same time when viewed from different perspectives, but they
always are a function of the total structure of power.[67]

By *instrumentalism* is meant, then, an open-ended evaluation of the
status quo, problems, and power structure, that is, evaluation not restrict-
ing change to the operation of status quo modes of change.[68] Instrumentalism is juxtaposed to the blind acceptance of the status quo as suppressive

of the learning process and testing of reality.[69] Along with empiricism, utilitarianism, and pragmatism, instrumentalism does not reject the values of continuity but augurs an open-ended valuational process. One can differentiate between the ideological or ceremonial invocation of the "market system" to canonize the existing power structure and/or business practices *and* the instrumental evaluation of markets in terms of their usefulness in achieving immediate or ultimate ends (in each case the end and relation thereto being carefully specified).[70] Markets can be instrumentally justified as a means to the enhancement of the life process through technological change and the diffusion of power, and institutions can have strengths and/or weaknesses, depending upon the instrumentalist criterion employed.

The technology-institutions dichotomy thus can be a framework for analysis and evaluation and as such can be an open or a closed system depending upon the criteria of interpretation and evaluation programmed into it. In practice, the dichotomy is always open in the sense that each practitioner is free (or has considerable latitude) to specify valuational elements. The dichotomy does not itself provide a settled body of conclusions immediately applicable to policy. At the least, it can help prevent both the erection of traditional prejudices into natural laws and the intrusion into the valuational process of unsubstantiated standards of fitness.[71] Systemic evolution and performance are a function of the tense interaction between technology and institutions.

The Significance of Technology

Technology enables the control and use of natural resources (the physical world) and governs the level of effectiveness thereof.[72] Technology governs input-output relations, influences the feasible and actual levels of real per capita income attained by society,[73] and indeed has been the major force in increasing per capita real income in the West and elsewhere. But this is subject to further evaluation (within extant institutions and attitudes) with regard to the subtler aspects of human welfare, both qualitative and substantive.[74]

Technology subtly and profoundly influences and transforms culture and values through the cumulative tool/machine process and organizational techniques. In recent centuries this has taken the form of the process and logic of industrialization, an imperative but not monolithic force. Industrialization is derived from the technological circumstances and has an inner logic and perhaps inherent tendencies arising from uniformities of the basic technology underlying the process.[75] For example, there is no one path of industrialization, but all seem to lead to what is perceived as an increasingly collectivist world.[76] Technology also is a source of challenges to established ways, a creator of externalities and of externality solutions, and a producer and resolver of social conflict,[77] always with distributional consequences. Technology thus influences the relation of man to nature *and* to man.

Apropos the dualism that institutions are a function of technology, and technology is a function of institutions, technological change creates opportunities and necessities for new property and other rights. Technological change is a function of research and development efforts which are a function of power structure-*cum*-capitalized expectations, both of which are a function of property and other rights. Technology is in part a function of price and power structures. Technological change is accompanied and facilitated by institutional change.[78] In the competition between institutions, technology performs a selection role. Materialist institutions abet technology, and technology abets materialist institutions. Technology can be used to promote large- or small-scale enterprises and administrative units, each with its relevant opportunity costs.

Technology is a key force influencing culture, society, and institutions, including power structure, but technology is comprised of an array of alternatives from which choice is made through the power structure, including hierarchical organizations and power operating through the cost-price structure in the market. Technology is both a dependent and independent variable. Individual creativity is the source of technology, but it is channeled by institutions and the power structure as well as by general culture.

The Significance of Institutions

Institutions perform, for good or ill, a number of important functions. They organize production and activity generally;[79] structure the incentive and reward system;[80] govern personal identity and behavior and influence preferences and personal conceptions of welfare; represent constellations of values;[81] generate and resolve conflict;[82] organize and distribute security,[83] in part coping with the radical indeterminacy arising from technological change, the nature of human choice processes, and the place of man in nature; provide social order;[84] structure power and apportion opportunity; and organize and channel human valuational and decision-making processes. Institutions function as the framework within which individual choice is formed, distributional decisions are made, and public purpose is defined.[85] Institutions govern the rate and pattern of economic development. Institutions govern technology: They both propel and brake technological change; help choose between technological alternatives, in part by governing definitions of output; govern information flows and thereby the assessment of technology and all other variables, indeed *are* informational systems;[86] control the discipline of the machine process, in part through legal-economic power play over technology and the absorption of technological change in existing institutions (however much the latter are themselves changed in the process); and govern the distribution of the "surplus" associated with the transfer of technology.[87] Institutions internalize externalities,[88] and they channel the capacity to organize for collective action.[89]

The market is formed by and gives effect to the institutions (power structure) which operate through it,[90] at the same time having an impact upon the evolution of these and other institutions, in part through calculations of advantage by individuals and groups. Among the ceremonial roles of institutions in our economy is the legitimization of the power relations entering the market; the legitimization of the organization and control system as a whole; the frequent masking of the volitional and choice character of the system; and the justification of the actual choices made and systemic performance produced. These notwithstanding, the ascendance of deliberative over nondeliberative (and symbolic) decision making and social control has been partially both a consequence and a reinforcement of an industrial-technological civilization, the incomplete substitution of matter-of-fact for ceremonial reasoning also being influenced, for example, by the spread of markets and accompanied by pecuniary (calculatory) habits of mind.

Institutions, such as the market, are not neutral. They are a function of power play both within and without.[91] They depend upon and also serve to re-create hierarchical structures intergenerationally.[92] One of the roles of tradition is to serve as a check upon abuse of power, but abuse of power can exist within traditional arrangements and, of course, is generally subjective. The valuational task is to adjudge which exercises of power, under what conditions, constitute abuse. Moreover, institutional change means distributional change.[93] The evaluation of institutions is more complex than a narrow conceptualization of technology can sustain, although that judgment includes more or less ambiguous normative elements.

In Conclusion

In preparing this article I have found it necessary to stress certain themes: the great diversity of treatment, even among those who are self-

886 Warren J. Samuels

consciously institutionalists; the great complexity of the materials; the fact that technology involves a valuational process not independent of institutions (human choice processes), which themselves can be judged ceremonial and/or instrumental as a consequence of valuation, and that we must differentiate between technology as a valuational process and the attributions of specific technological values by individual participant-observers.

Important doctrines and themes have been confronted with others, and some things have had to give at each point of conflict. The conflict already exists, of course, in the pages of the *JEI*. There are numerous other pertinent considerations as well. There has been an emphasis on methodological collectivist to the neglect of methodological individualist elements, hardly inappropriate given the topics of discussion, but nonetheless a limit. Moreover, I am expert in neither economic development (in which field so much analysis belongs) nor technology. It is also my view that the technology-institutions dichotomy can be interpreted in terms of a larger model of power, knowledge, and psychology in which technology and institutions can be explored in terms of each set of variables and with the interpretive problem of which is appropriate (or in what mix) in any particular case.

Paradigm development is not the only opportunity presented by the materials reviewed here. There are vast opportunities for both theoretical and empirical work: theories of the role of technology and of technological change, the role of institutions and of institutional change, the significance of alternative definitions and theories of technology and institutions and, *inter alia,* of capitalism and comparative economic system analysis. The available material is exceedingly rich, and the possibilities for research are no poorer. Investigation of the realities of technology, as both an imperative force and an array of alternatives subject to choice, provides ample research opportunities, and there are many others.

This article has attempted the systematic interpretation and integration of certain doctrines and themes found in the *JEI*. (Their relation to the more mainstream literature and to literature in other fields is also an area for further research.) Different people will produce different syntheses of those materials. The provision of one such synthesis for evaluation and testing by others has been another aim of this article.

Postscript

In this postscript, I want to report and comment on several reactions to an earlier draft of this article. My purpose is clarification, not erection and reinforcement of a "correct" interpretation of technology *vis-à-vis* institutions.

H. H. Liebhafsky strongly urges that I "ought to make the point and keep it constantly before the reader that the contributors to *JEI* have not employed consistent definitions or concepts of institutions or technology" and that the article, accordingly, is a survey of their "confusion."[94] I agree, to a point. that definitions and concepts in general should reflect the robustness, subtlety, complexity, and fecundity of the material to which they relate (see below).

Liebhafsky also stresses that many if not most of Ayres's students missed

> an understanding of his value theory and of what he and Dewey really meant by instrumentalism or "technological theory of value." The reason is that Clarence never really articulated his point of view clearly until he wrote *Toward a Reasonable Society*. . . . Instrumentalism is. as James said of Pragmatism, merely a state of mind, an attitude, a recognition of the idea that nothing shall be free from inquiry, including the question of whether or not freedom of inquiry is to be allowed. Put it another way: Basic postulate—there shall be no limitations on inquiry other than those imposed by the nature of the problem being investigated and this basic postulate applies also to the question of freedom of inquiry itself.[95]

Thus, Liebhafsky compares instrumentalism to the search by some economists for social welfare functions, a search he considers "merely natural law nonsense." In his view, the *actual* "social welfare function in our society is produced in a continuous process of negotiation and subjected to correction in that process as actions are taken on the basis of the negotiations completed. It is a process of self-correcting value judgments in an imperfectly democratic society."[96] I agree: The article stresses the social valuation process of which technology and institutions are each a part. The article also stresses the need to differentiate the overall operation of technology as a developmental force from the attribution of specific content and status to technology by particular interpreters.

Liebhafsky also urges "the point that some activities may have both institutional and technological aspects," and that Ayres distinguished between "two kinds of values; the culturally relativistic. ceremonial ones and the 'technological' or functional ones. A sharp knife is a sharp knife no matter what the cultural setting in which it is found." A sharp knife may be used to murder or cut meat. "So you see your point that institutions may perform functions is not really a critique of Ayres; it is when the institutions outlive the functions they perform that they become purely ceremonial and 'past binding.' Your paper also points to the confusion in the

JEI pieces between the concepts of innovation and technology. Innovation is not technological progress any more than engineering is science. Innovation is merely the exploitation of technology."[97]

This brings us close to the heart of the matter. The tension between technology and institutions is central to Veblenian-Ayresian thought. But it must be comprehended and applied on a sophisticated level. Technological determinism is incomplete and misleading (although technology, as above, is a major conditioning force). The determinations of (1) functional institutions *vis-à-vis* ceremonial past-binding and (2) technological progress *vis-à-vis* innovation require a valuational, choosing process. Technology and institutions, in their own complex ways, involve choice and the necessary study of choice. Once again I must stress the need to differentiate the overall operation of technology as a developmental force from the attribution of specific content and status to technology by particular interpreters.

In the relevant institutionalist literature there are three respects in which institutions have meaning: first, the dichotomy of technology-institutions; second, the role of institutions operating through the market to govern resource allocation; third, the historical permissive role of institutions to permit the industrial system to emerge. Expressed differently, culture is creative and ceremonial, in each respect "governing" performance. The technology-institutions dichotomy, given its essential normative and choice content, is basically a framework for both positive and normative analysis. Both technological and institutional developments can be judged foolish or wise, bad or good. The framework serves with regard to normative change and to explaining economic evolution, an evolutionary economics in the tradition of Veblen; with regard to the values and preferences which motivate activity; in the development of ideology (the culturally specific interpretations, tribal myths, and systemic ethos); and so on.

As for my stress on the ubiquity of the normative, Liebhafsky writes that "every point of view except that of instrumentalism which I have encountered involves a standard of evaluation external to the problem; but it is in the very definition of the problem itself that the standard of evaluation is embodied." He goes on to say that, "in general, it seems to me that most heterodox economists are guilty of just as much knowledge of the natural laws of justice, goodness, etc., as the orthodox economists. You are right if you are saying that there are normative elements in all these. But the kind of normative elements you find in Ayres and in instrumentalism are something different since the functional test of Peirce's clarity must be applied."[98]

I wrote to Liebhafsky: "I think that I comprehend the open instrumentalist conception, especially seen, as you put it, as a process of self-correcting value judgments in an imperfectly democratic society; a state of mind that subjects everything to inquiry. . . . It is an open question, to be worked out, as to when institutions become merely ceremonial and fail . . . the test of pragmatic or instrumental evaluation. The relativism may not be cultural, but it is; also, there is instrumental value to continuity and to that which promotes continuity, so 'past-binding' is not per se or *a priori* merely ceremonial." I also wrote that "the process is one of technology testing coupled with the socialization of preferences (with which testing is undertaken). The testing is instrumentalism in a larger context of the ends-means continuum."[99] Again the content of the instrumentally valuable is a product of a social valuational process and is to be differentiated from specific attributions of instrumental value by individual participant-observers.

Royall Brandis wrote that he sought but could not find treatment of "the measurement problem. What are the criteria by which we denote one technology as 'superior' to another? How do we know technological 'progress' has occurred? You recognize a normative element . . . as well as Boulding's suggestion of the role of relative prices."[100] My answer is that the ultimate valuational process involves the determination and application of the criteria by which one technology is deemed "superior" or "progressive." (The price system is *one* valuational mode.) *That* is the key process to which the technology-institutions dichotomy directs analysis, together, that is, with its counterpart in the determination and application of the criteria by which institutions are deemed "functional" or "ceremonial." This analysis relates to the role of participants in the valuational process; when observer-analysts perform evaluation, they become participants. Positively, the interplay of technology and institutions can be developed to "explain" evolution and performance.

Brandis finds the following unclear: "Institutions govern the choice of technology and thereby give effect to the power structure as to whose choices and interests will count." "Determinations of efficient technology (say, as the basis for removing institutional constraints) also require a specification of rights and interests, with policy and effective valuation a function of power structure." "Technology is comprised of an array of alternatives from which choice is made through the power structure, including hierarchical organizations and power operating through the cost-price structure in the market." My point is that technology is *chosen*. More specifically, a technology is chosen from a set of technological alternatives. The choosing process is a partial function of the power structure, to some extent embedded in institutions, and gives effect to judgments (decisions) as to whose interests are to count. Optimality, whether in terms of neo-classical price theory or institutionalist technology theory, requires an antecedent determination of interests (say, as rights). In actuality, rights redetermination, technology assessment, and optimal solutions are worked out simultaneously through joint processes. Insofar as the choice is made through the market, it is in part governed by the market's cost-price struc-ture, which itself is a function of the rights governing whose interests will count as a cost to others in the market.

Apropos the critique of the technology-institutions dichotomy, Paul Strassmann commented that "the real problem is explaining the non-technological." The point has to be interpreted, I think, in the context of his discussion of the functional-technological status of the ceremonial-institutional in Ayres's later work.[101] Surely, as Liebhafsky apparently feels, institutions serve functions beyond that of reinforcing the status quo.

Philip Klein wrote that

> I feel (as, no doubt does every other student of Ayres—perhaps each in his own way) that he knows what Ayres really meant by the dichotomy you have written about. Certainly you have touched on a number of the crucial factors. To me the critical ones have always been that the dyna-mism and the imperative to change derived from the technological or in-strumental continuum (very broadly defined) but that in its own way the institutional structure, though frequently tending to inhibit the release of the results of that process, are quite as necessary for society because that is where structure and stability come from. While Ayres was frequently scornful and derisive of how institutions in fact performed I don't think he ever denigrated their essential importance to an operative system.[102]

Rick Tilman commented: "At times [Ayres] wrote as though the tool continuum had a dynamism and an autonomy of its own—as though it were an independent force so to speak. Yet at other times, in almost iden-tical historical and social contexts, he emphasized the impingement of institutions and their impact on the development of technology."[103]

As I interpret the relevant materials in the *JEI* (and elsewhere), eco-nomic performance is influenced by both technology and institutions as well as their interaction; both technology and institutions may be judged functional or dysfunctional; and central to the role of each is a process of choice and selection in which the other is not unimportant. Technology may be adverse, and institutions may perform instrumentally.

A. W. Coats wrote that I am "quite wrong in identifying causal inter-dependence (e.g., mutual determination, which can be a static concept) with cumulative causation (which is, I think, though vaguer, inherently dynamic)."[104] I certainly use general (causal) interdependence, or mutual determination, as the analytical equivalent of cumulative causation, but only in a dynamic sense, with due allowance for the limited range of admitted variables.

Coats also reminds us that "the problems of definition . . . are by no means peculiar to technology." He says that the narrow-broad problem of exclusion *vis-à-vis* meaningfulness "could be applied to a great many key concepts."[105] I agree. This point brings us full circle to Liebhafsky's emphasis on the diversity of definitions and concepts—a major realm for the exercise of (valuational) choice. Accordingly, I have tried in this article to provide an integrative interpretation, emphasizing the role of choice and valuation, but I also have tried to reflect the great diversity of positions taken by authors in the *JEI*. This diversity reflects the real world, defines a predicament, and provides opportunity for further research and analysis.

Notes

1. I would like to acknowledge a wide range of published materials beyond the *JEI* in addition to numerous conversations over the past several years relating to the role of technology, technology *vis-à-vis* institutions, and "what Ayres really meant." I also have benefited from Edythe S. Miller, "The Institutionalist Methodology in Historical Perspective," and Joseph E. Pluta and Charles G. Leathers, "Veblen and Modern Radical Economics," both presented at meetings of the History and Economics Society, the former in 1975 and the latter in 1976, the latter to be published in a forthcoming issue of the *JEI*, and Wendell Gordon, "The Value Theory of Institutional Economics." I also am indebted to the comments upon an earlier draft made by Royall Brandis, A. W. Coats, Joseph Dorfman, Wendell Gordon, Philip Klein, H. H. Liebhafsky, Paul Strassmann, and Rick Tilman, as well as several anonymous referees. This article is an outgrowth of the author's report, "The *Journal of Economic Issues* and the Present State of Heterodox Economics." All references not otherwise cited are to the indicated earlier issue of this journal.
2. C. S. Friday (June 1967): 111.
3. P. R. Crosson (December 1974): 936; see also Abraham Hirsch (June 1967): 78–79.
4. Rick Tilman (December 1968): 424, n.3, 429. See also P. R. Crosson (December 1974): 936, and the articles by T. R. De Gregori and Wendell Gordon (June 1973): 267, 274, 277ff.
5. J. H. Street (June 1967): 54–55, 62, 59, and passim.
6. Wendell Gordon (June 1973): 281.
7. J. V. Cornehls and Edward Van Roy (September 1969): 16–32, and (December 1970): 86–87.
8. J. H. Street (December 1974): 707–28.

892   Warren J. Samuels

9. Wendell Gordon (June 1973) : 274, 278, 279, 281, 283–84.
10. Wendell Gordon (March 1969) : 86.
11. J. W. Christian (September 1968) : 298ff.
12. David Hamilton (June 1973) : 203.
13. David Hamilton (March 1970) : 35.
14. Ibid., pp. 38, 41; compare C. E. Ayres (June 1967) : 5–6.
15. David Hamilton (March 1970) : 41; see also Valdemar Carlson (March 1968) : 133, and David Hamilton (December 1967) : 320.
16. Rick Tilman (December 1974) : 689–706.
17. The technology-institutions dichotomy is also developed and/or discussed in John Gambs (March 1968) : 70; Louis Junker (December 1967) : 352–53; Lauchlin Currie (June 1969) : 170 and passim; M. D. Lower (September 1968) : 284; M. J. Davidson (December 1971) : 63–74; D. D. Martin (December 1974) : 773–74; T. R. De Gregori (June 1973) : 264; R. F. Neill (September 1969) : 5–6; and A. E. Scaperlanda (March 1971) : 78.
18. Rick Tilman (December 1968) : 431, n.14.
19. Ibid., p. 434.
20. Ibid., pp. 433–34.
21. Joel Jalladeau (March 1975) : 9.
22. See also David Hamilton (March 1968) : 135; and A. G. Gruchy (March 1969) : 14.
23. Glenn L. Johnson and Lewis K. Zerby, *What Economists Do about Values* (East Lansing: Center for Rural Manpower and Public Affairs, Michigan State University, 1973), pp. 19–21, 142, 162 and passim. See my review in this issue.
24. W. P. Strassmann (December 1974) : 671–87; and Manuel Gottlieb (December 1971) : 39.
25. W. P. Strassmann (December 1974) : 684.
26. R. D. Patton (September 1968) : 344.
27. Robert Solo (December 1974) : 859–76.
28. Benjamin Ward (March 1969) : 37–47.
29. For a recent study relating to this point, see John F. Kasson, *Civilizing the Machine: Technology and Republican Values in America, 1778–1900* (New York: Grossman, 1976), and the perceptive review by Neil Harris, *New Republic*, 12 June 1976, pp. 24–25.
30. W. P. Strassmann (June 1968) : 255–56.
31. A. G. Gruchy (March 1969) : 6, and (December 1976) : 952–55; P. R. Crosson (December 1974) : 939–40; and J. D. Shaffer (September 1974) : 610–13.
32. Compare Dudley Dillard (June 1967) : 115.
33. K. E. Boulding (June 1975) : 224.
34. Seymour Melman (March 1975) : 59–72; see also D. D. Martin (December 1974) : 771–84, and (June 1974) : 277; J. M. McCrea (March 1973) : 168–70; T. R. De Gregori (December 1968) : 403–15; A. E. Scaperlanda (March 1971) : 83; Vsevelod Holubnychy (September 1973) : 518–19; and R. L. Heilbroner (June 1974) : 252.
35. David Barkin (December 1970) : 82–86, juxtaposes to the explanation for lack of modernization and development (which emphasizes inflexible institutional arrangements, cultural characteristics, and attitudes) an

Technology vis-à-vis *Institutions* 893

alternative explanation in terms of the role of power groups at the top of the social structure in denying opportunities to those below. Instead of a lack of appreciation, stress is placed upon lack of opportunity. He argues that development institutions can be vehicles narrowly or widely distributing opportunities, in the former case when a modernizing elite uses the industrialization model for its own purposes and prevents (or does not encourage) the preparing of all the population for the industrial system. It is my personal view that the two explanations are not mutually exclusive, but that in any event what is said in or by one can be said in or by the other's terms.

36. Karl de Schweinitz (December 1974): 841–58.
37. D. R. Fusfeld et al. (December 1974): 909–33.
38. C. E. Ayres (September 1968): 343.
39. T. R. De Gregori (December 1974): 765.
40. Compare the positions taken by J. H. Street and Gunnar Myrdal (December 1974): 707–28 and 729–36.
41. J. L. Simon (March 1973): 130.
42. W. E. Kuhn (March 1973): 175.
43. John Gambs (December 1967): 368; and Karl de Schweinitz (December 1974): 841–58.
44. Robert Solo (December 1974): 859–76.
45. L. A. O'Donnell (March 1973): 156.
46. L. B. Jones (March 1968): 103.
47. Vernon Sorenson (September 1972): 152.
48. Robert Solo (December 1974): 859–76; M. I. Goldman (March 1974): 185; H. H. Villard (September 1972): 160–63; C. K. Wilber (September 1975): 546; see also Karl de Schweinitz (December 1972): 223; in general, see V. J. Tarascio (September 1969): 77; and Kalman Goldberg (March 1973): 149–51.
49. R. L. Heilbroner (June 1974): 252.
50. W. F. Mueller (June 1975): 160–65; and D. D. Martin (December 1974): 771–84.
51. For example, W. C. Peterson (June 1974): 492.
52. Emile Benoit (March 1972): 117–18.
53. For example, Ronald Müller (June 1975): 181–203; and Stephen Hymer (March 1972): 91–111.
54. P. A. Klein (June 1973): 212; and C. K. Wilber (June 1974): 449.
55. Gunnar Myrdal (December 1974): 729–36; Morris Singer (June 1969): 205; and E. A. J. Johnson (September 1967): 219–30.
56. Henry Oliver (December 1973): 543–51; T. B. Bottomore (March 1974): 152; and D. R. Fusfeld et al. (December 1974): 909, 913, 916, 919.
57. Wendell Gordon (March 1969): 86.
58. R. L. Heilbroner (December 1970): 16, 17.
59. Rick Tilman (December 1974): 690.
60. C. E. Ayres (September 1968): 342, 343.
61. P. A. Klein (December 1974): 785–811.
62. C. E. Ayres (June 1967): 10; see also Murray Wolfson (September 1972): 131; Gene Wunderlich (March 1973): 179–81; and David Hamilton (December 1967): 312–17.

63. Rick Tilman (December 1974): 702–703.
64. Compare W. S. Gramm (March 1973): 1–27.
65. A. A. Schmid (June 1974): 519–24. We must differentiate between the working out of rights structures by the social valuational process and the attribution of rights by individual interpreters.
66. See Louis Junker (December 1967): 352.
67. Seymour Melman (March 1975): 59–72; and Rick Tilman (December 1974): 697–702.
68. Robert Lekachman (September 1967): 256; Abraham Hirsch (June 1967): 79–82; and P. A. Klein (December 1974): 785–811.
69. Louis Junker (December 1967): 352.
70. D. D. Martin (December 1974): 771–84.
71. Abraham Hirsch (June 1967): 75–82.
72. On the relation of science and technology, see E. A. J. Johnson (September 1967): 228.
73. Bruce Glassburner (June 1967): 118–20; and T. R. De Gregori (June 1973): 262, 263.
74. See R. W. Pfouts (September 1973): 482, concerning technological advance as possibly only the postponement of high entropy. Also see William Breit and Kenneth Elzinga (December 1974): 818–23.
75. A. G. Gruchy (June 1974): 206; see also R. A. Gonce (September 1974): 608.
76. A. G. Gruchy (June 1974): 206.
77. Vernon Sorenson (September 1972): 152.
78. Louis Junker (December 1967): 353.
79. W. P. Strassmann (December 1974): 675–76.
80. K. H. Parsons (December 1974): 897–900; and Morris Copeland (December 1967): 337.
81. J. B. Herendeen (December 1974): 934.
82. K. H. Parsons (December 1974): 897ff.
83. See L. G. Harter, Jr. (June 1967): 64–66, concerning conflicting claims to security; and J. V. Cornehls and Edward Van Roy (September 1969): 22, 29.
84. C. E. Ayres (June 1967): 6; and K. H. Parsons (December 1974): 738–39.
85. R. H. Day (June 1975): 234–35.
86. Gene Wunderlich (September 1967): 199–210.
87. R. E. Smith (June 1974): 435.
88. Karl de Schweinitz (December 1974): 844ff.
89. Jack Barbash (June 1973): 294.
90. J. J. Spengler (September 1974): 534–35.
91. Compare Manuel Gottlieb (December 1971): 44–45.
92. H. M. Trebing (March 1969): 87–109.
93. Don Kanel (December 1974): 919–21.
94. H. H. Liebhafsky to W. J. Samuels, 18 August 1976, pp. 1, 3.
95. Ibid., p. 2.
96. Ibid.
97. Ibid., p. 4.
98. Ibid., pp. 4, 5.

Technology vis-à-vis *Institutions* 895

99. W. J. Samuels to H. H. Liebhafsky, 30 August 1976.
100. Royall Brandis to W. J. Samuels, 11 August 1976, p. 1.
101. Paul Strassmann (December 1974): 671–87.
102. Philip Klein to W. J. Samuels, 7 October 1976, p. 1.
103. Rick Tilman to W. J. Samuels, 28 July 1976, p. 2.
104. A. W. Coats to W. J. Samuels, 22 September 1976, p. 2.
105. Ibid., p. 3.

[6]

Jei JOURNAL OF ECONOMIC ISSUES
Vol. VIII No. 4 December 1974

Economics: Allocation or Valuation?

Philip A. Klein

*"Whether or not it continues to be a
science of price, economics must be a
science of value."*

Clarence E. Ayres
Theory of Economic Progress

Among the social sciences, economics long has suffered from a superiority complex. The economist's view of his field has been of a discipline that was rigorous and precise, with an advanced and pragmatic methodology leading to a highly developed theoretical structure. All this left far behind the imprecise and murky theoretical strivings of political scientists, sociologists, anthropologists, and historians.

The promised land which economic analysis made possible was known as equilibrium.[1] What sociologist or political scientist or anthropologist could offer any piece of analytical apparatus which for sheer beauty, precision, and logic could equal it? True, psychologists kept insisting that the behavioral assumptions of conventional economic theory—maximizing behavior, hedonism, rationality—all the characteristics of "Economic Man" which economics always has relied on for convenience, were fatally oversimplified. But economists mostly

The author is Professor of Economics, The Pennsylvania State University, University Park. He wishes to thank Lord Robbins for a very helpful and thought-provoking reading of this article.

have ignored the complaints of psychologists (who after all had problems of their own). Moreover, the psychologists were only too willing to follow the economist down the quantitative primrose path. Both disciplines once worried about their ancient roots in philosophy and could never quite rid themselves of the nagging suspicion that questions of subjective valuation could not be eliminated entirely so as to render each a 100 percent pure science. Both embraced mathematics as the true methodological Messiah come at last.[2] Together economists and psychologists measured all visibly quantifiable variables, developed models for all problems, and achieved intellectual orgasm through the contemplation of the possibilities of the electronic computer. By enshrining quantification, they believed they had set a standard of scientific excellence sufficiently ahead of their laggardly sister social sciences to enable them to continue virtually indefinitely to play the role of superego to the lowly id of sociology or history.

Without in any way demeaning the very real accomplishments of quantitative procedures in advancing knowledge in critical areas, I should like to suggest that at least in the case of economics, schizophrenia always has been latent in the discipline and has been kept that way only by sweeping under the rug important problems which increasingly have crept out to disturb the neat world of economist and econometrician alike. We can cope with any number of variables in ever more elaborate models, but we cannot cope with underlying questions of direction and meaning, of goals and objectives for the system. The excessive preoccupation with tools with which to cope with problems at best comprising a small corner of economics, and the obsessive need to believe these tools coped with the heart of economics, long has characterized the discipline. Facing up to this obsession involves the fundamental question of whether economics is a science of allocation or a science of valuation. For most of its existence economics has managed to equate the two, and there is a long and bloody literary road devoted to establishing that economics as a "science of price" thereby was coping with all the value problems with which it need legitimately concern itself.

Economics as a Science of Allocation

The central core of economic theory—at least microeconomic theory—was spelled out by Adam Smith and elaborated upon by the well-known nineteenth-century mainstream economists. The culmination was its restatement by Alfred Marshall, who not insignificantly changed the name of the descipline from political economy to economics. The profound changes of the past eighty years have left remarkably untouched much of the field which Marshall defined as "a study of mankind in the ordinary business of life; it examines that part of individual and social action which is most closely connected with the attainment and with the use of the material requisites of wellbeing."[3] Marshall added that economics "concerns itself chiefly with those motives which affect most powerfully and most steadily man's conduct in the business part of his life."[4] The latter is a far narrower perspective and considerably closer to what in fact Marshall's *Principles* dealt with. It was a critical reinforcement to the continued confusion between economics as allocation and economics as valuation.

Marshall's emphasis on materialism subsequently was questioned, for example, by Lionel Robbins, who wondered how a science concerned exclusively with the material could determine the wage rates for opera stars or orchestra conductors whose productivity is not quite so easily viewed as the more concretely material output of ditchdiggers, carpenters, and others among the myriad toilers in the economic vineyards. Robbins concluded that Marshall's materialism was a "pseudo-materialism"[5] and that what was really at the heart of economics was not materialism but allocation. Robbins then defined the field in the way which is customarily utilized to this day: "Economics is the science which studies human behaviour as a relationship between ends and scarce means which have alternative uses."[6] Such a formulation extricated economists from the materialism quagmire; by adding to this the deceptively simple assumption that the allocation process as carried out through the use of prices in the market disposed of all the ends and scarce means that the proper study of economics need embrace, economists thought they were home free.[7] The pricing process was assumed to be the vehicle by which the economic system expressed *all* the allocating priorities of concern to the economist. Thus price became, if it had not always been, the *only* measure of value with which economics had to concern itself.

Robbins himself reached this conclusion unequivocally by saying that the significance of economic science lay in the fact that "when we are faced with a choice between ultimates, it enables us to choose with a full awareness of the implications of what we are choosing." But he was very careful to add that "it is incapable of deciding between the desirability of different ends. It is fundamentally distinct from Ethics."[8] But even if the distinction between economics and ethics were accepted, the discipline must provide (if it is to permit us to choose with the "full awareness of the implications of our choice") mechanisms by which such "full awareness" choice can be made. The market alone cannot fill that bill in a modern industrial economy. Allocation and valuation are indeed different, and a discipline concerned only with the former can never permit "fully aware" choices to be made.

Those who view economics as a science of allocation customarily have argued that all participants in the economic process get their "values" from wherever they get them, that in fact societal values are of no concern to the economist. Thus all the economist need do is pontificate: "If an individual chooses to allocate his income in Direction A he must forego Direction B." "To achieve certain objectives, here is the most efficient way for society to achieve them, and here is what must be foregone in the process." Consequently, generations of economics students were taught that economics is not concerned with questions of "ought" but only with questions of "is." Economics as a science was not normative but positive.[9] Thus economics was viewed as the administrator of social options, in charge of calculating costs and predicting results, but without any normative participation in the process. The economist *qua* economist occupied a role in which normative judgments definitionally had no place. Only the economist *qua* citizen was permitted to be filled with the minimal requisite quantities of passion, prejudice, and "subjective valuation" that reside in the breast of other mere mortals.

This view of economics had some convenient side effects. For one, it enabled economic theory to blind itself to the implicit subjective valuations (previously alluded to) of what it did in the guise of pursuit of the scientific method, rigor, and precision. It therefore enabled economics to emulate the physical sciences and thus led to the coronation of equilibrium as normatively "good" in economics because in physics, from whence it came, it was "natural." If Keynes's notion of underemployment equilibrium represented a severe jolt to this notion, in microeconomics it survived because equilibrium prices led to market clearing, which was definitionally good. Finally, equilibrium could be viewed as an end in itself because the continued assumption that Adam Smith's Invisible Hand (developed for atomistic competition) could be appropriately if only approximately attached to emergent prices in actual markets rationalized away any lurking doubts about how economics disposed of the value problem. Individual selfishness was transmogrified into a process optimizing social welfare, and emergent prices did indeed express the values of society in the only way that need concern the economist.

Economics as a Science of Valuation

The simple world of the classical economist, familiar to all economists, was orderly and attractive, but unrelated to much of the economic
reality even of its own time. The history of economics has shown
a remarkable tendency to cling to that world, however, and to make
emendations only when pushed by a variety of inexorable forces.
Even in its own time, classical price theory developed with the
Industrial Revolution in England, and so Smith projected his Invisible
Hand on a world replete with, among other things, subhuman factory
conditions, child labor, widespread poverty, great inequality in the
distribution of both wealth and income, vast slums and urban ghettos,
and a rigid and uncompromising class system which severely restricted
labor mobility and economic opportunity. In short, it was a world
with a whole host of problems with which society still copes and
from all of which Smith's economics was structured to dissociate
itself.

It is interesting to note that this view of economics, based on
emulating the physical sciences, has in our own day seen the physical
sciences come to question the rigid distinction between the normative
and the positive. The dynamism of technology was such that by the
1940s the physicists had begun to realize that merely suggesting what
constitutes the most efficient way to destroy the world as we know
it might not thoroughly discharge the ultimate responsibility of the
physicist *qua* physicist.[10] So much for the model economics chose
to emulate.

To the extent that economics subsequently faced up to its value
problem (as opposed to its allocation problem) at all, it did so through
the introduction of the familiar notion of the Pareto optimum, which
fit extremely well the notion of the Invisible Hand. Pareto optimality
(however stated) never has been more than a very carefully hedged
statement: With given tastes, technology, and resources, no reallocation
of resources could better satisfy any member of the community without
someone else being less well satisfied. Such a view, even leaving
aside the old controversies about measuring satisfaction, nonetheless
fits well into the conventional perspective because it does not ask
how the distribution of satisfactions came to be what it is, what
the rules of the game are in which satisfaction-seeking is played,
and so forth. As was the case with the Invisible Hand, the Pareto
optimum was an attempt to define the value problem in economics
in sufficiently narrow terms to make it coterminous with resource
allocation in the market via prices.

To the extent that conventional theory altered its focus to cope with imperfect as opposed to pure competition, the following conclusions seem germane to our central concern with how economics copes with its value problem. Institutionalism in the past attacked the use of "competition" in conventional theory, but failed to note that *whatever* equilibrium might mean in competitive markets, it means something different in imperfect markets. Institutionalists were thus vulnerable to the charge of beating an ill if not dead horse. However, the charge that conventional economics continues to overemphasize the competitive model because it is elegant, precise, and deterministic while imperfect models have none of these characteristics is probably a fair one. Economists cling to the competitive model, partly at least as a child to a security blanket, and rationalize its continued emphasis in academic curricula by a variety of means. These contain enough truth to avoid broadside attacks on the theory as irrelevant, but enough error to prevent economists from easily addressing the modern world in a realistic, direct, and straightforward fashion.[11]

Economists always have been remarkably unconcerned about the allocational implication of how they spend their time and energy in price theory. Here, put in language the economist is uniquely qualified to understand, the institutionalist may have had a point: Price theory devotes a disproportionate amount of the economist's resources to competitive theory and too little to theories more generally applicable in the real world. To many economists no doubt price theory has the appeal of chess, and (importantly) it does permit the mechanics of the price system to be detailed. But even in the sector of the economy in which market prices still operate it leaves many questions untouched. Despite the failure of men like Clarence Ayres to recognize the development of noncompetitive models, the institutionalists still had a point in criticizing price theory. But this was in any case not the main import of what they were arguing.

The Frontiers of Economics: Valuation in the Market

If, as I believe, economics is and always has been primarily a science of valuation rather than merely allocation, it follows that price is not the only relevant measure of value, even in the areas where the price system still serves as the sole or primary allocative mechanism. There are many questions to which conventional economics should address itself in the areas where prices in fact do the allocating, but which many economists still prefer to ignore. For example, it is by now fairly clear that assuming that consumer wants are "given" assumes away many critical problems bearing on "the meaning of the price system." The normative implications of emergent prices in a system in which large corporate businesses produce whatever they choose to produce and then persuade consumers (through advertising, appeals to snobbery or class, or whatever) that this is also what they want are most assuredly *not* what they would be in a system in which prices reflected the efforts of business firms to adapt to the "sovereign" wishes of consumers. This would, of course, be true no matter where consumer wants came from provided only that they were not created by profit-seeking business firms themselves. This charge always has been levelled at price theory by institutionalists, beginning with Thorstein Veblen and including today J. K. Galbraith. He refers to demand manipulation as "the revised sequence" and comments: "The revised sequence sends to the museum of irrelevant ideas the notion of an equilibrium in consumer outlays which reflect the maximum of consumer satisfaction."[12]

It may be that Galbraith has exaggerated the degree of demand manipulation, as some have charged, but it is unlikely that any would argue that consumers and business firms interact on terms approaching parity. The attention given to Ralph Nader in recent years is due to the fact that consumerism is still so new and immature in our economy. Its rise is recognition that manipulation of consumers by firms unmatched by organized and informed consumer manipulation of firms seriously alters the normative implications of emergent prices. Only in economics as allocation can one argue that "the work or value of a thing is determined simply by what a person is willing to pay for it."[13] There is no need here to linger over this point except to note that what lies "beyond demand," to use John Gambs's phrase, is an integral part of economics as valuation and always has been.

A second inadequacy of the economist's analysis of how markets operate is closely related to the first and involves again the tremendous concentration of power in the modern business corporation. Economics as allocation has not been unduly concerned with economic power *per se*, but only with how "market imperfections affected the allocation of resources." Economics as valuation can make no such convenient division. There is by now a vast literature dealing with the rise of the modern corporation, its basis in great wealth, its *raison d'être* in its unique ability to exploit the fruits of ongoing technological development, and the concentration of power (economic but also political and social) to which these factors led. Certainly relatively little attention has been paid by mainstream economists to the impact of concentrated power on the meaning of the price system in operation.

Adolf Berle and Gardiner Means warned in the 1930s of the implications of separating ownership and control.[14] R. A. Brady some years later warned of the implications of concentrated corporate power to the fabric of the sociopolitical as well as the economic system[15] in a view anticipating Dwight Eisenhower's celebrated warning of the dangers to democracy inherent in the military-industrial complex. Despite the effort to develop models of imperfect competition, economics as allocation has never escaped from the dilemma posed by the dynamism of technology which simultaneously destroyed the world of Smithian competition, with its convenient assumptions of the Invisible Hand, and enormously increased the efficiency and productivity (but also the dangers to "sovereignty") of the system in fact operating.

This call to incorporate the realities of corporate economic power into conventional economics thus has a very old if relatively futile history. It may even be a cliché to mention, but like many clichés it represents an obvious necessity since it is still unrealized in economic theory. It is currently being urged most conspicuously by Galbraith.[16] Thus, if institutionalists erred in failing to recognize the impact of imperfect competition theory on the normative implications of "equilibrium," this error was small in the face of the problem they did perceive in the operation of prices to allocate resources in the market. The realities of concentrated power, the implications of an allocative mechanism based on "one dollar, one vote" operating amidst tremendous inequality in the distribution of both wealth and income, the degree to which concentration exercised a pervasive influence on both the flow of information and the "wants" assumed to be given—all these and related aspects of the economy were not so much unknown to economists as simply ignored definitionally by the profession in considering economic theory. The result was that even in its *terra cognita*, the domain of allocation in markets via prices, economists could not really deal with the value problem effectively. But the greatest inadequacies resulted from concentrating the attention of the economists unduly in this corner of their field, thereby ignoring the full implications of economics as valuation.

Institutional Economics and the Valuation Process

The meaning of the price system is only part of the strategy of economic progress, and it is the latter that lies at the heart of economics as valuation. It was this view, of course, that gave institutionalism its characteristic flavor, and Ayres in particular tried to pull the separate threads together to make a complete statement of economics as a science of valuation directed at developing a strategy of progress. From Veblen came his great sensitivity to the impact of institutional forces (economic and noneconomic) in shaping the development of priorities and the resultant futility of presuming wants to be given when in fact they are shaped by the economy. From the disputes in the physical sciences came his conviction that the Newtonian emphasis on equilibrium was far less significant for economics than was the Darwinian emphasis on conflict, process, and change. From John Dewey came the instrumental theory of value, which succeeded in producing a dynamic from which the valuation process in economics could be analyzed.

What Ayres saw better than anyone else, in my judgment, was that instead of concentrating on how resources are allocated in markets via prices, economists should subsume that problem in the larger and more compelling problem, namely: How does the economy shape as well as channel human choice, both during a given period and through time? What mechanisms does it provide both for the development and for the expression of values? When Kenneth Arrow considered welfare economics, he still viewed the economy as a transmission mechanism for expressing "values" exogenously determined—hence his title *Social Choice and Individual Values*. But a more meaningful title might well have been *Individual Choice and Social Values*. It is the latter which "the economy" represents. And I dare say that the fallacy of composition scarcely could be of greater critical importance than in the placid assumption of economists that the economy is an adequate and effective mechanism for summing individual values into social values. There is clearly a complex interaction between individual and social values, but the way in which the economy directs this interrelationship is far from clear, let alone necessarily satisfactory. (And "satisfactory" here may be interpreted only as certainty that the system accomplishes what each of its participants would prefer it to accomplish if they were "suitably" aggregated.)

The major critical frontier in economics, therefore, cannot be restricted even to market valuation; it lies in a far broader perspective.

The Frontiers of Political Economy: Individual Choice and Valuation in Society

Perhaps even Ayres took too narrow a view, in the sense that the ultimate concern of economics is not merely the meaning of the price system, but the meaning of the entire allocation pattern which emerges.[17] Increasingly it seems clear that economics as valuation cannot avoid concern with nonprice phenomena. The evidence is piling up on all sides that the old view of economics (as primarily concerned with how the market allocates resources via price under rigidly given assumptions) increasingly is being pushed aside by the necessity for facing many critical valuation problems.

This necessity has, however, only exaggerated the schizophrenia in economics. It is suddenly very fashionable in economics courses to include mention of urban blight, air and water pollution, conservation, the energy crisis, the population explosion, racial and sexual discrimination, and even "the quality of life." Our elementary texts exhibit the result brilliantly. They add chapters on these topics as each is pressed upon the professional consciousness in too forceful a manner to continue to be ignored, but these concerns are almost invariably grafted on at the end, in about chapter 37. The central chapters on the operation of the market are untouched, and the inadequacy of the theoretical framework in the field for coping with the valuation problems is glossed over. Price theory, particularly competitive theory, is our rosary. Critical areas of economic valuation are each given a chapter. That is our confession. The religion is intact.[18]

Thus Gunnar Myrdal recently suggested: "Modern establishment economists have retained the welfare theory from the earliest neoclassical authors, but have done their best to conceal and forget its foundation upon a particular and now obsolete moral philosophy."[19]

No better corroboration can be found for the thrust of the argument being advanced than to consider the history of the agricultural sector during the past several decades. Such perusal shows that price is by no means the same thing as value. It should suggest that welfare economics—even of the conventional type—cannot neatly separate allocative from distributive welfare problems, although it customarily tries to do so. It should support the notion that economics as valuation cannot easily isolate utility-based welfare economics, which is conventionally viewed as more manageable, from ethically based welfare economics, considered too ambiguous to be capable of economic analysis, but clearly involved in fact in determining resource allocation and distribution in this sector. It underscores the bases of essential allocative mechanisms in *both* the decision unit of one dollar-one vote and of one man-one vote, and it illustrates the manipulation of both to reveal and shape essential societal values. Finally, in the critical area of interrelationship between the origin and transmission of individual values, on the one hand, and the origin and transmission of societal values, on the other, it reminds us how every beginning student learns to corroborate the fallacy of composition. It is with the recognition that economic analysis shows that the result of individual farmers trying to lower their prices to increase their income may lower the prices and incomes of all. That being true, why is it so difficult to persuade economists who are not beginning students that they cannot blithely assume that individual choice, let alone values, will necessarily be transformed through simple summation into harmonious societal choice, let alone values? Is it not possible that in modern market-oriented economies, so far from atomistic competition, the Invisible Hand could fall victim to the fallacy of composition? Should we not at least attempt to develop a suitable analytical framework, specifically a realistic theory of political economy, in which the question could be pursued?

In fact the necessity for such an attempt is in process of being thrust upon us. Political economy as valuation is being forced to realize by the gap between the central concerns of the conventional analytical apparatus of economics and the central concerns of the economy that they need to be fused. Welfare economics never has been comfortable with notions of Pareto optimality, although it has elaborated them endlessly, because for one thing Pareto optimality never could cope satisfactorily with the Pandora's box Marshall so innocuously called externalities. Nor could it cope with welfare in any except a highly restricted sense involving the allocation of resources by prices with all the determinants of value given. The whole of the public sector, to which attention is shortly directed, is a monument to the limitations of Pareto optimality. Critical resource allocation decisions need to be—and in fact are—made constantly that cannot revolve easily about a market-price-measurable calculus. Pareto's maxim that the improvement in any member of the community improves social welfare if no one in consequence "feels himself worse off" is already inadequate if one must consider (as in all taxation questions, for example) the decrease in welfare of those whose taxes are increased and the increased welfare of those on whom the resultant revenues are spent.

Political economy as valuation then is ultimately as closely related to political science as economics always has been to psychology. Total allocation is made by both dollar votes and man votes.[20] To the conventional concern with how to measure the choices of individuals must be added the problem of how individuals influence each others' choices.[21] Even more crucial is the question of how individual and societal choices are interrelated. We lack a coherent developed

796   Philip A. Klein

theory here for static analysis, let alone for a dynamic theory capable
of coping with the notion of economic progress. These problems can
best be approached in turn.

The Valuation Process and the Public Sector

From what has been said, it is clear that the meaning of the political
economy as the instrument for valuation transcends the confines of
economics as allocation. One clear proof is the size of the public
sector in all advanced industrialized economies, even the most market-
oriented—our own. (More than 20 percent of 1972 U.S. GNP originated
in the public sector.[22])

Prices are utilized for the goods and services purchased in the
public sector, but we do not permit the price system to do the allocation
except in a trivial sense. Indeed, the public sector exists precisely
because here we have chosen to express our values through resource
allocation by fiat. The quintessential example always has been defense
expenditures. Collective consumption of any kind reflects the value
process as embedded in the political economy. Our system operates
in such a manner that military expenditures far more readily can
achieve a high priority justifying taxation for subsequent social
expenditures without being termed inflationary or "fiscally irresponsible" than can social welfare expenditures (note the term). The latter
run into far stiffer opposition. Elementary macroeconomic theory
suggests that a dollar's worth of government expenditure might, as
a first approximation, be viewed as being as inflationary as any other
dollar's worth of government expenditure. The terminology employed
is, therefore, merely obscuring differences in what one defines as
"necessary government expenditures." We conclude in effect that
we "need" national security "regardless of price"—a subjective value
judgment. We opt for stricter controls and limits on our definition
of "need" in other directions, also a value judgment and one essentially
nonprice determined. This can be illustrated by Charles Schultze's
comment that the 1969 Department of Defense appropriation of some
$78 billion involved only 50 different appropriations of which one
(for procurement and research and development), amounting to $22
billion, was justified by a single-page appropriation. In contrast, the
Health, Education and Welfare budget of a mere $14.5 billion (the
non–trust fund part) was covered in approximately 100 different
appropriations. HEW's budget is one-fifth the defense budget, but
requires twice the appropriations.[23] The same value orientation can
be substantiated by dozens of comparable illustrations. The point
here is neither to criticize nor approve any particular attitude toward

the resource allocation involved. It is only to underscore that because it concerns resource allocation, it is indubitably economic in nature; it involves political economy as valuation, and we have virtually nothing to contribute to the analysis as political economists.

Resource allocation is being carried out via *de facto* values, which both shape and are shaped by the economy and are no less integral because economics chooses to take them as given. A mixed economy is definitionally part market and part command, but most of the efforts made to bring the value problem into economics (except for the institutionalists) have centered on value as allocation in the market. This is true (as already noted) of Pareto optimal notions of welfare; and it is true of welfare economics in the Bergson-Arrow tradition.[24] Arrow made this point absolutely unambiguous: "We will assume in the present study that individual values are taken as data and are not capable of being altered by the nature of the decision process itself. This is . . . the standard view in economic theory."[25]

In short, virtually all would agree that modern welfare economics has been deliberately restricted to the interesting but extremely limited problem of defining and measuring social welfare only in cases for which individual values are given data and in which social welfare is restricted to the summation of these individual values. The "welfare" problem is confined to how to express and communicate individual values, how to sum them, and how to interpret the results. Whether individual values even so viewed can include collective consumption is not at all clear. The "social good" is surely deliberately eschewed. This brings us to the current concern with what is called cost-benefit analysis. On the face of it, it appears a potential step forward in coping with the value problem; perhaps it could be. But of crucial importance is the fact that cost-benefit analysis customarily is referred to as an application of welfare economics, and "social betterment" is viewed in terms of "a potential Pareto improvement." In short, social betterment cannot be separated from the summation and transmogrification of given individual values, which brings us back to the fallacy of composition, already commented upon.[26]

E. J. Mishan has suggested that Pareto-improvement notions of welfare are not very adequate until the economist decides whether to ground his welfare economics in utility or ethics.[27] This seems to obscure the issue somewhat, because one certainly could subsume utility under ethics, but what is needed is some more complete calculus than "the market" for expressing the underlying value system in economic decisions. This is more than cost-benefit analysis has ever claimed for itself.

Philip A. Klein

   Consideration of the public sector, therefore, suggests the magnitude
of the problem. The public sector represents a sizable part of the
total allocation of human and nonhuman resources in all market-orien-
tated economies. We have noted that although the resources so
allocated have prices attached to them, they are not fundamentally
allocated by prices, but by fiat. The fiat comes from the political
economy in the form of decisions to tax and to spend which are
made by various officials selected in various ways (most through
election, although by appointment in many critical areas, such as
the Office of Management and Budget), and by consumers and
producers organized into political units. What I am suggesting is that
the manner and degree to which the economy develops, conveys,
reacts to, and acts on societal values is as crucial to understanding
and evaluating the political economy as the psychological basis of
demand theory is to considering the behavior of individual consumers.
Whereas economics may worry at least on occasion about its psychological assumptions, both in demand theory and the theory of the firm
(the units involved in conventional economic "value" theory), little
concern is expressed for the assumptions or characteristics of the
political system through which individual and societal values are
intermingled in myriad complex but crucial ways. Here dollar votes
often are weighted by power considerations and in any case must
be combined with man votes to represent the total allocational
machinery—the political economy. Economics traditionally views "the
market" as the only such individual-social conduit with which it need
concern itself. But while it has concerned itself with its view of
the individual, it has been relatively oblivious to the character of
the other end of the conduit.
   Such analysis is a necessary prerequisite to a meaningful evaluation
of the performance of the economy in coping with its value problem.
This emphasis is what distinguishes the position taken here from that
taken by radicals, liberals, or conservatives, all of whom ultimately
would seem to advocate the substitution of their own values for those
they perceive in the system. The radical dissent involves, it is true,
much that customarily is considered out of the bailiwick of conventional
economic theory (the total distribution of power, for example). To
the extent that the argument here is that the political economist must
focus on the total allocation system, on how the political economy
both shapes and responds to emergent societal values if it is to
comprehend the meaning of the economy, our view, like that of the
radicals, is broader than that customarily taken. To the extent that
the radical critique is based on their dislike of the results they *perceive*

emerging from the system, judgments with which we may agree or disagree, the argument here is different from the radical dissent.[28]

Liberals such as Galbraith, who is disturbed by "private affluence and public squalor," object to how the public sector is being used. But he, as are radicals and conservatives, ultimately is arguing that he likes his own values better than those he views as emerging from the political economy. His impact, too, depends ultimately on his persuasiveness. But for the science of political economy, adopting the values of any participant is no substitute for developing techniques for ensuring that the economy moves in a way that is consistent with its *own* emerging values, no matter how individual participants may view them. Such a theory of political economy as valuation would suggest, incidentally, appropriate techniques to all groups for influencing it in the marketplace of valuational ideas.[29]

The same judgment is essentially applicable to the conservative critique. Milton Friedman, for example, no doubt would argue that his "positive economics" avoids subjective valuation. He has attempted, in effect, to elevate market allocation *per se* to a value premise on grounds that the results are, in his view, most efficient, or if not efficient more reliable and ultimately more in accord with his notion of what the economy should be doing than any other allocative mechanism. His argument is that one should "trust the market" because, whatever its flaws, it performs better than nonmarket mechanisms. Friedman has commented, for example, that "the role of the market . . . is that it permits unanimity without conformity; that it is a system of effectively proportional representation."[30] The word *effective* glosses over most of the problems considered earlier (the actual sovereignty of the consumer, the impact of concentration on the use of power in market allocation, and so forth) as well as being fairly irrelevant to collective consumption. The market cannot possibly allocate defense, "proportionally" or otherwise. Friedman, therefore, does find a role for political allocation (man votes). But he suggests that "fundamental differences in basic values can seldom if ever be resolved at the ballot box."[31] It seems inconsistent to place such faith in laissez-faire markets for economic allocation and so little in democratic processes for converting individual values into social policy.

In the end, reliance on the market, even if more consistent than reliance on any one individual, is no substitute for a theory of political economy as valuation. There still will be allocation for necessary collective consumption by political or administrative fiat. Social Security may be "necessary" to Galbraith, but not to Friedman.

National defense is "necessary" to them both (but how much and how to decide?). What shall be the criteria for determining "necessary"? The argument here is that these are crucial *economic* problems about which the economist remains mainly mute, that no single individual's values will suffice as acceptable criteria for these allocative decisions, and that the only solution is finally to face the total relevant value problem inherent in shaping and directing the destiny of the economy.

It might be added that Ayres's distinction between institutional and technological values was directed at just this point: that notions of welfare never can be appropriately resolved by the imposition of the "value system" of a single individual or group, nor (he argued) even of a given society. His failure was to suppose that emphasis on *process*, which eliminated the old problem of means and ends, could solve the value problem entirely. He argued that "the general welfare is not a condition; it is a process."[32] While he certainly was correct that values in this sense change, he underrated the practical need to develop an analytical technique by which emergent values in the political economy could be discerned. An adequate theory would constitute a mechanism through which emergent values are recognized, transmitted, and reflected in the ongoing operation of the economy. More important, economists then could judge both the accuracy and sensitivity with which the political economy expressed society's emerging values and how closely it conformed to any other preconceived "standard." This is why the emphasis here has been on the need to develop a more complete theory of the political economy as valuation.

The institutionalist emphasis on process was convenient in that one could assume that progressive development, as in technology, would constitute economic progress definitionally. It did not entirely serve to distinguish growth from progress, however, unless one assumes that in time society will make the "right" (that is, "technological") choices. (Ayres, of course, did indeed feel technological choices were eventually inevitable. By emphasizing the "continuum" he thought he had disposed of the value problem inherent in the notion of an end in itself ["ultimate values"].[33])

If the unsatisfactory way in which political economy currently copes with the value problem is illustrated by what it can offer in evaluating the public sector, its inadequacies for viewing the political economy through time are exemplified by considering the notion of economic progress.

The Frontiers of Dynamic Valuation:
Political Economy and the Meaning of Progress

We have proceeded by stages, and we come now to the last step. We have suggested that economics has concentrated its work in welfare theory on that which is measurable within the market through prices and with individual values assumed given. Consideration of the meaning of prices limited to that framework suggests that the institutionalist charge (but only this charge) that conventional equilibrium always meant competitive equilibrium can be partially rebutted. We also have argued that the economy as an overall allocative mechanism should be the proper focus of the economist and that to do so he must once more become a political economist and cope with the meaning of total allocation—that is, the problem of value. It is here that the question of the public sector is most instructive.

If, finally, the element of time is added, as it must be if questions such as pollution, conservation, and development are considered, even a simple Pareto optimality would become quite complex. Should we try to "dynamize Pareto optimality" by saying that "a dynamic Pareto optimality implies that a change which enhances the well-being of at least one member of the next generation without reducing the well-being of a single member of the present generation shall be defined as genuine economic progress"? If strategy X enhanced the well-being of the next generations as well as the present one, but at the expense of the $n + 1$ generation (the "limiting case" being the annihilation of the race in some future generation), what then? Intergenerational trade-offs are inherently complex even in the relatively simple Paretian world because tastes, technology, and resources at the very least must become dynamic givens.[34]

But just as Pareto optima cannot serve as adequate guides to the total value adequate problem in political economy in a single period, they cannot serve as adequate guides to progress. It is important to note that the customary emphasis in economic dynamics is on growth rather than progress for precisely the same reasons that the traditional emphasis in statics is on allocation rather than valuation. Progress involves valuation through time, while growth involves simply increase in whatever it is the economy happens to be doing.[35] Paul Samuelson, for example, in the ninth edition of his basic text tries finally to suggest that progress rather than growth is what concerns us, but his approach is to introduce a version of the Nordhaus-Tobin measure of economic welfare.[36] Samuelson suggests that increases in "per capita net economic welfare" are at a slower rate than increases in per capita GNP. The Nordhaus-Tobin suggestion that growth brings "disamenities" which need consideration is constructive. Techniques for distinguishing growth from progress, let alone measuring it, have very far to go, however.[37]

In short, the strategy of economic progress clearly suggests the primacy of political economy as a science of valuation. The focus is on a global inventory of human and nonhuman resources over time, their relations to changing technology, and the processes by which human beings create political economies. The latter are thus mechanisms through which emergent goals are determined through the interaction of individual and societal valuation processes. By explicitly comprehending the mechanisms in a theory of total allocation, the political economist thereby would enable the participants to direct all resources toward the goals which emerge and to evaluate them against any external criteria they individually might choose to employ. This emphasis on progress rather than growth currently is being debated both in developing economies, where institutionalists long have had an interest, and in the developed economies.

Ayres was one of the first (and still one of the few) to concern himself with economic progress rather than economic growth.[38] Technological progress has been such that we now can view the possibilities for the future with considerably greater awareness of the full implications of alternative strategies than was possible even thirty years ago, when Ayres outlined his theory of economic progress.[39] Economists increasingly recognize the distinction between growth and progress. Political economy as dynamic valuation focuses on where economies are headed. It is allocational in the broad sense that it begins with some fundamental notions: Accessible to human beings on the earth are a number of human and nonhuman inputs which an evolving technology converts into potential resources (in Zimmerman's sense); economies exist as channelling and conditioning mechanisms to assist in both determining and transmitting individual and social values as well as to provide techniques by which analysists can study the success or failure of economies in accomplishing what their participants expect of them. Political economy will develop criteria for making such judgments and at the same time will lay bare the techniques it develops for exposing the criteria so that advocates of diverse goals for economies (that is, with different views of what constitutes progress) will be better able to assess both the economy as the valuating mechanism it is and their own views for change.[40]

Implicit in this is ultimately a noneconomic value premise—that economic progress as dynamic valuation will emerge from within the system rather than be imposed from without by elitist or authoritarian agencies. Advocates of divergent strategies for progress will need to be able to dissect the existing strategy with reasonable accuracy so as to know whether their problem is to improve the way the existing economy reflects existing values or whether the problem is to change the values so as to produce a different path into the future.[41]

It should be noted that in advocating that political economy as dynamic valuation must confront the notion of progress in meaningful terms, we are not suggesting that there is no natural division of labor between economists and philosophers in approaching value. It seems consistent with the present position to argue that economists can continue to shunt off onto philosophers the more abstruse elements of the value controversy as it affects, for example, the debate over what constitutes the good life. If, however, we accept that resource allocation is the heart of economics, then economists need to confront all the value elements that bear directly on this central problem. So viewed, economics never has been "mere allocation," that is, concerned only with resource allocation via prices in markets.

Conclusions

It is perhaps possible to summarize the essential argument in a few propositions.

(1) Economics always has recognized that its distinctive emphasis has been on the need to make choices in a world where the energy crisis is only the most recent reminder that affluence has yet to replace scarcity as a basic conditioner of human existence.

(2) While economics, therefore, indubitably revolves about allocation, it is pre-eminently a science of valuation. To say this is to say something more specific than the philosopher's more cosmic concern with the ultimate destiny of man, but less specific than, say, Lionel Robbins's definition of economics would imply. Economic theory, in which market imperfections are noted, but values are assumed given, even when termed only "benchmark theory," is inadequate theory to cope with the economic problem.[42]

(3) Ayres well may have erred in his view of the meaning of modern market equilibria, but he surely was supremely correct in arguing that the central concern of economics is not how markets allocate resources, but rather how the total allocative thrust of the economy is perceived, determined, reviewed, transmitted, and altered over time.

(4) Economics long has given in to the tendency, therefore, to convert what is essentially a complex value problem into a relatively

simple and often mechanistic allocative problem because of the advantages of the latter in developing precise and rigorous models. But this effort has produced schizophrenia which has become ever more pronounced. The disproportionate attention given to theoretical apparatus which concentrated on simplistic allocation while the economy itself wrestled with valuation increasingly is being recognized. Perusal of any basic text will underscore this discrepancy between the complexity of our apparatus to deal with "markets" and the paucity of our apparatus to deal with value (in static terms) or progress (in dynamic terms).

(5) Only when economic theory concentrates on the meaning of the political economy—the problem of value—will we be able to assess the adequacy of our current allocation (outside as well as inside the market) to accomplish the evolving ends which the participants in the economy currently set for it. Only then can we criticize either the actual functioning of the economy or the expectations of its participants in effective fashion.

(6) If we accept consumer sovereignty as the important factor in economic allocation that classical and neoclassical economists assumed, the challenge is to turn their assumption into reality by developing a theory of political economy as valuation in terms of which the evolving total allocational thrust of society (its emerging values) can be expressed. In such terms economic performance can be judged by the only criteria that ultimately make sense: How effectively and accurately does the system reflect emergent choice?[43]

(7) The frontier of the political economy, therefore, is to be found in developing criteria by which economies can be judged in terms of their ability successfully to express the emergent values of society. In dynamic terms these criteria will provide an avenue for judging the economy through time as the embodiment of the evolving values of its participants, that is, economic progress. Only then can we comment meaningfully on whether the current structures in the economy constitute a road to serfdom, a road to utopia, or some halfway road, and whether, whatever the road may be, it is what (rightly or wrongly) its inhabitants choose.

Notes

1. That there were problems with the notion of equilibrium was not denied; they were simply ignored. For example: "Equilibrium economics describes a community without economic problems, because so far as it affects him, everybody knows how everyone else is going to behave." T. W. Hutchison, *The Significance and Basic Postulates of Economic Theory*

(1938) (New York: Augustus M. Kelley, 1965), p. 164.

2. In this connection, it is instructive to consider the views of Malthus, originally expressed in 1819. "It has been said, and perhaps with truth, that the conclusions of Political Economy partake more of the certainty of the stricter sciences than those of most of the other branches of human knowledge. . . . There are indeed in Political Economy great general principles . . . [but] we shall be compelled to acknowledge that the science of Political Economy bears a nearer resemblance to the science of morals and politics than to that of mathematics." T. R. Malthus, *Principles of Political Economy* (Tokyo: International Economic Circle, 1936), p. 1.

3. Alfred Marshall, *Principles of Economics*, 8th ed. (New York: The Macmillan Company, 1949), p. 1.

4. Ibid., p. 14.

5. Lionel Robbins, *An Essay on the Nature and Significance of Economic Science* (London: Macmillan and Company, 1946), p. 43.

6. Ibid., p. 16. Robbins thus explicitly related "means and ends" in the way which Ayres, with his notion of the "means-ends continuum," was to reject. The point is discussed below.

7. I do not suggest that Lord Robbins himself assumed that his definition so disposed of all means-ends problems, but only that this is what the profession customarily permitted his definition to lead them to.

8. Ibid., p. 152.

9. This view found expression, for example, in most of the editions of Paul Samuelson's widely used text, but significantly has dropped out of the last few.

10. The peril implicit in this view was aptly summarized by Tom Lehrer in his song about the ethics of Werner von Braun: "Once the rockets are up who cares where they come down? 'That's not my department,' said Werner von Braun." Developing such awesome technology carried with it uncomfortable responsibilities that could not be consigned to "society," and the physical sciences have been far less precise and certain, and far more factionally divided, ever since.

11. I myself some years ago argued strongly that institutionalism was failing to make much impact on the profession precisely because it attacked price theory as though no changes in the apparatus had occurred since Marshall. (Compare P. A. Klein, "A Critique of Contemporary Institutionalism," *Quarterly Review of Economics and Business* 1 [May 1961].) While I have not changed my view of the validity of that charge, I have changed my view of its importance, as the text may indicate.

12. John Kenneth Galbraith, *The New Industrial State* (New York: New American Library, 1967), p. 223.

13. The words are those of E. J. Mishan in *Cost-Benefit Analysis* (London: George Allen and Unwin, Ltd., 1971), p. 31, and represented his description of conventional "normative economics," not his concurrence with the definition.

14. Adolf A. Berle and Gardiner C. Means, *The Modern Corporation and Private Property* (New York: The Macmillan Company, 1932).

15. Robert A. Brady, *Business as a System of Power* (New York: Columbia University Press, 1943). In connection with the failure of economics

Philip A. Klein

as allocation ever adequately to come to grips with the value implications of emergent prices in concentrated markets, we may quote Robert S. Lynde's introduction to Brady's book: "For the most part, contemporary social scientists still exhibit toward the changing business world the encouraging moral optimism of Alfred Marshall. Nor are we helped by the fact that the crucial science of economics derives its data within the assumptions and concepts of a system conceived not in terms of such things as 'power' but of blander processes such as the automatic balancing of the market" (p. xvi). The economist would not make so simple a statement, lest he be accused of being simpleminded, but the charge strikes one as not only apt in 1942, when it was written, but discouragingly apt as well in 1974.

16. In his Presidential Address to the American Economic Association in December 1972, entitled, significantly, "Power and the Useful Economist," Galbraith reiterated the theme once more that modern corporations have obtained control of half the economic output in the United States and in the process have acquired so vast a network of control as to justify calling the result a "power or planning system." *American Economic Review* 63, no. 1 (1973): 4.

17. In this connection Allan Gruchy characterized Ayres's view as follows: "He shifts the center of attention from the individual as a choosing person to the whole economy as an evolving process in which individuals as a collective unit or body seek to cope with the problem of using scarce resources to serve culturally determined wants or needs." *Contemporary Economic Thought* (New York: The Macmillan Company, 1972), p. 95. The argument of the text is that the relationship between individuals and society cannot adequately be characterized as a one-way street in either direction, but is rather one of constant interaction through time.

18. In this connection Ayres wrote: "The truth is, it is impossible for economics to disavow the ethical implications of value theory or to dispense with the terminology in which those implications are imbedded, since economics is, and always has been, concerned primarily with the meaning of the price pattern." *The Theory of Economic Progress* (Chapel Hill: The University of North Carolina Press, 1944), p. 82. If by the "price pattern" one means the total pattern of allocation in an economy, then Ayres's view is identical with the view taken in the text.

19. Gunnar Myrdal, *Against the Wind, Critical Essays on Economics* (London: Macmillan Press, Ltd., 1974), p. vi.

20. T. W. Hutchison noted this many years ago. "The *political* side of politico-economic problems is represented sometimes as the 'weakness of the politician' in not putting through necessary but unpopular measures, or 'rigidities' or frictions. That is, the difficulties are not faced at all; it is implied simply that they ought not to be there." *Significance and Basic Postulates,* p. 165. We suggest only that the problem is not faced much more directly nearly forty years after Hutchison wrote because we still lack a coherent theory of political economy with which to view economics as valuation.

21. Game theory tends to be mechanistic rather than value oriented and to ignore the producer-consumer interractions alluded to earlier.

22. For a comparison of the role of the public sector in eleven market-oriented

economies during the 1960s, see P. A. Klein, *The Management of Market-Oriented Economies: A Comparative Perspective* (Belmont, Calif.: Wadsworth Publishing Company, 1973), Table 8-2, p. 179.

23. Charles Schultze, *The Politics and Economics of Public Spending* (Washington, D.C.: The Brookings Institution, 1968), p. 4.

    This value perspective continues critically to shape allocation through the public sector. Thus a Brookings Institution analysis of the fiscal 1974 budget proposals concluded that the administration's budget proposals, "while leaving the structure of federal taxes and the current defense posture unchanged . . . recommended a sweeping series of reductions in the domestic expenditures of the federal government, including elimination or sharp curtailment of many programs." Edward R. Freed, Alice M. Rivlin, Charles L. Schultze, and Nancy H. Teeters, *Setting National Priorities, The 1974 Budget* (Washington, D.C.: Brookings Institution, 1973), p. vii. This is not Friedman's "proportional representation" through the market (see text below), but economics as valuation masquerading as mere "fiscal orthodoxy."

24. Some years ago, Arrow suggested the difference between Abram Bergson's view and his own as follows: "But where Bergson seeks to locate social values in welfare judgments by individuals, I prefer to locate them in the actions taken by society through its rules for making social decisions." *Social Choice and Individual Values*, 2d ed. (New York: John Wiley and Sons, 1963), p. 106. Arrow appears, therefore, to come closer than Bergson to avoiding the possibility mentioned earlier that the Invisible Hand might be afflicted by the fallacy of composition. Arrow came close to recognizing that the real value problem in economics needs to be faced, but in the welfare economics he developed he generally appears to *assume* that the value problem somehow has been met and overcome (see text) and then concentrated on the mechanisms of its transmission through the economy under varying circumstances and assumptions.

25. Arrow, *Social Choice*, p. 7. Arrow goes on to note that this standard view has been attacked for its lack of realism by Veblen, Frank Knight, J. M. Clark, and others.

26. For a clear current statement of cost-benefit analysis and its view of social betterment, see Mishan, *Cost-Benefit Analysis*, especially p. 8.

    That efforts of this sort to develop applied welfare economics take too restricted a view of the required scope of economics as valuation may be noted in the following typical comment (this time from input-output analysis in welfare terms): "The analysis in this book has been concerned only with the implications of specifying a national objective such as maximizing production or consumption. Before one may examine how such an objective may be reached, it is first necessary to describe the actual operation of the economy in terms of a set of lagged behavior functions in market prices." Burgess Cameron, *Input-Output Analysis and Resource Allocation* (Cambridge: the Univeristy Press, 1968), pp. 94–95. Economics as valuation never can be encompassed simply by specifying a maximizing objective without some framework to suggest how specifying the character of the maxima reflects the value system, and that will never emerge from concentration on market prices alone, even if presented as a set of the most elegant of lagged behavior functions.

808   Philip A. Klein

27. Ibid., p. 311.
28. An interesting and illuminating exchange between a radical and a main-
    stream economist was that between John Gurley and Robert Solow in
    1971. Gurley argued that the establishment paradigm emphasized data
    and technique and ignored such factors as power and conflict and thereby
    "a large part of reality." Solow's rebuttal suggested that "knowledge
    of technique and acquaintance with data" was precisely what distinguished
    economists from others. See *American Economic Review* (May 1971):
    especially, 54 and 65.
29. Ayres would no doubt suggest a technique be devised for testing the
    degree to which the emerging societal values are consonant with evolving
    technological values. Sooner or later, in Ayres's view, they would have
    to match.
30. Milton Friedman, "The Role of Government in a Free Society," in
    Capitalism and Freedom (Chicago: University of Chicago Press, 1962),
    p. 23.
31. Ibid., p. 24.
32. C. E. Ayres, *The Industrial Economy* (New York: Houghton Mifflin
    Company, 1952), p. 315.
33. He compared our problem to that of medicine, where "health" is the
    only required criterion and good and bad become more or less in terms
    of the relevant value criterion. One wonders what he would have said
    about abortion and euthanasia, both currently highly debatable value
    propositions. If, as he argued, "as between institutional and technological
    systems of value, the technological values have always had the last word"
    (ibid., p. 314), which is the technological value side of these debates?
    Can one see far enough down "the continuum" to answer?
34. Institutionalists always have objected to the assumption of "given" tastes.
    Ayres stressed the inherently dynamic role of technology, and a funda-
    mentally dynamic view of resources as the only meaningful one for
    economists to take was stressed (although rather widely underrated and/or
    ignored by economists) many years ago by Erich W. Zimmerman in
    World Resources and Industries. It is the technological *process* which
    converts matter or energy into resources.
    As Zimmerman put it, "resources are dynamic not only in response
    to increased knowledge, improved arts, expanding science, but also in
    response to changing individual wants and social objectives." E. W.
    Zimmerman, *World Resources and Industries*, rev. ed. (New York: Harper
    and Row, 1951). In short, all the parameters within which economic
    models customarily are developed are essentially dynamic, and economics
    can hold them fixed indefinitely only at the peril of not developing in
    the most meaningful and viable way.
35. That the distinction is now attracting attention may be seen, for example,
    in *The Economic Growth Controversy*, edited by Andrew Weintraub.
    Eli Schwartz, and J. Richard Aronson (New York: Macmillan, International
    Arts and Science Press, 1973). In chapter 2, "Growth and Anti-Growth,"
    E. J. Mishan, for example, writes: "It is surpassingly convenient for
    the professional economist to interpret people's market choices, or their
    economic judgment generally, as reflecting their mature judgment about
    what is conducive to their happiness. But I hope he is not such a fool

as really to believe it" (p. 22). The central problem under discussion is: What can the professional economist bring to bear on perfecting the mechanisms by which market and nonmarket choices about resource allocation by individuals, and by society collectively, are directed toward any meaningful notion of what society wishes to achieve?

36. Compare P. A. Samuelson, *Economics*, 9th ed. (New York: McGraw Hill, 1973), pp. 195–96.

37. "Disamenities" is a slightly expanded view of Marshallian externalities. In view of the venerability of the notion of externalities in economics and its failure significantly to affect economic theory, one cannot be too sanguine about concern for per capita net welfare transforming the perspective or approach of economic analysis in the near future. See W. Nordhaus and J. Tobin, "Is Growth Obsolete?" in National Bureau of Economic Research Inc., *50th Anniversary Colloquium*, vol. 5 (New York: Columbia University Press, 1972).

38. It often has been said that institutionalists, including Ayres, did not develop their ideas in sufficiently precise form to command widespread acceptance among economists. Samuelson, for example, has said of institutionalism: "For the most part this school has not succeeded in reproducing itself and today it seems almost extinct." P. A. Samuelson, *Collected Scientific Papers of Paul A. Samuelson*, vol. 2, no. 125 (Cambridge, Mass.: MIT Press, 1966), p. 1736 (from an article, "Economic Thought and the New Industrialism," published in 1963). While one does not find copious references to Ayres in recent literature, there is considerable evidence that his ideas increasingly have worked themselves into current economic debate. For the views of one economist who argues this see Robert A. Gordon in Joseph Dorfman and others, *Institutional Economics* (Berkeley: University of California Press, 1963).

   An example of an unfortunate lack of specificity in Ayres in connection with his view of progress is the following: "Human progress consists in finding out how to do things, finding out how to do more things, and finding out how to do all things better." *The Theory of Economic Progress* (New York: Schocken Books, 1962), p. v of Ayres's new Introduction. That sounds more like growth. Without consideration of which, of all the things human beings can do, they should concentrate their relatively scarce resources upon (time, if nothing else), this can hardly be taken as a very useful description of progress.

39. A critical part of Ayres's theory of economic progress revolved around the dynamism which he derived from his instrumental theory of value, which was closely related to Dewey's means-end continuum. That this is closely related to the notion of progress emerging from valuation in an evolving political economy may be illustrated by Charles Schultze's comment: "We discover our objectives and the intensity we assign to them only in the process of considering particular programs of choices. We articulate ends as we indicate means." *Public Spending*, p. 38. Schultze suggests intuitively that economics is, after all, a science of value.

40. That this is the most likely perspective from which innovations in economic theory always have sprung is perhaps what Leo Rogin had in mind when he wrote that "new systems [of economic thought] first emerge in the guise of arguments in the context of social reform." *The Meaning and*

810   Philip A. Klein

Validity of Economic Theory (New York: Harper and Brothers, 1956), p. xiii.
41. A different path, in Ayresian terms, simply would be one more in accord now with emergent technological values.
42. The term is Samuelson's. "The competitive model is extremely important in providing a bench mark to appraise the efficiency of an economic system." *Economics,* 9th ed. (New York: McGraw Hill, 1973), p. 631.
43. An implicit assumption is that these emergent choices can embody Ayres's "technological values." Whatever they embody, it appears ultimately to be the only defensible system, short of any imposed authoritarianism.

References

Arrow, Kenneth J. *Social Choice and Individual Values.* 2d ed. New York: John Wiley and Sons, 1963.
Ayres, Clarence E. *The Industrial Economy.* New York: Houghton Mifflin Company, 1952.
_____. *The Theory of Economic Progress.* Chapel Hill: The University of North Carolina Press, 1944.
Berle, Adolf A., and Means, Gardiner C. *The Modern Corporation and Private Property.* New York: Macmillan, 1932.
Brady, Robert A. *Business as a System of Power.* New York: Columbia University Press, 1943.
Cameron, Burgess. *Input-Output Analysis and Resource Allocation.* Cambridge: the University Press, 1968.
Freed, Edward R.; Rivlin, Alice M.; Schultze, Charles L.; and Teeters, Nancy H. *Setting National Priorities, The 1974 Budget.* Washington, D.C.: The Brookings Institution, 1973.
Friedman, Milton. "The Role of Government in a Free Society." In *Capitalism and Freedom.* Chicago: University of Chicago Press, 1962.
Galbraith, John Kenneth. *The New Industrial State.* New York: New American Library, 1967.
_____. "Power and the Useful Economist." *American Economic Review* 63, no. 1 (March 1973).
Gordon, Robert A. In *Institutional Economics,* Joseph Dorfman and others. Berkeley: University of California Press, 1963.
Gruchy, Allan. *Contemporary Economic Thought.* New York: Macmillan. 1972.
Gurley, John. "The State of Economics." *American Economic Review* 62. no. 2 (May 1972): 53–62.
Hutchison, T. W. *The Significance and Basic Postulates of Economic Theory.* New York: Augustus M. Kelley, 1965.
Klein, Philip A. "A Critique of Contemporary Institutionalism." *Quarterly Review of Economics and Business* 1, no. 2 (May 1961).
_____. *The Management of Market-Oriented Economies: A Comparative Perspective.* Belmont, Calif.: Wadsworth Publishing Company, 1973.
Marshall, Alfred. *Principles of Economics.* 8th ed. New York: MacMillan. 1949.
Mishan, E. J. *Cost-Benefit Analysis.* London: George Allen and Unwin, Ltd.. 1971.

Myrdal, Gunnar. *Against the Wind; Critical Essays on Economics*. London: Macmillan, 1974.

Nordhaus, W., and Tobin, J. "Is Growth Obsolete?" In National Bureau of Economic Research, Inc., *Fiftieth Anniversary Colloquium*, volume 5. New York: Columbia University Press, 1972.

Robbins, Lionel. *An Essay on the Nature and Significance of Economic Science*. London: Macmillan, 1946.

Rogin, Leo. *The Meaning and Validity of Economic Theory*. New York: Harper and Brothers, 1956.

Samuelson, Paul A. "Economic Thought and the New Industrialism." Reprinted in *Collected Scientific Papers of Paul A. Samuelson*, volume 2, no. 125. Cambridge, Mass.: M.I.T. Press, 1966.

_____. *Economics*. 9th ed. New York: McGraw Hill Book Company, 1973.

Schultze, Charles. *The Politics and Economics of Public Spending*. Washington, D.C.: The Brookings Institution, 1968.

Weintraub, Andrew; Schwartz, Eli; and Aronson, J. Richard, eds. *The Economic Growth Controversy*. New York: Macmillan, International Arts and Science Press, 1973.

Zimmerman, Erich W. *World Resources and Industries*. Rev. ed. New York: Harper and Row, 1951.

7

Jei *JOURNAL OF ECONOMIC ISSUES*
Vol. VIII   No. 4   December 1974

Technology: A Culture Trait, a Logical Category, or Virtue Itself?

W. Paul Strassmann

During the 1940s anyone who tried to coax economists into meditations about technology was either naïve or a follower of Karl Marx, Joseph Schumpeter, or Clarence Ayres. Among these three, Ayres remains least well known; yet it seems to me that his approach to technology and human progress nevertheless will overtake class struggle determinism and entrepreneurial glorification. I am not predicting rising sales for *The Theory of Economic Progress* or *Toward a Reasonable Society*,[1] but certain mutually sharpening trends and potentialities in philosophy, economics, and anthropology do exist; these will keep fusing and evolving even if Ayres does not receive his rightful share of citations. But as he himself noted, given the trends in the arts of shipbuilding and navigation of 1492, someone was bound to have discovered America within a decade or two.

Introduction: Technology and Better Economics

Since the mid-1950s, independently of Marx, Schumpeter, or Ayres, a great vogue for technological studies has set economic hearts on fire. The growth of GNP, it appears, cannot be sufficiently explained by proliferating factors of production; recourse must be made to "technological" shifts of production functions. In international trade the Law of Comparative Advantage has been given a few technological

---

The author is Professor of Economics, Michigan State University, East Lansing.

amendments to heighten its luster and to safeguard its plausibility
Once technological effects were quantified, they had to be explainec
as yields from research and development expenditures or from humaı
investment, making one economic subdiscipline pop up after another
Not least of these is measuring elasticities of factor substitution ir
production, as well as finding *labor-intensive, intermediate,* and *appro·
priate* technologies for developing countries.

Much of this activity is useful, although Ayres doubtless saw it
as a futile, possibly reactionary, attempt to domesticate technology
in an individualistic, pre-Darwinian, equilibrium corral. But then Ayres
never bothered to be skilled at, nor fair to, middle run macro- and
microeconomics. In the spirit of Thorstein Veblen, he tended to see
money as a ceremonial fetish and capital as a tribal legend that ascribed
production to powerful people instead of to powerful machines. Capital
theory was "the apotheosis of a legendary power system." When
he quoted J. M. Keynes's byword that anything physically possible
was also financially possible, he seemed to think that financial
organization posed no more than trivial problems for men of good
will. "What counts is the volume of physical production. . . .
Everything else is incidental; or if it is not, it is . . . sand in the
bearings."[2] He seldom dealt with mundane questions such as deciding
what share of the labor force should build dwellings of what durability,
size, and quality for which occupants; and he surely would have
had a gallant word for the most hissed at capitalists, the mortgage
bankers and real estate developers.

But if Ayres was myopic on some questions posed by workaday
economists, they in turn have been blind to the fundamental issues
that he raised, questions about the "paradigm," as we would say
today. In 1962 he wrote: "The decisive issue is . . . a fundamental
misconception of the nature of the economy itself, one to which
Western society was committed by force of historic circumstances"
(*Theory*, p. xii). Market behavior was not synonymous with productive
behavior, and Ayres condemned the pretense that an amputated part
could account for the whole. To explain how northwestern Europe
had broken out of feudalism and industrialized, how other areas might
follow, and how growth everywhere might be accompanied by more
security and equality, he insisted on "the level of generalization of
cultural analysis" and asked: "What social functions and activities
are included in 'getting a living'?" (*Theory*, pp. 97–98.)

His anthropological approach to economic behavior nevertheless
rejected the concepts of "values" fashionable in either anthropology
or economics. With his doctoral training in philosophy, particularly

under the influence of John Dewey, Ayres maintained that "in spite of all the confusions of acculturation, the unity of value is inherent in the meaning of all values" (*Society*, p. 165). Thus a more sophisticated philosophy than value relativism supported the way he set economic behavior in the cultural life process of man. Much of it was a question of epistemology, and if Ayres's influence had been greater, Kenneth Boulding might not have grumbled in 1965 that, "unfortunately, the observations of economists on this question are for the most part simple-minded to the point of embarrassment."[3] As had Ayres, Boulding had come to realize that "economic development is not just a matter of capital accumulation or investment but is a matter of the large-scale transformation of the cognitive structure of large numbers of people . . . interaction between culture, cognition, and technology."[4]

In this article, I shall first review the way Ayres defined and extended his concept of technology from the 1940s to the 1960s. Next I will examine whether that concept came to be synonymous with rationality in general or even with virtue itself. Last is a brief review of the way some economists, anthropologists, and philosophers recently have dealt with the same issues. The conclusion is that many of us are beginning to talk the same language.

Artifacts and Symbols

Technology, as Ayres defined it, is central. It is the system of tool-using behavior, with a tool being any symbol or artifact that, whenever used in the prescribed manner, has the same observable effect, regardless of the culture or status of the user or observer. By contrast, a *fetish* is effective only in consecrated hands and in suitably conditioned eyes and nervous systems. The effectiveness of fetishes is thus limited and determined by past events, while that of tools is inherently developmental, meaning that tools can be combined and tested for improvements in a process reaching indefinitely into the future. Technological validity lies in consistency with scientific investigation generally, with procedures that compel acceptance for the time being, that is, until further inquiry compels modification.

This definition of *technology* is obviously broader than Webster's: "totality of the means employed by a people to provide itself with the objects of material culture." But Ayres thought that *material* and *nonmaterial* have "hidden meanings which have seriously aggravated our confusion" (*Society*, p. 79). In place of the material constraint, other definitions limit technology to "practical" or "useful" purposes, more or less crassly ruling out the acquisition of knowledge as too vague and intangible a result. In the *International Encyclopedia of the Social Sciences* (1968, vol. 15, p. 576), Robert Merrill has made this limitation explicit. He proposes that "technologies are bodies of skills, knowledge and procedures for making, using, and doing useful things [centering] on processes that are primarily biological and physical rather than on psychological or social processes."

These formulations may indeed reflect how most of us use the word, but Ayres thought it gave him no way of proceeding from the particular to the general, to issues of "increasingly great theoretical importance" (*Theory*, p. 117). He realized that technology "suffers from popular association with the most crudely mechanical 'techniques' " or with "physical apparatus" (*Theory*, p. 155; *Society*, pp. 277-78), yet he kept using the term because it suggested the reverse line of causation from industry to science: "All the achievements of the creative scientific imagination have been projections of industrial skills," not exercises in pure reason (*Society*, p. 278). Still, he conceded that John Dewey's word, *instrumentalism*, would have served as well, or better. Dewey himself disagreed.

From the 1940s through the 1960s Ayres did not change this concept of technology. Nevertheless, here and there he modified the emphasis. In the 1940s he stressed that technological "combinations are physical not less than ideational," apparently meaning rather more than equally: "The things they put together are physical objects" (*Theory*, p. 115). By the late 1950s, however, he ascribed a larger role to ways of thinking, "the symbolic process," and organizations *per se*. "Keeping the machines running" fades as a metaphor of cultural success, together with the more narrow behaviorist approach that apparently had been aimed at persistent and misleading metaphysical introspection. In his later works, Ayres thus already had gone beyond *Beyond Freedom and Dignity*, as proposed by B. F. Skinner in 1971.[5]

In the 1940s Ayres already had mentioned the symbolic tools used by mathematicians and artists. Their achievements would have been impossible without use of symbols, and at the same time these could not be genuinely appreciated by others with no understanding of what is actually, technically going on. But stress was more on the physical, rather than denotational, aspects of these tools.

Mention of the functional significance of organizations such as the city, the family, and even business administration likewise can be found by alert readers in *The Theory of Economic Progress*, but the context usually implies passive, logical, although not inevitable adaptation to use of some machine or artifact.

By 1958 symbols and organization had attained equal status with artifacts:

> But it does seem clear that the power of speech and the use of tools condition each other and that both likewise condition and are conditioned by patterns of interpersonal relationships. That is, the skillful use of tools is prodigiously enhanced by communication, which is itself an interpersonal relationship; while at the same time the effort to use tools is a powerful stimulus to communication and to interpersonal organization. . . . Each is essential to what is sometimes called operational efficiency.

> The . . . point that needs to be emphasized is the operational character of interpersonal relationships, or perhaps I should say the interpersonal character of operational relationships ("Theory," pp. 30–31).

In *Toward a Reasonable Society* we find not only that assembly lines and airline schedules are esteemed as operational or "technological," but also that even democracy, the apparatus of parliamentary procedure, is called "in its very essence technological . . . not the fact of majority rule, but rather the process by which majorities are formed [whenever] it registers the free choices of an informed electorate" (*Society*, p. 283). The sovereignty of the people must be the "sovereignty of the facts," and "equality before the law is a direct reflection of equality before the tool" (*Society*, p. 206). Without building the organizational apparatus of democracy, without developing "automatic" government by laws instead of men, throwing off the yoke of this or that tyrant is futile. Another comes to fill the power vacuum. Note that when democracy becomes a tool, its validity can become universal because it can be established like that of any other tool, by operational testing now and in the future, and not only by invoking a purely Western tradition.

Another development in Ayres's thought was increased understanding, one might almost say appreciation, of ceremonial thought and behavior patterns. In the 1940s he cursed these as pure humbug that allowed the strong to exploit the weak, and inefficiently at that. A decade or two later he came to see that the more numerous weak fell for the trick only because ceremonialism was pseudo-technological, "the imagined extrapolation of operational efficiency." This shift was more than reversion to Sir James Frazer's theory of magic as inferior science. At the heart of it once more was the "symbolic process":

> The apprehension of mystic powers is indissociable from any and all associational, or symbol-organized activity—activity of

which language is representative. It is so because such organized
activity is so astonishingly effective as to stir the feelings, and
because language (and the symbolic process generally) is therefore
inherently incantational no less than instrumental. All operational
procedures [give] expression to the sense of mysterious powers
which is evoked by the amazing effectiveness of symbolic operations . . . its persistence is attested by the practice—still quite
general in the twentieth century—of solving problems by giving
names to them. . . . From imputation it is only a step, and
seemingly an inevitable step, to reification, or thing-making.

[The ceremonial system] in origin . . . is an extrapolation of
tool causality and hence of the uniformities of nature, of which
it is a simulacrum. Hence the validity of the ceremonial system
cannot be asserted without indirect assertion of the reality of
the technological process and the validity of technological values.
When social scientists assert that values derive solely from the
convictions of the peoples who adhere to them, they are necessarily
and inevitably asserting the contrary (*Society*, pp. 96, 97, 133-34).

Tools, Reason, and Values

Is this cultural definition of technology too broad to be useful—as
a tool for inquiry? Has technology become a mere logical category?
What else remains when he says "the criterion of rightness is
technological, or intellectual" (*Society*, p. 147)? Is anything palpable
left when technology and ceremonialism become "two aspects of
culture [that] arose together and are obverse and reverse of the
symbolic process [and] go back to the very origins of man himself
and have persisted through all cultures" ("Theory," p. 33)? Perhaps
technology has become a mere synonym for rationality in general
or virtue itself.

Such diabolic questions make one flee to a ceremonial authority,
the dictionary. *Rational* defined as "the quality of possessing reason"
is not very helpful, but when defined as rejecting "what is unreasonable
or cannot be tested by reason in religion or custom" we are given
a mystifying clue. Can the irrational be tested reasonably?

At least rationality as a testing and perhaps rejecting process has,
like Ayres's technology, an operational definition. Rationality as a
condition, as Cartesian intuitive inner self-knowledge, is too unreal
to be reasonable. So if rationality is not taken in this pre-Darwinian
sense, the symbolic and physical testing activities that are implied
do become coextensive with Ayres's technological processes, and
they lead us virtuously *Toward a Reasonable Society*.

The idea that rationality is virtue itself is nothing new. *Virtue* is
defined as the voluntary observance of moral standards, the sort

of conduct required by duty and equity. Here duty tends to be ceremonial, based on deference and respect due to someone or something superior. If one has not been *properly* conditioned, duty is something one is *bound* to do but would rather not. On the other hand, equity implies fairness, something that can be tested empirically in specific cases and be used to supplement, correct, or even supersede purely legalistic (ceremonial) demands. The operational question that arises for virtue is: "How will the functioning of all involved individuals be affected?"

A sense of technological necessity, in Ayres's view, could even excite such emotional fervor that men would rise to acts of sublime virtue, going down with sinking ships after saving others (*Society*, pp. 141–42). Anything good, moral, or technological is a demonstrably effective tool for solving some problem, thus in general contributing to the problem-solving life process itself. Unfortunately, "the behavioral sciences have greatly exaggerated the moral role of fancy to the extent of virtually denying any moral significance to fact" ("Theory," p. 36).

This unified conception of value as a means-ends-means continuum is, as Ayres always acknowledged, John Dewey's theory of valuation. Ayres thought economists especially should try to think in such terms, but he did not hesitate to go further as an apostle to all other heathens as well. He admitted that it would be ridiculous to suppose that men could be inspired to virtue by an anthropological theory of culture. But then he did not believe that cosomological theories of the origin of the earth had intoxicated anybody either. "What has inspired them has been a vision that gave meaning to their own community existence and promise of an assured future not just for any one of them but for all, and for their children and their children's children" (*Society*, p. 190).

If Ayres had been less of a prophet, his lectures and writings might have been less gripping but more systematic, even technological, giving his reverential students workable postulates and theorems for humdrum research or "normal science." The Texas school of economists could have been more influential within the discipline. But given his myopia about middle run macro and micro, he probably was not equipped to communicate with the blind, so perhaps he followed the best strategy. As he himself wrote of John Dewey, scholars may not employ his "terminology, and many of his formulations may be superseded: but the unity of science will inevitably prevail over the dualisms of 'mind' and 'body' of instrumental values and 'moral' values, to correct which he has labored so long and valiantly" (*Theory*, p. 220).

Developments in Three Disciplines

Any attempt to show by selective quotation that the ideas of a man are prevailing is a dubious enterprise. One does not quote a random sample of the population but selects those leading thinkers who happen to have said something similar. Indeed, their saying similar things is what validates their "leading thinker" status.

Moreover, if the ideas happen to be part of a trend that is, in fact, coming to prevail, selecting one name as a fountainhead, even a David Ricardo or a J. M. Keynes, is misleading. Others had come before. In our case, Etienne Condillac, among several in the eighteenth century, rejected Cartesian fixed ideas and abstract principles. The Marquis de Condorcet wanted mathematics applied to the social sciences and saw human development as the spread of reason. Friedrich Hegel already had made individuality a social product and logical and moral principles, evolutionary phenomena. Marx made tools and machines central determinants of historical change. Charles Peirce brilliantly made truth an operational function of an indefinite community of investigators. The ceremonial-technological dichotomy lurks in all of Thorstein Veblen's ironies; and, of course, John Dewey provided the unified, instrumental theory of value.[6]

Assumptions as Frontiers in Economics

Without more preamble, but possibly with undue illusions, let us then single out a few promising developments in economics, anthropology, and philosophy. Among numerous other trends, economics has become less rigid. This is a result, first, of the sobering experience of trying to apply its methods to non-Western developing countries. Second, the fortunately interminable "F-twist" controversy has brought economists together with philosophers and made us more sophisticated about what is taboo in theory building.

In the 1940s Paul Samuelson shared the acultural hope of explaining market behavior "in terms of preferences which are in turn defined only by behavior."[7] Kenneth Arrow soon showed that no reasonable social welfare function could be derived from that approach.[8] But what started the major controversy (with a lag of a decade) was Milton Friedman's peculiar assertion that empirically tested confirmation of any theorem rendered acceptable any assumptions from which that theorem had been conveniently derived.[9] In other words, it did not matter whether psychologists and anthropologists agreed with his quaint view that human behavior was atomistic maximizing. That essentially was the F-twist.

From the resulting controversy, we all have been made aware that while valid assumptions do not assure a valid hypothesis, invalid assumptions do make an invalid theory regardless of successful hypothesis testing. We must simplify with assumptions, but not in a way that predetermines the outcome. If unexamined, unevaluated presuppositions are taken from the domain of other disciplines, our confidence in the adequacy of our theories must be qualified. The nominal boundaries among academic disciplines make it easier to formalize models since there is no limit to the nonscientific use of mathematics. But when the disciplinary boundaries let us cut off search prematurely, they can shelter our ignorance, prejudice, and sloth.[10]

Obviously it will be some time before the new safety standards of the building code for theories are widely used, since erecting theoretical shacks is easier and still respectably labeled "rigorous," even "elegant." Our "cognitive structure" must change. Meanwhile, it does not help when some writers swing from under-psychologizing to over-psychologizing economic behavior, making all major decisions a matter of resolving subconscious anxieties.[11] The profession is not likely to accept economic theorizing as the mere externalization of anal fantasies. But it seems equally unlikely that a sophisticated analysis of the motivation and behavior of the "technostructure" of large corporations will make our profession as huffy in a decade or two as it did when J. K. Galbraith coined the word.

Perhaps we will first be able to pose better questions calmly, not about our own society, menacing our own identities, but about people as remote as tropical subsistence farmers. When the development priority shifted toward agriculture around 1960, economists could not decide whether these folk were rational or not. They defined *rationality* as "maximizing economic returns or income." In allocating the small share of his output that was for sale, the peasant proved highly price-responsive in switching among beans, tomatoes, and cotton; hence he was rational. On the other hand, he seemed to be sluggish about larger investments and innovations. Did he have an irrationally limited time perspective or too much distrust and fatalism? Did he rationally consider alternative courses of action, and if not, why not? After editing a collection of papers on subsistence farmers, Clifton Wharton concluded:

> Innovation [has] been neglected, especially as it relates to risk and uncertainty. What is the relationship between risk resistances, and such variables as minimal levels of living, asset patterns, and the availability of alternative economic opportunities?

> Work on diffusion and adoption of new technology has . . .
> very limited participation by economists. This is particularly
> strange in view of the emphasis most economists place on new
> technology as being a primary force for the acceleration of the
> development of subsistence agriculture.
>
> How are institutional and cultural variables built into the
> indifference maps used by economists? Are subsistence farmers
> capable of discerning their best interests and of thinking logically
> regarding the means to achieve them?[12]

Trade and Work in Other Cultures

When economists begin raising such questions, anthropologists
should take it as a cordial welcome to speak up. Fortunately, it appears
that, under the promptings of George Peter Murdock, A. V. Kidder,
Clyde Kluckhohn, and others, anthropology began to abandon extreme
cultural relativism during the very 1940s when Ayres was grousing
about it. They began to see "common denominators" and "universal
categories" of culture.[13]

As economists also were observing, anthropologists found that
economic behavior is not inextricably embedded in general culture
patterns: Within limits, nonliterate folk can notice and react to "more"
and "less." Some truly ebullient outbursts of recantation went as
far as calling the "obsolete, anti-market mentality" "heroically muddled."[14] But surveying the literature once again, Marshall Sahlins
of the University of Michigan reaffirmed that "markets properly
so-called, competitive and price fixing, are universally absent from
primitive society." Nevertheless, exchange ratios among trading
partners do adjust to long-run demand and supply conditions despite
the traditional compulsion to "overreciprocate." Among the 'Gawa,
for example, "discussion of values is avoided, and the donor does
the best he can to convey the impression that no thought of a counter
gift has entered his head. Yet . . . hints are dropped [and] a careful
count is kept." Anthropology "has become more consistently rational
in its treatment of exchange," but, nevertheless, the underlying
rationale for the exchange process may be to preserve the peace.[15]
These developments go well beyond the horizons of Veblen or Ayres,
but they say little about rationality in technological innovation.

The scope for rationality and innovation, if any, should be observed
above all in the organization of production itself, which is a much
more central cultural phenomenon than trade. Conveniently, Stanley
Udy has tested hypotheses about the organization of work in 150
nonindustrial societies that had previous studies coded in the Human

Relations Area Files at Princeton University. He found almost forty relationships among pairs of variables that appeared to be valid cross culturally. Two examples follow. First, hunting and fishing tend to be carried on by organizations that emphasize roles with specific tasks for each individual; tillage, animal husbandry, and construction, by organizations emphasizing diffuseness. (Yule's $Q = .81$, $P < .001$.) Second, in organizations with three or more levels of authority, anyone above the lowest level is not likely to do ordinary work; but in organizations with only two levels (associations), leaders will do ordinary work. (Yule's $Q = .79$, $P < .01$.)

These two (and three dozen other) relationships seem not to vary in random fashion and therefore can be assumed not to be culturally relative. Udy suggested that "technological limitations on the possible forms which successful instrumental action can take, together with the interrelationships between such forms, constitute major sources of cross cultural uniformity."[16] Note that Udy used *technology* in the dictionary sense as referring to ways of providing and maintaining food supplies, roads, buildings, and other physical objects. These techniques will vary in complexity, uncertainty, effort per participant, and input of land, tools, and materials.

Taken in this sense, according to Udy's sample of cultures, technology fares quite well as a predictor of single, general tendencies. "In the area of authority structure it fares extremely well indeed—much better, it is submitted, than has generally been supposed." For example, tillage and animal husbandry involve a poorly understood, complex technological process, while effective hunting and fishing techniques are readily understood. Consequently, in tillage and animal husbandry, methods of recruitment, assignments of tasks, and authority systems that inhibit good performance are far more likely to be tolerated than in hunting and fishing.[17] This finding corresponds exactly to what Ayres asserted. Operational efficiency is likely to prevail where cause and effect are empirically obvious.

Where the operational effect is not clear, on the other hand, technology cannot explain organizational variations and may even be "downright misleading."[18] There are more traditionally rigid work organizations than one would otherwise expect, as Udy asserts, because of "the ways in which the property and political systems act on the structure of worker recruitment [with] a tendency to be inadequate both from a cognitive as well as a motivational standpoint [resulting] in a decline of over-all efficiency."[19] Given the opportunity, ritual, status, and irrationality, in some sense, creep in.

Myths and Rationality

About ritual and about possible limits to rationality, Stanley Udy's statistical survey says little. However, this topic, like the F-twist, has been the subject of a prolonged interdisciplinary debate; once again, philosophers started the trouble. Economists, it appears, are not their only targets. This time the philosophers had questions about "translating the meanings and the reason of one culture into the language of another, and of explaining super-empirically-oriented beliefs in scientific terms . . . the universality of the criteria of rationality as it has developed in Western society; of the comprehensibility of ritual acts." As were economists, many sociologists and anthropologists (including cultural relativists) were accused of "mindless lack of interest in the philosophical assumptions involved."[20]

The major contributions to the subsequent debate were gathered in the volume just cited by Bryan R. Wilson. Citations to C. E. Ayres (or to Peirce, Dewey, and Veblen) cannot be found in the volume, but a few quotations will suggest how close the consensus seems to Ayres's views. Rejected was I. C. Jarvie's and Joseph Agassi's view that there is such a thing as "false technology" that can nevertheless work. Also repudiated was the puzzle of how rational people can perform magical acts when the real question is "how primitive technology fits into the magical world view."[21] That question would have taken us back to Lucien Lévy-Bruhl, who thought primitive man had a "prelogical mentality."[22] Contrast this proposed retrogression with the following consensus quotations:

> Technology is itself the application of rational procedures (Bryan Wilson, p. x).

> Ultimate goals and values do not fit into the instrumental means-ends-means scheme of the self-perpetuating circle that characterizes formal rationality (Bryan Wilson, p. xvii).

> I agree with Lukes and Hollis that rationality and the rules of inference it implies are fundamental and universal. . . . When conclusions are drawn from religious or magical premises they are drawn *logically*; they could not be drawn any other way (J. H. M. Beattie, p. 259).

> No man can escape the tendency to see a unique and intimate link between words and things. For the traditional thinker this tendency has an overwhelming power. . . . the modern view [sees] words and reality as independent variables. With its advent, words come "unstuck" from reality and are no longer seen as acting magically upon it . . . [Descartes] crystallized a half-way phase in the transition from a personal to an impersonal cosmological

> idiom . . . after him we have "mind over matter"—just a new disguise for the old view (Robin Horton, pp. 156–58).

> Symbols are more than metaphors because . . . they frequently come to be imbued with a special potency . . . what are being distinguished are, usually, not so much actions as *aspects* of actions; the same pattern of behavior may have both empirically-grounded and symbolic components, and the way in which we classify it will reflect the aspect which predominates . . . these separate aspects must be distinguished analytically; our analytic categories are intended to resolve the confusions of reality, not merely to reproduce them (J. H. M. Beattie, pp. 242–58).

The similarity to Ayres's definitions, interpretations, and dichotomies are so clear that further commentary might affront the reader. Nevertheless, within the consensus, differences remain. Beattie believes that "while science analyzes experience, myth, magic, and religion dramatize it" and that the two approaches are "fundamentally different and mutually irreducible ways of looking at the world."[23] For Robin Horton this view is too dualistic. A main difference between myth and science for him is that myths are held in a deficient way, that is, they are not open to criticism or refutation by evidence because of taboos against disturbing a closed system, or even against seeing it as such. People everywhere "rationally" reject the obviously contradictory and the empirically false, and they pursue their goals with the most efficient means that they know about. In nonscientific cultures, however, they are conditioned not to be *open* to alternative explanations and to the examination of different goals.[24]

Popper's Three Open Worlds

Horton's use of the words *open* and *closed* explicitly conjures the name of Sir Karl Popper, and so we might close this discussion by opening his most recent book, *Objective Knowledge: An Evolutionary Approach,*[25] to see if he has enlisted himself in the cause.

Popper claims that human freedom can be understood only if there is "*causal openness* of . . . world 1 towards world 2, and the *causal openness* of world 2 towards world 3, and vice versa." These worlds are not the West, the Communists, and the Poor Nations. World 1 is the physical world of rocks and trees. World 2 is the psychological world of feelings and subjective experiences. World 3 consists of "objective knowledge," as the book's title suggests, not knowledge that is the mental state of individuals, but abstract things such as artistic concepts, ethical values, problems, theories, and arguments "including mistaken ones." This world 3 began with the evolution of numan language, and it is real because, using world 2 as an intermediary, its objects "can kick the physical objects of world 1; and they can also be kicked back."

Popper sees a powerful interrelation, even a feedback effect, between personal thought processes and the objective human language, but he insists that these two are not the same.[26] Their difference, the objective separateness of world 3, makes human freedom or creativity possible because it makes world 3 "intrinsically open," not completable. A trivial example: The man drawing a map of his room, including in his map the map he is drawing, *ad infinitum*, can never finish the job.

Through its effect on world 1, via world 2 and technology, objective knowledge makes the entire universe indeterminate, but not in the random sense of quantum mechanics. The universe inhabited by man is neither random nor deterministic general equilibrium; it is evolutionary, developmental, open. The implications for economics of this rediscovered insight have been clear to Ayres, Boulding, and other institutional, or better, evolutionary, economists for a long time.

Most people, according to Popper, cannot easily accept the existence of a world 3 because they are mind-matter dualists. Books are physical objects and language is a kind of noise for them that helps people have special kinds of subjective experiences. To prove the existence of world 3 to such stubborn folk, Popper has muddled up the concept by making it, Chomsky-like, partly autonomous with timeless, unalterable "inner structures," real and existing "independently of whether anybody has thought of them." This is quite different from saying, as Popper also does, that "world 3 problems and theories . . . are *not merely* our constructs, for their truth or falsity depends largely upon their relation to world 1, a relation which, in all important cases, we cannot alter." Oh, Plato, thou art mighty yet!

Conclusion

Perhaps Clarence Ayres was simply a belated nineteenth-century scientific humanist who bravely skirmished against humbug, cruelty, and squalor with original but unqualified statements. Perhaps he was simply a displaced philosopher who somehow had strayed into economics and found himself defining technology so broadly that he really should have called it something else. Perhaps he also did not keep abreast sufficiently with progress among his economic colleagues, who, while they had not bathed, were at least filling the tub. On the other hand—or at the same time—he might have been a man far ahead of his, and our, generation.

Technology: Trait, Category, or Virtue?   685

Notes

1. C. E. Ayres, *The Theory of Economic Progress* (1944) (New York: Schocken Books, 1962, 2d ed.), hereafter cited as *Theory*, and *Toward a Reasonable Society: The Values of Industrial Civilization* (Austin: University of Texas Press, 1961), hereafter cited as *Society*.
2. C. E. Ayres, "Veblen's Theory of Instincts Reconsidered," in *Thorstein Veblen: A Critical Reappraisal*, Douglas Dowd, ed. (Ithaca: Cornell University Press, 1958), p. 37, hereafter cited as "Theory."
3. Kenneth Boulding, "The Economics of Knowledge and the Knowledge of Economics," *American Economic Review* 56 (May 1966): 7.
4. Kenneth Boulding, Review of Robert A. Solo, *Economic Organizations and Social Systems, Science,* 8 September 1967, pp. 1158-59. He was explicit that "not only . . . price theory but even . . . macroeconomics, is sorely deficient, being based too firmly on equilibrium and comparative statics." This contrasts with Boulding's view during the 1940s when he still accepted the "method of economic analysis with very simple assumptions about human behavior." "The physical production functions, and the psychological laws of behavior, as expressed in the system of indifference curves [are] the ultimate determinants of [equilibrium]." *Economic Analysis* (New York: Harper, 1940), pp. 16, 767.
5. B. F. Skinner, *Beyond Freedom and Dignity* (New York: Knopf, 1971).
6. While the relativism of values at the individual or tribal level unquestionably had been carried to absurd lengths, making all values one is not wholly convincing in Dewey's and Ayres's work. In his sympathetic review of *Toward a Reasonable Society*, Sidney Hook found it "hardly plausible" that "all values are interrelated and compatible." Values might "conflict when men project new needs and revise old ones." "Can Science Light Up This Old Globe?" (*New York Times Book Review*, 25 March 1962). Hook nevertheless thought: "rarely in modern years has a full-bodied exposition of scientific humanism been presented with such refreshing orginality."

   Ayres sensed this issue of conflict when he wrote that "to treat security as an absolute is to sacrifice all other values . . . our problem is that of achieving a balance between what we have and what we hope to gain" (*Society*, p. 225). Yet he was not pleased when others tampered with value-unity or the technological-ceremonial dichotomy. Once I tried to divide consumption patterns into three operational categories: "status-conferring," "energy-conserving," and "awareness-yielding." Ayres wrote a generous letter about it but thought that the last two categories should be combined, presumably because conflict between them was inconceivable. (Strassmann, "Optimum Consumption Patterns in High-Income Nations," *Canadian Journal of Economics and Political Science* [August 1962]: 364-72.) Another former student, Phillip Nelson, has made a distinction between "experience goods" and "search goods" in his analysis of consumer quests for information about quality differences. Information about the consequences of consumption can correct consumer mistakes: Consumers with more information make better choices. They maximize utility subject to an information constraint. Nelson has blended the tradition of John Dewey with that of George Stigler and the Chicago School! "An Essay in Normative Economics," *Social Research* (Summer 1966): 314–31, and "Information and Consumer Behavior," *Journal of Political Economy* (March/April 1970): 311–29.

7. Paul Samuelson, *Foundations of Economic Analysis* (Cambridge, Mass.: Harvard University Press, 1948), p. 91.

8. Kenneth Arrow, "A Difficulty in the Concept of Social Welfare," *Journal of Political Economy* (August 1950): 328–46.

9. Milton Friedman, "The Methodology of Positive Economics," in *Essays in Positive Economics* (Chicago: University of Chicago Press, 1953).

10. Eugene Rotwein, "On the Methodology of Positive Economics," *Quarterly Journal of Economics* (November 1959); Ernest Nagel, "Assumptions in Economic Theory," and "Discussions" by Herbert A. Simon and Paul Samuelson, *American Economic Review* 53 (May 1963); Fritz Machlup, "Professor Samuelson on Theory Realism," and Paul Samuelson, "Reply," *American Economic Review* 55 (December 1965); Jack Melitz, "Friedman and Machlup on the Significance of Testing Economic Assumptions," *Journal of Political Economy* (February 1965); D. V. T. Bear and Daniel Orr, "Logic and Expediency in Economic Theorizing," *Journal of Political Economy* (April 1967): 188–96; and Louis de Alessi, "Reversals of Assumptions and Implications," *Journal of Political Economy* (July–August 1971): 867–77.

11. E. E. Hagen, *On the Theory of Social Change: How Economic Growth Begins* (Homewood: Dorsey, 1962). This approach is in the tradition of Freud, who thought all preoccupation with production was arrested development in the anal stage. The central concern of each discipline is easily seen as irrational in terms of other disciplines. Nevertheless, as Wilbert E. Moore said, "in some heavenly place there must be an accolade of angels for every economist who discovers human behavior." Review of Hagen's book in the *American Sociological Review* (April 1963).

12. Clifton Wharton, *Subsistence Agriculture and Economic Development* (Chicago: Aldine, 1970), pp. 459, 463, 465.

13. George Peter Murdock, "The Common Denominator of Cultures," in *The Science of Man in the World Crisis*, Ralph Linton, ed. (New York: Columbia University Press, 1945), pp. 124–41. See also articles written in 1939 and later by Murdock, A. V. Kidder, Clyde Kluckhohn, and others in *Readings in Cross Cultural Methodology*, Frank W. Moore, ed. (New Haven: Human Relations Area Files Press, 1961). The universal, mainly economic, elements are generally said to be (alphabetically): cooperative labor, division of labor, education, ethnobotany, feasting, gift giving, housing, inheritance rules, population policy, property rights, and tool making.

14. Scott Cook, "The Obsolete 'Anti-Market' Mentality: A Critique of the Substantive Approach to Economic Anthropology," *American Anthropologist* 63: 1–25; and Manning Nash, "Reply" to reviews of *Primitive and Peasant Economic Systems* in *Current Anthropology* 8 (1967): 249–50.

15. Marshall Sahlins, *Stone Age Economics* (Chicago-New York: Aldine-Atherton, 1972), pp. 171–83, 237, 301–303. See also Marcel Mauss, "Essai

sur le don" (1923–24), reprinted in *Sociologie et Anthropologie* (Paris: Presses Universitaires de France, 1966).

16. Stanley H. Udy, Jr., *Organization of Work: A Comparative Analysis of Production among Nonindustrial Peoples* (New Haven: Human Relations Area Files Press, 1959), pp. 38–43, 134.

17. Ibid., p. 53. See Ayres, *Society*, p. 101.

18. Udy, *Organization*, p. 53.

19. Ibid., p. 136.

20. Bryan R. Wilson, "A Sociologist's Introduction," in *Rationality*, Bryan R. Wilson, ed. (Oxford: Blackwell, 1970), pp. viii–ix.

21. Ibid., p. 190.

22. Lucien Lévy-Bruhl, *Les fonctions mentales dans les sociétés inférieures* (Paris: Presses Universitaires de France, 1910); English translation, *How Natives Think* (London: Allen and Unwin, 1926).

23. J. H. M. Beattie in Wilson, *Rationality*, pp. 261, 265.

24. Robin Horton and Steven Lukes in Wilson, *Rationality*, pp. 153, 207. See Ayres, *Society*, p. 101.

25. Karl R. Popper, *Objective Knowledge: An Evolutionary Approach* (Oxford: Clarendon Press, 1973). The key chapter, "Indeterminism Is Not Enough," was published in *Encounter* (April 1973), and a review article by Anthony Quinton appeared in *Encounter* (December 1973).

26. As Ayres said with a flourish: "[Culture] is not ourselves in a very real and definite sense. Not only is its existence independent of any particular individual; it is independent of his entire generation. . . . Indeed when a whole society lays down the torch—or has the torch snatched from its hands—another takes it over and carries on" (*Society*, p. 288).

8

Jei *JOURNAL OF ECONOMIC ISSUES*
Vol. VIII No. 4 December 1974

Technology, Ideology, and the State in Economic Development

Karl de Schweinitz, Jr.

Technology plays a pivotal role in economic growth. It offsets the deadening impact of diminishing returns and forestalls the onset of the stationary state that had so vexed Ricardian economists in the early years of the industrial epoch. By shifting old production functions and creating new ones it changes the organization of productive services and the structure of output even as it increases the size of markets and influences the preferences that sustain them. The contours of growth drawn by technological change historically have been extremely uneven in both the short and the long run. The investment embodying it expanded particular firms, industries, and sectors with forward, backward, and lateral linkages that focused incentives for subsequent investment in bunches and sequences, thus imparting to growth a discontinuous, disequilibrium quality. One only needs recall the mechanization of the cotton textile industry in eighteenth-century Great Britain and the succession of inventions and innovations triggered by the imbalances among the carding, spinning, weaving, and bleaching processes. Over very much longer periods of time the technology of the mechanical age has been augmented by the technologies of the chemical, electrical, atomic, and biological ages, each one of which has opened up new investment opportunities and quickened the pace of economic development.

The author is Professor of Economics, Northwestern University, Evanston, Illinois.

Whether *technology* is defined narrowly as the branch of knowledge that deals with the industrial arts or broadly as the "sort of information which improves man's capacity to control and to manipulate the natural environment," it is pervasively and interdependently caught up in the institutions of society.[1] There are, therefore, a number of ways of looking at it. One can, for example, analyze the history of inventions, explaining the technical problems that had to be surmounted, the training and background of the men and women who did so, the role of applied research and outside educational institutions in generating the knowledge essential for the endeavor, the legal characteristics of society which stimulate invention, and so on. To probe the roots of invention is to dig into the initiating factors in technological change, those institutional conditions in society that in the first instance encourage the creation of processes and products that may become the object of investment.[2] On the other hand, one can examine the consequences of technological change, the adaptations and adjustments among people who had little if anything to do with the initiating forces of invention. Joseph Schumpeter argued persuasively that the essence of historical capitalist growth was Creative Destruction in which "the opening up of new markets, foreign or domestic, and the organizational development from the craft shop and factory to such concerns as U.S. Steel . . . incessantly revolutionizes the economic structure *from within*, incessantly destroying the old one, incessantly creating a new one."[3] If technological change similarly is destructive as well as constructive, it is of some importance to the institutional characteristics of society how its ambivalent impact is accommodated. It is this issue that I wish to address in this article.

Schumpeter, of course, believed that the creative force of capitalist growth far outweighed its destructive force, but feared that in democratic society its benefits would not be so favorably assessed and that in the end the institutions of capitalism were likely to be replaced by socialism. Whatever one thinks of this prediction, it is hard to deny that in all contemporary economies the state is the critical institution that determines how markets are organized. Sometimes this is done in the name of socialism, but more often it seems to be a consequence of obdurate policy problems that are invariant to the great isms. At any rate a Friedmanian world in which the only limit to the autonomy of markets is the nondiscretionary powers of public officials is a dream, magnificent to be sure, but still a dream. I shall examine the long-run institutional response to the negative force of technological change in order to see if it may explain the relentless growth of the state during the industrial era.

Ideology and Organization

Presumably there are costs to technological change whenever real income is reduced by a changing production function. This may come about through a fall in money income, a loss in markets of valued consumption or job options, or a detrimental change in the physical or social environment. The latter occurs because of the external diseconomies of public and private choice. While these costs are objective to a degree, they also are subjective, depending on the preferences of the affected population. Just what these are, of course, is no easy matter to determine because they are amorphous, changing, and often inarticulate. Moreover, one person's economy may be another's diseconomy. During the industrial age, however, the means for expressing preferences have changed, as have the costs of technology. Technology has built upon itself cumulatively, altering the structure of output and jobs and irreversibly changing the environment, while our capacity to organize and to create ideologies that explain our relationship to the environment also has cumulated.

The fact that organization and ideology cumulate in the sequential process of industrial modernization may not be as clear as in the case of technology, for which there are visible structures and commodities that remind us of the way it has grown. Ideology has its monuments in learned texts, sacred exegeses, and the wisdom (and no doubt folly) of esteemed leaders and martyrs; just as technology may become obsolete, so may ideology. Yet, during the past two centuries there has been a tremendous increase in the stock of ideas from which we draw our normative views about how economy and polity, or more generally society, should be organized. Socialism of various types, anarchism, libertarianism, fascism, and other isms have proliferated, and the ideological vigor of neoclassical economics and the rising interest in arcane religious belief and communitarian life styles hardly bear out the expectations of those social scientists in the 1960s who heralded the end of ideology.

The cumulative effect of political and labor organizations is lateral, spreading from one interest group to another within and among countries. If organization is a learned form of social behavior, requiring discipline, commitment, and sustained involvement on the part of members, it needs the force of example—the demonstration effect—to overcome the inertia of private, traditional, or ancient customs. In the years since industrialization accelerated in the late-eighteenth century, the demonstration effect has functioned in this respect with astonishing force. In plural societies with decades of development

844   Karl de Schweinitz, Jr.

behind them there are few interests, economic, political, or social,
that are not to some extent embedded in organizations that can articulate
them continuously.

Ideology and organization, then, have worked hand in hand to mold
the institutions and markets in which technology ultimately becomes
part of the economic process. Where the one sharpens our sense
of right and the fitness of things, the other attempts to insinuate
these values into the performance of society. It should not be inferred
that institutional change is in consequence well ordered or purposive.
On the contrary, the cacophony of interests activated by technological
change expresses the hopes, fears, and resentments of those who
are willy-nilly caught up in its pervasive impact. Whether these interests
turn out to be functional or dysfunctional is not always easy to say.
In order to explore the cumulative and sequential force of technology,
ideology, and organization, I shall compare them in the familiar settings
of the Industrial Revolution in Great Britain and of the mature industrial
economy of the United States. While such a crude methology hardly
can generate a definitive explanation of the role of the state in the
growth of markets, it can be suggestive of the seminal influence of
technology in their relationship.

The Industrial Revolution in Great Britain

The Industrial Revolution was triggered by a series of mechanical
inventions that broke production bottlenecks in complementary industries whose markets benefited from both high income and price
elasticity of demand. The invention and perfection of the condenser
and the development of techniques for boring cyclinders accurately
raised the efficiency of the stationary steam engine so that James
Watt and Matthew Boulton could promote its use in coal mines by
contracting with the owners for a share of the fuel savings, using
the performance of the Newcomen engine as a standard. The mines
were cleared of water at less cost, increasing employment and the
output of coal at a time when the iron industry was becoming
increasingly hard pressed by the receding forests and the growing
scarcity of charcoal. Subsequent improvements in the steam engine.
notably its adaptation to rotary motion, increased the range of its
applications. Factories thus became independent of streams and rivers
as a source of power, and when the mounting of the steam engine
on whells increased the mobility of population and resources Great
Britain became exposed to the powerful forces of industrialization
and urbanization. The cumulative effects of the steam engine and
complementary inventions in manufacturing, metallurgy, textiles, and

transportation led to the relative growth of population in the cities of the midlands, Lancashire, and the West Riding of Yorkshire at a rate faster than was consistent with the maintenance of some appropriate level of urban amenities.

The arguments about the social consequences of the technology that spawned the new industrial order, of course, started at the creation. During the Industrial Revolution the fulsome enthusiasm of Andrew Ure was at least matched by the anger of Friedrich Engels, and in the post mortems that have been held ever since both sides have been well represented.[4] Against the grim portrayals of the older Arnold Toynbee and J. L. and Barbara Hammond can be set the favorable data of J. H. Clapham.[5] In our own day E. J. Hobsbawm, wearing the colors of Engels and the Hammonds, has entered the lists against the mainstream tradition of economic history as defended by T. S. Ashton and P. M. Hartwell.[6] As is so often the case with arguments that have polemical roots, the protagonists begin with different premises. Where the optimists are inclined to use real wages as a measure of well-being, the pessimists draw upon noneconomic criteria as well.

Whichever side one champions in this ancient feud, one cannot deny the structural impact of the interlinked technologies of the Industrial Revolution. Already in its early stages, before its urban consequences had become so evident, there were visible and defensive reactions—expressions of preferences—from skilled workers and artisans whose jobs were destroyed by labor-saving techniques in which capital was substituted against labor. Recall, for example, the machine-breaking during the late-eighteenth century in Great Britain, the smashing of Hargreaves's spinning jennies by workers at Blackburn, the burning of Arkwright's factories in Lancashire, the description by Josiah Wedgwood of an armed band of workers outside Bolton bent on destroying all the "engines" in the area.[7] Later, during the waning years of the Napoleonic wars, machine-breaking became wide-spread in the Luddite movement, a sufficiently violent response among workers to the new industrial technology to have raised the law-and-order fears of many middle-class Britons already apprehensive about Jacobin influence on working class behavior.[8]

Aside from being an affront to the legal and moral principles of private property, Luddism seemed to be an economic outrage, damaging to the interests of capital and labor alike, or at least it was so supposed by those who had become persuaded of the benefits of industrial technology. But in the very early stages of economic development when the historical rate of growth was low and there were no models from which to glean future patterns of industrial change, the uncertainty caused by the destruction of specific skills was very great indeed. The Luddites certainly broke the law, but at a time when Great Britain scarcely was organized for effectively representing working class interests, they were far from being eccentric, irrational troublemakers without support in society.[9] In the event, of course, Luddism was countered by vigorous oppression; habeas corpus was suspended, frame breaking was made a capital offense, and transportation of workers was imposed more frequently.

As the structural consequences of the Industrial Revolution became manifest in the nineteenth century, the specific costs of labor-saving technology were augmented by the diffuse costs of changes in the environment. Changes in housing conditions, working habits, and recreational opportunities created new ways of life for both the rich and the poor. To the extent that workers jammed into working class districts while the managerial and capitalist classes sought *lebensraum* in the outskirts of the growing cities, the distance between them became greater and hence the likelihood for the one to know, or know about, the other more remote.

Albert Hirschman has observed of nineteenth-century capitalism that it "is hard to beat: there was a minimum of internalization of external diseconomies and there was no limitation on the internalization of pecuniary external economies through acquisitions, combinations, or mergers with closely interdependent economic activities."[10] Thus, "it was the peculiar *lack* of internalization implicit in the private enterprise system—the way in which the institutions 'hid' certain costs from entrepreneurs—that was largely responsible for the dynamic economic changes that took place."[11] If the demographic force of industrial technology in the early-nineteenth century hid the condition of the "deserving poor" from the wealthier classes, the political-legal order was partly responsible. Since a political system institutionalizes the relationships between the rulers and ruled and the legal system defines the rights, obligations, privileges, and immunities of both, together they form a receptor that is more or less sensitive to stimuli originating in the social-economic environment. Until the Reform Bill of 1832 the overwhelming majority of the population were not included within the pale of the constitution.[12] The people suffering from the negative externalities of the expanding textile, metallurgical, transportation, and power sectors of the economy, therefore, lacked the access to governmental authority for redressing or at least for publicizing them.

Because of the social, economic, and political inequalities in Great

Britain at the time of its initial industrial transformation, the negative consequences of technological change, then, were borne disproportionately by people like those who crowd the pages of Henry Mayhew's *London Labour and the London Poor*. [13] Many, perhaps most, of them were brutalized by the uncertain and stifling environment of developing industrialism, but nonetheless there emerged in the years between the end of the Napoleonic wars and mid-century an extraordinary variety of protest movements, action organizations, and self-help groups, all of which expressed the anxieties of the age and, in very long historical perspective, laid the foundations of the welfare state. Friendly societies, trade unions, mechanics' institutes, cooperatives, Chartism, the Methodist revival, and Ricardian, Owenite, and Marxian socialism, as well as the ideologies that informed them, fashioned among working-class leaders various perceptions of how the economy and polity should be organized. These were turbulent years. From the Peterloo massacre in 1819 to the final Chartist campaign in 1848, when the aged Duke of Wellington defended Parliament in his last command, violence was an ever-present threat to the stability of society. Yet with its genius for accommodation Great Britain already had entered the reform age. The Reform Bill of 1832 was but the start of a continuing process of institutional change which adjusted ancient traditions and practices to the clamorous forces released by industrial technology and so spared Great Britain the greater violence of the Revolutions of 1848 on the Continent.

Great Britain's capacity to adjust to the structural changes brought about by technology in the nineteenth century may be said to have been eased by its front-runner position in industrialization. Before the age of durable goods and consumerism, wants were directed to the satisfaction of subsistence needs. Because so many people were uninvolved in society and had no continuing association with institutions that attempted to meet their needs, there was opportunity for institution building that had an integrating social influence. The gradual growth of trade unions organized the reaction of workers to job insecurity arising from technological change and mass unemployment within acceptable legal and social norms (which, of course, they helped form), thus reducing the incidence of industrial jacqueries like Luddism. The piecemeal extension of the franchise opened up the polity to a wider electorate and created expectations that political power could be used to mold the economic, social, and physical environment for the benefit of all rather than merely to preserve the privileges of a tiny minority. And the environment itself may have been more amenable to change than it subsequently became as population increased, the industrial capital structure hardened, and more interest groups developed institutional strength. The standard of living of the population in the conventional economic sense was a critical issue the reaction to which was conditioned by the prospects, if not always the reality, for meaningful participation of increasing numbers of people in the polity and economy. If per capita income or output rose slowly during those years, the future seemed less bleak because of growing "input" involvement.

The Post–World War II United States

Consider, now, the United States during the years since World War II. At mid-century few societies were better organized for involving its citizens in the economic and political processes affecting their lives. Universal suffrage formally had been achieved, and in the South there shortly would begin the great campaigns to extend this and other civil rights to the black population and other disadvantaged groups. Trade unions effectively had organized the manufacturing industries, and if there still remained unorganized sectors of the labor market, the principle of organization no longer was being resisted as it had been during the years prior to World War II. Labor belatedly had achieved what every other interest group—from veterans through bird watchers to physicians—had long since taken as a natural right. If not extended to their limits, the cumulative effect of ideology and organization was widespread. No one quarreled openly with the proposition that everyone should have participatory rights in society.

As for technology, it already had propelled the U.S. economy into the age of high mass consumption, as W. W. Rostow labeled it.[14] Twenty years of depression, war, and postwar conversion, however, had blunted its effect. Now there was about to be opened up a cornucopia of new products, new materials, and new processes that were the pay-off of applied chemical, electrical, electronic, biological, and nuclear research. Agriculture, transportation, construction, manufacturing, financial services, entertainment, health, education, and the knowledge industry all were affected. Indeed, it is difficult to think of sectors in the economy that were not to some extent transformed by the cumulative growth of technology in the twentieth century.

With all the developments in nonmechanical technology, the structural consequences of the interlinked technologies associated with the internal combustion engine, especially the automobile and the complementary services it requires and the new outputs it made possible, have become all the more profound. Even before World

War II the automobile was beginning to displace rail transportation as a prime determinant of the location of urban populations. After the war the decision of the U.S. government to subsidize the construction of an interstate highway system which would allow a motorist to drive from the east to the west coast without being inconvenienced by traffic lights and city congestion stimulated not only movement of population from city to suburb, but also the production of large automobiles with sealed interiors whose capacity for consuming miles and fuel extended exponentially the ambit of markets. The areas surrounding central cities became the focus of a boom in residential construction and investment in the marketing, maintenance, and entertainment facilities for serving the growing suburban population. Away from the central cities in so-called vacation areas, now easily reached by car, investment in motels, bars, ski runs and ski lifts, condominiums, tennis ranches, and weight-losing camps brought to the country the amenities of the city so that residents of the latter could enjoy the former without losing their urban identity.

Technology alone, of course, does not explain the enthusiasm with which America has taken to its cars. Mobility may not be as fundamental an urge as sex, but there is not much evidence that people try hard to resist it. Whether for roads, water, air, snow, or desert and beaches, new vehicles, contrivances, and machines that promise greater speed quickly find their following. Automobiles, in particular, may have great symbolic significance for people who for whatever reason have little control over their lives, perhaps because cars support aspirations for autonomy. At any rate, the complementary outputs linked with the internal combustion engine have fostered a life-style in the United States that many societies, wisely or unwisely, seek to emulate.

As we already have noted it is difficult to predict the consequences of technological change. These may be positive or negative, but at the moment of its development technical considerations in conjunction with short-run market considerations dominate. One must wait for technology to mature before its social costs and benefits can be assessed; in the meantime it may have achieved a momentum of its own which places it beyond constraint if it turns out that costs are severe. In the case of the Industrial Revolution in Great Britain the social costs of interlinked industrial technologies initially were muted because the political system did not articulate them effectively. This reflected the system's undemocratic nature as well as the immaturity of those organizations which might have been instruments for compelling the attention of political and social elites to the condition of those who bore the brunt of technological change. In the contemporary United States, where the cumulative force of ideology and organization amply has mobilized interest groups for which the polity may act as a sounding board and legislative medium, how does society respond to the costs of the interlinked technologies of the age of the automobile? Before answering the question, we must discuss these costs, although briefly, since they are so familiar a part of our every-day life.

Most widely perceived because of sensory contact with them is the loading of the atmosphere with pollutants that impair health and physical structures and the congesting of the transit and storage capacity of cities occasioned by the use in the United States (in 1972) of almost 120 million vehicles. In some areas the paving of the earth with roads and parking lots and the spread of suburban building have diminished the absorptive capacity of the earth so that once placid streams may turn into raging torrents, flooding surrounding areas, as they catch the run-off from heavy rains. With metropolitan areas becoming encased in concrete, nature, whether the potted plant at home or the forests, mountains, lakes, and beaches in summer retreats, has become more valued. Yet the internal combustion engine in protean guise has made it possible to penetrate nature in all its forms and in all seasons and leave behind the refuse of a so-called high standard of living. An aluminum beer can is not biodegradable and will foul the nest where it is thrown until it is removed by man.

Environmental costs such as those discussed above are a consequence of the vigorous search of households for a higher standard of living. There are other costs imposed on society by the exclusion of some people from this search, or at any rate the attenuation of their capacity to achieve the consumption standards set for them in the larger society. The mobility of population made possible by the automobile has altered the structure of jobs both with respect to their content and location. With the migration from city to suburb there has been a concomitant movement of firms that wish to be close to consumer and labor markets. Especially with respect to the latter, where skill requirements have increased as new techniques have facilitated the substitution of capital against many kinds of unskilled labor, firms seek locations in which they can take advantage of the external benefits generated by first-class educational systems. The people left behind in the cities are at once further removed from the markets for labor and from the schools that can prepare them for employment in modern industry. If they are black, Puerto Rican. or Mexican, they cannot easily move toward jobs and good schools because of discrimination in housing and education.

Meanwhile, as population and jobs are being restructured and relocated, technology relentlessly works on the wants of rich and poor alike, injecting into utility functions new options that render old consumption patterns obsolete. If the rich pioneer in devising new ways of consuming conspicuously, the poor, even if incarcerated in an urban ghetto, can become infected with the peculiar charm of the split-level home and its plethora of durable goods. Moreover, the responsiveness of wants to new consumption experiences may be all the greater because of the anesthetizing effect of technological change on job satisfaction in factory and office. A society already blessed with a high per capita income that continues to search for its El Dorado in growing output per unit of input (as opposed, say, to maximizing input satisfaction per unit of output) surely creates a population that is eager to be advised about how to live by advertisers and other arbiters of high taste.

Herbert Marcuse has observed that "a comfortable, smooth, reasonable, democratic unfreedom prevails in advanced industrial civilization, a token of technical progress."[15] E. J. Mishan is not sure that it is comfortable, smooth, or reasonable:

> No matter how rich he becomes a man has still but one pair of eyes, one pair of ears, one stomach, one sexual organ, a single brain and a single nervous system. In the face of this unremarkable fact of life, continuous material growth cannot be sustained by a system geared simply to producing ever larger quantities of the same goods. Hence the importance of product innovation. New and more expensive goods and services continuously supervene. And in the endeavour to ensure that men change their wants as rapidly, the economic system must be no less adept at creating dissatisfaction. Its success in this respect is symbolized by the post-war emergence of the "pace-setter"—an ideal type, hyperconscious of being in the van of fashion, and imbued with the new virtues of "dynamism," expertise and unlimited ambition. The more affluent a society the more covetous it needs to be. Keep a man convetous—"achievement-motivated" is the approved term—and he may be kept running to the last day of his life.[16]

What I wish to stress is the dysfunctional, possibly disintegrating, aspects of a society whose wants and job demands change constantly with the demands of technological change and in which a majority participates and a minority is left out. Benjamin Disraeli wrote of the Two Nations at a time when the reverse was true, and I have suggested that in that setting the struggle for involvement may have had an integrating influence on British society.[17] Kenneth Boulding recently has expressed concern about what he calls the "milk and cream" problem.

> Will the world separate out into two cultures, both within and between countries, in which a certain proportion of the people adapt through education to the world of modern technology and hence enjoy its fruits, while another proportion fail to adapt and perhaps become not only relatively worse off but even absolutely so, in the sense that what they have had in the past of traditional culture collapses under the impact of the technical superculture and leaves them disorganized, delinquent, anomic, and poor? . . . The depressed sector, however, may be large enough to be threatening not only to the consciences of the rich sector but even to its security, as frustration and anger lead to violence. [18]

We have had little experience in the industrial era, or any era for that matter, with systems where the majority has become economically and politically involved, while minorities have remained on the outside looking in. There is no doubt, however, that their reactions to the problem of a technologically changing world differ. In the mainstream of U.S. life, people belong to political, economic, or social organizations that articulate their preferences and direct their collective strength to realizing outcomes consistent with them. Not having to build and establish the legitimacy of these institutions, they can use them assiduously to seek job security, preserve environmental amenities, raise money income, or pursue whatever interest they represent. In consequence, there is built into society a mechanism—constructed, it hardly need be pointed out, largely from monopolistic parts—for raising costs and the demand on scarce resources that is incompatible with those full employment and price stability goals that were so confidently anticipated in the naïve Keynesian years. Underlying these frustrated expectations are the structural changes occasioned by technology which I have here symbolized with the automobile and the internal combustion engine. Their effect on wants, job opportunities, and population location is part of the transformation in which society has used up its reserves of unorganized, unrepresented, inarticulate people who could bear the residual burden of the equilibrating adjustment of macroeconomic variables. The price flexibility which once assured a degree of price stability was a function of a population institutionally incapable of resisting downward pressures on input prices.

If the dispossessed are outside the mainstream of U.S. life, they nonetheless are caught up in its problems. Whether the preservation of environmental amenities, for example, is sought by pricing output so that it bears social as well as private costs or by regulations and restrictions which specify how particular environments shall be used, the burden will fall disproportionately on them. Having had little chance to despoil nature during the prodigal years, they hardly can be expected to appreciate the social concerns of the affluent despoilers who have come to regret their past. Moreover, if their wants have been permeated by the values of high mass consumption, while a rising price level steadily increases the cost of subsistence, if they have been excluded from trade unions while their unemployment rates are far above average, if they have been denied meaningful participation in other majority organizations, they understandably question the legitimacy of the rules, laws, and behavioral norms that give these institutions life for the majority. Boulding's apprehension about the anomic and violent reaction of the dispossessed, a fear that the daily chronicle of events in the urban United States does little to allay, is easy to understand. The cumulative force of economic development, powered ultimately by product and process innovation, has created dysfunctional social groups whose problems are all the more intractable because of the oppressive weight of majority values and institutions.

Conclusion

From the vantage point of an affluent society where so many individuals and groups are adept in expressing their interests, and some in maximizing them, it is puzzling to observe in the subsistence societies of history that so few people tried systematically to increase their share of the social product. If the scarcity of resources threatened existence, one might have supposed the struggle over its division deep, bitter, and enervating. The puzzle no doubt is more apparent than real, for as Thomas Hobbes already was arguing in the seventeenth century, life in a state of nature was "solitary, poor, nasty, brutish, and short," necessitating the organization of political institutions that could constrain self-regarding behavior in the interests of security and civil amity. And, in fact, for most of history the majority of people have been excluded from the polity so that they had no opportunity to use its coercive powers to influence the allocation of resources and the distribution of income. To be sure, history abounds in jacqueries, price riots, rick burnings, and other instances of collective behavior, but while these manifested the harsh burden of subsistence, they also demonstrated the lack of institutional strength for doing much about it. Peasant revolts and riots came and went, but ruling elites maintained their grip on political power. Surely the latter were helped in this by widespread traditional outlooks which encouraged subservience to gods, rulers, and the environment, a cast of mind that perpetuated itself when there was no technological change or so little of it that the external world appeared to be much the same at the end of life as it was at the beginning.

Recently Professors Douglass North and Robert Thomas, in *The Rise of the Western World*, have argued that in the eight centuries preceding the Industrial Revolution in northwestern Europe the development of individual property rights and the concomitant emergence of the modern state out of feudal and manorial societies reduced transaction costs and so facilitated the growth of markets and the widening of exchange relationships, quite apart from technological change. [19] These same institutional arrangements also managed to take care of the struggle over the distribution of the social product, for, as Marx so clearly and abundantly noted, the assignment of property rights to individuals had its counterpart in the separation of most people from access to land and other durable assets, a condition enforced by the coercive powers of the state. The way thus was prepared for the technological changes that began to transform the British economy in the late-eighteenth century, for the security of property and the associated legal right to the financial returns from invention and innovation created an environment in which entrepreneurs were willing to experiment with new production functions.

One of the more important consequences of the Industrial Revolution was the freeing of society, not from the thralldom of scarcity, but from the belief that subsistence was a natural condition ordained by forces outside human control. With technology transforming the environment, it was not long before ideologies of progress began to transform values about how society should be arranged. People who, in the centuries'-long prelude to the Industrial Revolution, were resigned to subsistence now began to organize themselves for involvement in the polity and economy so that they could compete for a greater share of the social product, protect their occupational status, and mold the environment to their own needs. As we observed previously, in the nineteenth century this may have had an integrating influence in British society because a majority were seeking rights that had been privileges of a tiny minority since time immemorial. Inevitably, however, the struggle for involvement affected transaction costs. If in the years before the Industrial Revolution the law gradually reduced the encumbrances on property so that it could be exchanged more readily, in the years of the industrial age the institutional circumstances surrounding exchange have become more complex, especially the exchange of labor services. While real property was released from the grip of communal practices and traditions, labor became subject to rules of public and private groups which themselves were an institutional manifestation of the struggle for involvement.

Now in a highly interdependent economy such as the United States, where technology constantly produces new commodities and changes the structure of employment, and where few occupational, professional, or interest groups are left unorganized, the very institutional depth of the system affects transaction costs. On the one hand, the vigorous competition of legitimate organizations for shares of the social product has made cost-push inflation such a persistent phenomenon that however much our expectations are prepared for it we must try to hedge or protect ourselves against it. Whether this takes the form of negotiating contracts in real terms or using governmental authority to repress price increases, the conditions surrounding exchange become more complex, more subject to legal oversight. On the other hand, the disadvantaged minorities who have only limited access to the legitimate institutions of society may react to their oppression violently and in violation of the norms of the mainstream, thus raising demands for law and order and greater efficiency in the protection of property rights. Or if the mainstream responds to the plight of minorities, it may enact laws or otherwise take action to give minorities access to majority institutions. For this reason too the legal and political integument of exchange becomes more complex, more replete with opportunities for challenging the manner in which exchanges are consummated. In short, transaction costs in the contemporary United States may be said to be changing, and perhaps rising, because exchanges increasingly are being subject to the constraints of public and private groups.

One hardly can make sweeping generalizations about state and economy on the basis of the British experience in the late-eighteenth and early-nineteenth century and the American experience in the second half of the twentieth century Nonetheless, the spillover from the developmental process connecting eighteenth-century Great Britain and twentieth-century America has left few countries untouched. If technology has not transformed Third World economies, its ideological and organizational consequences have profoundly influenced mass values and the values of leadership elites. The gap between expectations and capabilities has widened as the visibility of industrial technological development and the concomitant environmental and social fall-out, perhaps best symbolized by the United States, have spread the desire to seek the one and avoid the other. The conflict between the distribution of income and the growth of social product, which early in the industrial age was muted by the slow rate of technological

856 Karl de Schweinitz, Jr.

change and the inchoate state of ideology and organization, therefore can become readily exacerbated. Thus Third World countries at early stages of development that already may be plagued by high transaction costs arising from the limited flow of information about market opportunities and from immobilizing systems of land tenure face the further costs of dealing with mass groups or parties whose goals have less to do with raising production capabilities than with seeking social and/or economic justice. In Great Britain and the United States these groups developed gradually in the wake of a growing economy and acquired great institutional depth. Nonetheless, as we have argued about the United States—and the argument applies to modern Great Britain—these groups as they mature politicize the economy in the sense that the costs of their self-regarding behavior almost inevitably draw government into its management.

In Third World countries, where the conflict between distribution and growth may be more severe because growth is not yet or only recently on a self-sustaining basis, a great institutional challenge is the devising of a system of governance which can resolve the conflict while building reserves of support and legitimacy in society. In the years since Indian independence in 1947 and the successful conclusion of the Chinese Revolution in 1949, Third World states have proliferated. So have military juntas, single-party dictatorships, and other forms of authoritarian government, developments that do not afford much comfort to crusaders for democracy, nor, indeed, to believers in socialism. Paradoxically, "the cry for justice," which has been vented the more vociferously because of the demonstrable capacity of technology to transform the environment and accelerate economic growth, often is being stilled by the claims of the state to being the custodian of both.[20] Whether one observes the experience of the mature or developing economies, it seems clear that the Marxian sequence has been revised, to borrow a phrase from Galbraith—the organization and direction of markets are coming to depend more and more on the use of political power.

Notes

1. Nathan Rosenberg, *Technology and American Economic Growth* (New York: Harper and Row, 1972), p. 18.
2. In this connection see Nathan Rosenberg's critique of Jacob Schmookler, *Invention and Economic Growth* (Cambridge, Mass.: Harvard University Press, 1966) in "Science, Invention, and Economic Growth," *Economic Journal* 84 (March 1974): 90–108.

3. Joseph A. Schumpeter, *Capitalism, Socialism, and Democracy*, 3d ed. (New York: Harper & Brothers, 1950), p. 83. Italics in original text.

4. Friedrich Engels, *The Condition of the Working-Class in England in 1844* (London: Allen and Unwin, 1950), English edition translated by Florence Kelley Wishnewetsky; and Andrew Ure, *The Philosophy of Manufacturers* (London: C. Knight, 1835).

5. J. H. Clapham, *An Economic History of Modern Britain*, volume 1, *The Early Railway Age, 1820–1850* (Cambridge: the University Press, 1926); J. L. and Barbara Hammond, *The Village Labourer, 1760–1830* (London: Longmans, Green and Co., 1911); idem, *The Town Labourer, 1760–1830* (London: V. Gollancz, 1937); and Arnold Toynbee, *Lectures on the Industrial Revolution in England* (London: Rivingtons, 1884).

6. T. S. Ashton, "The Standard of Life of the Workers in England, 1790–1830," in *Capitalism and the Historians*, F. A. Hayek, ed. (Chicago: University of Chicago Press, 1954), pp. 127–159; R. M. Hartwell, "Rising Standard of Living in England, 1800–1850," *Economic History Review* 13, 2nd series (April 1961): 397–416; E. J. Hobsbawm "The British Standard of Living, 1790–1830," *Economic History Review* 10, 2nd series (August 1957): 46–69; and E. J. Hobsbawm and R. M. Hartwell, "The Standard of Living during the Industrial Revolution: A Discussion," *Economic History Review* 16, 2nd series (August 1963): 120–46.

7. Paul Mantoux, *The Industrial Revolution in the Eighteenth Century*, rev. ed. (London: Jonathan Cape, 1952), translated by Marjorie Vernon, pp. 411–12.

8. Luddism early made its mark in literature, notably in Charlotte Bronte, *Shirley* (London: Smith, Elder and Co., 1888).

9. See E. J. Hobsbawm, "The Machine Breakers," *Past and Present*, no. 1 (February 1952): 57–70.

10. Albert O. Hirschman, *The Strategy of Economic Development* (New Haven: Yale University Press, 1958), p. 58.

11. Ibid., p. 59. Italics in original text.

12. According to Arthur Young, in the 1770s the electorate amounted to no more than 250,000, and by Richard Price's count, "5,723 persons chose half the members of the House of Commons." R. R. Palmer, *The Age of the Democratic Revolution, A Political History of Europe and America, 1760–1800: The Challenge* (Princeton: Princeton University Press, 1959), p. 168.

13. Henry Mayhew, *London Labour and the London Poor* (London: Griffin, Bohn and Co., 1861–1862).

14. W. W. Rostow, *The Stages of Economic Growth, a Non-Communist Manifesto*, 2d ed. (Cambridge: the University Press, 1971), pp. 73–92.

15. Herbert Marcuse, *One-Dimensional Man: Studies in the Ideology of Advanced Industrial Society* (Boston: Beacon Press, 1964), p. 1.

16. E. J. Mishan, *The Costs of Economic Growth* (London: Staples Press, 1967), pp. 122–23.

17. Benjamin Disraeli, *Sybil: or the Two Nations* (London: Nelson, 1957).

18. Kenneth E. Boulding, "Expecting the Unexpected: the Uncertain Future of Knowlege and Technology," in *Beyond Economics: Essays in Society, Religion, and Ethics* (Ann Arbor: University of Michigan Press, 1968), pp. 170–71, a paper prepared for a conference on Prospective Changes

858   Karl de Schweinitz, Jr.

in Society by 1980 on 29 June 1966 in Denver, Colorado.
19. Douglass C. North and Robert P. Thomas, *The Rise of the Western World—a New Economic History* (Cambridge: the University Press, 1973).
20. *The Cry for Justice* is the title of an anthology of the literature of social protest edited and published by Upton Sinclair in 1915 with an introduction by Jack London.

9

Jei *JOURNAL OF ECONOMIC ISSUES*
Vol. XVII No. 1 March 1983

Welfare Maxima in Economics

Wendell Gordon

In his 1981 presidential address to the American Economics Association, William Baumol said: "In the received analysis perfect competition serves as the one standard of welfare-maximizing structure and behavior."[1]

But some of the difficulty in which "the received analysis" currently finds itself is because of its difficulties in identifying these welfare maxima. Several examples follow to indicate that pure competition in a two-factor, two-product, Cobb-Douglas, or constant-elasticity-of-substitution (CES) production function setting, such as is frequently used in "the received analysis," cannot be counted on to produce a unique welfare maximum expressible by a common-denominator yardstick.

First, we compare alleged welfare maxima in the income-redistribution-possibility case:[2] In Figure 1, two commodities, X and Y (perhaps luxuries and necessities), are assumed. They are represented on the two axes as physical quantities of output, so the yardsticks on the axes are not the same. It is a two-commodity and two-factor-of-production world. $C'C$ is a production possibility curve. $A'A$ and $B'B$ are two in one family of community indifference curves, corresponding to which point P ostensibly represents a static welfare maximum. $D'D$ and $E'E$ are two in another family of community indifference curves (representing perhaps a situation where income has been redistributed to the poor by comparison with the $A'A$ and $B'B$ situation—the poor presumably buy relatively more necessities—or perhaps where there has merely been a difference in tastes as a result of alternative fashions) for which point P' ostensibly represents a static welfare maximum.

The author is Professor of Economics, University of Texas at Austin.

2   Wendell Gordon

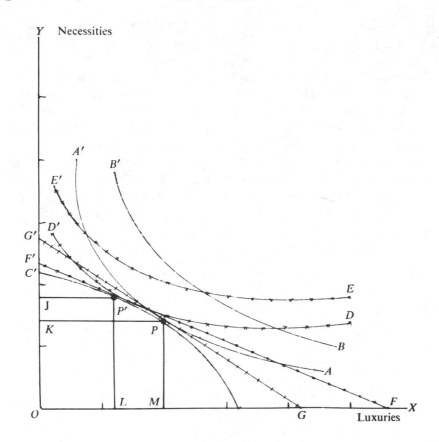

Figure 1. *Maximization: The Income Distribution Case*

Here one cannot make the standard welfare economics argument identifying a maximum (the tangency of the production possibility curve with
the furthest outlying community indifference curve it can reach) because
in the redistribution case the patterns of community indifference curves
cross each other. At this point one might merely say that the welfare maximum is indeterminate. But many economists feel an urge to say something
more meaningful than this.

Thinking thusly, one might proceed to try to identify a maximum by
identifying a common yardstick. If one alleges, as is common in general
equilibrium analysis, that the slopes of the tangents through P and P' represent equilibrium, market clearing, and prices, in the two cases one can
conceptualize gross national product (GNP = national income) using
either commodity Y or commodity X as the numeraire (money). If X
(necessities) is taken as the numeraire, the move from P to P', as a result

of the income redistribution, has lowered GNP from *OG'* to *OF'*. And one seems to have a firm, theoretically defensible, cardinal number to measure maximum welfare and welfare difference.

But if one takes *Y* (luxuries) as the numeraire, the move from *P* to *P'* has raised GNP from *OG* to *OF*. One gets contradictory signals as to the direction of change of GNP (not just a slight difference in magnitude) depending on which commodity is used as numeraire, and one has no definitive criterion for identifying the better numeraire.

Next, as a second example of the difficulty in identifying a maximum, there is the matter of the confusion created by the fact that the identity of the best-practice-technique is not unambiguously determined on the supply or technology side. Demand influences must be taken into account, as Figure 2 indicates.

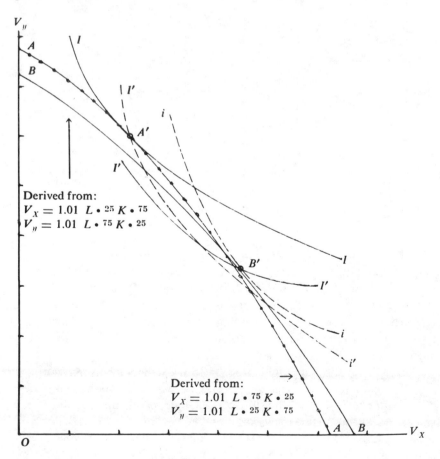

Figure 2. *Best Practice Technique*

4   Wendell Gordon

One is asked to accept that the indicated production functions, in a two-factor, two-product frame of reference, will generate the indicated production possibility curves AA and BB. In this case, the production possibility curves do cross each other. And this means that if the community indifference curve pattern II and $I'I'$ prevails, then the best-practice-techniques are represented by the production functions $V_x = 1.01 \, L \cdot {}^{75} K \cdot {}^{25}$ and $V_y = 1.01 \, L \cdot {}^{25} K \cdot {}^{75}$, and if the community indifference curve pattern ii and $i'i'$ prevails (perhaps representing alternative possible tastes), the best-practice-techniques are represented by the production functions $V_x = 1.01 \, L \cdot {}^{25} K \cdot {}^{75}$ and $V_y = 1.01 \, L \cdot {}^{75} K \cdot {}^{25}$.

The identification of the best-practice-techniques—which set of production functions is more productive—must wait on taking demand patterns into account.

A third example of a static contradiction, which arises in the quest for a welfare maximum, may be identified in an Edgeworth box where the contract line is derived from the production functions already used: $V_x = 1.01 \, L \cdot {}^{75} K \cdot {}^{25}$ and $V_y = 1.01 \, L \cdot {}^{25} K \cdot {}^{75}$. In this case one is comparing the GNP at Q with the GNP at Q' to ascertain whether there is a contradiction depending on the numeraire used. In this example capital (K) or labor (L) alternatively is used as the numeraire for measuring GNP. The slopes of the straight lines tangent to the isoquants at Q and Q' represent the wage/rate-of-return-to-capital (w/r) ratios at those points (on the full employment, etcetera, assumptions generally used in this paradigm). $M_K M_L$ has the same slope and therefore represents the same w/r ratio as prevails at Q. This means $O_x M_K$ corresponds to GNP using K as the numeraire when production is at Q. Similarly, if production is at Q', by similar reasoning, $O_x M'_K$ represents GNP. So GNP is lower at Q' than at Q.

But the direction of change is reversed if labor is used as the numeraire. $O_x M_L$ is GNP corresponding to Q and the greater amount $O_x M'_L$ is GNP at Q'.

It is worth noting and emphasizing that in the income redistribution case (Figure 1) and the Edgeworth box contract line case (Figure 3), not only does one get somewhat different orders of magnitude in the answers depending upon the choice of numeraire (under circumstances where there are no clear grounds for preferring one numeraire to another), but the *sign* (or the direction of change of GNP) is, in general, reversed. And the sign is reversed also if one merely orders the results instead of cardinalizing.

It is also worth noting the implication of this argument for the Marxist concept of socially necessary unit of labor time. Make the inputs two qualities of labor instead of capital and labor, and the concept of the so-

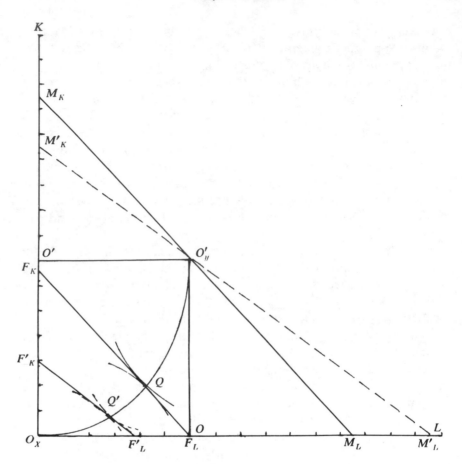

Figure 3. *The Edgeworth Box and Gross National Product (Alternative Pareto-Optimal Product Mixes under Full Employment)*

cially necessary unit of labor time (aggregating the two qualities of labor) loses its clarity. Whether the size of the product is increasing or decreasing (perhaps even whether exploitation is increasing or decreasing) depends on which quality of labor one uses as a numeraire. And, again, there is no clear criterion for identifying the better numeraire. So, one loses the ability to identify exploitation in the manner associated with Karl Marx. (Perhaps it would be better and simpler for those concerned for the poor merely to pass a value judgment on the degree of inequality in the distribution of income that one believes is appropriate and forget trying to quantify exploitation.)

Fourth, as yet another example of the inconsistencies that arise in the search for a welfare maximum, it may be helpful to consider the discus-

6   Wendell Gordon

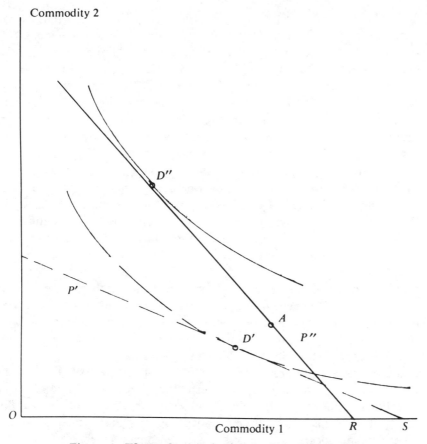

Figure 4. *The Welfare Criterion for Two Commodities*

sion of a "welfare criterion" in a standard textbook. The following example is from Richard Caves and Ronald Jones.[3] In Figure 4, the solid lines are from the Caves and Jones graph labeled: "The Welfare Criterion for Two Commodities." One may be intrigued to reconsider their effort to compare welfare in the two situations (involving their endorsement of commodity 2 as a measure of real income) and contrast their commodity 2 result with the implication of using commodity 1 as an alternative yardstick. Illustrating this possibility involves adding dashed lines to the Caves and Jones graph in a pattern that is not too implausible, given the solid lines they have already drawn. Their explanation is: "Two alternative consumption bundles are illustrated: D' and D''. The prices ruling when D'' is consumed are shown by line p''. The welfare criterion whereby situation double-prime is superior to situation single prime is shown by the fact that

D' lies below the line p'', which means $p''D'' - p''D' > O''$ (that is, price times quantity at D'' minus the same price times quantity at D' is greater than O). And yet this result is achieved only by claiming that the prices characterized by the slope of p'' are applicable to the D' situation, which is not reasonably the case. The price ratio at D' corresponds to the slope of dash line p'. (One may conjecture that a community indifference curve through D' might correspond [not too improbably] with the dotted community indifference curve, and the price ratio corresponding to D' correspond with the slope of the dotted price line p'.) And if one also decides to use commodity 1 as the numeraire, then D' represents a larger GNP than does D'' by the amount RS. And one has another example of different direction of movement of real GNP, depending on choice of numeraire, this time when one moves from one point on one community indifference curve to a different point on another community indifference curve.

Fifth, yet another situation: Consumer and producer surplus areas frequently are used in comparing whether a given policy or project (or commodity) will generate more or less welfare than another. Their use has been especially frequent in energy and resource studies since the 1973 energy crisis and in connection with evaluating efforts to stabilize prices in raw commodity control schemes.

It has been well understood for many years that the use of consumer and producer surplus areas under and over ordinary Marshallian demand and supply curves is theoretically questionable because of its inherent implication that the marginal utility of money is constant, when the marginal utility of money is clearly not constant in most of the relevant situations. (The areas in question are the cross-hatched region in Figure 5.)

In recent years it has been argued that this difficulty can be avoided by the use of compensated demand and supply curves. Such curves allegedly represent demand and supply on an assumption of unchanged utility or unchanged welfare. The consumer and producer surplus areas are then the areas under and over the compensated curves.

But the ability to draw such compensated curves requires the ability to identify unambiguously an amount of welfare or utility corresponding to a given mix of commodities, and to equate that amount of welfare to some amount of welfare corresponding to a different mix of commodities being consumed by different people. Difficulties involved in doing this have already been noted on both the demand and supply sides.

However, the argument developed above should not be interpreted as denying the rough and ready usefulness, in a ceteris paribus (not a general equilibrium) setting, of comparisons of areas under demand and over supply curves, provided one can identify demand and supply curves at all. But

8   Wendell Gordon

it does mean that the effort to validate such comparisons as being theoretically meaningful is unwarranted. It is worth quoting Kenneth Arrow in a related context: "What I want to emphasize here and repeat later in varying contexts is that this price adjustment mechanism is *not* independent of the choice of numeraire. More specifically, the movements of relative prices can be different with different numeraires."[4]

But then there is also an appropriate qualification to the qualification. If one looks only at the primary effects in microeconomic theory, it may be true that there is welfare gain implied when, if one also looked at some secondary effects, welfare loss would be implied. One can generate contradictory conclusions (antinomies) in both microeconomics and general equilibrium economics (and one might add macroeconomics) and under conditions with significant implications.

Sixth, another example of the problem involved in making logically consistent choices involves Arrow's (or Marie Marquis de Condorcet's, circa 1785) paradox of voting:[5]

> A natural way of arriving at the collective preference scale would be to say that one alternative is preferred to another if a majority of the community prefer the first alternative to the second, i.e., would choose the first over the second if those were the only two alternatives. Let A, B, and C be the three alternatives, and 1, 2, and 3 the three individuals. Suppose individual 1 prefers A to B and B to C (and therefore A to C), individual 2 prefers B to C and C to A (and therefore B to A), and individual 3 prefers C to A and A to B (and therefore C to B). Then a majority prefer A to B, and a majority prefer B to C. . . . If the community is to be regarded as behaving rationally, we are forced to say that A is preferred to C. But in fact a majority of the community prefer C to A. So the method just outlined for passing from individual to collective tastes fails to satisfy the condition of rationality, as we ordinarily understand it.

And yet Arrow has not proven that the democratic voting process should be abandoned because of its inability to guarantee a consistent solution. He has merely demonstrated that democracy is a somewhat more subtle process than mathematized decision-making processes allow for. I believe it likely that Arrow would now say that his subsequent thirty years of effort to work mathematical, general-equilibrium-type sense out of this paradox leaves the matter pretty much where it was in 1951.

Democracy is a process that permits popular, peaceful participation in the rule-changing process. It is not a static logical exercise.

It might seem that if static equilibrium, on conventionally reasonable assumptions, cannot generate a unique welfare maximum there would be a strong presumption that growth models cannot generate a meaningful unique, maximum solution either. Nevertheless, there have been efforts, going back at least to Frank Ramsey in the 1920s, to conceptualize a maximum to infinity. Also there have been less ambitious efforts. Such efforts are considered next.

First, there is the question as to whether an unambiguous increase in production capability in a setting of unchanged community indifference curves (and assuming full employment) produces an identifiable, consistent percentage growth rate by different, equally valid, yardsticks. In Figure 6, to make the case fairly strong it is assumed that the community indifference curves are linear homogeneous ($U = X \cdot {}^6 Y \cdot {}^4$), a fairly common assumption in "the received analysis." New technology is somewhat favorable to Y production and moves the production possibility curve from qq' to rr'. The welfare maximum, taken as tangencies between the production possibility curves and the furthest outlying community indifference curves that they can reach, moves from p to p'. This corresponds to moving the community indifference curve out by 50 percent relative to the origin. If one believes community indifference curves can only be ordered, that tells us nothing about providing a number for the percentage increase in welfare. If one believes these relations can be cardinalized, one might foresee a 50 percent increase in welfare.

But is "welfare in terms of what" a common denominator? If commodity X is then used as the numeraire, gross national product (in real terms) rises by about 27 percent from OB to OD. And if commodity Y is so used, it rises by approximately 92 percent from OA to OC. It makes considerable difference which commodity is used as numeraire. And yet governments of underdeveloped countries fall or survive on the difference between a 3 and a 4 percent growth rate.

Without departing too much from the way economists typically draw graphs, it is even possible to make GNP rise using one numeraire and fall using the other. Figure 7 illustrates the possibility.

Of course, in one way of looking at it, all this is merely an example of the well-known index number problem. It should be clearly acknowledged here that price level index numbers are still worth computing in spite of this difficulty. They are rough measures of something that it is important to measure as reasonably as possible. But price level index numbers are not and cannot be theoretically satisfactory, precise guides to changes in real value.

Second, "maximizing a growth rate" is a concept without much useful role in defining and determining future welfare. In Figure 8 the growth rate of per capita consumption starts off more slowly in track A than track B, perhaps because there is a higher rate of saving in relation to income in

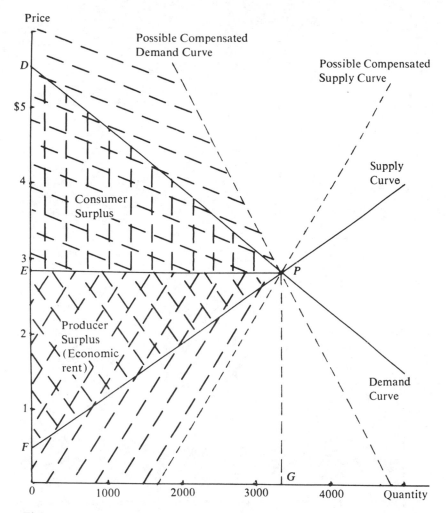

Figure 5. *Industry Demand and Supply: Consumer and Producer Surplus*

case *A*. But eventually, in the example allegedly in the tenth year, the earlier saving seems to pay off with a higher growth rate in per capita consumption along track *A* thereafter. Which track implies a high growth rate? It is not very helpful to put the question that way.

Other examples of the difficulty with maximization exercises include the Two-Cambridge Controversy and the maximization of bliss to infinity à la Frank Ramsey, Robert Solow, Trevor Swan, Edmund Phelps, and the golden rule of accumulation.

The preceding exercises have been intended to indicate that the concept

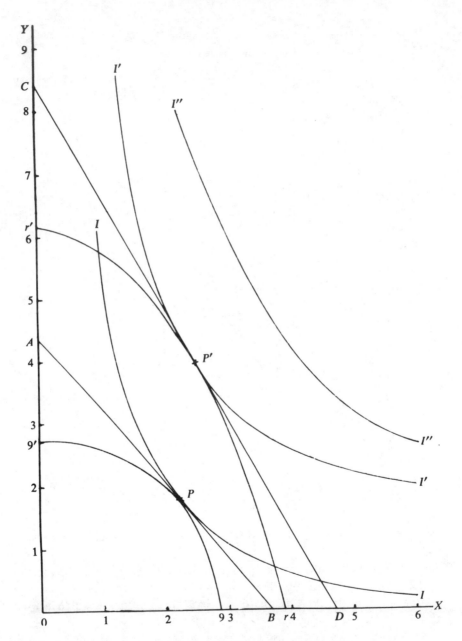

Figure 6. *Increase in Production Capability*

of a unique welfare maximum, expressible by a common yardstick, is not
and in general cannot be theoretically meaningful.

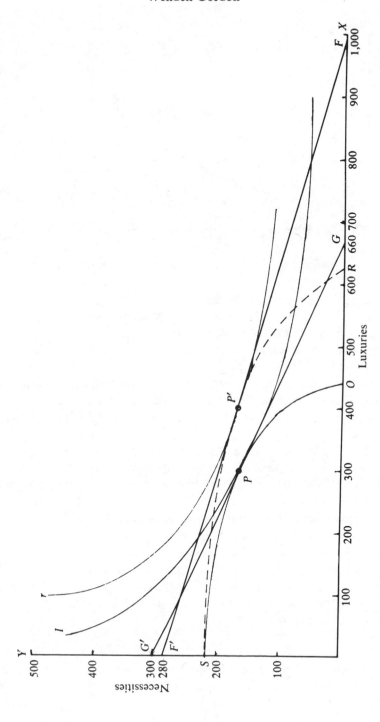

Figure 7. *Increase in Production Capability*

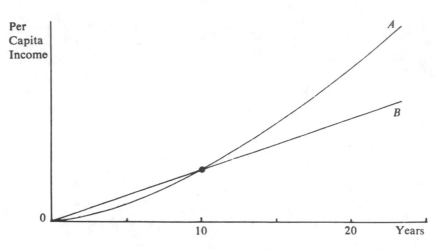

Figure 8. *Maximization of the Rate of Growth*

Changing conditions, changing knowledge, changing techniques, changing relative prices, changing relative use of factor inputs in given processes, in alternative processes, and in the production of different commodities, changing tastes, variations in tastes among people, decreasing (or increasing) utility, changing income distributions, and, above all, changing values mean that any attempt at a definitive conception of an overall, unique welfare maximum is a mirage. This is true both of alternative conditions at a given time (the static situation) and of changing conditions over time.

But, it should be added, these considerations do not deny the possibility that there may be situations where the solution of maximization problems is useful, particularly in decision making at the microeconomic level, in the short run, in a setting of some ceteris paribus assumptions. And none of the foregoing denies the importance of prices and profits. The individual buyer trying to pay less and the seller trying to get a higher price and higher profits may well be behaving in an intelligently rational manner. What has aborted in economics is the effort to aggregate these individual behavior patterns in an argument that leads to the conclusion that such behavior (in the setting of pure competition assumptions) tends automatically to be good for the general welfare.

Also one needs to shake the idea that the concept "marginal cost equals marginal revenue," at the microeconomics level, implies anything theoretically precise with regard to maximization of welfare at the general equilibrium level. $MC = MR$ may imply some useful perspective as to the rational behavior of firms. But one needs to be chary in applying any more general implications to that much abused concept.

Some may say that all this is well known and to keep repeating it serves no useful purpose.

And some, even many, economists working in general equilibrium analysis have certainly long been aware that in a setting of reasonably realistic assumptions pure competition cannot be counted on to generate a unique welfare maximum or even a unique solution—whether or not a maximum.

The difficulty in aggregating from individual indifference curves to community indifference curves has been well understood since Vilfredo Pareto. And Paul Samuelson has been acutely aware that the social welfare function he developed in his 1956 article did not provide a satisfactory alternative.[6] Max Weber has denied the meaning of welfare maximization. The same point has been made by E. J. Mishan and Thomas Schelling and many others.[7]

Frank Hahn has also denied meaning for the concept: "A bad nomenclature (Pareto-optimum) in the literature, together with much carelessness in textbooks, often misleads people into thinking that there is some theorem which claims that a competitive equilibrium is socially optimal. There is no such claim."[8]

Even Austrian/libertarians do not all subscribe to the proposition that the competitive general equilibrium maximizes the general welfare. Israel M. Kirzner of New York University writes that the "aggregate notions of social economic welfare [raise] well-nigh insuperable conceptual problems."[9] And Ludwig von Mises wrote: "If maximizing profits means that a man in all market transactions aims at increasing to the utmost the advantage derived, it is a pleonastic and periphrastic circumlocution. . . . Some economists believe that it is the task of economics to establish how in the whole of society the greatest satisfaction of all people or of the greatest number could be attained. They do not realize that there is no method which would allow us to measure the state of satisfaction attained by various individuals."[10] The implication of the statement is reasonably clear even if one temporarily stumbles over "pleonastic" and "periphrastic."

And there is Paul Samuelson's generous surrender to Joan Robinson in the Two-Cambridge Controversy: "We wish to make clear for the record that the nonswitching theorem associated with us is definitely false."[11]

What is the alternative if static general equilibrium analysis is dropped as the theoretical core of economics?

I believe there is a simple and meaningful answer. Society sometimes more or less democratically (and sometimes using dictators as intermediaries) dictates the institutionalized behavior norms people live by and determines the roles and relations of the market and the political process (democratic or otherwise) in making policy decisions. And in the background individuals play a role influencing this process and the modification of behavior norms. Their role becomes more meaningful the more they appreciate the nature of the process in which they are involved. In particular democracy is not merely a logical exercise that to be defensible requires that simple majorities produce consistent results. As was mentioned earlier, it is a subtle process in which the participants are continually readjusting the ground rules.

We live in a setting involving ongoing process. We are conditioned by this process and all that has gone before. We observe the present state of affairs and approve or disapprove, work for change or to prevent change, pass judgment on the changes and reconsider. And life is more interesting this way than if we were to live in an unchanging setting, with unchanging values tending toward equilibrium being the chief active influence. What a bore life would be if we really could solve the welfare maximization problem.

It is important to understand that in various important situations one *must* get contradictory allegations about direction of effect on welfare depending on choice of numeraire in a setting where there is no generally agreed-upon criterion for authoritatively identifying the better yardstick. And when one gets such reversals in the direction of change, the fundamental difficulty remains even if one is merely ordering according to the numeraire instead of quantifying in cardinal amounts.

Notes

1. William J. Baumol, "Contestable Markets: An Uprising in the Theory of Industry Structure," *American Economic Review* 72 (March 1982): 1–15 (especially p. 2).
2. Wendell Gordon, *Institutional Economics* (Austin: University of Texas Press, 1980), pp. 88–91.
3. Richard E. Caves and Ronald W. Jones, *World Trade and Payments*, 2d ed. (Boston: Little, Brown, 1977 [1973]), p. 447.
4. Kenneth J. Arrow, in Daniel Bell and Irving Kristol, eds., *The Crisis in Economic Theory* (New York: Basic Books, 1981), p. 142.
5. Kenneth J. Arrow, *Social Choice and Individual Values*, 2d ed. (New Haven: Yale University Press, 1963 [1951]), pp. 2–3; Marie Marquis de Condorcet, *Essai sur l'Application de l'Analyse à la Probabilité des Décisions Rendue à la Pluralité*, cc. 1785.

16 Wendell Gordon

6. Paul A. Samuelson, "Social Indifference Curves," *Quarterly Journal of Economics* 70 (February 1956): 1–22.
7. Max Weber, *Selections in Translation*, W. G. Runciman, ed. (Cambridge, Eng.: Cambridge University Press, 1978), pp. 83–88; Robin Marris, ed., *The Corporate Society* (New York: John Wiley, 1974). The latter publication includes articles by Mishan and Schelling.
8. Frank Hahn, in Bell and Kristol, *The Crisis*, p. 126.
9. Israel M. Kirzner, in Bell and Kristol, *The Crisis*, p. 119.
10. Ludwig von Mises, *Human Action* (New Haven: Yale University Press, 1949), p. 243.
11. Paul A. Samuelson and D. Levhari, "The Nonswitching Theorem is False," *Quarterly Journal of Economics* 80 (November 1966): 518–19.

[10]

Jei *JOURNAL OF ECONOMIC ISSUES*
Vol. IX   No. 1   March 1975

The Impact of Economics on Technology

Seymour Melman

Among economists and other social scientists, machine technology characteristically is viewed as an autonomously fixed condition in relation to human behavior. The typical treatment in the literature dealing with society and technology is of "the impact of technology on society." Indeed, historians of technology have noted a virtual absence of such titles as "the impact of society on technology."[1] There has been a general consensus among social scientists that technology has a direction and momentum of its own and, accordingly, that it sets limits that have a controlling effect on what is socially possible. In a volume entitled *The Technological Society*, Jacques Ellul succinctly expresses this viewpoint when he writes: "Capitalism did not create our world; the machine did."[2]

This article stands the above assumption on its head. I do not quarrel with the obvious fact that , once created and utilized, technology has wide-ranging economic and social consequences. I take issue, however, with the belief that it has an autonomous momentum and direction. Technology is man's creation. It is applied in accordance with specific social criteria wielded by those with economic decision power in the society. I propose here to indicate how the specific design and selection from among technological alternatives is controlled decisively by the industrial managers, private and governmental, on whose behalf technologies are researched, developed, and produced.

The author is Professor of Industrial Engineering, Columbia University, New York, New York.

One implication of this formulation, in contrast to assumptions about an autonomous technological momentum, is that technology is subject to major alternations as a consequence of variation in the economic and social criteria that are used to decide technology.

The differentiation between science, invention, and technology is useful for our discussion. *Science* is the body of knowledge and the process of discovery concerning the characteristics of the universe. *Invention* is the application of science to artifacts and methods for performing operations; it also refers to the research and development process whereby new artifacts and procedures are produced. By *technology*, I mean the application of science and invention in the service of some social requirement. The latter differentiation is crucial since museums of technology and the engineering literature world-wide are filled with inventions that never actually have been applied. New knowledge about the universe and free invention add to the options that conceivably can be siezed upon for application in the form of technology: products, means of production, or methods of organization. The present discussion is concerned with technology, not with the processes of science or invention.

By way of illustrating the characteristics of technology, let us draw on the experience of the automobile industry in the United States and other countries. The mass utilization of automobiles, *any kind of automobile*, would have generated profound effects on the distribution of population and the associated suburban life-style. These results would have been achieved had motor vehicles been large or small, expensive or inexpensive, energy efficient or inefficient, safe or unsafe. Needless to say, highways, suburbia, and the motor vehicles themselves include a host of humanly and socially destructive features and effects. These include unsafe vehicles and highways; grossly expensive, inefficient, and air-polluting vehicles; suburban configurations that are unreachable and unusable without the automobile; and the concommitant withdrawal of public capital from metropolitan centers. None of these results sprang autonomously from machine technology. All these features and effects were preferred selectively by the economic decision makers who determined which technology, in each instance, was most serviceable to their business advantage.

Throughout its history as a quantity-produced product, the design and hence the operating characteristics of the U.S. automobile have been stamped by the requirements of the directing managements of the major auto firms. They have sought to maximize the extension of their decision power as gauged by criteria of profit, capital investment, market share, and control over workers. However, the strategies used toward these ends have varied, and the changes of business strategy have been reflected in the technologies of the auto product and of the industry as a production system as well. First, the product.

The Automobile

In the industry dominated by the Ford Motor Company until the Great Depression, the mass-produced passenger car was a simplified, standardized, functional product. By the close of World War II, the industry was dominated by General Motors, whose business strategy, different from that of early Ford, favored a product technology of growing ornateness, a price-graded product line, and annual model changes that stressed numerous cosmetic alterations and dysfunctional innovations. Product standardization was deemphasized in favor of promoting product variation both in single years and through time. Product standardization was reduced, and the idea of auto simplification virtually was abandoned.

It is significant that during the period 1919–1929 the average price of U.S.-produced cars actually fell from $830 to $630 per car. By contrast, from 1949 to 1971 the average price per U.S.-produced passenger car was increased from $1,300 to $2,500.[3]

These changes in product (and prices) do not represent, in any sense, technology with direction and momentum of its own. All the changes in auto design were the result of elaborately developed management strategies. Tailfins, meaningless trim, horsepower beyond anything that could be used on any public road, failure-prone mechanisms, and quality control to ensure limited component and vehicle life, all these were ordered as part of a top management strategy for profits and expansion of decision power. A special kind of naïveté is required to accept the explanation for tailfins once offered to me by a former president of a major auto firm: The consumer wanted it.

By 1973 one of the Big Three had 43 models in its "low cost" line. The cost of auto transportation to the user was raised by the proliferation of body types, engines, transmissions, and seat controls, and the multitude of internal fittings produced a situation in which a major auto assembly plant could complete a year of work without actually building two identical cars. This kind of diversity killed the advantages of relatively low-cost quantity production and stable design that once had been the trademark of the U.S. auto industry.

It is worth noting some of the product technology characteristics that were avoided during the last decades. Vehicle economy was

Seymour Melman

foregone in favor of higher price tags and expensive maintenance. Safety considerations that would reduce highway deaths by at least half were foregone. Fuel economy was sacrificed for ever-higher horsepower. Convenient vehicle size was avoided in favor of styling considerations. Passenger comfort in the form of seating, head room, and leg room were given short shrift in preference to the "long, low look" and dysfunctional styling.

If product technology had a direction and momentum of its own, then it is unlikely that product design would have taken on precisely those characteristics that were serviceable to a particular business strategy rather than to the vehicle user. There is no escaping the fact that product technology did not just happen. It was selected, managed, ordered.

Criteria of choice play a key part in determining product design. Criteria determine the selection (and avoidance) of technology options from the array of alternatives that are available to industrial managers and to their engineer surrogates. With 97 million passenger cars in use by 1972, 83 percent of U.S. families depended on their cars. They obtained transportation at an average out-of-pocket vehicle cost of 15 cents per mile, annual vehicle costs of about $1,500, and a yearly toll of 56,000 highway deaths and 4,850,000 persons injured.[4] The medical and environmental cost of auto air pollution is unknown, but surely is large. All these costs of using conventional autos could have been diminished substantially by vehicles that were designed by engineers whose work assignments specified cheaper, safer, and less polluting passenger cars.

Imagine a row of engineers, each one given a different prime criterion for designing a gasoline-engined passenger car. The first must design with minimum money costs of operation in mind. The next with stress on safety for the driver. Another with the main emphasis on mechanical reliability, let us say, over an arbitrary period of fifteen years of use. The next must design with an eye toward maximizing fuel efficiency, another toward minimizing vehicle contribution to air pollution, and so on. The varying prime criteria of these assignments will cause the engineers to design, in each instance, a product that is manifestly different from others. By similar reasoning, change the criteria for automobile performance, and you will transform the familiar motor car.

In September 1973, the Porsche management in Germany displayed a prototype of a passenger car designed to last a full twenty years and run 180,000 miles. The car would cost about 30 percent more at the outset, but over the twenty-year period a reduction of 15 percent in full operating expenses could be expected. One of the engineers who developed this design stated that it is not based on exotic technology. "The components are either available or manufacturers will have them ready in the next several years." The car body would be aluminum, stainless steel, or recyclable plastic. Larger than normal components of many sorts would be used, and the engine would be a modest 75 horsepower with sophisticated mechanical and electrical features.[5]

Obviously, the production of such a vehicle is contrary to the U.S. auto industry's long sustained product and marketing strategy. But it reflects technological feasibility once there has been an enforced decision by a larger community that sets limits to the inefficiency of present motor vehicles. The fact is that the engineering literature includes an immense number of partial and full designs for motor vehicles that differ dramatically from the conventional products. They range from electrically driven to steam-powered cars. Whatever else, the Porsche design illustrates that management decision and not technological inevitability have determined automobile design.

In sum, several lines of evidence converge on the conclusion that auto products have no autonomous genesis or termination. Auto industry managers order their engineers to design products in keeping with their firms' general business strategy. Product designs that are not consistent with management policies are left to the limbo of office files, Patent Office drawings, engineering society papers, or museum models. All this spells product technology carrying the imprint of management's business strategy rather than any autonomous technological development. Similar patterns are visible in the shaping of the auto industry's production technologies.

Automobile Production

The belief that technology is autonomously determined generally includes the assumption that dehumanized and alienating conditions of work are intrinsic to the use of production machinery. Production work, it is assumed, must be inherently boring, dirty, and dangerous and must turn human beings into appendages of machines. Certainly contemporary conditions in the U.S. auto industry seem to be consistent with this belief. But are these conditions inevitable results of automotive production technology? Or, are they also heavily dependent on the choices of economic decision makers and hence subject to alteration given changed criteria and ways of decision making?

Managements whose traditions have included viewing the industrial worker as a species of replaceable, animated, special purpose machine

have not given priority attention to the impact of the physical conditions
of the workplace on human work performers. The result is a working
environment that is often dangerous, or noisy, or dirty, or poorly
ventilated, or too hot, or too cold, or some combination of these.
Long exposure to such conditions is bound to have a degrading effect
on the workers involved, especially while executive offices luxuriate
in a modern, air-conditioned decor. Think of spending the work day
in a place where, in order to speak to someone during working time,
you must shout at the top of your voice, or of ending each day
covered with grime.

As external pressures, such as liability for disabilities, have
compelled managers to order the reduction of noise in the factory,
for example, sustained attention has been given to developing new
techniques for this purpose. True, there are bound to be some limits
to what is possible in particular places. An iron foundry is certain
to be dirty because of the constant handling of large quantities of
fine sand. Areas around large presses are bound to be noisy and
vibration filled. Batteries of automatic lathes can produce a fearful
din. Even after considerable effort, a large amount of residual dirt,
vibration, and noise is sure to remain in such work areas. Even with
maximum effort it never will be like working in a library.

Nevertheless, very much could be done to reduce the tedium and
even the monotony of many industrial jobs by redesigning them and,
finally, by mechanizing difficult work hitherto done manually. In the
auto industry there could be economic justification for mechanizing
many monotonous jobs if the mania for annual model changes and
meaningless product variety were diminished, thereby increasing the
annual quantities of many components which could be standardized
over several years.

A U.S. visitor to the Saab-Scandia auto factories in Sweden has
commented on a four-year effort to organize automobile assembly
work on a small team basis. Engines, for example, are assembled
by three workers acting as a team. He further found that "the noise
level of the machinery was far below the decibel level of comparable
American machines . . . in contrast to the noisy and dirty conditions
of comparable American plants one could not help but be astonished."[6]

The production technology of the auto industry is sensibly considered
in two parts: the physical means of production and the techniques
for organizing and integrating the host of production operations. In
fact, these two aspects of production technology are intertwined and
are separable only analytically. Nevertheless, it is useful to distinguish

them for both purposes of engineering design and the present discussion. First, let us consider the means of production.

The Means of Production

The industrial manager who wants particular work done typically is confronted with the problem of choosing from among many alternative tools, devices, and machines available for accomplishing the given task. The availability of many methods stems from the accumulated body of science and invention and previous applications to technology.

Consider a very simple task, such as making a hole of specified size and shape in a one-inch thickness of wood. You immediately discover a great array of methods. You can start with a simple instrument such as a knife, advance to a device that has a drill bit, powered by hand, and move on to the same drill powered by a motor. Furthermore, the device can be held in place by a table or, beyond that, mounted on the floor. The alternatives extend to a device that automatically will put a work piece in place, perform the drilling operation, measure it for an acceptable dimension, remove the work piece, and transfer it to a stack of finished work.

To be sure, industrial managers and engineers often wish to accomplish a given task in a new manner; for example, by machine instead of human labor. Checking on the dimensions of a particular item long has been a manual task, but available knowledge and prior technology open the option for making this kind of product inspection a mechanical task. Thus new types of machines are designed and constructed to measure the dimensions of an object and segregate the bits that meet the required dimensions from those that fail. The development of new technology for production work enlarges the array of equipment options for accomplishing particular tasks. For engineers and managers the typical problem is: Which of the alternative available equipment options is most suitable to the particular work requirement?

This problem ordinarily is solved by applying a particular criterion to the range of alternatives. The usual one preferred by cost-minimizing managers is an estimate of the cost of doing the work with any particular machine. In such estimates, two factors have tended to dominate the scene in mechanical manufacturing operations: the price of the machine and the cost of labor per hour to the management. (In the process industries it is the ratio of raw materials to machinery costs.) Using these criteria, one usually can rank the alternative available machines according to the mix of labor and machinery costs involved,

66   Seymour Melman

that is, from those using most labor and least machine cost per unit of work done to those involving most machine and least labor cost. For a given quantity of work, the machine with the least combined cost will be determined by the prevailing pattern of wages and machinery prices.

During most of the twentieth century there has been a regular pattern of development of labor and machinery costs to U.S. management. The wages of labor have tended to grow on the average more rapidly than the prices of machinery. The result of this rise in the alternative cost of labor to machinery has favored ever more intense mechanization of work by cost-minimizing managers.[7] Average growth in output per worker man-hour has been the direct result of this process. Indeed, this criterion has been used to account for the considerable variation among countries in the productivity of labor.

If it were true that technology had a direction and momentum of its own, then it reasonably could be expected that the same sort of production methods and equipment would be used throughout the world. After all, the market for production machinery has long been an international one, training about science is similar in every land, and the literature of engineering (except for the secret military type) is available everywhere. Actually, the methods of mechanical manufacture have varied considerably among economies in a way that is not at all mysterious. I can illustrate the pattern of development by drawing on some of the data from my studies of comparative international productivity.

The Ford Motor Company is one of many corporations that owns and operates factories in different countries. During the 1950s I examined aspects of production operations in the Ford factories in Detroit, Michigan, and Dagenham, England.[8] I found striking differences between the two. The Detroit factories were using much more power equipment per worker. The factories at Dagenham, outside London, produced similar products but had work methods that required much more muscle power, more use of human sensory-motor capability than did those in Detroit. Stated differently, there was a much higher intensity of mechanization of production work in Detroit than in England. The similarities among these factories included: the same kind of product, the same company, the same underlying scientific knowledge in both places, the same ample staffs of engineers and ample access to technological knowledge in both, and ample access to capital for the purpose of designing and operating production facilities in both places. The differences in degree of mechanization remained to be explained.

I found that this variation in mechanization could be accounted for by the accompanying variation in the relative cost of labor to machinery in the two countries. Thus, in 1950 in the United States it was possible for an employer, at the cost of hiring a worker for one hour, to buy 157 kilowatt hours of electricity. In England, the employer could use the cost of employing a worker for one hour to buy only 37 kilowatt hours of electricity. Hence, employers interested in minimizing the total money cost of doing particular work were required to buy more electricity and fewer man-hours in Detroit and to buy more man-hours and less electricity in Dagenham.[9] Similar contrasts showed up in the ratio of labor to machine-hour costs.

Making the usual calculations of business cost, the managers of the Ford Motor Company and their counterparts in other firms made essentially the same decision: less mechanization in England than in Detroit. That was the result of the effort to minimize enterprise production costs in each case. There is no evidence here of production methods technology having a life of its own. No mysteries of self-actuated machine processes need to be invoked to account for the observed variation in the means of production, either in one country through time or among countries at a single time. The actual patterns of technological choice lend themselves to fairly straightforward explanation. Industrial managers and their engineer surrogates selected (or developed) those means of production which best satisfied the capitalist economic criteria for the operation of their enterprises. Similar considerations apply to the other major part of production technology—the organization and integration of production work.

Organizing and Integrating Work

A division of labor is an indispensable feature of automobile production. It is inconceivable that a single person could fabricate and assemble all of the main materials and functional components of a motor vehicle. Within that limitation, however, a great many alternatives are possible for the division of labor, both in ways of organizing and integrating the specialized work and in the decision processes that are needed to integrate the division of labor. To consider this matter, it is first necessary to overcome a considerable intellectual bias, namely, the assumption that the division of labor and the accompanying decision processes that have been characteristic of the auto industry are in some way integral to and essential for the utilization of any kind of machine technology.

The main elements of division of labor are, for each person, the task to be performed, the physical means to be used to perform

Seymour Melman

it, the variability that is possible in the performance of the work, the frequency of performance, and the ways by which the work of each person is linked to the work of others. In the auto industry (but also in mechanical manufacturing generally), the most characteristic pattern for division of labor has included three elements. The first is work simplification, which has meant ever smaller work tasks and more finely delimited work methods. The second is more specification, which has lessened variability in the ways of performing a work task. The third is maximum removal from the production worker of responsibility and authority for integrating his work with that of other workers. Terms such as *mass production* and *assembly line* have come to be used as generalized descriptions of this set of conditions.

The division of labor technology that selectively was installed and that operated for many years in the U.S. auto industries was particularly suited to the main objectives of managers who directed industrial operations. Thus, the micro division of unchanging work tasks first instituted by Henry Ford lowered production costs by raising the productivity of both capital and labor. More than that, by these means Ford was able to hire and quickly train workers with virtually no prior industrial experience. A new occupational category was invented: "semi-skilled." Getting work done with these rigorously controlled workers of limited skill broke the decision power of craft workers and craft unions in the industry. Management reigned supreme and unchallenged (until the CIO organizing of the 1930s) in its control of the growing industry, while being hailed as an industrial benefactor for paying the highest industrial wages and mass-producing the cars that transformed the U.S. life-style.

The U.S. auto industry's managers long were able to draw upon a large, new, industrially inexperienced work force from rural America, North and South. As its labor force increasingly comes from a more educated population, it is more than likely that the managers will confront increased worker opposition to their traditional pattern of work simplification plus mechanization plus work intensification plus work discipline policed by an ever-growing supervisory staff. New forms and intensities of worker resistance to these management policies manifested themselves recently in the General Motors factories in Lordstown, Ohio, where from 1972 on, a young, unusually well-educated work force rebelled against the managers of a much heralded showplace factory.

So common have work simplification and allied practices become in industry, and so dominant in the literature of industrial engineering, that they typically are assumed to be inevitable parts of industrialism. That is far from the truth. The progressive restriction of work tasks (work simplification) and repetition of identical tasks by workers are only two of many alternative ways of dividing work. Work tasks can be varied in content. Allocation of work tasks can be varied through time for each worker. Work tasks can be designed for performance by single workers or by small and large groups. Methods of working can include variations in the particular techniques employed. Workers can be decision makers in integrating their work tasks, including varying work assignments. Work simplification and task repetition have been preferred strategies of the auto industry managers bent on achieving both low production costs and maximum control over industrial workers. But there is no evidence of an autonomous technological imperative that has dictated these choices in division of labor.

Neither is there assurance that industrial productivity has been optimized by managerially controlled work simplification strategies. There has been little attention given to alternative conceivable ways for division of labor and decision making on production, within constraints of given intensities of mechanization.

The Locus of Decision Making

The prevailing methods of industrial decision making in the auto industry have led to little or no sense of connection or pride in the product and to alienation from the management and from the work-place. "Pride?" said one auto worker recently. "Nobody's proud of anything anymore. It's a job they come to because no one else will pay them more money." And further: "I think all blue-collar workers are taken for granted. I think deep down, most workers want to do a good job and take pride in their work, and if they're taken for granted this hurts them. If a car is built good, it's 'GM this and GM that,' but if something goes wrong it's always the fault of the workers."[10]

In the litany of the technology determinists, such worker attitudes derive from the mass-production process. The thrust of the present analysis is to distinguish between the methods of production and the decision processes that govern their characteristics and their use. The evidence from communities and industrial situations where workers have a substantial voice in industrial decisions indicates that both the reality and collateral feelings of alienation do not derive from the use of powered equipment in production or from a division

70   Seymour Melman

of labor. Rather, alienation is traceable to the absence of workers' decision power over their work.

There is no characteristic of industrial products or of production processes that vests decision-making authority over production in managerial occupations. The idea that there are many conceivable ways of dividing and organizing work is reflected in a growing literature that seeks to open new options for *Work in America*. [11] An increasing number of industrial consultants has been focusing on the feasibility and effects of widening and varying work tasks (job enrichment). There is evidence too of the feasibility of workers' mutual and democratic decision making over their own work rather than control over workers by separate managerial occupations operating through authoritarian hierarchies.

During the 1950s I examined and reported in some detail on the internal decision-making processes of workers and managers in the factories of the Standard Motor Company in Coventry, England. These factories employed thousands of workers and mass-produced passenger cars and tractors. An innovative top management and the local unions formalized the operation of a "gang system" of production organization for the factories in their collective bargaining agreements. Under the system a worker group rather than a single individual was responsible for the output. Payment varied with the output of the group rather than with the individual. Under the gang system as practiced in the Standard Motor Company, the size of particular work tasks could be regulated by a worker group. Management typically was agreeable to modification in tooling for work as the easing and the mechanization of work contributed to higher labor and capital productivity. Management substantially reduced its supervisory effort over the workers; in fact, these factories operated without supervisory foremen.

All these arrangements functioned within a framework of an agreed "price" per tractor or per car produced. This price was expressed in number of man-hours worked in the factory per vehicle completed. Hence, at the close of a week if the output was, for example, 50 percent greater in relation to man-hours worked than agreed upon labor times per unit, then a wage bonus of 50 percent was paid to all workers and other employees in the bargaining unit. These conditions gave the workers not only high pay but also a substantial voice in the detailed allocation and conduct of their work. Management agreed to this development in return for the high productivity of labor and capital and lowered administrative costs which accompanied the gang system of production organization. [12]

The successful operation of these factories under these conditions casts doubt on the assumption that work simplification enforced by authoritarian managerial control is a necessary condition for quantity production of motor vehicles. More recently, renewed interest in alternatives to work simplification has drawn attention to efforts by the managements of the Swedish Volvo and Saab companies to organize parts of the vehicle assembly operations on a group responsibility basis instead of on the basis of the traditional management-enforced, simplified, repetitive jobs performed along an assembly line.

The above examples of important variation in work organization have occurred within the framework and at the side of managerial-capitalist control over the enterprise. It is worth noting, however briefly, that there is evidence of the viability of industrial enterprises in which there is no formal separation between final authority over the enterprise and the performance of production work. The evolving industrial development in Israeli *kibbutzim* represents more than 200 factories in which control over the division of labor and the ways of integrating it is vested finally in the industrial workers themselves. Furthermore, an investigation of the relative efficiency of these enterprises has shown them to be as good or better than conventional capitalist enterprises in terms of productivity of labor and capital. [13] This experience from larger and smaller industrial enterprises is not accounted for by the conventional wisdom that says mechanized work only can be performed to the accompaniment of job simplification, or that a division of labor only can be organized and integrated by managerial controllers.

Conclusion

Drawing on the record of the prototypic industry of twentieth-century mass production, I have tried to respond to the mystique of technology which holds not only that society is powerfully affected by technology, but also that man and society have become the creatures of the machine. Fortunately, the reality is that our machines can be given varying characteristics by our machine designers and builders. [14] Technology, within the limits set by nature, is man-made and hence variable on order. If one wants to alter our technologies, then the place to look is not to molecular structure but to social structure, not to the chemistry of materials but to the rules of man, especially the economic rules of who decides on technology.

Man's social—especially economic—relations are imprinted upon technology. It cannot be otherwise because there is no way to make technology that is abstracted from human choice, hence from society. Given variety in our knowledge of nature, choices must be made

72   Seymour Melman

by and criteria for choice come from man and not from nature. Thus the product and the production system technologies of the auto industry have built into them the preferred economic criteria of the industry's decision makers.

It is therefore a warranted inference that technology does not, indeed cannot, determine itself. The physical and chemical properties of materials do not cause them to leap into the shape of man's artifacts. Only man, in fact, designs and shapes every particular technology. Once created and used, the given technologies have important bearing on man's life. But the location and direction of decisions to make particular use of our knowledge of nature derive from the power relations and the values which prevail in a given social system.

Notes

1. See the review article by George H. Daniels, "The Big Questions in the History of American Technology," *Technology and Culture* (January 1970), and the following papers.
2. Jacques Ellul, *The Technological Society* (New York: Vintage Books, 1964).
3. Emma Rothschild, *Paradise Lost: The Decline of the Auto-Industrial Age* (New York: Random House, 1973).
4. U.S. Bureau of the Census, *Statistical Abstract of the U.S., 1974*, pp. 550-53.
5. *Business Week,* 15 September 1973.
6. *New York Times,* 3 July 1974.
7. Seymour Melman, *Dynamic Factors in Industrial Productivity* (Oxford: Basil Blackwell; New York: John Wiley, 1956).
8. Ibid.
9. Ibid.
10. *Boston Globe,* 16 July 1972.
11. *Work in America: Report of a Special Task Force to the Secretary of Health, Education, and Welfare* (Cambridge, Mass.: The MIT Press, 1973).
12. Seymour Melman, *Decision-Making and Productivity* (Oxford: Basil Blackwell; New York: John Wiley, 1958).
13. Seymour Melman, "Managerial Versus Cooperative Decision-Making in Israel," *Studies in Comparative International Development,* vol. 6, 1970-1971, no. 3 (New Brunswick, N.J.: Rutgers University Press, 1971).
14. For numerous illustrations of the variability of design according to the criteria used, see Victor Papanek, *Design for the Real World* (New York: Pantheon Books, 1971). See the following Ph.D. dissertations which illustrate the detailed role of economic factors as determinants of design: John E. Ullmann, "Criteria of Change in Machinery Design," Columbia University, 1959; and George E. Watkins, "Cost Determinants of Process Plant Design—Central Station Boilers," Columbia University, 1957.

Part II
Institutional Economics
and
Economic Development

[11]

THE LATIN AMERICAN "STRUCTURALISTS" AND THE INSTITUTIONALISTS: CONVERGENCE IN DEVELOPMENT THEORY

James H. Street

Raúl Prebisch, prime mover among the economists loosely designated as the "structuralists," asserts that from the fluid, often confused state of economic thinking in Latin America a distinct and recognizable body of ideas is emerging. "In the midst of the depression," he observes, "we did not know the true nature of Latin America's difficulties; the dominant idea was simply to return to the past. Fifteen years ago we were already able to attempt to define the set of problems in question and to point with deep conviction to certain basic solutions. And today sufficient progress has been made to work out a system of ideas, a dynamic view of economic and social development leading to practical action. . . . What has to be done is to overcome the ideological poverty that prevails in our countries in this field, the traditional propensity to introduce from abroad nostrums that are largely alien to the real requirements of Latin America's situation."[1]

Some economists doubt that Latin America's problems are so unique that they require a new system of ideas and consider Prebisch's assessment defensive and tinged with regional parochialism. Others share his feeling that while economic doctrine formulated in the more developed countries has not adequately explained current processes nor provided effective formulas for policy, exponents of conventional theory nevertheless assume an attitude of expert knowledge and moral rectitude that is more than irksome to those confronted with the actualities. It becomes coercive when linked to the financial power of outside lending agencies and local interests, all insistent on applying prescriptive remedies where they will not serve.

Roberto Campos, while Brazilian ambassador to the United States, criticized the Anglo-Saxon inclination to regard Latin America's problems from "a moralistic and not a sociological view," adding that "there is little justification for a self-righteous attitude on the part of the lending countries, as if inflation and balance of payment troubles in Latin America were plain lack of guts or love of vice, and not the symptoms of difficult travail in face of adverse winds of trade, impatience of consumers and confused aspirations for the fruits of progress before the tree has matured to yield."[2]

The author is Professor of Economics at Rutgers, The State University. This paper was presented before the Association for Evolutionary Economics, San Francisco, December 28, 1966.

[1] *Towards a Dynamic Development Policy for Latin America* (New York: United Nations, 1963), p. 14.

[2] Address before Pan American Society, New York, December 19, 1962, *Brazilian Bulletin,* Vol. XIX, No. 424 (January 1, 1963), p. 6.

What is the basis for these complaints by Latin American economists? When one seeks a perspective on the bitter exchanges prompted by particular issues such as the terms of trade, inflation, and investment policy, one sees that the structuralists have been suffering much the same experience as befell the institutionalists, their North American counterparts, in an earlier period. Acting independently and apparently with little awareness of the relevant work of Thorstein Veblen, John Dewey, and C. E. Ayres, the Latin American structuralists have attacked identical weaknesses in orthodox theory, though understandably with special reference to their own problems. For a time they also endured the form of academic excommunication described by J. A. Hobson as a "conspiracy of silence," which in part accounts for the fact that institutionalist works are even yet rarely translated and hence infrequently read in Latin America. It also leads some structuralists to feel that more respectable economists in the advanced nations have relegated them to an intellectual doghouse for being hopelessly wrongheaded if not professionally irresponsible.

Yet from the recent work of the structuralists has emerged the outline of a body of positive thought that has much in common with institutionalist growth theory. It will be mutually beneficial for Latin American structuralists and North American evolutionary economists (not all of them, to be sure, institutionalists) to become better informed about their respective contributions to each other's work, remaining gaps in the fabric of thought, and potentials for cross-fertilization of ideas based on differing experiences. "Structures" and "institutions," meaningfully interpreted, have something in common and can form a bridge to a more adequate development theory. It is high time that the communications bridge between related schools of dissident thought surmount problems of distance, language, and environment.

STRUCTURALIST CRITICISMS OF ORTHODOX THEORY

Structuralism, like institutionalism, began with an attack on deficiencies in neoclassical economic doctrine or on policies derived from that doctrine. That this controversy should still continue is perhaps surprising, after the upheaval in economic thinking of the 1930s in the more developed countries, but this is in part attributable to the power of old ideas to persist long after new conceptions overtake them. It is also due to the special forms that orthodox theory has taken in the underdeveloped countries, where the problems are of growth more than of cyclical fluctuations, of technological dependence more than industrial unemployment. Even the Keynesian reformulation of neoclassical thought does not seem to meet the requirements of the structuralists.[3]

[3] For an effort in this direction, see Celso Furtado, *Development and Underdevelopment* (Berkeley: University of California Press, 1964), pp. 52–56, 59–60, 72, 115–116.

Structuralist objections to concepts imported from the industrially more advanced countries, though diverse, can usefully be summarized in four points of attack that in their general form will be recognized by students of Veblenian criticism. They question the static analysis of the external growth process, the efficacy of automatic market forces to provide needed external and internal adjustments, the use of conventional measures to correct deep-seated secular problems, and the reduction of the general standard of living as a way of promoting growth.

The static view of the external growth process. To the structuralists, orthodox theory has described essentially static international economic relations and has not explained or provided for dynamic changes over time involving shifts in the use of resources. For Latin America, still emerging from neocolonialism and hence subject to strong outside influences, this criticism first bore upon international trade and investment theory. The key element in the orthodox explanation of growth was the principle of comparative advantage, by which less developed countries had been assured, since at least the time of Adam Smith, a greater share in the wealth of nations if they would specialize and exchange—even with highly industrialized trade partners. This theory, coupled with the understanding that private foreign investment would provide the necessary transfers of industrial know-how and equipment, implied that the less developed countries could only harm themselves by any efforts to regulate the free flow of trade and investment, since both the operation of comparative advantage and the theory of mobility of capital transfers depended upon the absence of market restrictions. These ideas have been little affected by the Keynesian revolution, except insofar as Keynes pointed out that foreign trade may be used in time of depression to export unemployment and thus become exploitative of weaker countries.

Raúl Prebisch, in his seminal essay on "The Economic Development of Latin America and Its Principal Problems" in 1950, challenged the validity of the neoclassical claim that "The benefits of technical progress tend to be distributed alike over the whole [international] community, either by the lowering of prices or the corresponding raising of incomes."[4] Prebisch sought to demonstrate in his now familiar "worsening terms of trade" argument that because the relative prices of manufactured goods produced by the industrialized "center" countries and of primary products supplied by the underdeveloped "periphery" countries had tended to run in favor of the industrialized countries, the underdeveloped countries had not obtained the promised benefits of higher productivity in the center. The industrial countries had resorted to labor organization and administered pricing to raise their own incomes rather than to lower the prices of their export products. Moreover, the same relative price movements had obliged the weaker peri-

[4] *The Economic Development of Latin America and Its Principal Problems* (New York: United Nations, 1950), p. 1.

phery countries, incapable of using similar defensive techniques, to pass on any gains in their own productivity to the center.

Hans W. Singer pursued a similar argument in an article appearing about the same time as Prebisch's study.[5] Singer further questioned whether foreign private investment had actually contributed to the internal development of the capital-receiving countries. Such investment, Singer felt, was too highly specialized to have general effects. Prebisch later referred to such investment as "characteristic types of foreign enclave which do not spread technical progress to the internal economy."[6]

The criticisms by Prebisch and Singer of the orthodox explanations of externally originated growth set off two lines of counterattack—one empirical, the other theoretical—that largely missed the main issue. The question was, as Prebisch had made clear, how could the benefits of advancing technology in the more developed countries best be transferred to retarded economies as they sought to shake off neocolonial limitations? The protracted empirical controversy over the secular deterioration of the terms of trade has been inconclusive, bogging down on definitional questions and the interpretation of long waves.[7] Prebisch, conceding that the terms of trade may fluctuate for particular products and particular countries, has since accepted Gunnar Myrdal's view that differing income elasticities of demand for raw materials and manufactured goods in the respective export markets chiefly account for "a cumulative process toward the impoverishment and stagnation" of raw-materials producing countries.[8] It can hardly be denied on empirical evidence that the Latin American countries suffer sharp variations in foreign-exchange earnings because they depend on a limited number of primary-product exports whose prices fluctuate widely in world markets. These fluctuations in earnings alone are sufficient to impede any sustained and coherent internal development program.

Efforts to preserve the applicability of the principle of comparative advantage on theoretical grounds also leave the impression that the writers are less interested in explaining the dynamics of development than in defending the logical unassailability of the theory and its implications for free trade.[9] These arguments offer little to counter the belief of structuralists that strict reliance on comparative advantage would condemn the countries of

[5] "The Distribution of Gains between Investing and Borrowing Countries," *American Economic Review*, Vol. XL, No. 2 (May, 1950), pp. 473–485.

[6] *Towards a Dynamic Development Policy*, pp. 7, 53–54.

[7] M. K. Atallah, *The Long-term Movement of the Terms of Trade between Agricultural and Industrial Products* (Rotterdam: Nederlandsche Economische Hoogeschool, 1958).

[8] *Rich Lands and Poor* (New York: Harper and Brothers, 1957), pp. 52, 101.

[9] M. June Flanders, "Prebisch on Protectionism: An Evaluation," *The Economic Journal*, Vol. LXXIV, No. 294 (June, 1964), pp. 305–326. See also Gottfried Haberler, "International Trade and Economic Development," National Bank of Egypt Fiftieth Anniversary Commemoration Lectures, Cairo, 1959, reprinted in Theodore Morgan, George W. Betz, and N. K. Choudhry, eds., *Readings in Economic Development* (Belmont, California: Wadsworth Publishing Co., 1963), pp. 240–249.

Latin America to the existing overspecialized and labor-exploitative use of resources in the face of pressing internal changes, and thus offer no key to a strategy for progress.

The remaining structuralist criticisms concern internal stimulants to growth. As in the case of external forces, they question the automatic operation of market influences.

Reliance on free market forces for internal adjustments. The trust in the free play of the market, which we have so much modified in our own practices, is still one of our principal exports to the developing countries. Professor Gottfried Haberler at a conference in Rio de Janeiro counseled the assembled economists from all parts of the region that to achieve a proper internal diversification of industry, "the simplest method would be for each of the Latin-American countries to adopt a fairly uniform ad valorem import tariff over a wide range of commodities. Then, inside this framework, free enterprise, the forces of demand and supply, would automatically select the industries which would specialize here and there. That, it seems to me, would be the ideal solution."[10]

One need not be a structuralist to find such advice unrealistic in light of the wide disparities in income distribution in Latin America, the persistent tendency for aggregate demand to outrun supply, and the flooding of Latin American markets with superficial "demonstration effect" goods for which modern marketing techniques build an enormous desire.[11] Under these circumstances market demand is hardly a reliable guide to expenditures that will promote maximum development. Structuralists generally accept the need for intervention to correct the pattern of demand, though they are not agreed on the best means of carrying it out. José Figueres, a former president of Costa Rica and architect of major economic reforms in his country, has cautioned that the more successful the Central American Common Market becomes in integrating the economies of its five member countries, the more vulnerable it is to the marketing skills of foreign sellers, who can stimulate demand for nonessential imports much faster than the Common Market can generate domestic productive capacity.[12]

Perhaps what really underlies the yearning for a return to free markets is the belief that the present tangle of pricing arrangements in Latin America is so dominated by special interests and so indefensible on rational grounds

---

[10] "Panel: International Policies," *Inflation and Growth in Latin America*, ed. Werner Baer and Isaac Kerstenetzky (Homewood, Illinois: R. D. Irwin, 1964), p. 465. See also, in English and Spanish editions, *How Low Income Countries Can Advance Their Own Growth* (New York: Committee for Economic Development, September, 1966), pp. 23–29.

[11] The income distribution problem is discussed by Prebisch in *Towards a Dynamic Development Policy*, pp. 4–6, and by Osvaldo Sunkel in "The Structural Background of Development Problems in Latin America," *Weltwertschaftliches Archiv* (Kiel), Vol. 97, No. 1 (1966), pp. 45–47.

[12] Personal conversation with the author, August 25, 1966.

that it should be entirely discarded. But few governments can seriously entertain such a possibility. The question is not one of a return to free markets, but how the system of regulation can best be overhauled.

Short-run solutions for long-run problems. The most prominent issue which has involved the structuralists as a group is the explanation of chronic inflation in Latin America and the means of its control.[13] In the recent critical phases of their development, several of the larger, partially industrialized countries such as Chile, Brazil and Argentina (but also some of the smaller countries, notably Bolivia and Uruguay) have experienced persistent overt increases in price levels, associated at times with disguised inflation in the form of unsustainable imports of consumer goods. A succession of stabilization plans, usually known locally as austerity programs, were launched on the assumption that the inflation could be corrected by monetary and fiscal measures derived chiefly from European and North American experience.

The failure of one of these programs carried on under the advice of the Klein-Saks mission in Chile from 1955 to 1958 provoked a series of analytical studies of the inflationary process by Osvaldo Sunkel and Aníbal Pinto Santa Cruz, Chilean associates of Prebisch in the Economic Commission for Latin America, who thereby became charter members of the structuralist school.[14] As similar stabilization plans were initiated in other countries, the structuralists centered their attention on recommendations of the advisory staff of the International Monetary Fund, who established guidelines based on orthodox monetary policy as a basis for granting loans. These recommendations had profound consequences when the International Bank for Reconstruction and Development, the American government, and foreign private lenders began to condition their assistance on the observance of IMF guidelines. Governments concerned were left with little alternative but to accept the policies suggested or forego outside assistance.

Sunkel and Pinto concluded from their studies that the basic causes of the inflationary problem in Latin America lay deeper than in the aberrant

---

[13] The literature on the structuralist-monetarist controversy is extensive and is well summarized in Joseph Grunwald, "The 'Structuralist' School on Price Stability and Development: The Chilean Case," *Latin American Issues: Essays and Comments*, ed. Albert O. Hirschman (New York: Twentieth Century Fund, 1961), pp. 95–123. See also Dudley Seers, "A Theory of Inflation and Growth in Under-developed Economies Based on the Experience of Latin America," *Oxford Economic Papers*, N. S., Vol. 14, No. 2 (June, 1962), pp. 173–195.

[14] The key studies were Osvaldo Sunkel, "La inflación chilena—Un enfoque heterodoxo," *El Trimestre Económico* (Mexico, D. F.), Vol. XXV, No. 4 (October-December, 1958), pp. 570 ff.; and Aníbal Pinto Santa Cruz, *Ni estabilidad ni desarrollo—La política del Fondo Monetario Internacional* (Santiago, Chile: Editorial Universitaria, 1960). The Sunkel article has since appeared in English in *International Economic Papers*, No. 10 (1960). Without being aware of the emergence of the structuralist school, the writer published a two-part article at about the same time applying what was essentially a structural analysis to inflation as observed in Argentina: James A. Street, "La inflación en los paises en desarrollo," *Selección Contable* (Buenos Aires), Vol. XIV (July, 1958), pp. 466–472, and Vol. XV (August, 1958), pp. 74–83.

fiscal and monetary practices of irresponsible governments. Strong secular inflationary tendencies were imbedded in the uneven process of growth itself —in structural limitations and rigidities within the economic system that have impeded an adjustment of domestic output to growing demand over relatively long periods of time. To attempt to suppress such demand by conventional measures would not only impose great social costs but also interfere with the development process itself. Moreover, the tools which were developed for countries that experience alternating periods of boom and recession become blunted when they must always operate in one direction, to counter inflation. Surface stabilization efforts, because they do not go deep enough, must eventually fail.

Those countries which have experienced stabilization plans since the mid-1950s, according to Sunkel, "find themselves anew where they were five or six years ago, but with much larger external debts, having regrettably lost the opportunity to begin correcting some of their structural problems. Moreover, as a direct consequence of stabilization policy, the concentration of property and incomes has tended to be accentuated, a surplus of unemployed and underemployed manpower has been created or increased, investment for the replacement and enlargement of infrastructure capital has continued to be neglected, and the deep deficiencies in housing, health and education have been intensified. Little or nothing has been done in the way of increasing the return or improving the elasticity of supply of the agricultural sector, nor has the necessary revision of the structure of the tax system been approached."[15]

Hence the stabilization efforts were largely misdirected. "The difficulty," Sunkel continues, "rests in the fact that the structural deficiencies have roots and solutions that are long-term, while the traditional anti-inflationary mechanisms are typically short-term."[16]

Once more the issue became obscured as the structuralists were accused of advocating deliberate inflation as a means to development, a position indeed taken by some theorists, but specifically disavowed by Prebisch for the ECLA group.[17] Prebisch complained of the moralizing tone of critics who refused to see in the stresses of the Latin American growth problem more than a popular desire to live beyond one's means. "Those who profess [orthodox] . . . anti-inflationary policy—both those who suggest it from outside and those who live in the midst of this harsh and hazardous reality of Latin America—sometimes entertain the esoteric notion that sin can be redeemed by sacrifice."[18]

The "salvation through sacrifice" theme not only provides justification for stabilization programs but recurs in a related theory of the development process which the structuralists have assailed.

[15] El fracaso de las políticas de estabilización en el contexto del proceso de desarrollo latinoamericano," *El Trimestre Económico,* Vol. XXX, No. 4 (October–December, 1963), p. 637. Translation by the writer.

[16] *Ibid.,* p. 638.

[17] "Economic Development or Monetary Stability: The False Dilemma," *Economic Bulletin for Latin America,* Vol. VI, No. 1 (March, 1961), p. 1.

[18] *Ibid.*

*The orthodox theory of capital formation through a reduction in the
general level of consumption.* The abstinence theory of capital formation, so
effectively dealt with by Ayres in *The Theory of Economic Progress*,[19] is here
applied to Latin America. While denied by experience, the idea persists that
the only way a people can raise the necessary investment funds to insure their
own industrial expansion is by a prior and widespread reduction in the level
of consumption. Somehow, as a principle, this idea has escaped the Keynesian as well as the institutional onslaught. Thus Paul Samuelson in the
popular textbook which is still one of the few post-Keynesian texts available
in both Spanish and Portuguese for adoption by the more progressive Latin
American economics faculties, puts it with characteristic clarity: "To the extent that people are willing to save—to abstain from present consumption
and wait for future consumption—to that extent society can devote resources
to new capital formation. And to the extent that people are unconcerned as
to the future, they may at any time try to 'dissave'—to snatch present pleas-
ures at the expense of the future."[20]

Not only is this misrepresentation of the observed relation between consumption and investment in growing economies firmly implanted in the basic
textbooks, but it pervades much of the writing of economic historians, who
have ample evidence to the contrary. Phyllis Deane's admirable account of
The First Industrial Revolution contains a theoretical passage to the same
effect, which is elsewhere put into question by her own description of the
technological revolution, the means of its financing, and the attendant social
effects.[21]

In actual historical experience (except perhaps in collectivized economies
operating under forced draft), the formation of capital—both real and financial—has expanded simultaneously with a rise in general consumption.
In time of depression, a reduction in consumption, far from permitting investment to expand, tends to force a decline in capital formation. In short,
the growth of investment and consumption are dependent on each other. The
theoretical problem in a dynamic economy therefore is not how to stimu-

[19] Chapel Hill: University of North Carolina Press, 1944, Chapter III.

[20] *Economics: An Introductory Analysis* (New York: McGraw-Hill, 6th ed., 1964),
p. 47. In a footnote, Samuelson takes note of the "paradox of thrift" which the first
edition of his text brought to widespread attention, but he does not suggest the greater
paradox that consumption and investment can and do increase simultaneously. (Only
the fourth edition has been translated.)

[21] Cambridge: Cambridge University Press, 1965. "A community spends its income
on consumption or investment: or to put it another way, it takes up its output in the
form of consumption goods or capital goods. If it was possible for the nation to build
up new capital goods on the scale that it did, it was possible only because some of its
citizens were willing or obliged to abstain from consuming their full incomes by a corresponding amount" (p. 160). But subsequent discussion suggests that the financing
of early industries did not rely exclusively on personal savings or require a general
decline in living standards. See especially Chapters 10, 11, and 15. Robert L. Heilbroner in *The Making of Economic Society* (Englewood Cliffs, N. J.: Prentice-Hall,
1961) also sets forth the abstinence theory (pp. 94–96), which he later contradicts with
statistical evidence (p. 156).

late investment *at the expense of consumption*, but how to coordinate *simultaneous expansion* in both sectors at rates that will maintain maximum sustainable growth. This in itself is a formidable set of problems, but materially shifts the emphasis in development policy.

The structuralists have concentrated their fire on the "where is the money coming from?" aspect of the capital formation process. As we shall see, this is a secondary problem, yet it occupies an overwhelming part of the time and energies of development planners and reinforces the conviction that industrial growth cannot go forward without an endless succession of austerity measures which seem to the public at large to be a contradiction in terms. "To be sure, in the short-run we can tighten our belts," one structuralist paraphrasing Keynes has remarked, "but in the long-run we all starve to death."

Prebisch argues that present income levels of the mass of consumers are too low for domestic investment funds to come from this group. (One of the difficulties with the "forced saving" approach of the inflationists is that it likewise places the burden of development on the low income groups.) According to Prebisch's estimates, "while 50 per cent of the population [in Latin America] accounts for approximately two-tenths of total personal consumption, at the other end of the scale of distribution 5 per cent of the inhabitants of the region enjoy nearly three-tenths of that total."[22] "Among these upper strata . . . average consumption per household is fifteen times greater than that of the lower strata. . . ."[23]

"This impressive disproportion in the consumption of the groups in question, and in the income transferred abroad for investment and hoarding," Prebisch believes, "implies an ample savings potential which would permit a sharp increase in the rate of development, provided other conditions were met at the same time."[24] One of the conditions, of course, would be an improvement in the terms of trade to supplement domestic taxes on upper incomes with earnings in foreign exchange; another, a program to insure the application of these funds to strategic capital formation. In these proposals for a systematic redistribution of income to foster economic growth, Prebisch touches a sensitive nerve and parallels the institutionalists of the 1930s, who also called for income redistribution, though with the aim of remedying the gap in consumption rather than investment. "Technology," he declares, "has made this dynamic concept of redistribution viable for the first time in history, for without the immense potential it places at the disposal of developing countries, the effects of the redistribution operation will be very limited in their scope."[25]

In recognizing that technological progress is the key to Latin America's real growth, Prebisch has placed his finger on the heart of the capital formation problem. The misleading effect of abstinence theory—and policies

---

[22] *Towards a Dynamic Development Policy*, p. 5.
[23] *Ibid.*, p. 6.
[24] *Ibid.*, p. 32.
[25] *Ibid.*, p. 5.

based upon it—is that it emphasizes the primarily financial obstacles to development, rather than the necessity of raising total output and productivity. It thus directs attention away from such questions as, why has Latin America's technological performance been so poor, and what can be done about it?

Osvaldo Sunkel points out that "the rate of [financial] capital formation, which is usually assumed to be the main determinant of growth, does not appear to be associated with growth rates in any clear-cut fashion. The Argentine, for instance, which has a very high and growing rate of capital formation, has become an almost stagnant economy in recent years; Mexico has been increasing its investment rate, but the growth rate has been falling until the last two years; Brazil, which shows a lower rate of investment than Argentina, Colombia, and Central America, has nevertheless had higher rates of growth than these countries."[26] Evidently it is not the availability or lack of availability of investment funds which chiefly underlies the growth process.

The four major points of criticism of conventional economic doctrine which have been reviewed by no means exhaust the dissatisfaction of the structuralists with received ideas. What began as a controversy over the application of isolated concepts has since become a questioning of the entire fabric of orthodox economic ideology and its derivation. Dudley Seers, who sought to interpret the new way of thinking of the structuralists before it had fully taken form,[27] perceived that the controversy over inflation has broader implications than are commonly realized. "This is not just a technical issue in economic theory," he notes. "At the heart of the controversy between 'monetarists' and 'structuralists' are two different ways of looking at economic development, in fact two completely different attitudes toward the nature of social change, two different sets of value judgments about the purposes of economic activity and the ends of economic policy, and two incompatible views on what is politically possible."[28]

POSITIVE CONTRIBUTIONS OF THE STRUCTURALISTS

Because structuralism was born in criticism of received doctrine and has been embroiled in controversy ever since, it was not at first apparent that the school had any positive roots as an organism of its own. The chief claim to originality of the structuralists, aside from their polemic positions, was that they were trying to be more accurately descriptive of the economic system in Latin America than the general theorists with their standard preconceptions. To some, therefore, structuralist analysis, like institutional economics, has become synonymous with "mere description."

[26] "The Structural Background of Economic Problems," p. 26.
[27] "A Theory of Inflation," pp. 173–195.
[28] Seers, "Inflation and Growth: The Heart of the Controversy," *Inflation and Growth in Latin America,* p. 89.

Yet, more accurate description is a good place to begin, since it leads to better diagnosis. The structuralists are characterized as a group by their impatience with stereotyped descriptions of Latin American economies. Living in the environment, they see important distinctions between national economic units, available resources, cultural backgrounds, and accidental historical factors that the newcomer to Latin America is likely to overlook or to regard as insignificant. They know that these very differences condition the respective capacities of some countries to make more rapid progress than others. Most of the recognized structuralists are painstakingly empirical in their research, in a region where reliable data are distinguished by their rarity. The statistical output of ECLA, as well as such other agencies as the Getulio Vargas Foundation, while still limited, is becoming an invaluable basis for research on Latin American problems.

Structuralists have tried to be rigorously inductive in their reasoning from the available data. As all economic historians and evolutionary economists know, this procedure is not the easiest of tasks, because the data impose constraints and they do not readily fall into patterns when viewed afresh. Often the most significant facts, being qualitative in nature, are elusive as a basis for tight chains of reasoning and for the quantitative models which the profession now prefers. Although many of the structuralist studies would no doubt be classified by some as more "sociological" than "economic," they are often of a very high order. An example is Sunkel's recent article on "Change and Frustration in Chile," a perceptive account of the very rapid and intense changes that have occurred in Chile during the recent third of a century, while in the final analysis, as he says, "the fundamental elements which determine the generation of the power structure and thus the orientation of economic and social policy have not changed at all."[29]

The related series of studies of the Chilean economy conducted by Aníbal Pinto since 1958 are also an important contribution, particularly as they concern the long-term factors underlying inflation.[30] Unfortunately most of these articles are not yet available in English. Others, associated with the structuralist school, whose major works, principally in the field of economic history, have recently been translated are Aldo Ferrer (Argentina), Víctor Urquidi (Mexico), and Celso Furtado (Brazil).[31]

Raúl Prebisch's work, much of which appeared under the aegis of the Economic Commission for Latin America, is for that reason more familiar to North American readers. Prebisch has been criticized as too "simplistic" in

[29] Claudio Véliz, ed., *Obstacles to Change in Latin America* (London: Oxford University Press, 1965), pp. 116–144.

[30] The most recent of these is "En torno a Chile—Una economía deficil," *El Trimestre Económico*, Vol. XXXIII, No. 130 (April–June, 1966), pp. 171–186.

[31] Aldo Ferrer, *The Argentine Economy* (Berkeley: University of California Press, 1966); Víctor L. Urquidi, *The Challenge of Development in Latin America* (New York: Frederick A. Praeger, 1964); Furtado, *The Economic Growth of Brazil: A Survey from Colonial to Modern Times* (Berkeley: University of California Press, 1963); and *Development and Underdevelopment*.

his approach because he has from time to time fastened on one or another of the maladies of Latin America as the "key problem," has occasionally shifted ground, and has offered a variety of solutions. Few economists, however, have revealed a more fertile mind or more consistently pragmatic approach in looking at the problems of Latin America from a fresh point of view, in suggesting new ways of coping with these problems, and in persistently directing attention to the obstacles, often represented by powerful vested interests, standing in the way of change.

Conceptually, the structuralists are best known for their diagnoses of the "structural deficiencies," "bottlenecks," or "internal maladjustments" which they believe account for the lags in Latin American development. Individual members of the school will differ in the relative importance they assign to the respective factors, but all agree that they are basically of two sorts: bottlenecks originating outside the countries concerned, such as the adverse terms of trade and the limited capacity to import; and maladjustments which occur internally, such as accelerated population growth, premature urbanization and expansion of the service sectors of employment, lag in agricultural production, the limited size of domestic markets, ineffective tax systems, and politically significant shifts in class structure. The approach is pragmatic. The structuralists have not come up with a standard list of structural maladjustments or bottlenecks, since circumstances vary from country to country and over time, but the maladies they describe are recurrent.

To the North American economist with an institutionalist background, many of the descriptions of structural problems have a strong "institutional" flavor. While in a significant sense the structural maladjustments are a result of differing rates of historical acceleration among sectors of the economy and thus seem to be uniquely associated with the present epoch of chaotic change in Latin America, they also represent traditional modes of organized behavior that have not been equally responsive to changed conditions. That is to say, they reflect the inertia of *institutions*.

Indeed, it is common to read in the structuralist literature references to structures *and* institutions as obstacles to change, with no differentiation between the two. Thus when Prebisch says, "The social structure prevalent in Latin America constitutes a serious obstacle to technical progress and, consequently, to economic and social development,"[32] the passage might have been written by an institutionalist. This would not be remarkable if it were not for the fact that the bibliographic citations for structuralist literature reveal a striking innocence of acquaintanceship with North American institutionalist writing, whether derived from Veblen, Commons, or Mitchell. Personal conversations with leading structuralists have confirmed that they have arrived at their concern with institutional inertia as a social force by a quite independent and convergent course. "Structures" are indeed "institutions" in some uses of the term, and "structural maladjustment" is often equivalent to "cultural lag" as American sociologists have employed the phrase.

[32] *Towards a Dynamic Development Policy*, p. 4.

Among the positive achievements of the structuralists, their persistence as critics has probably already had some significant though unacknowledged impact on policy. The International Monetary Fund, for example, has evidently reexamined the larger effects of its monetary and fiscal recommendations on internal economic growth and reveals somewhat greater flexibility in its guidelines. Recently the Fund announced a significant change in lending policy which takes into account the fluctuation in export earnings of member countries as a basis for compensatory financing, thus yielding a point to Prebisch.[33]

GAPS IN STRUCTURALIST THEORY

Areas for fruitful interchange may develop between structuralists and institutionalists (as well as other evolutionary economists) based on the relative emphases they have given to their respective lines of investigation. Institutionalists have particular contributions to make with respect to the nature of technological change, institutional adjustment, and an instrumental system of values.

The structuralists seem to have become aware only recently of the potential significance of technological change in the domestic development process, and this oversight may reflect a cultural hiatus in their own background. In the earlier writings of Prebisch, for example, one detects a feeling that technological innovation is something available exclusively to the center, something to be withheld from the periphery or employed only as an instrument of neocolonial exploitation. When he speaks of "technological enclaves" in the underdeveloped countries, he again implies that the institutional power of the industrial countries has given them exclusive access to the fruits of technology and that these fruits can be tightly contained once they are introduced into the less developed countries. It is doubtful whether such a conclusion is warranted.

There are, of course, no more striking contrasts between North America and Latin America than in the degree of use of technology and in the circumstance that nearly all modern technology in Latin America is borrowed, or alien to her culture. This gulf is not easily explained, since in pre-Columbian times both Middle and South America supported rich and inventive cultures and in modern times the region has had continuous contact with European civilization. Why and under what circumstances did the interest in maintaining and elaborating an indigenous process of discovery, invention, and application die? The Spanish conquest and its suffocating institutions no doubt played a major role, yet probably do not constitute a sufficient explanation. Nevertheless, the long absence of a native technological interest

---

[33] "Compensatory Financing of Export Fluctuations: Developments in the Fund's Facility," *International Financial News Survey*, Vol. XVIII, No. 41 (October 14, 1966), p. 1. The new policy was first applied to Brazil in 1963, and was announced as a general measure in *The New York Times* on September 24, 1966.

has been a key bottleneck in Latin American development worthy of historical study and explanation.

We know from other experience, notably our relations with the Soviet Union, that knowledge of science and technology cannot be withheld from those determined to make use of it. What is clearly needed in Latin America is to domesticate or "internalize" the technological process so that it becomes part of the indigenous culture (or so that Latin America becomes truly part of western industrial culture, depending on the relative importance attached to other goals). This is what Japan has done, so that she is no longer dependent on cultural borrowing, but is innovative in her own right. Given modern communications, the stock of technological know-how is not institutionally confined, is accessible, and can become liberating rather than exploitative.

That the integration of modern technology into Latin American civilization has been delayed may be partly attributable to the long orientation of the region to Spain and Portugal, which were similarly retarded, rather than to other parts of Europe and the United States. But it is also probably due to a lack of local exposure to Veblen's "discipline of the machine," for which the paucity of existing industry and the inadequacy of educational substitutes have been responsible.

Countries with relatively high literacy rates, such as Argentina, Chile and Uruguay, in recent years have had low rates of growth amounting to stagnation. This anomaly suggests that the educational system, though not solely responsible, is not working very well. According to Ayres, "the most important factor in the economic life of any people is the educational level, as we now call it, of the community. A technically sophisticated community can and will equip itself with the instrumentalities of an industrial economy."[34]

It has always seemed to me to be particularly unfortunate that Domingo F. Sarmiento's introduction of popular education into Argentina in the 1870s coincided with the rise of a social class who had no understanding of a technologically based culture (although they benefited handsomely from it) and no interest in mastering the requirements of an industrial system. The *estancieros* of Argentina laid down a pattern for education, especially higher education, that Sunkel has aptly labeled "ornamental rather than functional and technical."[35] In sending their sons to Madrid or to the Sorbonne to acquire the attributes of gentlemen, to the Faculty of Law in preference to Engineering or Agronomy, they implanted a structural defect of enduring influence on the future development of their country. Similar misconceptions of the role of education in relation to development are common in other Latin American countries.

This situation is changing, and the process should be accelerated. Under the impetus of the Alliance for Progress, the construction of urban and rural

---

[34] *Theory of Economic Progress,* 2nd ed. (New York: Schocken Books, 1962), p. xxi.
[35] Sunkel, "Desarrollo Económico," notes for a course in economic development (mimeo.), p. 27.

schools has been stepped up significantly. In Guatemala, for example, where 65 per cent of the school-age children have never attended school,[36] the number of classrooms constructed since 1960 exceeds the number built during the entire previous period from the time of the Spanish conquest in 1524.[37] But vastly more important than the building of schools is what is taught in them. Rote instruction by poorly prepared teachers is still common and anything comparable to the Deweyan revolution in education has yet to touch many parts of Latin America.

In Mexico, where a revolution in education is in full swing, leaders of the popular education movement have rediscovered the philosophy of Enrique C. Rébsamen, a Swiss educator who established the first normal school at Jalapa in 1885. Rébsamen's ideas were akin to Dewey's precept of "learning by doing." He believed that children should have a broad exposure to materials and their practical and esthetic uses throughout their learning career. As a result, the state of Vera Cruz, where the Rébsamen movement started, has an exceptionally fine teachers' college, well equipped with shops and laboratories and following a progressive program of instruction. The pattern is extended to numerous rural elementary schools scattered through the state. This is but an instance of the sort of change that will have to occur on a large scale in Latin America if the technical and industrial revolutions are to become part of the basic culture.

The agricultural sector, as the structuralists have repeatedly emphasized, is one of the principal bottlenecks in Latin American growth and becomes more critical as the population surges upward. Lauchlin Currie, a severe critic of the development program inaugurated in Colombia in 1961 under the tutelage of ECLA advisers, asserts that "The chief weakness of the ECLA-Prebisch Approach in Latin America lies in its failure to grasp the significance or potentialities of the technical revolution in agriculture."[38] In view of other constraints prevailing in Colombia the criticism may be unduly harsh, but Currie is correct that to identify a sector as a "bottleneck" is not to concede that it cannot be broken. Special techniques of education which reach rural adults as well as children can wear down the traditional resistance to improved agricultural methods, and as we know from our own experience, an abundance of extension and other informational methods is feasible. The recent remarkable achievements of Mexico in raising agricultural yields and total output through a combination of domestic research and the dissemination of its findings are promising evidence that a concerted effort can overcome this bottleneck. With an estimated two million transistor radios now distributed among the isolated rural people of Latin America, it should be possible to utilize means of communication never before available.[39]

[36] *Economic Development of Central America* (New York: Committee for Economic Development, November, 1964), p. 34.

[37] *Perfiles de progreso en Centroamérica y Panamá* (Guatemala City: U. S. Agency for International Development, 1965), pp. 26–27.

[38] *Accelerating Development: The Necessity and the Means* (New York: McGraw-Hill, 1966), p. 60.

[39] An estimate by Roger Vekemans, S. J., Center for the Economic and Social De-

"Technology" is so broad a term as at times to seem an abstraction, and hence a mysterious force available only to the initiated. This conception has often given Latin Americans a sense of hopeless inferiority in the face of the overwhelming technological dominance of the more advanced countries. Actually, however, technology is made up of a multitude of discrete methods and techniques, interrelated to be sure, but accessible "by the piece." This circumstance permits the less developed countries to select their own tools, based upon their peculiar needs at each stage of development and according to their respective complements of resources.

Technology, taken as a whole, is a distinctive way of thinking and acting, and it includes new modes of social organization and managerial skill in which the emphasis is on operational efficiency.[40] The absorption of technology into the culture of less developed countries must therefore proceed at various levels more or less simultaneously. Some of the structuralists have lately begun to investigate the means by which the process can be accelerated. A recent study by Aníbal Pinto examines the reasons for the unbalanced concentration of technical progress which characterizes the dual economies of Latin America and suggests ways that the disparities might be alleviated.[41] A conference on the application of science and technology to Latin American development was held in 1965 in Santiago, Chile, under the joint sponsorship of ECLA and UNESCO, and it recommended that the Latin American countries allocate as much as one percent of their national revenue to scientific and technical research. Although this is a much smaller amount than the industrial countries regularly spend on such activities, it would mean a substantial increase over present levels in Latin America.[42]

Institutionalists and structuralists can reinforce each other's investigations in another area. A dynamic program of development requires effective techniques of institutional reform and reconstruction. As Simon Kuznets has said in a particularly lucid passage, "The transformation of an underdeveloped country into a developed country is not merely the mechanical addition of a stock of physical capital; it is a thoroughgoing revolution in the patterns of life and a cardinal change in the relative power and position of various groups in the population. . . the growth to higher levels of population and per capita income involves a revolutionary change in many aspects of life and must overcome the resistance of a whole complex of established interests and values."[43]

Since the structuralists are dealing with just such aspects of society, their

---

velopment of Latin America (DESAL), Santiago, Chile: personal interview, June 14, 1966.

[40] Cf. Ayres, *The Industrial Economy* (Boston: Houghton Mifflin, 1952), Chapter XII.

[41] "Concentración del progreso técnico y sus frutos en el desarrollo latinoamericano," *El Trimestre Económico*, Vol. XXXII, No. 125 (January–March, 1965), pp. 3–69.

[42] Felipe Herrera, statement at second plenary session of the Inter-American Development Bank, Washington, D. C., April 26, 1966 (mimeo.), p. 26.

[43] "Toward a Theory of Economic Growth," *Economic Growth and Structure* (New York: W. W. Norton, 1965), p. 30.

diagnoses and prescriptions are certain to have revolutionary implications. But in what sense are their conclusions revolutionary? While clearly "left of center," structuralist views as a whole are not readily identified with a particular political position in the traditional Latin American spectrum. Their ideology, still in formation, is not cast in the Marxist mold of violent class conflict and is refreshingly free of the sloganizing which has infected most Latin American revolutionary and political reform movements. Yet specific proposals for income redistribution, agricultural reform, and other forms of economic intervention are bound to generate political opposition.

It may be helpful for the structuralists to draw on the problem-solving experience of such figures as John R. Commons, Gardiner C. Means, and Rexford G. Tugwell, whose contributions to administrative and legal reform are well summarized in Allan Gruchy's *Modern Economic Thought: The American Contribution*.[44] Although these institutionalists were concerned with problems of organizational and political reform in another cultural context, they developed well defined conceptions of the general tactics of induced social change. Another valuable type of investigation is represented by Albert O. Hirschman's *Journeys Toward Progress*, which in three concrete problem situations in Brazil, Chile, and Colombia seeks to unearth successful instances of contrived reforms, illustrating tactics which he labels "reformmongering."[45] Hirschman's studies concern the informal political and cultural mechanisms by which economic decisions are actually carried out, or frustrated, and hence go far beyond conventional methods of economic investigation.

Still another area—possibly the most important—in which institutionalists have something to contribute to structuralists is the formulation of a more comprehensive system of values. Institutionalists have long discarded the system of market prices as the ultimate basis of valuation in making normative judgments about the economy. So, it appears, have the structuralists. But many have expressed uneasiness about the lack of a new orientation, once they had cut themselves loose from economic orthodoxy. No doubt this is what Raúl Prebisch has in mind when he complains about the "ideological poverty that prevails in our countries." The same state of mind has often been described in Latin America as a "crisis of confidence." Latin Americans understandably cherish the cultural uniqueness of their civilization, yet many of their intellectual leaders, being products of that culture, seem unable to distinguish purely sentimental and ceremonial values from those that are vital to the evolution of the society.

Celso Furtado, identified with the Brazilian wing of structuralism, explains that this uncertainty is one of the reasons that Marxism has had a wide appeal among the younger generation in Brazil: "Marxism, in any of its varieties, affords a diagnosis of the social reality and a guide to action."[46]

---

[44] New York: Prentice-Hall, 1947.

[45] *Journeys Toward Progress: Studies of Economic Policy-making in Latin America* (New York: Twentieth Century Fund, 1963).

[46] "Brazil: What Kind of Revolution?" *Foreign Affairs*, Vol. 41, No. 3 (April, 1963), pp. 527–528.

By association with these emphases, some structuralists, among them social critics and activists such as Furtado himself, have been charged with being crypto-Communists (an experience not unknown to institutionalists). Furtado, however, explicitly rejects Marxism because in its own way, particularly when applied to agricultural reform, it is a "theory of salvation through punishment" much like orthodox economics. Furtado believes that the new outlook must be rooted in "humanism and optimism concerning the material development of society."[47] What the structuralists may be looking for is the instrumentalist philosophy derived by Ayres from Dewey and illuminatingly applied to economics. Indeed, Sidney Hook has identified Ayres' philosophy as a form of "scientific humanism," though it is more than that term suggests.

Other approaches to the value problem have resulted in one form or another of sterility. The Marxist approach, because it pits class against class and insists that all virtue rests with those below, threatens the destruction of the social fabric without revealing the mechanism by which positive gains are to result. Institutionalists recognize that while it is the historic role of the upper classes to defend their privileges, they are not the exclusive carriers of evil. The entire culture, encompassing *all* social classes, is the victim of past-binding ways of feeling and acting, as well as the potential user of the instrumental continuum. It is the culture that must be updated, rather than merely a class to be overthrown. Marxist agitation is therefore generally misdirected: it seeks to fasten the blame on the domestic culprit class, or the foreign imperialists, and consequently in many concrete instances it has denied the society access to the instruments most readily at hand for making progress.

A case in point is the extended controversy in Argentina in which Communists were joined by nationalists to oppose the hire of foreign companies (and engineers) to assist in the production of petroleum under conditions that could have been closely regulated in the public interest. Another case is the fear of "cultural penetration"—meaning imperialist political domination —expressed by leftist students that prevents some Latin American universities from establishing stable, mutually beneficial and nonexploitative relations with foreign scholars and universities.

The attempts of neoclassical welfare economists to solve the value problem are equally unsatisfactory.[48] In their approach, all value judgments are construed as uniquely personal and therefore "given." The task for the economist as analyst and even as policy planner is value-free; he merely makes a diagnosis on an "objective" (positivist) basis as to which of several alternatives will give consumers what *they* want, insofar as limited resources permit. Their preferences continue to be best registered in markets. But, as we have seen, this solution is an evasion, since the normative inclinations of neoclassicism still underlie the analytical and prescriptive apparatus. And the structuralists insist that the fate of the less developed countries cannot be

---

[47] *Ibid.*, p. 529.
[48] For a discussion of this issue by an economist who accepts the positivist *wertfreiheit* position as applied to pure price theory but not as applied to development, see Benjamin Higgins, *Economic Development* (New York: W. W. Norton, 1959), pp. 310–311.

left to the random forces of the market. The object of removing existing restrictions on growth is to release the economy not to the dynamics of the market but to the dynamics of productive technology in all its forms. The prescriptions in each case will be very different.

Even those who seek to take a purely *ad hoc* approach to Latin American development problems, without a systematic theoretical base, fail to do justice to the value problem. Because the trend is to apply purely quantitative standards to growth, these analysts often reduce the goals of development to an increase in per capita gross domestic product, a low capital-output ratio, and similar criteria. To structuralists such as Sunkel the result is a narrow and inadequate definition of the goals of development, which involve shifting relations among sectors and regions of the economy as the process moves along. Often these shifting relationships can be described only in qualitative terms. Sunkel is evidently calling for an approach which Gruchy termed "holistic."[49] In this view, economic activity is part of a larger and evolving cultural whole, and its values are derived from the requirements of that whole. Among countries with differing degrees of development, Gruchy declares, the structure and functioning of each field of economic relations are in many ways "unique cultural products."

What system of values is broad enough to encompass these differences in cultural circumstances and yet is based upon principles that have universal validity? Ayres has shown that these requirements are met in the instrumental logic of technology, which accommodates both quantitative and qualitative goals in an endless array of complexes. The specific forms that the objectives of development take at each evolutionary stage are defined by the current social problems and the disposable means of their solution— not by any preconceived notion of natural order or natural process. The "disposable means of their solution" are the world storehouse of tools, machines, instruments, and modes of organization, which have universal serviceability.

A study of the instrumental system of values, which is beyond the scope of this paper, commends itself to the structuralists precisely because, like other technological borrowings, it is largely alien to the Latin American culture as it has developed historically. Such a study can contribute to a better understanding of the strategy and tactics of economic development itself. Thus structures and institutions, which are after all negative aspects of the development process, are not the only bridge to a better theory. A common quest for a more serviceable set of values—instrumental and humanistic—may also form a bridge to a deeper comprehension of the positive forces of social change.

[49] *Modern Economic Thought*, pp. 550–553.

Jel *JOURNAL OF ECONOMIC ISSUES*
Vol. XVI   No. 3   September 1982

Institutionalism, Structuralism, and Dependency in Latin America

James H. Street
and
Dilmus D. James

In the past three decades there has been a convergence of two strains of thought regarding the process of economic development, particularly in the less developed countries, derived from two quite independent sources: North American institutional economics, beginning with the seminal work of Thorstein Veblen in the early part of the century, and more recent conceptions of the Latin American structuralists inspired by Raúl Prebisch. Both these streams of ideas depart significantly from conventional neoclassical formulations and are more useful in understanding economic development in Latin America, as well as in other regions, as an evolutionary process.

In common, institutionalism and structuralism represent holistic approaches to economic investigation, as Allan G. Gruchy applied that term to institutionalism.[1] Students of institutionalist theory are aware that the holistic approach embraces two basic conceptions, one relating to the economic system as a whole, and the other to the nature of human behavior. The first conception regards the economic system as an evolving process rather than an equilibrating mechanism of stable economic relations centering on market activities. The second conceives of human behavior as characterized by habitual patterns resulting from cultural conditioning but

---

The authors are, respectively, Professor of Economics, Rutgers University, and Professor of Economics, University of Texas, El Paso.

674   James H. Street and Dilmus D. James

capable of intelligent response to changing realities. It is thus distinguished from the conventional economic view that human behavior is primarily devoted to utilitarian motivation and pecuniary calculation in a static system of markets. Both of these conceptions are distinctively incorporated into institutionalism and structuralism as they relate to developing economies.

However, the two schools reflect important differences in emphasis, especially as the attention of structuralists has shifted away from maladjustments within the Latin American region toward a study of the dependency mechanism, which concentrates on foreign institutional controls over trade, financial investment, and the international transfer of technology. Moreover, institutionalism has always stressed the technological process as the motor force in economic growth, while the structuralists were slower to recognize the dynamic character of technological innovation.

When first brought into contact, institutionalists and structuralists found more in common in examining existing structures of power and control and their inhibiting effects on growth, even though these differed in detail betwen the United States and Latin America, with their distinct cultural heritages. The structuralists, in turn, added a dimension to institutionalism with their description of significant unbalancing shifts in the internal structure of growing economies, by sectors and by interest groups. This contribution to development theory was later echoed in the United States in the empirical work of Simon Kuznets on the rate, structure, and spread of world development in the modern period.[2]

Dependency theory, an outgrowth of structuralism, has added new insights into the powerful influence of the unequal structure of nation states, the rising multinational corporation, and by extension, the resource cartel, on world development and underdevelopment. Yet by its shift in emphasis and possibly because of its exploitative conception of the growth process, dependency theory tends to minimize indigenous growth forces that persist in the Latin American environment and that show vitality despite bottlenecks that impede these efforts to break out of traditional institutional restraints and modes of thought. There thus appears to be continued promise in *each* of the lines of investigation laid down by institutionalists, structuralists, and dependency theorists. This, we believe, may lead to further theoretical convergence.

Since readers of this journal will be familiar with the main features of institutionalist analysis, no detailed elaboration will be undertaken here. Following a brief survey of the current stage of development in Latin

America, we shall turn rather to a review of the emerging characteristics of structuralist and dependency analysis for comparison with the application of institutionalist theory to developing countries.

The Current Situation in Latin America

It is a paradox that although Latin America as a whole has experienced strong economic expansion during the past decade and has shown remarkable powers of recuperation from major external shocks administered by the energy crises of 1973–74 and 1979–80, there are evidences of growing social imbalance and heightened political tensions resulting from failure to meet commonly accepted goals of socio-economic development, as opposed to mere growth of output. These goals include a reduction in income inequality, a diminution in the "marginalization" of excluded social groups, the elimination of gross violations of human rights, broader public participation in the political process, and greater autonomy for Latin Americans in the control of their internal and external affairs. The intensity of social pressures arising from failures in the development process has given rise to sharp policy debates over alternative strategies and has led, particularly in the Southern Cone, to the re-establishment of highly authoritarian regimes intent on recovering control of the distributive system, even at extreme social cost.

Latin America and the Caribbean region attained an annual average growth in real gross domestic product of 7 percent during the period from 1967 to 1972, and per capita output also rose during this period.[3] Under the impact of the rise in oil prices in 1973 and the subsequent world recession, which severely affected Latin American exports, the regional growth rate declined to 3 percent in 1975. (Venezuela, a major oil exporter, is excluded from this comparison.) Real growth recovered steadily over the next four years to reach 6.5 percent in 1979, but further rounds of oil price increases in 1979 and 1980 once more slowed the rate to 5.7 percent in 1980 and a projected 5.5 percent in 1981. There was considerable variation from country to country, and Argentina suffered negative growth in 1976, 1978, and 1981.

The general growth record is remarkable in light of the balance-of-payments difficulties, internal inflationary pressures, and a growing debt-servicing burden that simultaneously afflicted the region. The current account deficit for the chiefly oil-importing nations (again excluding Venezuela) nearly quadrupled from $4.5 billion in 1973 to $16.5 billion in 1975, although subsequently it was reduced to about $10 billion by

1978. After the second round of oil price increases, the region's current account deficit more than doubled to $21 billion in 1979 and tripled to reach $33 billion in 1980.

Despite a large flow of foreign investment, principally to Brazil and Mexico, the overall balance of payments showed a net deficit of $2 billion for the region in 1980, the first such deficit in five years. The outstanding long-term external debt of the region increased by $19 billion in 1979 and by about the same amount in 1980 to reach an unprecedented total of $153 billion at the end of the latter year. For many countries the cost of servicing the external debt has required a large share of current export earnings and the need to borrow to meet current energy requirements has sharply curtailed access to these funds for development purposes.

Although several countries, notably Argentina, Brazil, Chile, and Uruguay, have been troubled with chronic price instability, inflation is a relatively new phenomenon in most of the region. From 1966 until 1970, the annual rise in the cost of living in fifteen Latin American countries did not exceed 5 percent.[4] By 1974, the price level rose by more than 15 percent in eighteen countries, and inflation became a common malady. An estimate of the average increase in prices for the region as a whole shows a rise of 55 percent in 1976, a slight reduction to 42 percent in 1978, and a renewed upsurge to 61 percent in 1980.[5] Again, there is variation by countries, but the inflationary trend seems strongly established.

The spread of inflation and the recent setbacks to growth have manifested themselves as unemployment, underemployment, and widening disparities in income distribution. Data on unemployment by countries are not uniformly available, but a survey by the International Labor Office for the mid-1970s concluded that unemployment and underemployment for the region as a whole amounted to an "unemployment equivalent" of about one-fourth of the labor force.[6]

Distribution of income is heavily concentrated in favor of upper income groups, and there is some evidence that these disparities may have increased during the recent growth period.[7] In the early 1970s, the wealthiest 10 percent of households in Argentina received 35.2 percent of the total post-tax income; in Brazil, 50.6 percent; Chile, 34.8 percent; Mexico, 40.6 percent; Peru, 42.9 percent; and Venezuela, 35.7 percent.[8] (These figures may be compared with 26.6 percent for the United States and 23.5 percent for the United Kingdom.)

The persistence of price inflation has probably increased disparities in real rates of consumption because of the differential effects of price increases on the more vulnerable lower income groups in the money-using sectors. Although Mexico, for example, had enjoyed four decades of growth averaging more than 6 percent a year, the National Council on Science and Technology reported in 1976 that "available information on nutritional levels in the country indicates that at least two-thirds of the population is undernourished."[9]

Such data are often accepted as commonplace, yet they lend little support to the concept that economic growth is by nature a self-equilibrating process whose fruits automatically are widely shared as economic expansion takes place. They suggest rather that the longer run imbalances in the growth process require public attention to alleviating these effects, and to establishing social priorities that will spread the benefits of growth without bringing the process to a halt or to a social explosion. These conclusions are reflected in policy aspects of institutionalist and structuralist economics.

Institutionalism and the Development Problem

Institutional economists such as Thorstein Veblen, C. E. Ayres, John R. Commons, and Wesley C. Mitchell in the main utilized their analytical frameworks to understand the forces at work in advanced capitalist, industrial society. Those who followed them in what Gruchy has identified as modern neo-institutionalism have likewise concentrated their investigations and their policy formulations on developed, rather than developing, countries.

Yet by the time the second edition of *The Theory of Economic Progress* appeared in 1962, Ayres recognized in a new foreword that his theory had acquired general applicability, and he added a significant subtitle: "A Study of the Fundamentals of Economic Development and Cultural Change."[10] Nevertheless, few institutionalists confronted the peculiar problems of less developed countries and applied theory and method to them in a distinctively institutionalist analysis.

Notable exceptions are Wendell C. Gordon, who in 1950 incorporated an institutionalist view in his study of *The Economy of Latin America*, and William P. Glade. Glade's *The Latin American Economies: A Study of their Institutional Evolution* is a comprehensive historical and interdisciplinary account of the evolution of institutional structures and ideologies that have affected the course of economic development in Latin America.[11]

The applicability of the institutions-technology dichotomy to the historical process underway in Latin America is, if anything, heightened by the recrudescence since the 1960s of extreme measures of authoritarian, police-state control, especially in the Southern Cone and in some countries of Central America. These events bring to mind Veblen's phrase "The triumph of imbecile institutions over life and culture," and suggest the urgency of more effective policies grounded in the realities of the society.

The Development of Structuralism

Structuralism, as an organized body of thought, originated in the work of Raúl Prebisch and his associates in the United Nations Economic Commission for Latin America, centered in Santiago, Chile, in the 1950s. Like institutionalism in an earlier era, structuralism began with an attack on deficiencies in neoclassical economic doctrine or on policies derived from that doctrine.

Prebisch, in an illuminating essay on "The Economic Development of Latin America and its Principal Problems" in 1950, challenged the validity of the neoclassical claim that "the benefits of technical progress tend to be distributed alike over the whole [international] community, either by the lowering of prices or the corresponding raising of incomes."[12] He did not consider the static descriptions of the operation of the principle of comparative advantage and the international investment process to reflect adequately what had been happening over time in the relations between the industrially advanced countries (the "center") and the countries supplying food and raw materials (the "periphery").

Based on an empirical investigation, Prebisch concluded that because the relative prices of manufactured goods produced by the industrialized countries under increasingly oligopolized conditions tended to outrun the prices of primary products supplied by the periphery, subject to competitive conditions, the underdeveloped countries had not obtained the promised benefits of higher productivity in the center. Thus, over an extended period the adverse terms of trade had not only deprived the underdeveloped countries of a stable share of income but of the financial and technical means of their own internal transformation and growth.

Prebisch's criticism of neoclassical doctrine was eventually seen as the beginning of an independently derived conception of the economy as a dynamic, rather than static, process and one not necessarily subject to equilibrating forces over time. This became a major principle of structuralism. Moreover, because Prebisch was in essence describing a secular shift in the nature of the international power structure, his contribution is now also recognized as an important element in modern dependency theory.

The structuralists waged a number of other attacks on economic orthodoxy, perhaps the most telling of which was their criticism of the monetarist explanation of domestic inflation in several Latin American countries, which underlay policies prescribed for those countries by technicians of the International Monetary Fund. Beginning with the strictures of the Chilean economists Osvaldo Sunkel and Aníbal Pinto Santa Cruz, the structuralists offered an alternative explanation of secular inflation, rooting the causes in internal structural imbalances common to the Latin American growth experience.[13] They sought to show, using empirical studies for each case, that these imbalances had occurred in the course of an uneven growth process, which became particularly critical in the most dynamic examples—Argentina, Brazil, and Chile. In each instance definable constrictions, or "bottlenecks," impeded a smooth and balanced growth and remained unrelieved by conventional monetary and fiscal policy. Among these internal bottlenecks were the effects on aggregate demand of highly accelerated population growth, premature urbanization and expansion in the service sectors of employment, lagging agricultural production, deficient development of the energy sector, the limited size of domestic markets, ineffective tax systems, and politically significant shifts in class structure. Internal adjustments were complicated by bottlenecks originating outside the countries concerned: adverse terms of trade and limited capacity to import.

In seeking to understand and cope with these bottlenecks, the structuralists conducted studies of the functioning of social institutions that resembled earlier investigations carried on by North American institutionalists in their own milieu. Some structuralists concluded that without new social structures, probably on the scale of regional economic integration rather than mere reform within existing national units, chronic inflation and other distributional maladies would likely remain endemic and the growth process would continue to function by fits and starts.

The Emergence of Dependency Theory

Increasingly the structuralists turned their attention to the international level and became participants in the Dependency School.[14] In common, members of this school accept the definition provided by Theotonio Dos Santos: "By dependence we mean a situation in which the economy of certain countries is conditioned by the development and expansion of another country to which the former is subjected."[15] To the question, Do forces largely external to developing countries account for the perpetuation of conditions of underdevelopment? dependency theorists answer resoundingly in the affirmative.

Yet dependency theory takes a number of forms related to a variety of distinct influences on writers who make up the school. Moreover, each version leads to correspondingly dissimilar policy conclusions.

In its simplest form, dependency theory is little more than a historical description of the evolution of neocolonial institutions in regions that were formerly parts of extensive imperial systems. Such a contribution is *The Colonial Heritage: Essays on Economic Dependence in Perspective*, by Stanley J. Stein and Barbara Stein, who are historians.[16]

In a more expanded, yet still moderately critical form, dependency analysis draws on the work of the Latin American structuralists, who include, besides those already named, Celso Furtado, Fernando Henrique Cardoso, Helio Jaguaribe, Aldo Ferrer, and Miguel S. Wionczek.[17] Included are sociologists and political theorists, as well as economists. Other significant contributors from outside Latin America have been Hans Singer, Gunnar Myrdal, and Dudley Seers.[18] Building on the pioneering analysis by Raúl Prebisch of the secular deterioration in the terms of trade between the center and periphery countries, dependency theorists extended the study of structural maladjustments within the Latin American region to incorporate a world economic structure that had become increasingly unbalanced as its units grew inextricably more interdependent.

Osvaldo Sunkel has placed the principal shift in economic power relations as occurring after World War II.[19] Prior to this period, in the neocolonial era, western imperialist governments and international banking houses played predominant roles in the dependency relationship. More recently, international capitalism has become much more highly organized in the hands of multinational corporations, and governments and international lending organizations have often served as agents of a network of supranational interests to dominate weaker national economies.

Sunkel describes a pattern in which research and development are concentrated and tightly controlled in advanced countries, so that foreign users are obliged to buy entire packages of entrepreneurship, financing, management skills, designs, technological processes, and marketing techniques from monopolistic or oligopolistic firms. No longer can they assemble their own technological components piecemeal from a variety of competitive sources. Even domestic brainpower, credit agencies, import substitution restrictions, and other preferential arrangements become co-opted for the benefit of foreign firms. The result is a widening of the technological gap and increasingly complex forms of dependency. Most other dependency theorists would share this conclusion.

Some dependency writers, taking their inspiration from Marxist-Leninist sources and particularly Lenin's theory of imperialism, would go even further.[20] They interpret underdevelopment as a deliberate form of international exploitation, by which the dominant capitalist countries extract the surpluses and even the *potential* surpluses of the periphery to increase their own power and wealth. Foreign investment and foreign aid alike are means of appropriating income, and the native capitalist classes ("lumpen-bourgeoisie") of the less developed countries are merely the agents of their overlords in the imperialist countries.[21] In the absence of international capitalist exploitation, the less developed countries would no doubt have developed their own industrial systems along more egalitarian lines, but these inherent growth impulses were suffocated as the capitalist countries established exclusive control over the required technology. A potential investible surplus that would have been created within the developing countries has been drained by luxury consumption or aborted by monopoly control.

Despite a wide diversity of detail and emphasis within the writings of the more radical dependency theorists, they tend to agree on a number of conclusions. First, the condition of widespread underdevelopment is an outcome of the expansive and exploitative development of industrial market economies. Second, development and underdevelopment are seen as counterparts in a single, unified world system. Third, underdevelopment is not a temporary stage leading to ultimate development; the established pattern of center-periphery exploitative relationships is likely to endure. Fourth, even though the mechanisms of transmission of influence may vary, underdeveloped countries will continue to be deprived of autonomy over internal political, social, and economic decisions that might rectify existing inequalities. In short, according to the most pessimistic view, dependency is a persistent historical expression of capitalist contradictions and class conflict from which there is no escape short of social revolution.

The dependency literature continues to grow, and to become richer in specific applications to cases. For example, in a comprehensive review of the evolution of dependent development in Brazil, Peter Evans contends that Latin American governments and domestic entrepreneurs do not completely identify with the interests of international elite groups, nor are they wholly at the mercy of admittedly powerful multinational enterprises.[22] Local financial direction is able to survive and even thrive in many, although not all, sectors. Rapid industrial progress takes place within a context of partial dependency in which influential blocs with diverse goals and interests are able to share in a mutually beneficial growth process. Nonetheless, the process excludes the majority of the population from a proportionate increase in welfare or any participation in decision-making.

Evans refines earlier dependency literature by explaining how growth can take place over an extended period without significant general socio-economic development, how internal support for rapid industrialization can be marshalled without the co-optation of domestic elite groups by foreign capitalists, and how domestic enterprise has managed to survive the "denationalization" of foreign investment control. His analysis resembles John Kenneth Galbraith's description of "countervailing power," and in contrast with more dogmatic forms of dependency analysis, recognizes that there are ways in which governments and interest groups in less powerful countries can achieve some elements of autonomy over their own affairs.

Dependency and Institutionalism

As heterodox explanations of economic development and underdevelopment, institutionalism and structuralism-cum-dependency share certain characteristics. Both are holistic, in Gruchy's sense. They do not conceive of development narrowly in conventional terms, but look upon the economic system as "an evolving, unified whole or synthesis, in the light of which the system's parts take on their full meaning."[23] The approach is interdisciplinary, drawing on anthropology, history, politics, and sociology, as well as economics, for an understanding of development. Historical evolution, shifting class structures, and modes of political control are central to the economic analysis, not extraneous to it, as in much standard economics.

Moreover, neither institutionalists nor dependency theorists are reluctant to make explicit normative judgments, in contrast with economists who still assert a preference for positivism and eschew explicit value judgments while at the same time implicitly upholding the accepted values of a market system. This willingness to take into account the value aspects of the development process—indeed, an insistence that development has no meaning without reference to social objectives—is critical to the analysis, since considerations of income distribution, access to education, availability of productive jobs, and conditions of health and nutrition are at the heart of the debate over appropriate strategies to convert mere growth in Latin America into genuine socio-economic development.

Both institutionalism and dependency theory are deeply critical of orthodox economic doctrine on the grounds that it fails to provide an adequate historical explanation of the development process and that it is too narrowly based, in its preoccupation with the market, to serve as a useful guide for development policy.

They are similar in yet another aspect. Both institutionalism and dependency theory recognize the importance of long-term trends and are more concerned with their explanation than with that of short-term crises, which often spring from immediate and particularistic political dilemmas. Some of the failures of policies applied by military bureaucratic governments in Latin America may be attributed to their crisis-management nature, in which short-range objectives tend to supercede long-range development strategy. The result is a succession of stop-go measures from which there does not appear to be any escape into sustained growth.

Yet while institutionalism and dependency theory have much in common, the former provides a more comprehensive explanation of the development process, and they differ significantly in the interpretation of how growth takes place. In concentrating almost exclusively on the exogenous factors influencing the development process, the Dependency School has tended to lose interest in domestic, and often deeply cultural, factors that have also contributed to economic retardation. This was not true of earlier structuralist analysis.

There is little doubt that the present control of most high technology and the means of its propagation by multinational corporations poses difficulties in the international transfer and acquisition of useful knowledge, and thus reinforces existing dependency relationships. However, in focusing attention on this comparatively recent development, dependency theory has neglected to explain the long-retarded nature of indigenous scientific and technological activity within the underdeveloped world, or to suggest means by which such activity could be stimulated as a way to overcome continued dependency. In Latin America, institutionalists would investigate the reasons for the disappearance during the colonial period of the native innovative spirit characteristic of the Aztec and Inca civilizations and the subsequent failure to revive it, or a similar creative movement, in modern times.[24] They would question whether, without concrete efforts to implant a domestically stimulated scientific and technological strategy to cope with the region's problems, the widening development gap can be overcome.

Moreover, institutionalists would not abandon the promising study of domestic bottlenecks undertaken by the structuralists in favor of a recent preoccupation with outside influences. They find that many of the obstacles to economic development remain in the repressive features of local institutions, in which nationalistic military intervention and control, reverence for the *caudillo*, or charismatic leader, and a preference for ceremonial over functional behavior in nearly all strata of society play a large part.

Institutionalists are less ideologically committed than radical dependency theorists to a Marxist view of historical inevitability, the class strug-gle, and the probability or desirability of a violent solution. While they recognize the powerful force of institutions, they are more inclined to think that the historical process can be altered through the application of collective intelligence, or the conscious search for useful institutional in-novations and alternatives. They note that authoritarian and unprogres-sive behavior may be observed among the lower classes as well as among dominant elites, and among Third World countries as well as among cap-italist. Thus the pricing, marketing, and investment decisions of the Or-ganization of Petroleum Exporting Countries, in their impact since 1973 on other underdeveloped countries that must import oil, showed little to distinguish them from forms of monopolistic behavior originating in in-dustrial countries.

Much dependency analysis, in its profound pessimism, tends to rein-force the fatalistic mood traditionally present in Latin American society. In contrast, institutionalism seeks to discover ways in which social effort may be redirected constructively and formal institutions reshaped to be-come functionally useful. This is more than a preference for optimism over pessimism; it stems from a strong belief in the efficacy of technology in all its forms, and in the progressive evolutionary character of society.

The efficacy of technology rests upon two principles elaborated by C. E. Ayres: that technology is essentially an autonomous, self-sustaining pro-cess, and that the potential for fruitful discoveries will be enhanced in a receptive environment.[25] Ayres rejected the conventional notion that in-vention and discovery are best explained in market terms; that is, that they depend chiefly on consumer demand or on financial investment. Instead, technology is an independent continuum of interrelated discoveries and applications, whose extension depends on a pre-existing milieu filled with artifacts and with informed investigators who constantly manipulate and recombine them and examine the results. Thus the greater the stock of existing technological devices, the greater the number of permutations and recombinations in the form of new inventions that are likely to occur.

In addition, such an environment of widespread research and develop-ment increases the chances of serendipity—the faculty of making desir-able but unsought-for discoveries by accident. Ayres has cited many such instances of "accidental" discoveries rendered virtually predictable by the facilitating conditions of the cultural environment. A survey of the tech-nological history of Latin America and sub-Saharan Africa would reveal that such an environment has existed in few places in the respective re-gions, and in modern times over only relatively short periods. This cultural hiatus helps to explain the paucity of technological creativity, with a few notable exceptions.

However, a third principle laid down by Ayres suggests that Latin America and Africa may benefit from the circumstance that growth is now taking place under frontier conditions.[26] Ayres has shown that the possibilities for cross-fertilization of techniques is increased when a new frontier is penetrated. A frontier is a region that offers the space for expansion of population in movement, for a rupture with old institutions, and for the application of techniques brought from other regions to achieve an accelerated rate of development. Given the increased cultural contact, and the special challenges posed by frontier conditions, new combinations and adaptations of useful knowledge are almost certain to occur. There is mounting evidence that such inventions and adaptations, particularly in agricultural biology and in industrial techniques, are occurring with increasing frequency in Latin America.[27] The Dependency School has tended to overlook or to minimize the significance of these achievements.

The Task Ahead

What now remains to solidify the contribution of economic heterodoxy to the solution of Latin American development problems? The main outlines of a general understanding of the economic evolutionary process have been laid down, and in view of the acute conditions described in Latin America, it is necessary to attempt a fresh analysis of the specific institutional deficiencies and the technological needs now confronting the region. This will require a coordinated effort to provide the necessary empirical data, and fortunately many of these are currently being supplied by such agencies as the Economic Commission for Latin America, the Inter-American Development Bank, and a number of specialized research centers.

Yet it is precisely the study of prevalent *institutions*, such as the authoritarian bureaucratic governments, the multinational corporations, the international lending agencies, and other centers of control, that pose the most delicate problems for effective research. Because economic heterodoxy recognizes the crucial nature of these institutions and their effect on development, it cannot neglect their further investigation.

Some useful work has already been done in this direction. Two unpublished dissertations can serve as models. One, a study by Asim Sen of the development of the Japanese economy after the Meiji restoration, in the latter part of the nineteenth century, is an acute analysis of the intricate

686 James H. Street and Dilmus D. James

relation between Japanese social institutions and the introduction of European technology into a feudal society.[28] The other is Milton D. Lower's dissertation on *The Institutional Bases of Economic Stagnation in Chile*, which could well be updated for the decade of the 1970s.[29] Such updating would surely include a series of five studies carried out at considerable personal risk by a group of economists associated with the private Corporación de Investigaciones Económicas para América Latina (CIEPLAN) in Santiago.[30] These studies, using independently derived empirical data, raise serious questions about the reliability of official data published by the government concerning the recent performance of the Chilean economy.

Harry Martin Greenberg has made a thorough investigation of the operation of the Mexican Secretariat of Hydraulic Resources, an agency with a great deal of de facto power, which could be replicated for other cases.[31] A document that eschews a narrow technical focus for a more inclusive examination of historical, economic, legal, and political circumstances shaping scientific and technological capabilities in Mexico is the *National Indicative Plan for Science and Technology* produced by a team headed by the structuralist economist Miguel Wionczek.[32] An exemplary series of reports emerged from a major project by the Canadian International Development Research Centre in the mid-1970s to explore ways in which institutions impinge on efforts to stimulate scientific and technological progress in less developed countries.[33]

It is admittedly difficult for the academic researcher to "get inside" the powerful institutional structures that are to be investigated. However, the task is not impossible, and the results are often fruitful in understanding the realities of the development process. There is ample room for collaboration among institutionalists, structuralists, and dependency theorists in carrying out this task.

Notes

1. Allan G. Gruchy, *Modern Economic Thought: The American Contribution* (New York: Prentice-Hall, 1947), p. viii.
2. Simon S. Kuznets, *Modern Economic Growth: Rate, Structure, and Spread* (New Haven: Yale University Press, 1966). Kuznets's contribution to economic development theory extends to many other works.
3. This and following compilations, which exclude Venezuela because of its weight during the period as a major exporter of petroleum, are based on data from national sources. Carlos E. Sansón, "Latin America and the Caribbean: A Medium-term Outlook," *Finance & Development* 18 (September 1981): 34–37.

4. *Economic and Social Progress in Latin America: 1977 Report* (Washington, D.C.: Inter-American Development Bank, 1978), p. 11.
5. Sansón, "Latin America and the Caribbean," p. 35.
6. Regional Employment Programme for Latin America and the Caribbean (PREALC), *The Employment Problem in Latin America: Facts, Outlooks, and Policies* (Santiago, Chile: International Labor Office, 1976). See also Peter Gregory, "An Assessment of Changes in Employment Conditions in Less Developed Countries," *Economic Development and Cultural Change* 28 (July 1980): 673–700.
7. Irma Adelman and Cynthia T. Morris, *Economic Growth and Social Equity in Developing Countries* (Stanford: Stanford University Press, 1973); Hollis B. Chenery, et al., *Redistribution with Growth* (New York: Oxford University Press, 1974); David Felix, "Income Inequality in Mexico," *Current History* 72 (March 1977): 111–14, 136.
8. These estimates must be treated with the usual caution regarding reliability and comparability. *World Bank Development Report, 1980* (Washington, D.C.: The World Bank, August 1980), pp. 156–57.
9. National Council for Science and Technology, *National Indicative Plan for Science and Technology* (Mexico, D.F.: Editorial CONACYT, 1976), p. 112. The Pan American Health Organization reported that during the period from 1971 to 1975, an estimated 61.4 percent of the children under five in 19 Latin American countries suffered from protein-calorie malnutrition. *Economic and Social Progress in Latin America: 1978 Report* (Washington, D.C.: Inter-American Development Bank, 1979), p. 138.
10. C. E. Ayres, *The Theory of Economic Progress*, 2d ed. (New York: Schocken Books, 1962).
11. Wendell C. Gordon, *The Economy of Latin America* (New York: Columbia University Press, 1950); William P. Glade, *The Latin American Economies: A Study of their Institutional Evolution* (New York: American Book; Van Nostrand, Reinhold, 1969).
12. Raúl Prebisch, "The Economic Development of Latin America and Its Principal Problems," *Economic Bulletin for Latin America* 7 (February 1962): 1–22. Originally published in Spanish in 1950. See also Werner Baer, "The Economics of Prebisch and ECLA," *Economic Development and Cultural Change* 10 (January 1962): 169–82.
13. The key studies were Osvaldo Sunkel, "La inflación chilena—Un enfoque heterodoxo," *El Trimestre Económico* 25 (Mexico, D.F., October-December 1958): 570 ff.; and Aníbal Pinto Santa Cruz, *Ni estabilidad ni desarrollo—La política del Fondo Monetario Internacional* (Santiago, Chile: Editorial Universitaria, 1960). The Sunkel article has since appeared in English in *International Economic Papers*, no. 10 (1960). See also Werner Baer, "The Inflation Controversy in Latin America: A Survey," *Latin American Research Review* 2 (Spring 1967): 3–35; and James H. Street, "The Latin American 'Structuralists' and the Institutionalists: Convergence in Development Theory," *Journal of Economic Issues* 1 (June 1967): 44–62.
14. For a comprehensive bibliography and critique of the Dependency School, see C. Richard Bath and Dilmus D. James, "Dependency Analysis of

688   James H. Street and Dilmus D. James

Latin America: Some Criticisms, Some Suggestions," *Latin American Research Review* 11 (Fall 1976): 3–54.

15. Theotonio Dos Santos, "The Structure of Dependence," *American Economic Review* 60 (May 1970): 231.

16. Stanley J. Stein and Barbara Stein, *The Colonial Heritage: Essays on Economic Dependence in Perspective* (New York: Oxford University Press, 1970).

17. For a detailed delineation of the origins of dependency theory as it grew out of active discussions among Latin American scholars, see Fernando Henrique Cardoso, "The Consumption of Dependency Theory in the United States," *Latin American Research Review* 12 (Fall 1977): 7–24. See also Helio Jaguaribe, Aldo Ferrer, Miguel S. Wionczek, and Theotonio Dos Santos, *La dependencia político-económica de América Latina* (Mexico, D.F.: Siglo Veintiúno Editores, 1970).

18. The major early contributions are cited in Street, "The Latin American 'Structuralists,' " pp. 47–9.

19. Osvaldo Sunkel, "Transnational Capitalism and National Disintegration in Latin America," *Social and Economic Studies* 22 (1973): 132–76.

20. André Gunder Frank, *Capitalism and Underdevelopment in Latin America: Historical Studies of Chile and Brazil* (New York: Monthly Review Press, 1967); James Petras, ed., *Latin America: From Dependence to Revolution* (New York: John Wiley and Sons, 1973). See also the bibliography in Ronald H. Chilcote and Joel C. Edelstein, eds., *Latin America: The Struggle with Dependency and Beyond* (New York: John Wiley and Sons, 1974).

21. André Gunder Frank, *Lumpenbourgeoisie: Lumpendevelopment, Dependence, Class, and Politics in Latin America* (New York: Monthly Review Press, 1972).

22. Peter Evans, *Dependent Development: The Alliance of Multinational, State, and Local Capital in Brazil* (Princeton, N.J.: University of Princeton Press, 1979).

23. Allan G. Gruchy, *Modern Economic Thought*, p. viii.

24. The destructive nature of the Conquest has, of course, been fully described by many historians and by structuralist economists such as Osvaldo Sunkel, but few have addressed themselves to an explanation of the paucity of innovative effort and results over long succeeding periods of time. See David Felix, "On the Diffusion of Technology in Latin America," in *Technological Progress in Latin America: The Prospects for Overcoming Dependency*, ed. James H. Street and Dilmus D. James (Boulder, Colo.: Westview Press, 1979), pp. 29–62.

25. Ayres, *Economic Progress*, pp. 125–54.

26. Ibid., pp. 133–54; James H. Street, "The Technological Frontier in Latin America: Creativity and Productivity," *Journal of Economic Issues* 10 (September 1976): 538–58.

27. Street and James, *Technological Progress*.

28. Asim Sen, "The Role of Technological Change in Economic Development: The Lessons of Japan for Presently Developing Countries" (Ph.D. diss., Rutgers University, 1979).

29. Milton D. Lower, "The Institutional Bases of Economic Stagnation in Chile" (Ph.D. diss., University of Texas, Austin, 1970).
30. Alejandro Foxley, Ricardo Ffrench-Davis, et al., "Cinco estudios sobre la economía chilena desde 1973," *Colección Estudios CIEPLAN* 4 (November 1980): 5–201.
31. Harry Martin Greenberg, *Bureaucracy and Development: A Mexican Case Study* (Lexington, Mass.: Heath, 1975).
32. National Council for Science and Technology, *Indicative Plan.*
33. See, for example, Francisco Sagasti and Alberto Aráoz, *Science and Technology Policy Implementation in Less-developed Countries: Methodological Guidelines for the STPI Project* (Ottawa: International Development Research Centre, 1975).

[13]

Jei JOURNAL OF ECONOMIC ISSUES
Vol. XI No. 4 December 1977

The Development of Economic Institutions

Daniel R. Fusfeld

This interpretive essay seeks to clarify the questions that need to be asked about the development of economic institutions. The approach is macroeconomic in nature. That is, the object of inquiry is the economic system as a whole, concentrating on how a particular type of economy such as modern industrial capitalism changes over the course of time. In this context one of the chief issues is the process by which one type of economy is replaced by another type, for example, the transition from feudalism to capitalism or capitalism to socialism.

The development of individual segments or elements of the larger economy is important in understanding the changes that take place in the larger economy, but they are not included in this inquiry. We do not consider, for example, the process by which subsistence farming is replaced by commercial farms, the emergence of fractional reserve banking, or even a topic like the rise of large enterprise in modern capitalism. These and similar microeconomic issues are important for an understanding of the changes that have occurred in modern capitalism, but we are after bigger game: We want to understand the theoretical principles that underlie the global shifts that take place in economic systems as a whole. Once those principles are understood the lesser dimensions of the problem can be fitted into the analysis of any specific case.

In following this inquiry, then, we leave aside two very rich bodies of

The author is Professor of Economics, University of Michigan, Ann Arbor.

743

knowledge. One is the large literature of economic history. The other is the almost as comprehensive literature on economic development. Except insofar as writings in these fields contain a strong and explicit theoretical analysis of institutional change at the level of economic systems as a whole, they are not included in this study.

Nor do we start with an attempt to define the concepts *development* and *economic institutions,* for there is no consensus among scholars about the meaning of those terms. Rather, one of the objectives of this essay is to try to derive a reasonable operational definition from the inquiry itself. This may bother readers addicted to Aristotelian logic, Kantian idealism, or logical positivism. If so, grit your teeth and read on, assuming the existence of a stochastic, existential universe.

The first section examines the analysis in orthodox or mainstream economics of the development of economic institutions. The second is a brief overview of the dissent from that position on the part of the English and German historical-institutionalist schools of the nineteenth century and notes two important contributions made by Henry Sumner Maine and Ferdinand Tönnies. The third section treats the American institutionalist school, concentrating on Thorstein Veblen, John R. Commons, and Clarence Ayres. It notes their important insights into fundamental issues, but also their failure to produce a comprehensive theory of institutional change. The fourth section deals with Marx's writings on the issue: Here we find the only attempt to develop a thorough-going theory of institutional change applicable broadly across historical eras and cultural watersheds. Section five, where we examine the work of Max Weber and Karl Polanyi, shows that Marx did not have all the answers, nor even ask all the relevant questions. Section six focuses on the key relationships between economic base and ideological-political superstructure (to use Marx's formulation) in the work of Richard H. Tawney, Barrington Moore, Jr., and Immanuel Wallerstein. The final section attempts to synthesize these diverse elements and draw some conclusions.

The Orthodox View

Theoretical analysis of the development of economic institutions has never been a central concern in mainstream economics. Among the classical economists, Adam Smith, Friedrich List, and John Stuart Mill, among others, made use of information about the institutional structure of society as the framework for their analysis.[1] These writers did not make significant contributions to a theory of institutional change, but they did provide some starting points for later writers.

Smith's chief contribution was the idea of stages of economic development. Capital accumulation and widening of the market promoted a "progress of opulence" that could transform an agricultural economy into one with agriculture and commerce and ultimately to a diversified economy of agriculture, commerce, and manufacturing. This transformation from rural to urban society was caused by a single driving force, the acquisitive nature of the individual. It was not seen as a self-generating process in which a variety of social forces interacts to produce institutional change. The state played an important facilitating role in the process, however, providing the legal framework that would give free play to the acquisitive motive and protecting property rights in the gains.

Implicit in Smith's argument was a hidden assumption about economic institutions: The institutional structure within which acquisitive behavior would lead to progress was either there to begin with or would itself be created by individual action. This was tantamount to assuming either the prior existence of a system of self-adjusting markets or that such an institutional structure would naturally evolve over time as part of the progress of opulence. Smith was apparently aware of this gap in his logic when he gave to human beings the "propensity to truck, barter and exchange." Although Smith did not show exactly how that propensity would manifest itself in the self-adjusting markets through which his "system of natural liberty" functioned, it is possible to interpolate such a history into his schema. In essence, Smith substituted a "propensity" in the psychological or behavioral makeup of human beings for an analysis of institutional change.

List took over Smith's development sequence, but gave it a different twist. Economic progress was attributed not only to individual acquisitiveness, but also to the national spirit expressed through community action. Government had a positive role to play in List's schema, for it was the chief instrument through which noneconomic institutions and the economic infrastructure could be structured to take full advantage of a nation's development potential. The institutional framework within which acquisitiveness could lead to economic progress did not just appear by itself; it had to be created by community action. List, however, applied this idea only to the infrastructure of institutions within which a system of self-adjusting markets functions, not to the system of markets itself. As did Smith, he assumed that to be a natural development, if government was able to create the proper environment for individual action.

John Stuart Mill, who compromised on most basic problems, straddled the issue of the relationship between government and economic institutions. As did all the classical economists, he took an economy of self-adjusting markets for granted. However, he argued that progress in production was the result of immutable laws of production, while patterns of income distribution were man-made. Going on to describe the societal or institutional arrangements that affected patterns of income distribution, he did not analyze the forces that brought them about, and he thereby missed an opportunity to build a theory of institutional change into the body of mainstream economics.

Although Smith, List, and Mill provided space for analysis of the development of economic institutions in the logic of their analyses, David Ricardo did not, and his ideas dominated the classical school.[2] Ricardo argued that capital accumulation under conditions of diminishing returns would lead ultimately to a stationary economy, but he analyzed the path to the stationary state within the institutional framework of an individualistic private enterprise economy that did not change its structure as it moved through time. One might justify such an approach by arguing that holding the institutional structure constant enables the theoretician to isolate the effects of "pure" economic variables such as capial accumulation under conditions of diminishing returns. But the penalty is to ignore the effects of the economic variables on the institutional structure, and the impact of institutional changes on economic variables, thereby setting aside institutional change as a subject for economic analysis. For example, the process of capital accumulations, which is the driving force of Ricardo's model, also involves technological change, which can bring decreasing costs and monopoly, thereby changing the economic structure and the path of economic development. Ricardo did not explore this line of reasoning, but it was taken up by Karl Marx, Arnold Toynbee, and the American institutionalists, among others.

Neoclassical economics went even further. The central questions of economics shifted after 1870 away from analysis of capital accumulation and production toward market exchange. Buyers and sellers facing each other in competitive markets, modified later to include imperfect competition and related market structures, became the heart of economic analysis. Even the effects of diminishing returns (increasing costs) in the long run were eliminated by the assumption of constant costs as an essential element in general equilibrium analysis. This assumption also eliminated the gap in Ricardo's analysis created by the possibility that capital accumulation (and technical change) might bring changes in the competitive structure of markets. Alfred Marshall, of course, had allowed space for this type of institutional change in his analytical model: partial rather than general equilibrium; the concept of the representative firm; increasing and decreasing cost industries. These concepts might have opened up a line of inquiry into the emergence of big business out of competitive markets and the impact of monopoloid elements on the market economy and on the political-social structure, and a beginning was made with analysis of imperfect competition by Joan Robinson, E. H. Chamberlin, Heinrich von Stackelberg, and others. But this potential opening for analysis of change in economic institutions was closed by the almost universal acceptance of general equilibrium models following publication of John R. Hicks's *Value and Capital* (1939) and Paul Samuelson's *Foundations of Economics* (1947). Now, more than ever, economic orthodoxy has excluded from analysis the processes by which the institutional structure of the economy changes.[3]

There have been two notable attempts by neoclassical economists to deal with the problem of institutional change within the framework of equilibrium assumptions. Joseph Schumpeter was the first.[4] His *Theory of Economic Development* starts with a perfectly competitive capitalist economy in general equilibrium. This static situation is broken by one or more entrepreneurs, who devise improved ways of obtaining profits. The enlarged profits disturb the equilibrium, while the new product, production technique, or form of organization spreads through the economy. Ultimately, a new equilibrium can be established. Innovations lead to economic fluctuations, however, and to the rise of giant enterprise, government intervention, and ultimately the demise of capitalism. Schumpeter finds that the ills of modern capitalism are the direct result of its successes—economic growth, new products, new technology, and so forth—which is merely a new twist to an old Marxist argument. Schumpeter's basic point, however, was that the operation of the competitive private enterprise economy would create conditions that bring fundamental changes in the institutional structure of that economy. Schumpeter had defined one of the key problems: Is it possible for a competitive market economy to reproduce itself over time, or will it create conditions that force a change to some other type of economic system? His ideas never became part of the accepted canon of orthodox neoclassical economics.

The second effort to deal with institutional change in a neoclassical framework was made by Douglass C. North, first in collaboration with Lance E. Davis and then with Robert Paul Thomas.[5] The first version was frankly neoclassical, involving comparative statics (movement from one general equilibrium to another), profit maximization, and Pareto optimality. Introduce into a Pareto optimal equilibrium an exogenous change that makes it possible to obtain profits that cannot be obtained within the existing institutional arrangements. Economic units will then reorganize the institutional arrangements to obtain the potential gains. This first approximation applies to Pareto superior solutions, in which one group can gain without worsening another group's position. A second approximation applies to Pareto inferior situations, in which one group's gain can be achieved only at the expense of another group. This type of institutional rearrangement requires the coercive use of government on behalf of the side seeking to gain from the resultant redistribution of income. This North-Davis model had some serious flaws: The initiating force for institutional change is endogenous to the model and therefore incapable of accounting for the historical presence of continuing change, and the model is limited by its behavioral assumptions to those systems dominated by market exchange. Its applicability would be very limited in socioeconomic systems in which economic relationships are "mediated by" noneconomic forces (Marx) or "embedded in" noneconomic institutions (Polanyi).

North's second effort, in collaboration with Thomas, took a somewhat different approach.[6] It was based on the theory of property rights, in particular on the proposition that economic development is promoted when the gains from innovation can be appropriated privately. The development of the institution of private property is seen as the key change that led from feudalism to capitalism. The driving force, however, was change in the relative scarcities of factors of production. North and Thomas argued that the economic efficiency of feudal Europe's production arrangements was reduced in the thirteenth century because of population growth that changed the relative scarcity of labor and land. This brought on a period of crisis that led to the breakup of feudal society and was not overcome until population growth began once more in the late fifteenth century. But the changing scarcity relationships among factors of production now made it possible to achieve large economic gains if private property replaced feudal property. The lure of these gains brought strong pressure to change the legal basis of property, and, with the assistance of the national state, the change was made. The theory has been broadened in this version; it attempts to deal with large transformations from one type of economy to another; it brings the role of the state into a central position; it focuses on legal changes in property relations; and basic economic relationships of relative scarcity are the sources of institutional change. In many of its outlines it is compatible with Marx's analysis of the same period in history and is similar in some respects to Wallerstein's treatment (which we shall examine later). The basic reason for these similarities is that North and Thomas move back to the classical school's treatment of value: Relative scarcities of factors do not merely generate relative prices in the markets, but bring changes in real costs of production. The neoclassical model of pure exchange in the first version of North's theory becomes a classical theory of production costs in the second. This change made the theory applicable to a wider variety of historical situations: Costs of production, measured in amounts of input of human effort, are a fundamental element in any economy, but market prices are relevant only in an economy organized around markets as the chief element in the institutional framework. It was not the introduction of property rights that strengthened the theory, but a shift from relative prices to real costs of production as the economic force setting institutional change in motion.

The North-Thomas theory fits into the logical gap in classical economics created by the institutional assumption of self-adjusting allocative markets. An historical analysis specific to Western Europe can be substituted for that assumption, or for Smith's assumption of a human propensity to exchange, to explain the appearance of a market economy. Furthermore, the North-Davis theory can be used to explain institutional change within the framework of a market economy, once it is established.

Nevertheless, the North theories have some serious limitations. Perhaps the most important is the implication that the economy of self-adjusting allocative markets is a final term in institutional change: Since shifts in relative scarcities of factors of production are the basic driving force of systemic institutional change, and a system of self-adjusting markets can adapt to changes in relative scarcities, there seems to be no reason for further systemic change. One doubts that the authors of the theory would take such a position so baldly stated, but it is inherent in the argument. Expressed another way, the North theories set aside problems of conflict arising from within the institutional structure itself as a source of institutional change, the question of values in a market economy versus larger concepts of human values, and the role of technological change, to mention only a few sources of institutional change emphasized by other writers. Nor do the North theories deal with the internal dynamics described by Schumpeter: the successes of capitalism creating conditions inimical to the continuation of capitalism. We conclude that North's efforts to graft an institutional dynamics onto an essentially static equilibrium analysis have not been successful.

The English and German
Historical Schools

There had always been dissent from an economics that ignored institutional change. The English and German historical-institutionalist school had attacked the Ricardian assumptions of a static institutional structure as early as the 1830s and 1840s. Indeed, the institutionalism of Walter

Bagehot and Arnold Toynbee helped to weaken the classical position and prepare the way for acceptance of the neoclassical approach.[7] Those writers attacked the assumptions of Ricardian economics as historically invalid and empirically inaccurate. They were among the first to argue that the rapid pace of technological change invalidated theories based on a given institutional structure. But while they were able to show that industrialization and the development of financial markets had so changed the economic environment that the Ricardian model was increasingly out of tune with reality, and that capital accumulation and economic development created an ever changing institutional framework, Toynbee and Bagehot did not develop a theoretical analysis of why institutional change occurs and the patterns it is likely to follow.

The German historical school took simultaneously a broader and a narrower view. The earlier writers in this group, Wilhelm Roscher, Friedrich von Hermann, Bruno Hildebrand, and Karl Knies,[8] put great stress on the interplay between economic, political, and social forces in determining patterns of development of economic institutions. They emphasized the proposition that each nation had a unique historical heritage, that its institutional structure differed from that of other nations because of its heritage, and that the theory and economic policies appropriate to one country would not necessarily be applicable to others. They used this argument to reject Ricardian economics and free trade as inapplicable to the central European economy.

The later German historical writers, particularly Gustav Schmoller,[9] were responsible for narrowing rather than broadening this beginning. They narrowed it in two ways: toward detailed historical studies of particular aspects of the institutional structure, and into studies of specific areas of economic policy such as public finance, tariff policy, social insurance, and related matters. In doing so, the broad generalizations about the interrelatedness of economic, political, and social forces in generating institutional change bequeathed to them by the first generation of the historical school were left largely undeveloped.

The most important contribution in the nineteenth century to an understanding of institutional change was the idea that an economy based on market exchange and driven by the profit motive was something new in human history. Moralists such as Thomas Carlyle and John Ruskin criticized the commercialization of social values, Honoré de Balzac satirized the commercial classes and their attitudes, Charles Dickens savaged both the values and the results of the industrial economy, and it was the substitution of market-oriented values for the older truths that Edmund Burke criticized when he wrote: "The age of chivalry is dead, that of sophisters, œconomists and calculators has succeeded, and the glory of Europe is extinguished forever." Many people understood that the nineteenth century had brought a fundamental change to the economy and society of Europe.

It is not surpising, then, to find scholars analyzing the change, despite the implicit assumption of the classical economists that the institutional structure of a system of allocative markets could be taken for granted. The most sophisticated analysis of the development of an exchange economy was devised by Karl Marx, and we shall examine his approach shortly. But two other versions of the same transition were also published at about the same time, by the English legal scholar Henry Sumner Maine and a German sociologist, Ferdinand Tönnies.

Main's classic work, *Ancient Law,* argued that "the movement of the progressive societies has hitherto been a move *from Status to Contract.*"[10] That is, in earlier social systems such as those of the feudal period, ancient society, and primitive communities, the position of the individual was determined by his status at birth—by his initial position in family, tribe, city-state, or other hierarchic structure. In Maine's view, human progress is largely the history of how those elements of status are replaced by voluntary association or agreement—by contract. The legal system of private property, contractual relationships, and exchange grew up as the social order slowly (and sometimes not so slowly) evolved away from systems of status.

Maine's essentially optimistic view that human freedom and a society based on contract or exchange developed together differed from the critical views of Ferdinand Tönnies. His *Gemeinschaft und Gesellschaft*[11] argued that the old order was an integrated society in which the individual had a known and accepted place in the community that provided meaningfulness and satisfaction to the individual. The new society, however, cut off the individual from meaningful relationships with other people, severed his ties with the community as a whole, and left people isolated and alone in a world of only material values.

The work of Maine and Tönnies shows that the institutional assumptions of classical economics were not shared by other social scientists. Maine approached the problem from the viewpoint of a moderate liberal who liked the path that the development of institutions had taken; Tönnies was a conservative who looked with affection on the old social order and was critical of the new era; Marx, of course, was a radical who disliked the old, hated the new, and looked forward to the next social revolution. Maine was a legal historian interested in the effects of the British legal system on the traditional society of India; Tönnies was an academician in nineteenth-century Germany, which was caught up in the economics and politics of the transition from a quasi-feudal to a modern society; Marx was the quintessential philosopher-radical. Yet, all three had diagnosed the same transition to an individualistic society oriented around market transactions and motivated by private gain. They understood that this social order had appeared only recently, and that it had profound implications for human happiness. From three different starting points, with three different social-philosophical orientations, they had defined one key issue in analysis of the development of economic institutions: the nature and origins of modern capitalism.

Veblen, Commons, and Ayres

In the United States, the institutional economists also dissented from the orthodox assumption of a given institutional framework. Henry Carter Adams's studies of the state, the law, and the corporation showed how new forms of economic organization arose to meet the needs of an expanding business civilization.[12] Richard T. Ely examined the relationships between the forces of economic growth and technological change, on the one hand, and property relationships as defined by law, on the other, to argue that government regulation was necessary to solve the problems of a rapidly industrializing society.[13] Both Ely and Adams were active participants in the growth of government regulation of the private sector and the development of legal constraints on big business in the late nineteenth and early twentieth century.

The institutionalist emphasis on a changing institutional framework was formulated most effectively by Thorstein Veblen, John R. Commons, and Clarence E. Ayres. These writers, although different in many ways, had two basic and common points of view. First, they believed that the static approach of orthodox economics was invalidated by the observed fact of institutional change. They rejected a theory that excluded consideration of what they believed was the most important aspect of social reality. Second, their center of interest lay in the problems created by industrialization and economic development and not in an analysis of how an exchange economy functions.[14] Veblen, Commons, and Ayres identified a different central question for economics than did Marshall, Léon Walras, or J. B. Clark, arguing that the orthodox approach was narrow and trivial, while orthodoxy responded that the institutionalists were dealing with sociology, not economics.

Veblen, Commons, and Ayres were concerned primarily with the nature, development, and future of modern industrial capitalism. They saw the emergence of big business as the dominant economic force of their time, driven by a rapidly advancing industrial technology, and leading to a new set of class relationships. The small farmer and small business enterprise were being driven to the wall; mass labor and its unions were a new force to be reckoned with; great wealth for a few and economic power concentrated in their hands transformed patterns of income distribution. These changes were accompanied by great economic instability. Furthermore, changes in the economic structure of society brought a shift in the locus of political power, and political conflict, as the new centers of economic interest struggled with each other. Clearly, the economy was changing rapidly, affecting the everyday lives and satisfactions of ordinary people, the way people thought about the world and themselves, and the locus and structure of power. What would be the outcome? How could the direction of change be molded? These issues were central to the thinking of the first generation of institutionalists.

Veblen, Commons, and Ayres did not create a general theory of the development of economic institutions, nor did they attempt to do so. They had little to say, for example, about the transition from feudalism to capitalism or from tribal to feudal economies. Nevertheless, several analytical problems were common to their analyses. All involved conflict as the source of change. If the institutionalists may be said to have developed a cohesive theory of institutional change, it is to be found here.

First, a distinction is made between social forces and institutional arrangements that lead to cohesion and stability in the social order and those that lead to conflict, instability, and change. In Veblen's schema, for example, the "vested interests" seek to preserve an existing institutional structure because it gives them a favored position. On the other hand, disadvantaged groups and individuals desire changes favorable to themselves. Meanwhile, science and technological change are continually driving toward new patterns of production relationships, pushed by the urge of curious people seeking new experiences and innovation as ends in themselves, as well as by the instinct of workmanship that continually seeks more effective ways of doing things. New patterns and relations of production undermine the existing position of the vested interests, weaken them in relationship to a growing majority that seeks change, and as conflict grows tensions build until institutional change becomes inevitable. Depending upon circumstances, it might be either peaceful or violent.[15]

Commons viewed the contrast between stability and change somewhat differently. Any economy constitutes a system of arrangements and working rules that enables a complex system of transactions (which need not be monetary) to be carried on. Production and distribution of useful things are carried on in this framework. In this sense the economy is a "going concern" that enables people to satisfy their wants. However, in the modern world industrial technology and corporate organization have disturbed the balance of the economy as a going concern, bringing a need for labor and farmer organizations and for government regulation to restore balance. Commons believed that a plurality of economic interests would develop collective management of the economy to make and keep it "reasonable" and therefore viable. Mutual interests in maintaining the going concern would prevail over selfish interests in self- and group aggrandizement.

Ayres took still another position. On the one hand, inherited beliefs and values are passed on from one generation to the next through the entire institutional structure. On the other hand, scientific and technological change, driven by a desire for improvement and abundance, creates a need for new institutional arrangements, beliefs, and values. Emergence of the new is hampered by irrational allegiance to the old. With Ayres, reason is the force for change, emotional attachment to tradition the force for stability.

The three leading institutionalists analyzed the conflict between forces of stability and change at three different levels. Veblen saw the conflict primarily in economic and social class terms, between the economic benefits gained by the vested interests and the needs of the common man, between existing production relations and the innovation generated by the instinct of workmanship. Commons saw the conflict as essentially political, resolved by compromise among organized economic interest groups who have a common need to keep the system going. With Ayres the conflict is ultimately in the ideal realm, between rationality as expressed in the advance of science and technology and irrationality as expressed by support for the status quo in institutions and values.

The second source of institutional change analyzed by the institutionalists was conflict between the motivations and wants of people as many-faceted social beings and the more limited and narrower economic motives characteristic of an acquisitive capitalistic economy. Economic motives were placed within a larger context of social motivations as a whole. Veblen, for example, felt that human behavior was founded on people's needs for subsistence, but that human subsistence was always obtained in a social context, by group behavior. This meant that the desire for social cohesiveness, maintenance of family, clan, and tribe, and mutuality of relationships were as much built into the pattern of economic motivations as was subsistence itself. It therefore becomes impossible to isolate specifically acquisitive or economic behavior distinct from the larger pattern of social motivations. Although Veblen phrased these ideas in the terminology of instincts, we should not let outmoded phrases obsure the underlying holistic concepts.

Commons and Ayres used different phraseology, but they shared Veblen's *Gestalt* approach to human motivations. Commons argued that the social system had collective as well as individual needs. Among them was the necessity to keep the economy functioning adequately so that individual needs could be met. This included maintenance of reasonable levels of prosperity and the resolution of class conflict between capital and labor. These collective needs could be fulfilled only by collective action, however, which meant government action to promote economic stability and labor peace. Ayres stressed a different aspect of human psychology, the creative, seeking, problem-solving nature of the human mind. This behavior lay behind the advance of science and a changing technology. In one respect, Ayres tended to agree with the utilitarians: People sought new ways of doing things in order to improve themselves or their society. But in another respect he was more modern: People tended to do new things simply because they were new and different. Although he argued that human behavior could be understood only in the context of the particular social and cultural institutions of the time and place, the operation of human creative intelligence was an independent and autonomous force for institutional change.

Veblen, Commons, and Ayres also saw a conflict between the values and attitudes generated in a market economy and those inherent in their broader view of human nature. Veblen contrasted social with private utility, material with pecuniary values, making goods with making money, the instinct of workmanship with the acquisitive instinct. He argued that the emphasis in modern industrial society on making money represented a denial or negation of the broader aspects of human motives. As a result, modern capitalism would ultimately have to give way to different institutional forms—or else be sustained by force.

Commons saw the conflicts somewhat differently. Economic life was essentially collective and social in nature, not individualistic, and so were its motivational pattern and attitudes. This was particularly true of modern industrial capitalism. But the theory, property relations, and ideology of capitalism were individualistic in nature. The resultant conflict had to be resolved, and Commons saw a developing compromise that included judicial limitation of unchecked individualism and government management of a variety of economic activities.

Ayres contrasted the "price values" of the market system with "real values." The former reflect not only market adjustment processes, but also the class, status, and property relations of the economy. In particular, they reflect the power of big business and finance to distort competitive market forces in favor of special interests. Real values, by contrast, are related to the efficient functioning of the production system, its expansion and advancement through improved technology. As did Veblen, Ayres felt that there was a conflict between these two aspects of the modern economy and that price values impede the growth of real values. There was a need, Ayres argued, to replace direction of the economy by people wishing to maximize price values with people oriented toward real values.

The third aspect of institutional change dealt with by the institutionalists was the interplay between economic and political institutions. Unlike the mainstream economists, they did not develop a purely economistic model in which economic forces worked themselves out independently of politics and power, with a government sector grafted on as a modification of the basic model. Nor did they see a simplistic relationship between economic base and political superstructure similar to that of official Marxism in the Engels-Lenin-Stalin line of development. Rather, like the more sophisticated analysis of Marx himself, they postulated a complex pattern of mutual cause and effect between economic forces and political institutions, which they placed within a continually changing institutional framework rather than a class structure.

As did Marx, Veblen saw the national state as an instrument for serving the interests of those who held wealth and power. Writing in a period of colonial imperialism, he argued that colonies were acquired to provide profitable outlets for investment and sources of cheap raw materials. Colonies were too poor to offer significant markets, but colonial wars, navies, and armies promoted the increased purchasing power necessary for domestic prosperity. Furthermore, the nationalism generated by imperial ventures, stimulating patriotism among the masses, served to bolster loyalty to the state. The modern industrial economy was essentially unstable because of its pursuit of pecuniary values and financial gain; as these tendencies developed further with increased industrialization, there was a growing need for the centralized state power that could mount imperial ventures and maintain military power. Veblen argued that the vested interests of industrial capitalism were increasingly supporting a centralized, militarized state rather than the laissez-faire state. Nevertheless, the national state was seen as only a passing phase. The industrial economy was spreading worldwide: This spread would soon make the national state obsolete, and it would ultimately disappear along with the private enterprise economy.

Commons also postulated a mutual pattern of cause and effect between economic and political institutions. The disharmony in economic affairs caused by the development of big enterprise, big finance, and organized labor, along with the economic instability of prosperity and depression, required management in order to preserve the economy as a going concern. This need for imposed harmony was leading, he argued, to a collective capitalism in which a combination of government regulation, legislation, and judicial rules would bring about a reasonable adjustment of conflicting interests. "Banker capitalism" was leading to a "reasonable capitalism" as the class struggle gave way to class collaboration. This optimistic view of a pluralist political solution was at odds with Veblen's pessimistic forecast of a possible authoritarian militarized state.[16] Commons's position implies that people have a large degree of control over their political institutions and can mold the basic outlines as well as the details of the political superstructure. Furthermore, it suggests that political (and legal) institutions have a great deal to do with the operation of economic institutions. In this respect, Commons and Veblen are very similar: Both take the position that economic changes are reflected in changes in political institutions *and* that political institutions strongly affect the operation of the economy.

Ayres shared this emphasis, but with even greater stress on the malleability of political institutions and their ability to control economic forces. Private enterprise capitalism, he argued, was unable to take full advantage of the advancement of science and the improvement of technology, largely because of its stress on price values rather than real values. Its deficiencies lead to demand for economic planning, and with the growth of planning comes a growing dominance of social decision making over private. Ayres foresaw the ultimate triumph of political institutions over the economic, or, expressed perhaps more accurately, a combination or melding of the two.

That is the same outcome postulated by Veblen and Commons, albeit in different form. Veblen expected an authoritarian militarism in the interests of private wealth and power to take over direction of the economy (although he hoped a technocratic socialism run by the engineers might succeed). In either case there would be a unification of economic and political power. Commons expected a pluralistic unification of economic interests under the aegis of government and law. Ayres hoped for planning of the economy under the auspices of democratic political institutions. In all three versions of the destiny of the modern industrial economy, economics and politics were institutionally intertwined.

Although the American institutionalists did not evolve a comprehensive analysis of the development of economic institutions, they pointed the way by isolating three important variables: the tension between forces promoting maintenance of existing institutional patterns versus forces leading to change; the conflict between market or pecuniary values and attitudes, on the one hand, and broader, more humane values and attitudes on the other; and, finally, the interrelationships between economic and political institutions, particularly a trend toward unification of political and economic power.

Marx's Schema

Karl Marx developed the most comprehensive theoretical schema for analysis of the development of economic institutions. The basic outlines are familiar. The constant striving of humankind to produce material things from a recalcitrant nature has led to continuing improvement in the forces of production that can ultimately bring economic abundance. However, scarcity brings on a struggle for control of resources, including people. This struggle, together with the forces of production, generates relations of production, that is, a class structure appropriate to the prevailing forces of production. Taken together, the forces and relations of production form the economic base on which is built a superstructure of political, social, and ideological institutions, which exists in a mutually reinforcing relationship with the economic base. These structural patterns tend to reproduce themselves through time. However, they are continually changing as the forces of production change, driven by the human effort to find better methods of production and distribution. But the social relations of production tend to retain their existing structure as the dominant class seeks to hold its position. Ultimately, the changing forces of production will triumph, bringing a new class structure (this is the social revolution, and it may take centuries). The social revolution also transforms the superstructure, with part of that transformation being a political revolution that transfers political power to the newly dominant economic class.[17]

Several subsidiary points help fill out the basic model. First, the new superstructure that emerges during the period of active revolutionary change is developed in rudimentary form during the preceding period of social revolution. As a rising social class moves slowly toward economic dominance through transformation of the forces of production, it gradually builds the new ideologies, political institutions, legal forms, and so forth, that will ultimately form the new superstructure.[18] Second, a rising social class becomes aware of itself as a class, with its own special interests and goals, as a result of its conflict with the established class or classes that are initially dominant. This class consciousness, and the ideologies associated with it, develops out of the historical experience of the class struggle.

Indeed, a social class is not a social class until it has achieved the consciousness that enables it to function as a class in the political arena. The historical development of a social class not only depends upon changes in the forces of production, but also is affected by the historically unique class struggle out of which class consciousness and class action develop.[19] Third, institutional change is the outcome of actions taken by individual people, each one of whom is motivated by a desire to improve his or her position. The alternatives open to individuals, however, are limited by the specific historical situation prevailing at the time, and the individual actions that succeed are those that move progressively toward human improvement. For example, actions that increase production will be institutionalized, while those that do not will be abandoned; types of political action that fail will be modified or abandoned, while those that succeed will be repeated or expanded. Individual action creates social forces, and social forces channel individual action. In Marx's words, "men make their own history, but they do not make it just as they please."[20] This general schema of institutional change and its chief corollaries, stripped of their philosophical jargon, comprise Marx's often misconstrued concept of "historical materialism."

Unfortunately, Marx's analytical schema has been terribly distorted into what might be called "official" Marxism. A line of development running from Engels's later writings through Lenin and Stalin created a highly rigid interpretation of Marxism, designed primarily for political purposes, that has moved far from Marx's richer and more flexible analytical framework. Official Marxism has its origins in Marx's own writings, but only by ignoring much of other parts of his work. For example, the famous Marxist model of the development of society from primitive communism through slavery, feudalism, and capitalism to socialism is found in Marx and Engels's *Manifesto of the Communist Party* (1848), developed further in Engels's *Origin of the Family, Private Property and the State* (1884), has a central position in the writings of Lenin and Stalin, and is featured in the Soviet Union's textbooks on political economy. Many Western commentators and critics of Marx assume that this schema is a central proposition in Marx's own writings, but that is not the case. It can hardly be found anywhere in Marx's writings outside the *Manifesto,* which is clearly a political pamphlet and not a piece of theoretical analysis. Marx did indeed feel that socialism would follow capitalism (but only if the correct political action were taken), but he did not confine himself to the simplistic linear theory of development postulated by official Marxism.

Marx's position on this matter is contained in *Pre-Capitalist Economic Formations,* which is composed of selections from Marx's *Grundrisse,* a series of notebooks unpublished until long after his death.[21] The development presented there is multilinear. The analytical model is so important that it will be summarized here.

The starting point is primitive society, which is not described at all, but which, by implication, is characterized by such complete integration of all aspects of society that it is impossible to distinguish among economic, political, religious, or any other institutional structures. This stage is succeeded—Marx does not describe the transition—by four other types, depending on the region in which they are found: the Asiatic, Ancient, Germanic, and Slavonic economic modes. The Asiatic is characterized by communal property, the Ancient by private property, and the Germanic by a mixture of both (for example, the village commons as well as the "private" rights of the lord of the village). The Slavonic type is not described at all and drops out of Marx's writings. Development of the other three forms is based on their property relationships, on which rests a class structure, out of which comes the conflict that leads to institutional change.

The Asiatic form, with communal property, does not have a class structure and therefore lacks the conflict necessary to produce change. The communal village goes on indefinitely. However, it is possible for the village to be conquered by marauders from outside who are then able to appropriate the economic surplus and use it for their own purposes, perhaps to conquer more villages. A ruling class of warriors and an oriental despotism can develop: gigantic empires based on internal loot through taxation and external loot via warfare. Meanwhile, the economic base remains unchanged; technological change is prevented because any improvement would only increase the surplus appropriated by the warrior class; and the only economic improvements come from massive public works programs organized by the rulers. Marx used this analytical framework in later writings on British rule in India and on China.

The Ancient economy was based on private property in the agricultural city-state, and the dynamics were different from the Asiatic form. Population growth, requiring more land, led to military conquest of neighboring areas and the introduction of slavery. A ruling class of slaveowners developed which could enrich itself by further conquest. The result was the ancient empire, typified by Rome, whose extent was limited only by the technologies of transportation and war. But production technology was stagnant, because those who produce—the slaves—had no interest in producing a larger surplus, and the ruling class gained only through war and conquest. No class had an interest in improved technology. Ultimately, the heightened conflict between a growing slave class and a tiny slaveholding ruling class, together with inherent overextension of the frontier, led to growing internal conflict and border warfare. The ancient empires ended in chaos. In this case, as in the case of the Asiatic economy, there is no next stage, no continuing progress of human society.

Only the Germanic type was truly progressive. Its progressiveness originated in the contradictions inherent in its property relationships: common property in the village itself, private rights of the lord of the village, and the mixture of private rights in common (village) property held by individual families. These relationships led both to technological change (because communal property rights limit appropriation of the surplus by the lord) and to feudalism (as the rights and duties of lord and villagers develop over time). Feudalism, in turn, led to capitalism, as Marx describes in detail in *Capital,* volume I.

Human progress, then, did not follow the simplistic stages of the *Manifesto,* but took the more complex path of primitive society–Germanic mode–feudalism–capitalism, with exploration of two dead ends in the Asiatic and Ancient modes. (Perhaps three if the unexplained Slavonic type is included.) The driving force for change rested in the economic base—in property relationships and their accompanying class structure—and the conflicts found there. In one case, the Asiatic, the economic base remained unchanged, while the political superstructure moved from decentralization in village communes to centralization in regional states or military empires, and back again. Ancient society developed a pattern of imperial conquest and geographical expansion, only to break down because of internal conflict and a stagnant production technology. Only Western civilization, originating in the Germanic mode, was able to generate continuing progress, avoiding both the stability of the Asiatic mode and the explosion followed by collapse of Ancient society.

The progressive nature of Western civilization is indicated by the continuing expansion of the forces of production at each stage of development. The expansion is the result of both capital accumulation and technological change. Each transformation of society brings forces and relations of production that are more efficient in meeting human needs, releasing productive forces that the previous social order held in check. This was true of the transition from Germanic mode to feudalism, from feudalism to capitalism, and will also characterize the transition from capitalism to socialism. And, as Marx insisted, no economic system gives way to another until the elements of progress inherent in it are fully worked out.

However, this history of economic progress was accompanied by growing alienation. Primitive people lived in a social order in which the individual's life activity was embedded fully within an integrated social system. There was no distinction, at this stage, between base and superstructure, between political and economic institutions. Labor, as an economic activity, could not be said to exist at all. Only human action could be identified, in which economic, political, religious, social, and all other aspects of life were inextricably intertwined with each other. The institutional development of the social order ever since this original stage has involved a continuing structural separation of functions. In Marxist terminology, as the forces of production developed, the relations of production (social classes) became more clearly defined, and the differences between economic base and political-ideological superstructure became more distinct. In the process, three crucial changes occurred: The producer was increasingly separated from his product, first by feudal dues and then by market relations; the worker was increasingly separated from the means of production, first by development of feudal relations and then by the rise of private property under capitalism; and distinct social classes emerged in conflict with each other over products and means of production. Industrial capitalism represents the culmination of these trends, with the greatest degree of alienation of producers from products and means of production, and of class conflict. Production for use has been transformed into production for exchange, and an economy in which economic activity was "mediated by" social institutions has been transformed into an exchange economy that dominates other social institutions.

In this schema, economic forces completely determine the historical pattern only in the fully developed industrial economy. In all previous economic formations, economic activity is mediated by other social institutions, thereby reducing the impact of economic forces. As we move backward in time, the significance of these mediating noneconomic institutions increases relative to that of the economic. In primitive society, production and distribution are so intricately embedded in the social fabric that it becomes impossible to define a separate economic sector or to distinguish economic forces from others. By contrast, in the late capitalist era the last of these mediating institutions have been stripped away, the exchange economy dominates the entire social order, and individuals are completely at the mercy of the economic forces of the market. The real meaning of the "economic interpretation of history" is clarified here. In one sense, it is only in fully developed industrial capitalism that economic forces reign supreme, while the role of noneconomic institutions in determining historical events increases as we move backward in time. In another sense, however, it is always true that the driving force of institutional change is the human effort to produce material things from a niggardly natural environment. There is an economic force underlying all social change.

It is within this larger framework of the analysis of institutional change that Marx discusses the origins, development, and ultimate breakdown of capitalism.[22] He describes the rise of the capitalist class and the decline of the feudal nobility, the formation of a system of self-regulating markets, the institutionalization of capital accumulation as an economic process, the emergence of private property out of feudal property relations, and the building of a working class. The theme is the ruthlessness and brutality with which workers were finally separated from control over their tools and the products of their labor and subjected fully to wage labor as the means of obtaining their livelihood.

One subtheme in this discussion is often overlooked: It concerns the interplay between economic base and political superstructure. In the early years of the rise of capitalism, the capitalist class transformed the economic base of society by gaining control over the processes of production. The development of a labor market in which labor power could be bought enabled employers to move work out of the home to shops directly supervised by the employer. Production, hours of work, and all other aspects of the workplace were placed under the direct command of the supervisor.[23] During this period in which capital gained control over labor, capitalists were content with a political alliance with the monarchy that furthered their joint interests in opposition to the feudal nobility—an era of authoritarian central governments in alliance with, but not dominated by, the capitalist class. But once the feudal nobility had been eliminated or reduced to impotence *and* control over the workplace and the working class had been achieved, the capitalist class moved to gain direct control over political institutions in the era of the bourgeois revolutions in England and France. Then the capitalist class was free to complete its revolution by using the power of government to increase its wealth, power, and control over the social order and to exploit the working class more fully. In Marx's analysis there was a multistage economic and social revolution in which the transfer of political power was the penultimate act, preceded by perfection of control over the production unit and a period of political alliance directed against two class enemies.

Even in the industrial era, political economy was no simple matter of natural class alignments; rather, it was a complex pattern of coalitions. For example, in analyzing French politics in the mid-nineteenth century, Marx shows how a political adventurer, Louis Napoleon, was able to put together a coalition of big industry and big finance (whose interests did not always coincide) with small shopkeepers (whose economic interests were in conflict with those of big industry and finance), together with the independent farmer (who had other interests altogether), cementing the whole with psychological appeals to nationalism, religion, and family solidarity. The key interest groups, however, were big industry and finance, which were well served by Louis Napoleon, but the government could not serve those capitalist interests single-mindedly since it had to keep the coalition together by compromise.[24] Thus, Marx pictures the political superstructure as serving the interests of the class that holds the reins of economic power, but not in the single-minded simplistic pattern of "official" Marxism.

Finally, we note Marx's treatment of the forces leading to stability and change. The scheme of simple reproduction developed in *Capital* shows a capitalist economy reproducing itself over time at exactly the same level and mix of output, with no capital accumulation (only replacement of capital used up in production). This was a purely theoretical exercise designed by Marx to show that his analysis of value and production were logically correct; that is, they were consistent with a continuing and viable economy. But capitalism has institutionalized reinvestment of the economic surplus, leading to expanded reproduction. In this part of the analysis Marx defines the conditions necessary for balanced economic growth and shows that they are not possible in a capitalist economy. He also shows, in his treatment of the transformation problem, that prices in a capitalist economy must diverge from values based on inputs of labor time.[25] There are, then, two fundamental contradictions within the operation of a capitalist economy, but Marx explored only one in detail, unbalanced growth.

In Marx's analysis, capital accumulation is institutionalized in the business firm, which exploits its labor to accumulate surplus value and uses the surplus to enlarge its operations. The same forces that drive it to expansion also drive it to substitute capital for labor, so that capital accumulation and technical change go hand in hand. These forces, together with inadequate purchasing power, bring on business cycles of increasing severity, a secular decline in the rate of profit (probably: Marx is not sure of this), a growing reserve army of the unemployed, and polarization of the social order into an ever smaller but increasingly wealthy capitalist class facing a growing and increasingly immiserated working class.[26] These economic trends, analyzed in purely theoretical terms in the three volumes of *Capital*, are modified in the real world by imperialism, labor unions, social legislation, and so forth, which were discussed by Marx in his other writings, for the most part. For our purposes, however, it is important to note that in a capitalist economy the forces for change are economic in nature, related to capital accumulation, and rooted in exploitation of labor, out of which comes class conflict, while the stabilizing forces tend to be found in the political and ideological superstructure.

Marxism can be interpreted from many points of view. Seen in terms of revolutionary politics, it degenerated into the "official" Marxism-Leninism of Soviety ideology. Seen from the vantage point of orthodox economic theory, it was a threat to be fought against, and, since it was based on an objective, cost-oriented theory of value, it could be ignored by theorists interested in developing a subjective theory of price. If we are interested in analyzing the process of institutional change, however, we find in Marxism the only general theory from which to start. Its scope is as broad as the whole history of human society. It asks key questions: What are the chief modes of economic organization? What causes them to retain their basic forms, and what are the tensions within them that produce change? What are the relationships between economic and noneconomic institutions and forces in producing institutional stability and change? How can all of this be applied to an understanding of our own times? How does it affect the welfare and happiness of human beings? The answers to these questions in Marx's writings may be at once sophisticated and crude, fundamental and superficial, broad and limited (this is hardly the place for a thorough-going critique of Marx's accomplishments and limitations), but we should recognize that Marx presented us with a framework within which fall most of the relevant questions.

Max Weber and Karl Polanyi

Many Marxists, particularly the "official" ones, are scornful of the work of non-Marxist scholars, calling it "bourgeois" social science, which, in their schema, is the tool of the capitalist ruling class. This was not Marx's way, at least in his scholarly writings, although he was a polemicist par excellence in his political writings. He quoted extensively from non-Marxist scholars and government research reports. Some contemporary Marxist writers, such as Immanuel Wallerstein, who uses the ideas of non-Marxists such as Karl Polanyi and Fernand Braudel, are less provincial, and the cross-fertilization has been highly significant. Marxist scorn for bourgeois social science is often reciprocated, particularly where the target is official Marxism. For example, Selig Perlman's rejection and critique of Marxism is an attack on the official Marxism of his day.[27]

When Marxists and non-Marxists deal with similar issues, much might be gained by combining ideas. For example, the institutionalists developed the proposition that pecuniary values in a competitive market do not reflect real values, but they have a difficult time defining and quantifying the latter. They are open to criticism from orthodox theorists that the idea of real value is vague, value laden, culture bound, and unscientific; furthermore, the concept of real value cannot be objectively defined or analytically specified. Marx can help here. He showed that prices in a capitalist society diverge from values based on socially necessary labor time. One may wish to disagree with the specifics of Marx's theory on this point, but if the labor theory of value can be generalized to include the cost of production of all inputs, Marx has produced an economic analytic proof of one of the key points in the institutionalist analysis of modern capitalism.

It is also worthwhile to examine the contribution that non-Marxist social scientists can make to the development of a general theory of institutional change. We begin with Max Weber. First, Weber challenged Marx's definition of social class. He argued that any social order has three dimensions, each with its own pattern of stratification. The economic system is stratified according to income, the status system according to rank, and the political system according to control of power. Each of these systems has a different institutional structure and performs different functions within the social order as a whole. Although interrelated, they can be separated both structurally and functionally. Adding a value system underlying and unifying the whole, we arrive at Talcott Parsons's structural-functional theory of the social order.[28]

Weber used this framework to develop the concept of ideal types as a way of defining social and economic systems. The essential elements of a social system can be classified under the three (or four) chief institutional sectors and the distinguishing functional relationships defined. Institutional change can then be analyzed as the way in which one pattern of structural and functional elements gives way to another. Note, however, that this approach uses the method of comparative statics, of movement from one ideal type to another. It may help us analyze the elements in the process of change, but we must be careful not to let it prejudice our understanding of that process. Weber's method has another limitation. One assumption of the ideal type concept is that there is a logical and rational relationship between the various institutional elements of the type, rather than just historical-developmental relationships. But that problem can be resolved through the concept of the "real" type, pioneered by Arthur Speithoff, in which the logic of the purely theoretical structural and functional relationships of the ideal type is modified by chance events and historical development peculiar to any one case of historical change.[29]

Weber's ideal type leaves unresolved such questions as the sources and patterns of institutional change and whether change is evolutionary, developmental, or revolutionary. Weber himself tended to think in terms of nonrevolutionary change, and Parsons's development of Weber's ideas into a full-blown structural-functional theory of society hardly had space for any institutional change at all, although Neil Smelser made a valiant effort to fit the Industrial Revolution and technological change into the model.[30] Weber also puts great stress on ideology and social values in his definition of ideal types, and much of his research on institutional change concerned the religious ideologies of Western Europe and Asia. Weber's studies of religion tended to emphasize the independent or autonomous role of religious belief in institutional change; independent, that is, of economic forces. Ideology was a force to be reckoned as equal to that of the economic.[31]

From the viewpoint of a general analysis of the development of economic institutions, Weber's approach has another serious flaw. In particular, the emergence of a discrete economic sector of society, distinguishable from the political, social, or ideological sectors and carrying out distinctive economic functions, is itself part of the historical development of human society, as Marx, among others, argued. The structural and functional distinctions so clearly seen in modern society by Weber and Parsons are obscured in earlier eras. It is possible, of course, to identify social functions institutionalized in concrete ways in modern society, define them carefully, and then identify those same functions in earlier social systems. But doing that imposes the categories and concepts of modern society on other societies and their economies, fitting them to the Procrustean bed of definitions relevant to us but not necessarily to them. In doing so an ideal or theoretical construct is substituted for the concrete reality.

Karl Polanyi pointed this out. In nonmarket economies, he argued, economic activity is embedded in noneconomic institutions and is at least partly motivated by noneconomic factors.[32] This concept is analogous to Marx's idea that in precapitalist economic systems economic activity is "mediated" by noneconomic institutions, thereby protecting the individual from the full impact of economic forces (and, in so doing, modifying the principle of simple economic determinism). This embeddedness of economic activity in the noneconomic makes it impossible to define a discrete set of economic institutions or to isolate purely economic motives. That is possible only in the modern market economy, a system of self-regulating markets that generates patterns of production and distribution independently of other social institutions. This independence becomes dominance, according to Polanyi, since the very existence of the great majority of families depends on the outcome of market exchanges. In that situation, everything else is subordinated to the dictates of market forces. Polanyi, like Marx, felt that the predominance of economic forces was characteristic of modern society and that it developed over time as part of the process of institutional change.[33]

Polanyi made a second and more important contribution to the analysis of institutional change. Where Marx concentrated on property relations and economic classes to distinguish his types of economic systems, Polanyi focused on patterns of exchange. Reciprocity, redistribution, and market exchange are Polanyi's three ideal types. A fourth type, autarchy (the self-sufficient economic unit, an analog to Marx's Asiatic mode) was abandoned by Polanyi, perhaps prematurely. Following Marcel Mauss,[34] Polanyi argued that reciprocity was the dominant feature of tribal societies, although it was almost always mixed with redistributive elements. Following Richard Thurnwald,[35] he found redistribution the dominant feature of the ancient empires and the African kingdoms. In both cases, market exchange was restricted largely to petty trade in local surpluses, where it was heavily regulated by both custom and political authorities, and to external trade with other social units. In neither case were market forces predominant within the social system itself, where both reciprocity and redistribution were embedded in a variety of social and political institutions.

Thurnwald had pointed out that there were logical stages of development from homogeneous tribal societies based on reciprocity to complex graded societies based on redistribution. From tribe to empire, so to speak. Technological changes were important in that development, particularly the domestication of plants and animals and the emergence of peasant agriculture. But the logic of the development stops with the redistributive empires, which can oscillate between centralized despotisms and decentralized feudalisms (an analog to the political aspect of Marx's Asiatic mode). There does not seem to be any reasonable developmental path to an economy based on market exchange.[36]

Polanyi took up this challenge, exploring the only known case of that transition, Western Europe, and one case of an abortive transition, ancient Greece. He stressed the uniqueness of the transition. Even though the entire civilized world in the fifteenth century, stretching from Western Europe through southern Asia to Japan, had a peasant economy with a variety of feudal and quasi-feudal social forms that enabled an aristocracy to appropriate the surplus, and with a variety of centralized and decentralized political structures, it was only in Western Europe that the transition to a self-adjusting market economy occurred. Why at that time, in that place? What unique concurrence of events put Western Europe on the path to an institutional structure that humankind had never successfully devised? This is perhaps the most intriguing question that the historian can ask about the development of economic institutions.

Polanyi's chief contribution, however, was further development of

Marx's idea that the rise of market institutions had brought economic forces to dominate the entire social order and complete the institutional separation between base and superstructure. The formation of a market economy in Western Europe, accompanying the rise of capitalism, transformed labor, land, and money into commodities. These elements in the economy were not commodities in nonmarket economies, but part of the continuing life of people and the social order. Even money was used as part of the social structure oriented toward subsistence, survival, and continuity and was a secondary element in nonmarket economies. These "natural" relationships were disrupted by the artificial imposition of a system of competitive self-adjusting markets upon the social order in the eighteenth and nineteenth century after an earlier era of gestation from about 1450 to 1700. In the case of labor, the last element to yield to the self-adjusting market, the price of the transformation was immiseration and poverty for the great majority. Land, likewise, was transformed into a commodity through a long and slow process of legal changes (the rise of private property) and the agricultural revolutions. In the monetary system, the international gold standard enabled the self-adjusting market to reflect patterns of international trade.

Inclusion of land, labor, and money in the system of markets transformed the economy into the dominant institutional structure of society. All aspects of the social order were subjected to use and disposition according to the dictates of cost, demand, and relative prices. As a result, all other social institutions—family, religion, political structures—were fitted into the needs of the market. In particular, the survival, welfare, and development of individuals were subjected to market forces.

Polanyi did not use Marx's term, *alienation,* but did use the concept. Economic life embedded in family, clan, and tribal organization, characteristic of patterns of reciprocity and redistribution, met a social need that could not be met through market exchange. Reciprocity and redistribution stress mutually supportive human relationships, not economic gain, and they reinforce the protective framework of the social structure, while the rivalry and competition of market exchange are essentially hostile in nature and disruptive of the social fabric. The birth of market economy meant the death of society.

Polanyi also argued that the growth of government intervention in the economy from the second half of the nineteenth century onward was a reaction against the breakup of those social institutions that stand between individuals and market forces. The poverty, economic instability, and other problems created for people by the market economy no longer were "mediated" (to use Marx's term) by the social institutions in which economic activity had formerly been "embedded" (to use Polanyi's term). However, government intervention to ameliorate the human problems of the market economy interfered with the processes of market adjustment and prevented the economy from functioning effectively. The failures of the market economy brought a breakdown in the international financial system, setting in motion the age of imperialism, world wars, and fascism. Polanyi sees modern capitalism developing into a crisis, a social revolutionary situation, but the path to it is different from the path of class struggle driven by capital accumulation as described by Marx in *Capital*. Rather, the rise of an exchange economy and the growth of alienation— themes developed by Marx in *Precapitalist Economic Formations* and the *Grundrisse*—are at the root of the crisis.

Polanyi's work is valuable from another point of view. His categories of economic modes—reciprocity, redistribution, and market exchange— make possible the definition of real economic types subject to investigation by anthropologists, historians, and economists. Each economic mode was connected with particular types of social institutions—reciprocity with duality in social relations, redistribution with centricity, and market exchange with the institutions of the self-adjusting market economy. This schema defined a set of institutional relationships to be explored in detail. Pursuing this line of reasoning, a group of real economic types emerges. The simplest form is tribal society, characterized by reciprocity and redistribution and a pattern of economic life deeply embedded in kinship, religious, and other social institutions. The second is peasant society. We know of some peasant societies of independent agricultural villages, but the great majority are characterized by dependent agricultural villages ruled by an aristocracy that uses a variety of devices to extract a surplus from the peasant farmers.[37] The surplus is then used to trade for luxury products, enabling most peasant societies to support urban manufacturing and trade, which can develop as "capitalist islands in a non-capitalist world," to use Eileen Powers's felicitous characterization of medieval cities.[38] These societies can develop as feudalisms or as centralized monarchies. It was out of one complex peasant society that Western Europe began to develop modern capitalism, which is the third major type. This historical sequence is similar to Marx's postulated sequence of primitive society–Germanic mode–feudalism–capitalism, but it has a worldwide scope and, with some modification, could include Marx's Asiatic and Ancient modes in a unified sequence. Whether such a schema is too broad to encompass the great variety of economic patterns characteristic of human social organization, even if a variety of subtypes is postulated, remains to be seen.

Tawney, Moore, and Wallerstein

We have explored the central core of the problem of the development of economic institutions, namely, the definition and sequence of types of economic systems. We turn now to a second problem that has occupied the attention of theoreticians: the relationship between changes in economic institutions, on the one hand, and changes in the ideological and political superstructure, on the other. We use the Marxist concept here, but only for convenience, raising the question rather than assuming any pattern of cause and effect.

Richard H. Tawney developed perhaps the most sophisticated analysis of the relationship between religious ideology and economic institutions. His *Religion and the Rise of Capitalism* is written at three different levels:[39] It is a polemic against the role of religion and religious ethics in twentieth-century capitalist society; it is a detailed historical study of the relationship between religious thought and economic life in early capitalist England; and it contains an implicit theoretical framework for analyzing relationships between the economic base and ideological aspects of the superstructure. This theoretic aspect of Tawney's work has hardly been commented on, so it will be useful to outline his schema.

First, he defined the field of inquiry and the relationships prevailing within the field, in this case the medieval economy with its social classes, ideology, and relationships between them. Since religious ideology is the main topic, it is placed in a central position in the field, and relationships are sketched between it and other institutional structures. Second, the field of inquiry is set in motion by examining forces within the socioeconomic system that induced change, along with forces operating upon the society from outside: endogenous and exogenous forces promoting change, so to speak. Third, the crucial changes are those that involve social classes, in this case the rise of the merchant capitalist and banker and the decline of the feudal nobility. Coalitions are important also, particularly the political alliance between commercial and banking interests and the kings. Fourth, the interests of the rising social classes require support and rationalization in the realm of ideology, social philosophy, and ethics. The result is the emergence of a new ethic that explains and justifies the newly emerging social order. Ultimately, a new constellation of economic relations, social classes, and ideology appears.

In the specific case of the rise of a Protestant ethic in early modern times, Tawney documented a complex pattern. The Catholic Church attempted to adapt its ideology to the needs of the emerging capitalist class, without changing the fundamental propositions that were in conflict with capitalist goals. This compromise produced a reaction from religious conservatives, led by Martin Luther, who wished to go back to ideological fundamentals. The conservatives obtained the political support of local interests opposed to the centralization of religious authority (and finance) in Rome, as well as the support of rulers opposed to papal claims of temporal authority. The new religious conservatism was modified by John Calvin in a manner highly useful to urban commercial interests, and it was this reformed ethic that became the basis for the new ideology. The ethical foundations of the new economic order emerged out of a complex pattern of historical change that involved interrelationships between economic institutions, social classes, political institutions, and ideologies. The changes in religion did not follow the simple line of a new social class bringing with it a new ethic; rather, the pattern of change was one of mutual and interrelated causation between economic base and political-ideological superstructure.

Nevertheless, Tawney is in the tradition of economic determinism: Every economic system, with its classes and property relations, develops an ethic that serves to justify the system. This was the basic point in Tawney's polemic against modern Protestantism: It sought to justify an unjust economic system.

Barrington Moore, Jr., explored a different aspect of base-superstructure relationships.[40] He was concerned with political aspects of modernization: why political democracy developed with modern capitalism and industrialization in England, France, and the United States and why modernization brought authoritarian governments in Germany, Russia, Japan, and China. Three paths to modernization were defined: capitalism plus parliamentary democracy; capitalism with reactionary authoritarian government culminating in fascism; and communism based on peasant revolution. The starting point of all three was essentially the same, a peasant society with an aristocracy that appropriated the surplus, together with an urban-commercial sector. The outcomes differed largely because of the accommodations made by the agricultural system to the forces of economic change and the political alliances made among the chief interest groups: aristocracy, rulers, commercial interests, and farmers. Moore's great insight was that the political institutions of modern society resulted not only from the rise of new social classes and class conflict, but also from the accommodation the new classes made with the chief economic and political interests of the earlier social order, particularly the landed aristocracy and peasants.

The peasantry could be transformed into commercial farmers (England) or coerced in ways that allowed the aristocracy to continue extracting a surplus (Eastern Europe and Russia). The aristocracy might transform its estates into large commercial farms (England) or plantations (southern United States) or remain essentially feudal (eastern Germany and Russia). Depending on the economic transformations that occurred in agriculture, the agricultural classes entered the political economy of a modernizing nation in a variety of ways, which heavily affected the ultimate political pattern after modernization. Moore argues, for example, that before the English Civil War the commercial interests of the landed and urban upper classes converged "in such a way as to favor the cause of freedom." In Germany, however, these classes remained in conflict, enabling the ruler to play them off against each other and establish the authoritarian pattern that was ultimately to develop into twentieth-century fascism.

In this century Russia and China entered the modernizing process with economies based on peasant agriculture. These countries lacked a commercial revolution in agriculture, leaving the peasant economy to bear the burden of the stresses and strains of the modern era, while the landlords continued to extract the economic surplus. In both countries a Marxist revolutionary movement was able to unite rural and urban discontent around the communist ideology and achieve political power.

The great weakness of Moore's analysis is lack of a comprehensive theoretical framework on which to base his treatment of the relationships between politics and economics. This leads him to derive generalizations by finding similarities among specific cases of comparable phenomena, a procedure that depends very heavily on individual judgment and a persuasive literary style, and that inevitably leads to disagreement. For example, his treatment of the role of the landed aristocracy in the creation of German authoritarianism pales by comparison with that of Theodore S. Hamerow, who uses a far more sophisticated theory of base-superstructure relationships.[41] In particular, Moore fails to take adequately into account the international economic and political forces at work in his analysis of Western European, Russian, and Chinese developments. The international position of Germany was crucial to the formation of the modern German political economy, as Hamerow makes clear. And the position of Russia and China in an imperialist world system was a major influence on the peasant revolts there, as pointed out by Eric Wolf.[42] The sophisticated accounts of German political economy and twentieth-century peasant revolutions are to be found in Hamerow and Wolf, not Moore. Nevertheless, Moore isolated an important factor in the political economy of the transition to capitalism: The form taken by political institutions and the structure of power depended very heavily on the manner in which agriculture was brought into the emerging industrial capitalist order.

Immanuel Wallerstein deals with many of the same issues as Moore, but with a more sophisticated analytical approach derived heavily from Marx, and influences from Karl Polanyi and Fernand Braudel. Wallerstein's *The Modern World-System* examines the origins of capitalism out of European feudalism, concentrating on the role of the state in the transition.[43] Following Braudel, he develops the idea that European feudalism was in a crisis in the mid-fifteenth century: diminishing returns in appropriation of the economic surplus of peasant agriculture, a cyclical contraction related to the failure of technology to improve, reduced agricultural productivity related to changes in climate, and epidemics that decimated the productive population. The crisis was overcome by the overseas expansion of Europe, which provided a tremendous opportunity for gain on the part of the proto-capitalist urban sector of the feudal economy. A new "world system" was in the process of creation, made possible by geographical expansion, the development of a variety of methods of labor control, and the emergence of the national state. All three were essential elements in the new system.

A worldwide pattern of core, semiperiphery, and periphery characterizes the modern world system, an idea also derived from Braudel.[44] In the core, the capitalist nations of Western Europe, the characteristic form of labor control was the wage system of market exchange; in the semiperiphery, the former core states of Spain and Portugal as well as Italy, sharecropping was the form of labor control; in the periphery of Hispanic America and eastern Europe, coerced labor was the rule: slavery, debt tenure, and related forms of coercion. The core states were the centers of commerce, finance, and manufacturing, with regional subcenters in the semiperiphery that were only partially independent of the core, at best. Production tended to be more capital intensive in the core, more labor intensive as it emerged in the semiperiphery. The core states developed strong, well-organized central governments that successfully helped national economic groups to further their own interests *vis-à-vis* the two outer rings. In particular, the capitalist interests of the core states were able to promote the development of strong national governments and then use these to protect and extend their own interests at home and abroad. A symbiotic relationship between capitalist class and national state was crucial to the development of the new world system. Extraction of the economic surplus, and its use in expanding economic activity—what we have called institutionalization of capital accumulation—is seen by Wallerstein as a joint effort on the part of capitalist enterprise and the national state.

The core countries perfected this pattern early on, the semiperipheral states only imperfectly, and the periphery never had a chance to do so because of domination by the core.

But the role of the state was limited. One of Wallerstein's most important insights was that the success of the capitalist world system was facilitated by the dispersal of political power among numerous national states. There was no single political structure to rule over the whole. This left the economic appropriation of surplus through the market largely free of political control and limited the ability of the state to appropriate the surplus through taxation. For example, the coerced labor of the periphery produced a surplus appropriated by capitalists of the core (and semiperiphery) and not by national states. Capital accumulation was therefore channeled primarily into economic expansion rather than political aggrandizement. The national state was the handmaiden of capitalism, but could not develop into the parasitic authoritarianism of the precapitalist world systems.

Wallerstein makes several other important contributions. Even in its early stages the emergence of the capitalist world system should be looked at as a whole, not merely as a phenomenon developing in the core. The structure of core, semiperiphery, and periphery was there from the very beginning and did not develop only in the period of imperialism in the nineteenth and twentieth century. Second, the working class was fractionated from the start, and not only by the development of modern technology and methods of management. Free, semifree, and coerced labor was part of the system from the start. Third, the special role of the national state was crucial: strong enough to promote the development of the new economy, but not extensive or strong enough to interfere significantly with private accumulation of capital.

Conclusions

Some general observations about the development of economic institutions are now in order. First, economic institutions are part of a larger social structure in which all the parts are related to each other. Any meaningful inquiry into one portion, such as the economic, must therefore be based on a general theory of social structure or social organization. Second, since we are interested in development and change, the general theory should not be essentially static in nature, but should have a dynamic of change built into the analytical structure itself. Third, the analysis of change embodied in the underlying theory should not prejudice the conclusions by excluding either evolutionary (gradual) or revolutionary (sudden and comprehensive) change. Fourth, the theory should be general enough to encompass the full range of known types of social organization, while at the same time specific enough to analyze concrete historic situations such as the origins of modern capitalism or changes in the structure of the modern industrial economy. Finally, the theoretical framework should encompass both continuous, self-generating or self-sustaining processes of change as well as the comparative statics of movement from one equilibrium situation to another implied by the use of concepts of ideal or real types.

Needless to say, no existing theory fully satisfies all of these requirements. Marx's framework of analysis certainly comes close, and in some respects at least it partially satisfies all of the requirements listed above. Its chief drawback is that it is very commonly misunderstood because of its narrow and rigid use in the "official" Marxist variant. A first task is to strip away those aspects of the theory, for example, the "official" Marxist postulate that all change is the result of class conflict. In the more sophisticated analysis of Marx himself, that proposition is seen as a tremendous oversimplification, at best, even under the conditions of developed industrial capitalism.

Marx's theoretical framework has some other difficulties. His writings are in the tradition of the enlightenment of the eighteenth century in that he sees a pattern of long-run progress in the human condition. This emphasis is built into the theoretical analysis: It is presumed that people seek a better way of life, material betterment, ease. The need for subsistence and a continuation of the social order is at the root of the drive toward betterment, and it is essentially economic in nature, since it rests on the economic activity of production of material things. The progress of society as a whole rests on the progress of the economy. Progress, in Marx's analysis, also has psychological and ideological foundations. People have the intellectual capacity to understand their relationship to the physical world, enabling them to make a conscious effort to remake the world to benefit themselves. Technological and scientific progress is rooted in this consciousness of people-nature relationships. We find here an ingenious combination of economic and ideological variables, although both are based on the material condition of people in their everyday lives. However, to the twentieth-century mind there appears to be too much emphasis on purposive human action, too much determinism in the result. Where does random action, idle curiosity, or pure chance fit into the analysis? If we start with the Marxist model, a modern investigator might wish to modify it to account more fully for those aspects of reality.

The starting point of Marx's analysis prejudices the conclusions. If the progress of society is rooted in the human need for subsistence and the desire for greater ease, if scarcity of material things is the source of human progress, change will stop and progress will cease when full economic abundance is achieved. Furthermore, abundance brings an end to conflict among people, and a harmonious society without the conflict that leads to change will ultimately develop, presumably some form of communal society. This teleology is also difficult for the modern social scientist to accept. If we use the Marxist model, can it be modified to drop its implications of a final term, embodying instead a process of continuing and unending change, while still retaining its highly useful analytical framework?

Those modifications can probably be made. One starting point might be the findings of modern dynamic psychology that a certain amount of human behavior is not purposive but random and exploratory, seeking new experience as an end in itself. A second possibility is to build chance events into the basic theoretical framework. Some Marxist scholars and philosophers are already engaged in these inquiries.

Marx was not the only scholar to define the chief problem that motivates analysis of the development of economic institutions. The central issue concerns the origins, development, and future of the modern industrial economy. The entire inquiry focuses on the present problems and future possibilities of modern society. Estimation of future prospects requires understanding of the present, which rests upon knowledge of how the present came to be. If we think of the present as a point in space and time, we can examine the past in terms of how a variety of processes and forces combined to produce the present situation. The present, in turn, contains within itself a variety of paths into the future, some of which are more probable or more feasible than others. This continuum connecting the past with the future identifies the development process.

At this point Marx's Hegelian background makes an important contribution. The forces of the past that have produced the present cannot be understood fully until we know what their impact on the future will be. A simple illustration: Our understanding of the New Deal era is better in 1977 than it was in, say, 1940 because we are able to perceive some of the effects that had not yet happened. Our understanding of the past unfolds and deepens as events themselves occur; that understanding must always be incomplete and tentative; knowledge itself is part of the unfolding and development of our social system and can never be complete.

Another contribution of the Marxian approach is the proposition that the principles of institutional change themselves may change over time. An assessment of the forces leading to change and those promoting stability in the modern industrial economy may take into account the forces

unleashed by capital accumulation and technological change, clashes between social classes or other economic interest groups, the role of government and ideology, and the other chief variables discussed in the earlier
parts of this article. Will those forces and their relationships be similar to
the ones that are found in a precapitalist society of peasant farmers dominated by an aristocracy, or in a tribal society organized around reciprocity
and redistribution? Marx's analysis as well as Polanyi's suggest that they
will not, that the specific model of change and the relationships between
variables that are appropriate for a fully developed industrial society may
be different from the model and relationships appropriate to another type
of economic system. Change in economic institutions involves alterations
in the process of change itself, as well as in the institutions.

That proposition is implied by the shifting relationship of economic and
noneconomic institutions within the social system. In a tribal society, in
which economic activity is heavily embedded in noneconomic institutions
and economic relationships between people are heavily mediated by noneconomic social relations, it is difficult and perhaps impossible to isolate
changes in the purely economic aspects of society. However, as the market
economy emerges in the modern world, it becomes easier to isolate and
identify that part of the institutional structure that can be termed economic. The presence of economic activity (production and distribution of
useful things and services) does not necessarily mean the presence of
economic institutions. The emergence of economic institutions within the
total institutional structure of society is itself a part of the process to be
studied.

We return then to our starting point. We can define the term *economic
institutions* fairly readily in the case of the modern industrial economy
and can analyze relationships between the economic base and the "noneconomic" superstructure. But those institutions and relationships are the
product of an historical process in which the economic activities of the
social order are institutionalized separately from other aspects of human
activity. In this way, the subject of our inquiry emerges out of the inquiry
itself.

Notes

1. Adam Smith, *An Enquiry into the Nature and Causes of the Wealth of
   Nations* (New York: Modern Library, 1937 [1776]). Smith's discussion
   of the institutional framework of the economy is to be found chiefly
   in Book III, "Of the different Progress of Opulence in different Nations," Book IV, "Of Systems of Political Economy," and Book V, "Of
   the Revenue of the Sovereign or Commonwealth." Friedrich List, *The*

National System of Political Economy (London: Longmans, Green, 1928 [1841–1844]), particularly chapters 11–15. John Stuart Mill, *Principles of Political Economy*, 5th ed. (New York: Appleton, 1895 [1847]); the chief institutional material is in Mill's discussion of income distribution, Book II, chapters 1–10, and Book IV, "Influence of the Progress of Society on Production and Distribution," chapters 1–7. Mill is one of the few classical economists who discussed at length the effect of changes in the institutional framework on the processes of capital accumulation and technological change.

2. David Ricardo, *On the Principles of Political Economy and Taxation*, edited by Piero Sraffa (Cambridge: the University Press 1953), particularly chapter 21, in which Ricardo sketches his stationary state. Mill, *Principles*, has a more complete statement in Book IV.

3. Recent work on economic growth by James Meade, Robert Solow, Edmund Phelps, and others shows how the neoclassical model can be set in motion. General equilibrium theory as developed by Kenneth Arrow, Gerard Debreu, and Edmund Malinvaud introduces time into the model by considering a good purchased at different times as different goods: this assumption reduces all of the variables in the system to relative prices. Both of these efforts to introduce dynamics into the theory retain the simplifying assumption that the institutional structure consists only of a system of self-adjusting markets that does not change as a result of either economic adjustments or growth. The assumption of constant costs is therefore essential to these models. The critique of capital theory by the Cambridge school, particularly by Piero Sraffa, Joan Robinson, and Luigi Pasinetti, has shown that neither of these approaches has a valid theory of production, leaving the theory of exchange hanging in metaphysical space. The goods that are exchanged cannot be shown to have been produced; and since the incomes spent in markets are based on production, even the theory of exchange is not logically complete.

4. Joseph Schumpeter, *The Theory of Economic Development: An Inquiry into Profits, Capital, Credit, Interest and the Business Cycle* (Cambridge, Mass.: Harvard University Press, 1934), *Business Cycles: A Theoretical, Historical and Statistical Analysis of the Capitalist Process* (New York: McGraw-Hill, 1939), and *Capitalism, Socialism and Democracy*, 3d ed. (New York: Harper, 1952 [1942]).

5. Lance E. Davis and Douglass C. North, *Institutional Change and American Economic Growth* (Cambridge: the University Press, 1971), chapters 1–4.

6. Douglass C. North and Robert Paul Thomas, "The Rise and Fall of the Manorial System: A Theoretical Model," *Journal of Economic History* 31 (December 1971): 777–803, and *The Rise of the Western World: A New Economic History* (Cambridge: the University Press, 1973).

7. Walter Bagehot, "The Postulates of English Political Economy" and "The Preliminaries of Political Economy," in *Economic Studies* (London: Longmans Green, 1879); and Arnold Toynebee, *Lectures on the Industrial Revolution in England* (London: Rivingtons, 1884).

8. The only systematic treatise of the German historical school that has

been translated into English is Wilhelm Roscher, *Principles of Political Economy* (New York: Henry Holt, 1878), which consists of the first two volumes of his *System der Volkswirtschaft* (Stuttgart: J. G. Cotta, 1864–1903, 5 vols. in 6). Other important works include Friedrich von Hermann, *Staatswirtschaftliche Untersuchungen über Vermogen, Wirtschaft, Productivität der Arbeiten, Kapital, Preis, Gewinn, Einkomen und Verbrauch* (Munich: A. Weber, 1832), which contains a remarkably modern bargaining theory of wages; Bruno Hildebrand, *Die Nationalökonomie der Gegenwart und Zukunft* (Frankfurt am Main: J. Rutten, 1848); and Karl Knies, *Die Politische Oekonomie vom Standpunkte der Gegenschichtlichen Methode* (Braunschweig: C. S. Schwetschke, 1853), which makes the case for an historical approach to economics without developing an analytical framework for such an approach.

9. Typical of the detailed studies of the later historical school in Germany were monographs by Gustav Schmoller on German economic history, Adolf Wagner on public finance, Ludwig Brentano on labor, and Georg F. Knapp on money and agriculture. Their students produced numerous monographs on public policy issues such as the social insurance system that the German government developed in the late nineteenth century. In this respect, the German historical school went down a path to be followed later by the American institutionalists, moving from general treatises to applied studies. Only Schmoller tried to construct a general treatise based on historical studies, his *Grundriss der Allgemeinen Volkswirtschaftslehre* (Leipzig: Duncker and Humblot, 1901 and 1904, 2 vols.). Much interesting work was done on the development of capitalism by Karl Bucher, Richard Ehrenberg, Jakob Streider, and Werner Sombart, among others, but they did not contribute significantly to a general theory of institutional change. Max Weber, *General Economic History* (London: Allen and Unwin, n.d.) went back to the beginnings made by the older school, searching for a broader approach, but that book is a summary of lectures based on student notes, with all the limitations such a book has.

10. Henry Sumner Maine, *Ancient Law: Its Connection with the Early History of Society and Its Relation to Modern Ideas* (London: Oxford University Press, 1931 [1861]), p. 141, italics in the original. Two other works by Maine fill out the empirical basis of his argument: *Village-Communities in the East and West* (1871) and *Lectures on the Early History of Institutions* (1875).

11. Ferdinand Tönnies, *Community and Society* (East Lansing: Michigan State University Press, 1957 [1887]).

12. Henry Carter Adams, *Relation of the State to Industrial Action and Jurisprudence* (New York: Columbia University Press, 1954 [1887 and 1897]).

13. Richard T. Ely, *Property and Contract in Their Relations to the Distribution of Wealth* (Port Washington, N. Y.: Kennikat Press, 1971 [1914]).

14. Excellent summaries of the ideas of Veblen, Commons, and Ayres, along with other institutionalists, are found in Allen G. Gruchy, *Modern*

Economic Thought: The American Contribution (New York: Prentice Hall, 1947) and *Contemporary Economic Thought: The Contribution of Neo-Institutionalist Economics* (Clifton, N. J.: Augustus M. Kelley, 1972). The chief works of the institutionalists related to the discussion in this essay are noted below. Thorstein Veblen, *The Place of Science in Modern Civilization and Other Essays* (New York: B. W. Huebsch, 1919), *The Theory of the Leisure Class* (New York: Macmillan, 1899), *The Theory of Business Enterprise* (New York: Charles Scribner's Sons, 1904), *The Instinct of Workmanship and the State of the Industrial Arts* (New York: B. W. Huebsch, 1918), *The Vested Interests and the Common Man* (New York: B. W. Huebsch, 1919), and *The Engineers and the Price System* (New York: B. W. Huebsch, 1921); John R. Commons, *Legal Foundations of Capitalism* (New York: Macmillan, 1924), *Institutional Economics: Its Place in Political Economy* (New York: Macmillan, 1934), and *The Economics of Collective Action* (New York: Macmillan, 1950); and Clarence E. Ayres, *The Theory of Economic Progress* (Chapel Hill: University of North Carolina Press, 1944), and *The Industrial Economy* (Boston: Houghton Mifflin, 1952).

15. In *Theory of Business Enterprise* (1904) Veblen suggests that an authoritarian military regime is the fate of capitalism, although he does not close the door to socialism. By the time he wrote *Engineers and the Price System* (1921), planning by technical experts was the expected result.

16. Both may have been correct, Commons for New Deal America and Veblen for fascist Europe, although it is by no means clear after the Nixon administration that Veblen's pattern may not develop in the United States as well. Seen in retrospect, Veblen and Commons may have defined best the chief alternatives open to modern society.

17. The classic statements of the Marxist theory of historical materialism are Karl Marx, *A Contribution to the Critique of Political Economy* (Chicago: Charles Kerr, 1904 [1859]), "Introduction"; Karl Marx and Friedrich Engels, *The German Ideology* (New York: International Publishers, 1947), Part I, "Feuerbach: Opposition of the Materialistic and Idealistic Outlook"; and Friedrich Engels, *On Historical Materialism* (New York: International Publishers, 1940 [1878]). The Engels essay already starts the reduction of the theory that culminated in contemporary "official" Marxism.

18. Marx's writings on French politics in the nineteenth century show how the working class builds its own patterns of class action and political structures out of the hurly-burly of class conflict. See *The Class Struggles in France* (New York: International Publishers, n.d.), *The Eighteenth Brumaire of Louis Bonaparte* (ibid.), and *The Civil War in France* (ibid., 1940).

19. The classic case study is Edward P. Thompson, *The Making of the English Working Class* (London: Gollancz, 1963).

20. Marx, *Eighteenth Brumaire*, p. 13.

21. Karl Marx, *Pre-Capitalist Economic Formation* (London: Lawrence and Wishart, 1964), and *Grundrisse* (New York: Random House, 1973).

22. Karl Marx, *Capital: A Critical Analysis of Capitalist Production* (Moscow: Foreign Languages Publishing House, n.d. [1869]), vol. I, Part VIII, "The So-Called Primitive Accumulation."

23. Some recent writings reemphasize the importance of control over the workplace as a central objective of the capitalist enterprise. See Stephen A. Marglin, "What Do Bosses Do? The Origins and Functions of Hierarchy in Capitalist Production," *Review of Radical Political Economics* 6 (Summer 1974): 60–112; and Harry Braverman, *Labor and Monopoly Capital:The Degradation of Work in the Twentieth Century* (New York: Monthly Review Press, 1974), especially chapters 1–6.

24. Marx, *Class Struggles in France* and *Eighteenth Brumaire.*

25. Marx, *Capital,* vol. 1, chapter 19, "The Transformation of the Value (and Respectively the Price) of Labour-Power into Wages," Part VII, "The Accumulation of Capital," vol. 2, chapter 20, "Simple Reproduction" and chapter 21, "Accumulation and Reproduction on an Extended Scale," and vol. 3, Part II, "Conversion of Profit into Average Profit." In the voluminous literature on the transformation problem, the point made here, that in a capitalist economy prices must diverge from values, has gone almost unnoticed as theoreticians tried to correct Marx in order to eliminate the disparity.

26. Marx, *Capital,* vol. 1, Part VII, "The Accumulation of Capital," and vol. 3, Part III, "The Law of the Tendency of the Rate of Profit to Fall."

27. A. L. Riesch Owen, *Selig Perlman's Lectures on Capitalism and Socialism* (Madison: University of Wisconsin Press, 1976).

28. Max Weber, *From Max Weber: Essays in Sociology* (New York: Oxford University Press, 1946), pp. 180–244, and *The Theory of Social and Economic Organization* (ibid., 1947), pp. 424–30; and Talcott Parsons, *The Social System* (Glencoe, Ill.: Free Press, 1951), especially chapters 3–5.

29. The best presentation of Weber's theory of ideal types is his own application of it in *The Protestant Ethic and the Spirit of Capitalism* (London: Allen and Unwin, 1930); the theory is developed in J.E.T. Eldridge, ed., *Max Weber: The Interpretation of Social Reality* (New York: Scribner, 1975). On real types see Arthur Speithoff, "Pure Theory and Economic Gestalt Theory: Ideal Types and Real Types," in Frederic C. Lane and Jelle C. Riemersma, eds., *Enterprise and Secular Change: Readings in Economic History* (Homewood, Ill.: Richard D. Irwin, 1953), pp. 444–63.

30. Neil J. Smelser, *Social Change in the Industrial Revolution: An Application of Theory to the British Cotton Industry* (Chicago: University of Chicago Press, 1959). The effort to graft change onto the static Parsons model is found in Parsons, *Social Systems,* chapter 11, "The Processes of Change in Social Systems"; Talcott Parsons and Neil J. Smelser, *Economy and Society* (New York: Free Press, 1956), chapter 5; and Neil J. Smelser, *The Sociology of Economic Life,* 2d ed. (Englewood Cliffs, N. J.: Prentice-Hall, 1976), chapter 5.

31. Weber, *Protestant Ethic, Ancient Judaism* (Glencoe, Ill.: Free Press, 1952), *The Religion of China: Confucianism and Taoism* (ibid., 1951), *The Religion of India: The Sociology of Hinduism and Buddhism* (ibid.,

1958), and *The Sociology of Religion* (Boston: Beacon Press, 1963).

32. Karl Polanyi, "Our Obsolete Market Mentality," in *Primitive, Archaic and Modern Economies: Essays of Karl Polanyi,* edited by George Dalton (Garden City, N. Y.: Doubleday, 1968), pp. 59–77.

33. Karl Polanyi, C. M. Arensberg, and H. W. Pearson, "The Place of Economies in Societies," in ibid., pp. 116–38.

34. Marcel Mauss, *The Gift: Forms and Functions of Exchange in Archaic Societies* (Glencoe, Ill.: Free Press, 1954).

35. Richard Thurnwald. "Staat und Wirtschaft im alten Aegypten," *Zeitschrift für Sozialwissenschaft* 4 (1901), and "Staat und Wirtschaft in Babylon zu Hammurabis Zeit," *Jahrbücher für Nationalökonomie und Statistik* 26–27 (1903–1904).

36. Richard Thurnwald, *Economics in Primitive Communities* (London: Oxford University Press, 1932), pp. 59–104 and 289–98.

37. Karl Polanyi, *The Great Transformation* (New York: Farrar and Rinehart, 1944), "The Self-Regulating Market and the Ficticious Commodities: Land, Labor and Money," in Dalton, ed., *Essays,* pp. 26–37, and "The Economy as Instituted Process," in ibid., pp. 139–74.

38. Eileen Power, *The Wool Trade in English Medieval History* (London: Oxford University Press, 1941), p. 4.

39. Richard H. Tawney, *Religion and the Rise of Capitalism* (New York: Harcourt Brace, 1926). For further studies of the relationship between the Protestant reformation and the origins of capitalism see Weber, *Religion and the Rise of Capitalism,* and the bibliographies in Tawney's study and in Robert W. Green, ed., *Protestantism and Capitalism: The Weber Thesis and Its Critics* (Boston: D. C. Heath, 1959). Kurt Samuelsson, *Religion and Economic Action: A Critique of Max Weber* (New York: Basic Books, 1961), rightly puts the problem into the framework of general processes of historical change rather than a simple relationship between religion and economy. That is exactly what Tawney did, but his general theory, not stated explicitly in his book, has gone unnoticed.

40. Barrington Moore, Jr., *Social Origins of Dictatorship and Democracy: Lord and Peasant in the Making of the Modern World* (Boston: Beacon Press, 1967).

41. Theodore S. Hamerow, *Restoration, Revolution, Reaction: Economics and Politics in Germany, 1815–1871* (Princeton, N. J.: Princeton University Press, 1958), and *The Social Foundations of German Unification, 1858–1871* (ibid., 1969).

42. Eric R. Wolf, *Peasant Wars of the Twentieth Century* (New York: Harper and Row, 1969).

43. Immanuel Wallerstein, *The Modern World-System: Capitalist Agriculture and the Origins of the European World-Economy in the Sixteenth Century* (New York: Academic Press, 1974).

44. Fernand Braudel, *The Mediterranean in the Age of Philip II* (New York: Harper and Row, 1973), and "European Expansion and Capitalism: 1450–1650," in *Chapters in Western Civilization,* 3d ed. (New York: Columbia University Press, 1966), vol. 1. Braudel develops the idea of world system with core, semiperiphery, and periphery. He also stresses the

role of natural resources and environment in limiting change and stabilizing the economic base of the social order, which suggests that changing science and technology, which tends to free the economy from reliance on the natural order, is a key element in the process of institutional change.

[14]

Jei JOURNAL OF ECONOMIC ISSUES
Vol. XI   No. 4   December 1977

An Institutionalist View of
Development Economics

Philip A. Klein

By common assent, the most significant visible impact of American institutionalism has been in the field of what is now called development economics.[1] This relatively favorable assessment of the influence of institutionalism in this increasingly important field is in rather considerable contrast to the prevailing impression concerning the impact of institutionalism on economics generally. Paul Samuelson, in his elementary text, dismisses it with the comment that, "although Veblen and the Institutionalists had some followers in American academic life . . . 40 years ago Institutionalism withered away as an effective counterforce in economics."[2]

It will be the argument of this article that despite the denial of the validity and/or relevance and usefulness of much of what institutionalism has to offer economics generally, in the field of development economics the victory has been so complete that many economists fail to realize it or to credit institutionalists with contributing any part of the current analytical framework of development economics. This failure has wider implications as well.

The author is Professor of Economics, The Pennsylvania State University, University Park. He wishes to thank his colleague, Professor Warren C. Robinson, for his helpful comments.

Modern Origins of Economic Development

There are references to economic development throughout post–Adam Smith economics, but customarily economists tend to date its modern incarnation to the days of reconstruction following World War II, when there was much ferment in the Third World and "what to do about the backward nations" was a popular topic for economic debate. At that time development usually referred to the quest by countries with low per capita levels of income to raise their levels. Thus, an early Samuelson definition: "An underdeveloped nation is simply one with real per capita income that is low relative to the present-day per capita incomes of such nations as Canada, the United States, Great Britain, France, and Western Europe generally. Usually an underdeveloped nation is one regarded as being capable of substantial improvement in its income level."[3]

Except that "underdeveloped" is now renamed "less developed," the definition is substantially unchanged in the tenth (1976) edition. Earlier basic texts, of course, ignored the subject.[4] Therefore, while mainstream economics has had the problem of economic development in its modern form pushed to its attention for more than a quarter century, it early dealt with the subject with some confusion, which institutionalists should be able to explain. Simon Kuznets indicated the nature of the confusion a decade ago when he suggested that underdevelopment can signify (1) "failure to utilize fully the productive potential warranted by the existing state of technical knowledge—a failure resulting from the resistance of social institutions"; (2) "the backwardness of economic performance compared with a few leading countries"; and (3) "economic poverty in the sense of failure to assure subsistence and material comfort to most of the country's population."[5] As Kuznets correctly points out, the first definition applies to most countries most of the time; many of the Third World countries made the problem acute by their qualification under the third definition; but the second is the working definition favored by most economists. The possibility of improvement in the per capita income levels is crucial because it suggests the possibility of change. Change is precisely where modern development begins; it is the fundamental premise, and it is what initially distinguishes development economics from the central thrust of mainstream equilibrium economics. Change enters mainstream economics, if at all, through the notion of "dynamic equilibrium," and that is a vastly different notion than the kind of change involved in development economics. One can argue with considerable cogency that this difference in initial premise is still far too little appreciated. Many economists would argue more simply that modern development economics is merely the application of mainstream economics to the problems facing the new and/or industrializing countries of Asia, Africa, and Latin America. To so argue is to miss a critical point. We shall here maintain that the adjustments required in applying mainstream economics to development economics are precisely the sort that institutional economists have long advocated for economics generally. The widespread acceptance of the necessity for these adjustments by development economists is the reason it becomes difficult, if not impossible, to distinguish "mainstream" from "institutionalist" development economics.

Some Crucial Definitions

Immediately after World War II economists were fond of referring to "the backward countries" or "underdeveloped economies." Because these terms appear to have carried pejorative connotations, at least in the eyes of the countries so characterized, they have been replaced by "less developed countries" (LDCs) or more often now "developing economies." As Kuznets pointed out,[6] *all* economies are developing if for no other reason than that technology is always changing, just as resources are always being discovered both in reaction to and as stimulus to changing technology, as well as because of the vagaries of "the instinct of workmanship" among geologists, chemists, and others. So what Western economists often mean by "developing economies" is assisting (or observing) Third World economies in exploiting their own resources so as to adapt modern technology to a version of industrialization which is compatible with moving beyond agriculture alone and toward an industrialization which is believed possible for them to achieve. The implications of this view of development will be explored shortly. Two other common terms are *growth* and *development*. They are customarily used in tandem (as in the title of Samuelson's chapter 38, "Problems of Economic Growth and Development"[7]). The implication is clear, if not at the outset, then very soon thereafter. *Growth* refers to the rate by which real per capita income or output increases; underdeveloped economies have low real GNP per capita, and the process of development is a technique whereby the rate of increase in real per capita income and output can be speeded up.

While the terms *growth* and *development* are, therefore, often used interchangeably, it can be argued that a good deal is lost thereby, and much is to be gained by differentiating them. Sherman Robinson, for example, recently wrote: " 'Economic growth' is defined as increases in aggregate product, either total or per capita, without reference to changes in the structure of the economy or in social and cultural value systems (which are called 'aggregate preference structures.' . . . 'Economic development' is defined to include not only growth but also social and cultural changes which occur in the development process."[8] In short, "growth" refers to mere quantitative increase in whatever the economy is currently doing. "Development" refers to directing the economy toward objectives which have both qualitative and quantitative dimensions. Hence, economies customarily—but not invariably—grow. Mainstream economists are usually comfortable coping with growth and consider the directing of growth one of their primary preoccupations. Development, as we shall see, is a very different matter. Why should this be the case?

The Institutionalist Foundations of
Modern Development Economics

In his *Theory of Business Enterprise* Thorstein Veblen pitted the machine process and the requirements of the industrial process against business enterprise motivated by pecuniary gain. It was dominance for long periods of the former by the latter which created the kind of tension capitalist economies all exhibit.[9] It was this notion, coupled with John Dewey's emphasis on "the means-end continuum" and the instrumental theory of value, that formed the core of Clarence Ayres's perspective. The relationship between technology and institutions permeated all of Ayres's work as, for example, his comment on Veblen:

> He conceived the economy as the system of related activities by which the people of any community get their living. This system embraces a body of knowledge and of skills and a stock of physical equipment; it also embraces a complex network of personal relations reinforced by custom, ritual, sentiment, and dogma. This conception of the economy—one that is applicable to a paleolithic culture no less than to our own, and to our own no less than to any other—is Thorstein Veblen's principal bequest to succeeding generations.[10]

The hallmark by which institutional economics can be differentiated from mainstream economics is, therefore, that the economist qua economist must pay attention to all of these factors. It is precisely here that mainstream economists prefer to part company with institutionalists.

Peter Bauer and Basil Yamey, for example, commenting on the origins of modern development economics, write:

> There are no special economic theories or methods of analysis for the study of the underdeveloped world. . . . In the half century before the

Second World War the advances in economic theory were largely in fields of equilibrium analysis. . . . The discussion was generally at a high level of abstraction, so much so, indeed, that the principal long term determinants of income and wealth, such as the factors underlying growth of capital, the size of population, the attitude toward work, saving and risk-bearing, the quality of entrepreneurship and the extent of markets, were considered as institutional facts given, as data, to the economist.[11]

In short, precisely these factors which mainstream economists were most comfortable assuming as "given" were the crucial factors from which any study of development economics had to begin. The result was a change in the approach of development economists, a change carried out thus far without producing a corresponding change in the approach of other mainstream economists. The argument here is that development economists embraced the fundamental tenets of institutionalism for their own specialty without calling it that, without influencing other mainstream economists (until, perhaps, relatively recently), and without institutionalists themselves paying as much attention as they might have to what had happened, or to its significance.

The dynamism of technological development, the resistance of institutions, the inevitability of change—these are basic elements of modern evolutionary economics. They are, for example, what Joseph Schumpeter had in mind when he distinguished invention (a technological process) from innovation (the incorporation of an invention into the business enterprise economy) and noted that the process involved "creative destruction."[12]

What remains to be said, however, is that "creative destruction" or, if one prefers, economic change as a result of the confrontation of the essential dynamism which characterizes technology with the institutional framework which provides at one and the same time both resistance to change and the requisite stability without which no society can function, is a *ceaseless* process. From that point of view the term *underdeveloped* is far less satisfactory than the term *developing* because the former connotes a static state, whereas the latter connotes a process. But the same comment can be made of the term *developed*. Kuznets is correct because, in the Veblen-Ayres tradition, he recognizes that *all* economies are in process of change at all times. In precisely the same way that Dewey's means-end continuum provided the most appropriate undergirding for what Ayres liked to call the instrumental theory of value, modern economics could benefit from acceptance of the notion that industrialization is not a process with a finite end. Indeed, the value problems with which "developed"

economies are currently wrestling exist precisely because the development process is on-going and presents them, therefore, with problems that
could be more amenable to analysis and possibly even resolution were we
all to stop regarding the task confronting "underdeveloped" countries as
primarily one of achieving for themselves the closest possible approximation to our own current state.

Is There an Institutional Theory of Growth?

The implications of the preceding discussion for growth theory are important. Not only is there an institutional theory of growth, but also, however else they may differ, all widely espoused growth theories must begin
from an institutionalist perspective. "Growth theory" here, following but
extending a distinction made by John R. Hicks, refers to the process by
which economies change and develop over time rather than what mainstream economists mean by the term when they discuss "dynamic economics." Thus, Hicks is able to write: "Underdevelopment economics is
a vastly important subject, but it is not a formal or theoretical subject. It
is a practical subject which must expect to call upon any branch of theory
(including non-economic, for instance sociological, theory) which has any
relevance to it."[13] He then proceeds to make it clear that the former is not
his concern—he means economic dynamics, a far more circumscribed
endeavor. The analysis of equilibrium, whether static or dynamic, has
never received high priority among evolutionary economists, and so the
question of whether there is an institutional growth theory is here addressed to the larger view of growth. It will be argued that development
economists are essentially institutionalist whether they know it or not,
and thus many of them may find that, like Moliere's *bourgeois gentil-
homme,* who was surprised to discover he had been speaking prose all
his life, they may always have been writing institutional economics without knowing it.

Several years ago A. W. Coats argued that institutionalism must mean
more than that "social and cultural influences play a crucial role in the
process of economic development."[14] Surely it does. Institutionalism em-
bodies a fundamental notion of the economy, namely, an institution as a
dynamic entity is subject to influences far broader than "the market" with
all its attendant givens. Coats went on to suggest that it would be interesting to compare the contents of the *Journal of Economic Issues* with that,
for example, of *Economic Development and Cultural Change* for clues
as to the degree to which institutionalism can be differentiated from main-

stream economics.[15] The term "institutionalist growth theory" is rarely encountered even in the *JEI*.[16] Still, Coats's notion is a reasonable one. Do
writers in the *JEI* mean something different by the terms "economic
growth" or "economic development" than do other economists in the development field? My conclusion, based on something less than an exhaustive analysis of both journals, is negative, with the possible exception of
one area.

Progress in Development Economics

In general, work in economic development in the past quarter century
has taken one of two directions; either it has been an effort to further our
understanding of the development process through case studies of particular economies in process of development, or it has been an attempt
to further our understanding by refinements in development theory in
general. Often the former involve consideration of obstacles to industrialization. These efforts appear in a variety of publications, of course, but
my contention here, following Coats's suggestion, is that customarily it is
impossible to guess *a priori* whether they would be published in the *Journal
of Economic Issues* or in "mainstream" publications typified by *Economic
Development and Cultural Change* according to the method the studies
adopt or their general thrust. A number of members of the Association
for Evolutionary Economics have themselves published in *Economic Development and Cultural Change,* among them Clarence Ayres,[17] Karl de
Schweinitz,[18] William Glade,[19] Abraham Hirsch,[20] K. William Kapp,[21]
Peter McLaughlin,[22] Robert A. Solo,[23] and W. Paul Strassmann.[24] Most
of these articles have been case studies, but the critical point is that they
might with equal logic have appeared in the *Journal of Economic Issues.*

Economic Development and Cultural Change is the house organ of the
University of Chicago in the field of development economics, just as the
JEI bears that relationship to the Association of Evolutionary Economics.
The distinctions in emphasis, point of view, subject matter, and policy
orientation between the two journals as regards development economics
are relatively minor in my opinion precisely because the divisions in the
development field (and there are a number) do not follow the customary
division between establishment economics (where the University of Chicago and its *Journal of Political Economy* can surely be placed in the fore-
front) and evolutionary economics. Corroboration of this position as well
as suggesting its implications are the subjects of the remainder of this
article.

The Journal of Economic Issues *and*
Development Economics

JEI *Case Studies*

What have been the concerns of development economists writing in the *Journal of Economic Issues*? There have, to begin with, been a number of case studies involving various countries of Asia, Africa, and Latin America in process of developing. We shall cite several of these, commenting as necessary in order to show that their general perspectives, as well as their method and conclusions, do not clearly distinguish them from other case studies in economic development appearing in journals such as *Economic Development and Cultural Change,* which do not purport to be institutionalist. We shall endeavor to substantiate the conclusion that *all* such studies are essentially institutionalist of necessity because they concern themselves with some aspect of the clash between dynamic technology and institutional barriers to economic change and/or with the implications of economic development for the overall direction in which a particular developing economy is moving. To conclude that a particular case study is "not institutionalist" is another way of saying that it cannot be differentiated from case studies in economic development generally, because the field itself is institutionalist.

One such study involved the comparison of economic development in Mexico and Thailand, concentrating on the difficulty of grafting Western methods and objectives onto countries with different institutions. While the study (in two parts) was subtitled "An Institutional Analysis," it is not notably institutionalist except insofar as it is concerned with the juxtaposition of modern technology to the diverse institutions of developing economies. But this is precisely what almost all modern development economics is concerned with, no doubt in response to the relatively simplistic notion after World War II that an infusion of Western technology and/or money was all that backward economies needed "to develop."[25] The articles, in short, are a contribution to development economics appearing in the pages of the *Journal of Economic Issues* but cannot be said to have attempted to differentiate an institutionalist development theory from standard development theory. The reason, to repeat, it is argued here, is because such a distinction, with the exception of one possible area, discussed below, cannot easily be made.

There have, of course, been many similar case studies published in the *JEI*. Indeed, almost half of its issues have contained one or more articles on problems of economic development. Because, with few exceptions,

they have not attempted a differentiation of institutionalist from mainstream development economics, they would in principle be as appropriate
in *Economic Development and Cultural Change* (EDCC) as in the *JEI*.

Among these one could include Glade's "The Employment Question
and Development Policies in Latin America" and Milton Lower's "Institutional Bases of Economic Stagnation in Chile."[26] Glade's study is a
straightforward attempt to describe the employment aspects of Latin
American development policy; it is not more or less institutionalist than
most such studies wherever they have been published. Lower purports
from the onset to explain Chilean stagnation from an Ayres-Veblen perspective:

> Technology, conceived of as a universalistic process of accumulation and
> assimilation of tools and knowledge is the dynamic force in economic
> development and cultural change. To account for a past or present in-
> stance of sustained development would require a heavy emphasis upon
> what might be called its "technological bases," though it would also
> require some independent explanation of the relative permissiveness of
> the institutions in the face of this advancing "cultural incidence of the
> machine process."[27]

This is, of course, a familiar notion to institutional economists, interesting as well because it incorporates the title of Chicago's economic development journal. The article itself considers the institutional difficulties
involved in Chilean economic development and concludes ultimately that
although "the institutional barriers that must yet be overcome are awesome, . . . there is ground for cautious optimism."[28] The case study, therefore, makes a contribution to understanding problems of economic development but not, it would appear, to distinguishing institutionalist
development theory from standard or establishment development theory.
Thomas De Gregori, to cite one more study, examined post-war British
colonial Africa and concluded that experience there "has clearly shown us
that capital or foreign investment alone cannot engender development."[29]
This conclusion is one widely reached by development economists and,
while important, again provides no basis for distinguishing institutionalist
from standard development economics.

General Studies in Development

In addition to these case studies, there have been a number of contributions in the *Journal of Economic Issues* to the general theoretical literature
of development economics. Some of these have concerned themselves
with general problems of development or stabilizing relationships between

developed and developing economies. Deena Khatkhate, for example, wrote an article suggesting that a system of dual exchange rates could provide useful interim assistance in the development process.[30] Whatever the merits of the argument, it is clearly general in nature and no more (or less) "standard" than institutionalist.

Similarly, William Miller has written on the general question of the role of education in economic development, discussing a number of controversies concerning current views on the subject but not readily classifiable as "institutionalist" as opposed to "standard." The writers whose views he analyzes are development economists generally, and the article, in principle, could appear anywhere.[31] The same can be said of Robert Alexander's discussion of import-substitution strategy or W. T. Wilford's examination of the relation between nutrition levels and economic development.[32] Mention may be made similarly of Solo's examination of the hypothesis that low wages in developing countries lead to a trade-off favoring relatively labor-intensive technologies.[33] All these studies, in terms of both approach and subject, would in principle be as appropriate to *Economic Development and Cultural Change* as they are to the *Journal of Economic Issues*. Much the same conclusion is appropriate for William Thweatt's study of world poverty and the continued increase in the gap between the income levels of the richer and poorer nations.[34]

Finally, Steven Barsby has examined Alexander Gerschenkron's hypotheses concerning generalizing Western Europe's growth experience to other countries. Barsby considers the United States, Canada, Japan, Australia, and South Africa. His attempt to refute Gerschenkron by suggesting that the Western European growth experience can indeed be generalized to other countries is interesting, but like the other studies cited, only with tortuous difficulty can it be classified as "institutionalist" rather than "mainstream."[35]

It is no doubt true that evolutionary economists are more likely than others—even other development economists—to make specific reference to Ayres or Veblen. Some studies state that they will concern themselves with some aspect of Veblenian or Ayresian theory, but in the final analysis they are not noticeably different from conventional development economics. (The reader will recall, however, that we are here arguing that this is because the mainstream of development economics is institutionalist.[36])

A number of economists have examined the general problem of technological change and diffusion, often in terminology which might disturb "nondevelopment" institutionalists, but this is clearly a major area where development economics must be and is institutionalist, with no clear way to distinguish the mainstream from evolutionary economics. For example, James Christian's study of institutional alterations required by changing technology is surely supremely Ayresian in point of view, but the methodology and terminology are derived from mainstream economics with results that can only be viewed as an effort to contribute to evolutionary development theory.[37]

Similar concern with the obstacles to diffusion is expressed by James Street in his study of the Latin American technological frontier. He writes from a far more explicitly institutionalist perspective than does Christian, but his study is not radically different, except for some terminology, from the work of other development economists (both in the *JEI* and elsewhere) on the subject.[38]

The Role of Savings

In one area some have attempted to argue in the *JEI* that there exists an institutionalist as opposed to a mainstream position in economic development. It concerns the role of savings in economic growth and development. Primary participants in this controversy appear to be Louis Junker, Street, and De Gregori,[39] although others have commented on the matter.

The issue is customarily expressed in terms of whether or not an increase in savings is a prerequisite for an increase in the growth rate. While the question is here applied to less developed countries, it can, of course, with equal logic be applied to any economy.

This question is scarcely new in economics. If we go back no farther than J. M. Keynes, his basic system,

$$C + I = Y, \qquad (1)$$
$$Y - C = S, \qquad (2)$$
$$I = S, \qquad (3)$$

would suggest at least two ways to increase the rate of investment. One could reduce consumption and so increase savings which might be invested. Or one could increase the income level with consumption unchanged, and so provide increase in savings and investment. The mathematics is identical, but the economics radically different, and it is around this that the controversy appears to revolve.

Junker stated the matter clearly by suggesting that Joan Robinson had indeed posed the critical question relating to development theory, and it was concerned essentially with capital theory. Asked Robinson: "What governs the overall rate of accumulation of capital?"[40] Her answer was that in contrast to far better known theories of capital accumulation, "there is a less well-known theory that seems more promising. This is put forward by a disciple of Veblen, Professor C. E. Ayres."[41] It is Junker's contention that there is an institutionalist theory of capital accumulation which can be differentiated from the standard theory. How treacherous the categories and the terminology can be in this area is illustrated by Junker's decision to use Robert Heilbroner's argument in *The Great Ascent* as typifying the standard theory that the inability of poor countries to accumulate capital is their basic obstacle to development and growth. The argument continues that the inability to accumulate capital is due to the inability to save when the level of economic activity is at or near the subsistence level.[42]

Junker thus views Heilbroner as representative of many development economists on this matter. He specifically names Bauer and Yamey, Irma Adelman, Barbara Ward, and Henry Bruton as having ensnared themselves somehow or other in the "low-level equilibrium trap"—without saving there can be no growth, and economic performance is at too low a level to permit any saving. In Junker's opinion, Robinson's view of capital, how it is accumulated, and the relationship of capital accumulation to economic growth is far closer to an appropriate nonsavings centered theory of economic development. Others whom Junker sees as on the right track include A. K. Cairncross, John P. Lewis, and Wendell Gordon.[43] Junker's essential argument is that the factors which permit growth to accelerate create a whole constellation of dynamic changes among which increase in savings is one, and the chain of causation runs from these factors to changes in savings, not the other way around. Indeed, *a priori,* an increase in savings alone might well depress investment incentive because it would indicate a diminution in the consumption rate. This is also Robinson's argument, and a number of other economic theorists in general as well as development economics have joined in the debate.

Street underscores the same issue in his effort to prove that the overall approach of Latin American "structuralists" parallels that of North American institutionalists. Ayres's view concerning the inadequacy of "the abstinence theory of capital formation" discussed in *The Theory of Economic Progress* has, in Street's view, been echoed more recently in the views of the Latin American structuralists: "While denied by experience, the idea persists that the only way a people can raise the necessary investment funds to insure their own industrial expansion is by a prior and widespread reduction in the level of consumption. Somehow, as a principle this idea has escaped the Keynesian as well as the institutional onslaught."[44]

This is the essential thrust as well of De Gregori's insistence about the "wrongheadedness" of the view that savings is necessary for economic development.[45] Wendell Gordon finally has joined the debate, arguing that the view that "the institutional adjustment problem . . . is an insuperable barrier to . . . fostering economic development" is itself part of the explanation for the slowness of development since World War II.[46] While there is a certain ambiguity to Gordon's argument as he originally stated it, eventually it becomes clear. He writes that the attitude which regards raising the rate of saving as an "impossible task" is one of the barriers to growth, but he does not appear to be suggesting that the *necessity* to raise the rate of saving as a prerequisite to growth is invalid.[47] The rest of his argument seems unambiguous and is very much what one expects of an institutionalist—technology (the accumulation of knowledge) is dynamic, its implementation involves overcoming "firmly entrenched domestic institutional resistance," and, finally, "one of the real contributions of Keynesian theory was its demonstration that prior personal monetary saving is not necessary to set moving the wheels of investment, production, rising income, and rising welfare."[48]

All this leaves the savings question, narrowly construed, and its relation to institutional economics somewhat confused. As Alan Nichols (a non-institutionalist who has written for the *JEI*) has aptly noted in commenting on Junker's discussion on the savings question,

> if Professor Junker means that private savings, both domestically and through international transfer, are not up to the job of economic development, we may nod, though for the nth time, in agreement. If he means that know-how is indispensable, who will dissent? If he means that "cultural patterns" can be an obstacle, how can we say otherwise? But if he means that savings as understood by nearly everyone in the profession are not required, I must suggest that he believes that he has found a very cheap way indeed to development. And he really ought to tell us about it.[49]

What is one to make of all this? Part of the problem is the ambiguity over "savings as understood by nearly everyone." Gordon in the previous quotation is careful to refer to his interpretation that Keynes believed "prior personal monetary saving is not necessary" for development. Junker and Street seem to have attacked the notion that increased real saving (real reductions in consumption) are a prerequisite to capital accumulation and increases in the growth rate. In short, if one wishes to argue that an implication of the Veblen-Ayres views on economic progress is that the way to increase economic growth rates depends primarily on adjusting institutions to changing technology so as to establish the ferment from which both increase in consumption and investment emerge (the Junker-Street position, I think), then one must conclude that Gordon's position is ambiguous, Nichols and Heilbroner are probably in disagreement, and Robinson may well side with Junker and Street. De Gregori, as we have seen, argues that the savings-is-necessary-for-development position is "wrongheaded," but in an earlier article on economic development in British colonial Africa he takes a middle position, saying that "it is possible if not probable that current emphasis on saving and foreign investment may be misplaced" as prime factors in increasing economic growth. "An economic policy that encourages domestic saving and foreign investment is frequently aligned with a political and social oligarchy that restricts the utilization of modern technology."[50] This much would be clear to all. But what if "an economic policy that encourages domestic saving" were aligned with otherwise ideal dynamic social and political institutions sympathetic to introducing new technology? De Gregori's later article would appear to argue that such a savings policy would nonetheless be "wrongheaded," but in the British Africa article he does not say, stating only that emphasis on savings may "possibly" be misplaced. The Junker-Street position would clearly be that such emphasis is surely misplaced. In sum, on the issues raised by the narrowly construed savings-centered theory, institutionalists Heilbroner and possibly Gordon, plus Nichols (not an institutionalist) argue that real savings are probably a critical part of the capital accumulation–development process, whereas Junker, De Gregori, Street, and Robinson (an institutionalist?) take the opposing view.

More broadly construed, institutionalism does not assign primary importance to savings as an essential incentive to more rapid growth. (Non-institutionalists, probably for somewhat different reasons, might agree.)

Institutionalists generally stress the primary importance of institutional flexibility and adaptability to a dynamic changing technology as a major, if not *the* major, prerequisite to economic growth and development. On the narrower question of the role of savings there is confusion. All writers in the *JEI* do not take the same position, and in the process of discussion the most ardent opponents of savings-centered capital accumulation theory align themselves with similarly minded economists who are not customarily viewed as institutionalists. Gordon, finally, regards "the conventional Keynesian position" as disposing of the matter. One must conclude that a narrowly construed savings-centered theory *per se* is at best a tenuous reed on which to hang a possible distinction between institutional development economists and other development economists. Concerning the general necessity of permitting technological developments to emerge in order for economic development to occur, virtually all development economists appear to be in agreement.

Institutionalism and Current
Development Economics

In a recent discussion entitled "Development Economics from a Chicago Perspective"—a perspective which, in most any other field of economics, should differentiate evolutionary from mainstream economics in about as clear-cut a fashion as can be imagined—W. Paul Strassmann comments: "Compared with the mainstream and Marxist approaches to economic development in the past quarter of a century, the Chicago anti-interventionists do not come off badly."[51] That a distinguishing characteristic of the Chicago School is a preference for relying on the market will surprise no one. What is not so immediately unsurprising, however, is that Strassmann, both an institutionalist and a development economist, here includes no "institutionalist approach to development economics"—only mainstream, Marxist, and Chicago. I suggest this is because, as previously noted, in development economics in general the mainstream *is* institutionalist. It is true that he notes that Gunnar Myrdal (an institutionalist) is "infuriating" to Chicago when he writes that "the price system as a part of a very irrational whole, namely the economy of a backward and stagnating country, can hardly have any great claim on rationality to begin with."[52] The point to note is that the comment of institutionalist Myrdal might be infuriating to Chicago, but hardly to the mainstream of development economists.

Strassmann offers a long quotation from Chicago's Arnold Harberger:

> While simple theoretical models have been developed in which the bottleneck to progress turns out to be, depending on the circumstances, either a shortage of domestic resources (a "savings gap") or a shortage of imported goods (a "foreign exchange gap") there are at most only a few countries and periods to which such models can be applied in practice. In general, as is well-known the modernization of backward economies is a time-consuming process. Barriers to growth abound: social and political elites unreceptive to change, gross deficiencies of the technical skills and capacities required by modernization, markets that are poorly organized and whose functioning is further impaired by ill-conceived public policies, systems of fiscal and also foreign-trade policy that in their present state are if anything impediments to rather than promoters of modernization—these constitute only a partial listing.[53]

Strassmann's eminently appropriate comment is: "What institutional economist could quarrel with that list?"[54] And here we come to the point precisely. Even Chicago economists in the development field are not "Chicago economists" specializing in development but are mainstream development economists. What we have been suggesting is that in this field "mainstream economists" are institutionalist economists. The controversies one finds in development economics are those which, in general, begin *beyond* the basic premises which, although they clearly separate mainstream from institutional economists in most of our discipline, are pretty clearly agreed to in general by most development economists. In terms, therefore, of Coats's notion that one might find clues to basic orientation in development economics by comparing relevant work published in the *Journal of Economics Issues* with that published in *Economic Development and Cultural Change,* one can reasonably conclude that the differences between them are far smaller than the differences, say, between *both* of them and Chicago's *Journal of Political Economy*. In this sense, therefore, development economics can with considerable accuracy be called "the least orthodox field in economics."[55]

Contemporary Institutionalism, Development Economics, and Beyond

Economic development is, in the final analysis, a process. Despite the misleading nature of much of the terminology, few if any economies have never changed or developed at all. "Underdeveloped" and "backward" are, therefore, not the absolutes they seem to suggest, but are relative terms, as the more recent and appropriate term, "developing," clearly is. At the other extreme, we speak of Western Europe, the United States, and Japan as "developed," and this, too, is misleading—they are merely *more* developed. This emphasis on process has always been a major characteristic of evolutionary economics. Institutionalists have historically expended most of their energies in trying to pursuade economists to look at our own economy from an evolutionary or processual perspective. It has not been an easy struggle. This survey has attempted to show that because change and development—process—is the very fundamental premise from which development economics must begin, almost all economists, regardless of what they call themselves when they are not being "development economists"—whether Chicagoans, mainstream economists, Keynesians, whatever—have been drawn ineluctably to operate from within far more of the framework of evolutionary economics than many (both institutionalists and others) realize. Ayres always maintained that the changing interface between the dynamic technology and the resistant institutional fabric was far easier to see in other cultures than in one's own. Nowhere is this truth more strikingly borne out than in the contrast between the relative ease with which development economists can adopt an evolutionary perspective and the relative difficulty most economists (including, one supposes, a number of these same development economists) have in accepting this perspective for the study of their own economies.

Recently, mainstream economists have been forced increasingly to accept an evolutionary perspective as they contemplate the consequences of economic growth in their own economies. This is a position a number of economists have recently argued, including Ezra Mishan, myself, and others.[56] In effect, the essential dynamic underlying the economy as a developing entity, with all that this entails and on which evolutionary economists have insisted for decades, is now pretty clearly accepted by the mainstream, both when looking at economies in relatively early stages of development and, increasingly, when looking at postindustrial development. It is only in the "middle," when considering mostly static economics for their own advanced industrialized economies, that the disagreement between evolutionary and mainstream economists continues. The acceptance, therefore, of evolutionary principles is perhaps far more complete than many of us have realized.

Conclusions

Several main propositions about the current state of development economics and its relationship to evolutionary economics emerge from the work of development economists who are avowedly institutionalists or who may classify themselves otherwise.

Development economics is the subdiscipline in which institutionalism has thus far had its greatest influence. It is the "least orthodox" field in economics; hence, it is argued, it is the most heterodox, which is to say institutionalist.

If mainstream development economics is basically institutionalist, it is because evolutionary or institutional economics and development economics must begin with *change* as the basic premise and with explicit disavowal of the conventional givens of mainstream economics—tastes, resources, population, technology, a closed economy, rationality, and emphasis on the interaction of these givens in one mechanism, the market. In precisely the same way that institutionalists have always examined the interaction of these factors partly as determining and partly emerging from the economy, so, too, this is the only sensible perspective from which to view economies less developed than our own.

Thorstein Veblen emphasized process as the motive force in the economy and ineluctably, therefore, in the science which studies the economy. In his view economics has always been an evolutionary science. Ayres, commenting on Veblen's work, wrote: "Workmanship implies not only working with the hands but with tools, and tools are always capable of combination and elaboration. Growth, development, evolution—all are implicit in that type of activity."[57] And "that type of activity" is precisely what all economies organize. Hence, "growth, development, and evolution" are characteristics of *all* economies—not just those of the Third World.

This unity of process is in constant need of emphasis by evolutionary economics. The process is nonteleological, and "backward" countries are merely at an earlier point on the continuum than "developed" countries. No nations, as we are all finally aware, are "developed" in the sense of having reached any "end."

The word *industrialization* in connection with economic development is, therefore, used ambiguously. It may appropriately be employed to denote a critical part of the tool developing process, but it is often used inappropriately to suggest some finite technological state, as in "underdeveloped countries must strive to achieve industrialization." All economies constantly cope with the ongoing adjustments which technological change presents to them.

At the heart of economic development, in consequence, lies the process of technological change. The wheel and the missile are on the same technological continuum. The "most primitive" and "most advanced" economies are on the same development path. This explains why, in the end, the distinction between "development economics," used to refer to the problems of converting agricultural into industrial economies, and "growth economics," used to consider the range of problems faced by highly industrialized economies as they contemplate their futures, is ultimately a phony distinction. None of this is really new. Schumpeter's "perennial gale of creative destruction" as inventions press institutional constraints to become "innovations" suggests the primary institutionalist notion about how dynamic technological possibilities are adapted via institutional adjustment into societally diverse patterns of change.

The challenge to institutionalists or evolutionary economists is to make the economics profession ever more aware of precisely how institutionalist "mainstream" economics has become. The distinction, indeed, can today be clearly maintained only for a shrinking area of static economics dealing (increasingly unrealistically) with the here and now in the highly industrialized economies of the world. For those which lie in the East, our "establishment economics" must contend with the conflicting jurisdictional claims of Marxists and central planners of various stripes. In the capitalist or at least market-oriented economies of the West, "establishment economists," as we have endeavored here to show, are already largely institutionalist when they contemplate economic process outside their own countries in less developed economies. Only in relatively more developed industrialized economies are the conventional assumptions associated with mainstream micro- and macroeconomics, and against which institutionalists have been railing for many decades, still being seriously propounded. Finally, as concern with the future of postindustrial society increases, problems involving pollution, conservation, the quality of life, the energy crisis, and our newfound interest in the possibly dubious virtues of what we have previously called "growth" all suggest overwhelmingly that at the more "advanced" end of the spectrum precisely the same fundamental questions must be faced as development economists have overwhelmingly accepted as essential for the analysis of economies at the less advanced end. Ultimately, the institutionalist perspective emerges as consistently appropriate for evaluating, as well as directing, "the economy" as it moves along the entire spectrum from less to ever more developed.

Notes

1. For example, R. A. Gordon, noting the upsurge in interest in economic development since World War II, writes: "Here economics has truly 'gone institutional.' " "Institutional Elements in Contemporary Economics," in *Institutional Economics: Veblen, Commons, and Mitchell Reconsidered* (Berkeley and Los Angeles: University of California Press, 1963), p. 129.
2. Paul Samuelson, *Economics*, 10th ed. (New York: McGraw-Hill, 1976), p. 847.
3. Ibid., 5th ed. (New York: McGraw-Hill, 1961), p. 776.
4. It is interesting to note that in the first edition of his widely adopted basic text, which appeared in 1948, there was no chapter at all on economic development. As for other texts, see, for example, W. J. Baumol and Lester Chandler, *Economic Processes and Policies* (New York: Harper, 1954); or John Ise, *Economics*, rev. ed. (New York: Harper, 1956).
5. Simon Kuznets, *Toward a Theory of Economic Growth* (New York: W. W. Norton, 1968), p. 2.
6. See definition above.
7. Samuelson, *Economics*, 10th ed., p. 759.
8. Sherman Robinson, "Theories of Economic Growth and Development: Methodology and Content," *Economic Development and Cultural Change* 21 (October 1972): 54. Because of the distinction made between growth and development in the text, it should be clear that we are distinguishing

growth theory in the sense used by modern adaptors of classical Ricardo-Marx growth models from development theory. This latter is the theory of how preindustrial economies increase their per capita outputs by industrializing in some fashion appropriate to each economy's particular institutional characteristics and cope with the attendant problems such economic transformation invariably brings. The former type of growth theory does not necessarily presuppose any institutional changes but concentrates instead on the implications for productivity and increased output per capita of varying the input proportions, frequently spelling out these implications in highly mathematical models. Examples would include the work of R. M. Solow, in particular, "A Contribution to the Theory of Growth," *Quarterly Journal of Economics* 70 (February 1956): 65–94; or Hirofumi Uzawa, "On a Two-Sector Model of Economic Growth," *Review of Economic Studies* 29 (October 1961): 40–47. See also the discussion below on pp. 790–91.

 9. Thorstein Veblen, *The Theory of Business Enterprise* (New York: Scribner, 1904), especially chapters 2 and 3.

10. Clarence E. Ayres, "The Legacy of Thorstein Veblen," in *Institutional Economics: Veblen, Commons, and Mitchell Reconsidered* (Berkeley and Los Angeles: University of California Press, 1963), p. 61.

11. Peter T. Bauer and Basil S. Yamey, *The Economics of Underdeveloped Countries,* Cambridge Economic Handbooks (Chicago: University of Chicago Press, 1957), pp. 8–10.

12. See, for example, Joseph A. Schumpeter, *Capitalism, Socialism and Democracy,* 2d ed. (New York Harper, 1948), chapter 7.

13. John R. Hicks, *Capital and Growth* (New York: Oxford University Press, 1965), p. 3.

14. A. W. Coats, review of Allan Gruchy's *Contemporary Economic Thought, Journal of Economic Issues* 8 (September 1974): 599.

15. Ibid.

16. One who does use it is James H. Street. See "The Latin American 'Structuralists' and the Institutionalists: Convergence in Development Theory," *Journal of Economic Issues* 1 (June 1967): 45.

17. Clarence E. Ayres, review of W. H. Nicholls, *Southern Tradition and Regional Progress, Economic Development and Cultural Change* 9 (January 1961): 197–99.

18. Karl de Schweinitz, Jr., "Industrialization, Labor Controls, and Democracy," *Economic Development and Cultural Change* 7 (July 1959): 385–404; "A Rejoinder," ibid., vol. 8 (January 1960): 197–98; and "Ethics of Economic Development," ibid., vol. 21 (July 1973): 717–21.

19. William Glade, review of Ray Vernon, *Dilemma of Mexico's Development: The Roles of the Private and Public Sectors, Economic Development and Cultural Change* 13 (April 1965): 366-75.

20. Eva and Abraham Hirsch, "Changes in Agricultural Output Per Capita of Rural Population in Turkey, 1927–60," *Economic Development and Cultural Change* 11 (July 1963): 372-94, and "Changes in Terms of Trade of Farmers and Their Effect on Real Family Income Per Capita of Rural Population in Turkey," ibid., vol. 14 (July 1966): 440-57.

21. K. William Kapp, "River Valley Projects in India: Their Direct Effects,"

Economic Development and Cultural Change 8 (October 1959): 24–47.

22. Peter F. M. McLaughlin, "The Sudan's Three Towns: A Demographic and Economic Profile of an African Urban Complex. Part I. Introduction and Demography," "Part II. Output and Expenditure," and "Part III. Labor Force Occupations, Occupational Income, Income Distribution," *Economic Development and Cultural Change* 12 (October 1963): 70–83, 12 (January 1964): 158–73, and 12 (April 1964): 286–304.

23. Robert A. Solo, "Anthropomorphism and Entropy," *Economic Development and Cultural Change* 22 (April 1974): 510-17.

24. W. Paul Strassmann, "Measuring the Employment Effects of Housing Policies in Developing Countries," *Economic Development and Cultural Change* 24 (April 1976): 623–32.

25. The articles in question are Edward Van Roy and James V. Cornehls, "Economic Development in Mexico and Thailand: An Institutional Analysis," Part One, *Journal of Economic Issues* 3 (September 1969): 16–32, and Part Two, 3 (December 1969): 21–38.

26. William P. Glade, "The Development Question and Development Policies in Latin America," *Journal of Economic Issues* 3 (September 1969): 43–62; and Milton D. Lower, "Institutional Bases of Economic Stagnation in Chile," *Journal of Economic Issues* 2 (September 1968): 283–97.

27. Lower, "Institutional Bases," pp. 283–84. The last phrase is an interior quotation from Veblen, *Theory of Business Enterprise*, chapter 9.

28. Lower, "Institutional Bases," p. 297.

29. Thomas R. De Gregori, "Foreign Investment and Technological Diffusion; The Case of British Colonial Africa," *Journal of Economic Issues* 2 (December 1968): 403–15.

30. Deena R. Khatkhate, "Economic Development and the Cost of Foreign Trade and Exchange Controls," *Journal of Economic Issues* 4 (December 1970): 56–67.

31. William L. Miller, "Education as a Source of Economic Growth," *Journal of Economic Issues* 1 (December 1967): 280–96.

32. Robert J. Alexander, "The Import-Substitution Strategy of Economic Development," *Journal of Economic Issues* 1 (December 1967): 297–308; and W. T. Wilford, "Nutrition Levels and Economic Growth: Some Empirical Measures," *Journal of Economic Issues* 7 (September 1973): 437–58.

33. Robert Solo, "Capital and Labor Intensive Technology in Developing Countries," *Journal of Economic Issues* 3 (December 1969): 96–103.

34. William O. Thweatt, "The Inevitability and Irrelevancy of the Increasing Income Gap," *Journal of Economic Issues* 4 (June/September 1970): 17–24. As his title suggests, Thweatt argues that the increase in gap is irrelevant even if poorer nations grow at twice the rate of the richer nations for the next century. Reducing poverty (per capita income increases) can occur nonetheless.

35. Steven L. Barsby, "Great Spurts and the Experience of Non-European Countries," *Journal of Economic Issues* 7 (September 1973): 459–74.

36. In this connection, one example, referred to earlier, is the Lower study of Chilean development.

37. James W. Christian, "The Dynamics of Economic Growth, Technological

Progress, and Institutional Change," *Journal of Economic Issues* 2 (September 1968): 298–311. Christian begins by considering the views of a whole list of development economists who have concerned themselves with the relationship between technological change and economic growth (Robert Solow, Edward F. Denison, William Fellner, Eli Ginzberg, Edwin Mansfield) and argues that equal attention should be paid to institutional changes required for growth. However, from this "evolutionary" perspective, Christian pursues conventional techniques, beginning with a Harrod-type model, to develop a "dynamic general equilibrium model." He emerged with three variables—work-leisure preference patterns, labor force participation rates, and population as affecting the full employment growth rate. The terminology and approach are anything but institutionalist, but the essential thrust is an effort to contribute to a problem that Clarence Ayres regarded as critical in economic development.

38. James H. Street, "The Technological Frontier in Latin America: Creativity and Productivity," *Journal of Economic Issues* 10 (September 1976): 538–58.

39. Louis J. Junker, "Capital Accumulation, Savings-Centered Theory and Economic Development," *Journal of Economic Issues* 1 (June 1967): 28–43; James H. Street, "The Latin American 'Structuralists' and Institutionalists: Convergence in Development Theory," ibid., pp. 44–62; and Thomas R. De Gregori, "Prodigality or Parsimony: The False Dilemma in Economic Development Theory," ibid., vol. 7 (June 1973): 259–66.

40. Joan Robinson, *Economic Philosophy* (London: C. A. Watts, 1962), p. 105, quoted in Junker, "Capital Accumulation," p. 25. In short, Robinson, perhaps a "radical economist" now, but not customarily viewed as an institutionalist, agrees with the Junker position. She says of the basic Harrodian equation $G = S/V$ that it has "made a great negative contribution to the development of economics" by making it appear that a primary determinant of growth is the savings rate (ibid., p. 105).

41. Robinson, *Economic Philosophy*, pp. 109–10, quoted in Junker, "Capital Accumulation," pp. 25–26.

42. Junker, "Capital Accumulation," pp. 26–27. Junker argues that Heilbroner, a former board member of AFEE, reflects the "almost universal position when he writes, 'It is for the lack of capital of every sort, not just for lack of capital on the land, that the underdeveloped nations are unable to produce adequate incomes' " (quoted in ibid., p. 27, from Heilbroner's *The Great Ascent*). The argument of the text is simply that whatever the merits of the debate this puts institutionalist Heilbroner in direct opposition to institutionalists Junker, Street, and De Gregori (see text below) and so makes the narrow question of the role of savings in capital accumulation and ultimate economic development a very treacherous way to try and differentiate institutionalist from standard development economics.

43. The references in Junker's article are to A. K. Cairncross, "Capital Formation in the Take-Off," in *Factors in Economic Development* (London: George Allen and Unwin, 1962); John P. Lewis, *Quiet Crisis in India* (Washington, D.C.: The Brookings Institution, 1962); and Wendell

Gordon, *The Political Economy of Latin America* (New York: Columbia University Press, 1965).

44. Street, "The Latin American 'Structuralists,' " p. 51.
45. De Gregori, "Prodigality or Parsimony," pp. 259–66.
46. Wendell Gordon, "Institutionalized Consumption Patterns in Underdeveloped Countries," *Journal of Economic Issues* 7 (June 1973): 278.
47. Compare ibid., pp. 278–79.
48. Ibid., p. 284.
49. Alan Nichols, "On Savings and Non-Institutionalism," *Journal of Economic Issues* 3 (September 1969): 65.
50. De Gregori, "Foreign Investment and Technological Diffusion," pp. 403–404.
51. W. Paul Strassmann, "Development Economics from a Chicago Perspective," *Journal of Economic Issues* 10 (March 1976): 63–80.
52. Ibid., p. 65.
53. Quoted in ibid., p. 66.
54. Ibid.
55. De Gregori, "Prodigality or Parsimony," p. 261. De Gregori is probably correct as well that development economists, in ridding themselves of the vestiges of savings-centered theory, can do so with benefit to development economics by recognizing clearly that "every time phenomena fall outside traditional categories, orthodox economists do not rethink the issues, they merely rename them. We are left with the whole of economic development. . . . We are left at the point where every evolutionary economist begins: an evolutionary theory of value, a cumulative theory of technology, an interdisciplinary analysis of social institutions with special emphasis on their resistance to change, and a theory of growth and dissemination of knowledge and skills. We do have theory that conforms to reality." Ibid., pp. 263–64.
    The only point in contention, as previously discussed, is, on the one hand, the comment that all the institutionalist development economists have clearly not yet "rid themselves of the vestiges of savings-centered theory" to the degree De Gregori asserts (see the previous section of the text) is appropriate. On the other hand, the degree to which the majority of development economists, however they label themselves otherwise, have accepted the central thrust of these basic propositions of evolutionary economics may be larger than De Gregori and some other institutionalists have realized.
56. See E. J. Mishan, *The Cost of Economic Growth* (London: Staples Press, 1967), and the review article by Krishan G. Saini, "A Critique of Affluence: Mishan on *The Costs of Economic Growth*," *Journal of Economic Issues* 2 (December 1968): 393–402. See also P. A. Klein, "Economics: Allocation or Valuation?" *Journal of Economic Issues* 8 (December 1974): 785–811.
57. Ayres, "Legacy of Thorstein Veblen," p. 57.

Part III
The Study of Institutions

15

JƏİ *JOURNAL OF ECONOMIC ISSUES*
Vol. VII   No. 2   June 1973

Institutionalized Consumption Patterns in Underdeveloped Countries

Wendell Gordon

This article attempts to study consumption problems in underdeveloped countries. These problems are a result of (1) inadequate supplies of the right kinds of food and of (2) consumption habits. These habits are conceived, here, as representing institutionalized behavior patterns which frustrate the introduction of desirable new consumption practices. The inadequacy of protein in the diet is used as a whipping boy through most of the discussion.

David Hamilton writes: "Wants are social phenomena, the product of cultural conditioning. . . . Veblen contended that consumption was peculiarly conditioned by the system of status. . . . Thus our wants are affected by both institutional (symbolic) and technological (tool using) considerations."[1]

We need to eat to live; and yet, what we eat, and how much, and when is heavily conditioned by custom, habit, and social pressure. Muzafer Sherif says:

> Like other organisms, man is born with certain needs, such as the needs for nutrition, shelter, and, later, mating. . . . Along with this, we note another fact. When we observe people in the search for food, shelter, or mates, we conclude that these activities run in certain prescribed channels. People do eat, mate and enjoy

The author is Professor of Economics, University of Texas, Austin. This article was presented at the Annual Meeting of the Association for Evolutionary Economics, Toronto, Canada, 27-29 December 1972.

> the security of shelter; but how and under what circumstances
> they will eat, mate and enjoy shelter are, to a great extent, regulated
> by customs, traditions, laws and social standards. This is true
> for every individual, living in every society we know, primitive
> or highly developed. If an individual does not come under this
> category to any important degree, he cannot be said to be a
> member of society.[2]

To the proposition that wants are in large measure socially or
institutionally determined, we add the perhaps self-evident proposition
that there is want.

The Problem of Want

Much of the world's population is semistarved, lives in squalor
and chronic sickness, and dies young. This is true despite the fantastic
technical progress mankind has made since the Industrial Revolution.
In particular, millions of small children begin life starved for protein
and are deformed and mentally retarded in consequence before they
ever have a chance to do anything about it for themselves, if they
ever could.

I will regale you with only one quotation because you all know
that there is starvation and want in much of the world and that
malnutrition (and especially lack of protein in early years) adversely
affects intelligence, resistance to disease, human growth, and human
energy. The quotation is from Pedro Belli:

> Recent investigations indicate that a woman who suffers from
> malnutrition during gestation will give birth to a child who will
> be weaker, smaller, less resistant to disease, and less intelligent
> than a child whose mother ate well during its sojourn in the
> womb. Similarly, there is ample evidence suggesting that children
> who suffer from malnutrition, especially during the first months
> of life, will grow up into weaker, smaller, more disease-prone,
> and less intelligent adults than those who were well fed from
> the moment that they were born. The main economic implication
> of these findings is quite clear. Countries where the incidence
> of malnutrition is high will have populations that are less productive
> than countries where malnutrition is rare.[3]

A concern of this article is with the problem of bringing the very
poor up to a decent minimum level of living (not with the obtaining
of ever higher levels of living above the decent minimum). The
analytical problems involve (1) the reluctance or inability of the poor
to spend wisely such purchasing power as they may have, and (2)
the related question as to whether there are enough of the basic

necessities available so that in all reason the poor should have adequate supplies.

The answer to the question of potential overall goods availability must be that, in the current state of the arts, the world is quite capable of producing more than enough of the basic necessities for all. The problem is not the ability to produce and has not been since about 1900. Income redistribution, or consumption redistribution, and producing to capacity (or perhaps less than capacity) will suffice. The goods are or can be available. The problem is to deliver them to the needy and to have the needy consume them after they have them.

Despite this abundance and despite the Green Revolution, however, per capita food production does not seem to be growing in the underdeveloped countries.[4] For whatever the reasons (whether the rigidities of the land tenure arrangements or other causes for failure to take advantage of known technologies), there remain serious problems in implementing production.

The Protein Question

Protein Requirements

As an example of what is involved, there is the matter of protein starvation. Protein lack, especially in the very young, is, as has been mentioned, one of the great problems. A United Nations report says: ''Protein malnutrition, which is a problem of crisis proportions for the developing countries, must be recognized by the entire world community as a threat to world peace and stability which it can ignore only at its own peril. It is imperative that each developing country understand the magnitude and appalling implications of the problem now.''[5]

Tables 1 and 2 provide some information on estimated protein and calory requirements. Needs in hotter and colder countries vary, and they also vary according to the amount of work done by the individual, and according to his or her age, sex, and physical size. But there seems no reason to believe that they vary with the pigmentation of the skin.

At a rough estimate, the very poor person in an underdeveloped country needs about 25 grams of supplementary protein to approximate the acceptable minimum of 65 grams (55–75 grams or so).[6] Twenty-five grams is about one-twentieth of a pound, it is less than an ounce; by weight it is something less than half of a ten-cent Baby Ruth candy bar. One might, very roughly, quantify the magnitude of the problem in the following way. In this world of three and one half

Table 1. Calorie and Protein Supplies and Requirements by Sub-Regions (as Estimated in Early 1960s)

	Calories			Proteins			
	Supplies	Requirements	Supplies as percentages of requirements	Supplies in total proteins	Supplies of animal proteins	Requirements (practical allowances)	Supplies as percentages of requirements
	Per caput per day			Grams per caput per day			
Zone A							
North America	3090	2710	114	91	64	74	123
Western Europe	2950	2660	111	87	42	74	116
Japan	2250	2390	94	70	17	65	108
Oceania	3200	2540	126	93	62	73	127
South Africa	2830	2420	117	81	32	65	124
Zone B							
USSR	3010	(2600)	116	86	30		
Eastern Europe	3020	(2570)	118	94	34		
Mainland China	2180			63	7		
Zone C							
	2130	2260	94	57	11	61	93
Zone C							
Latin America	2600	2380	109	68	25	65	105
Central America	2440	2310	106	62	15	62	101
South America	2650	2400	111	70	28	66	106
Zone C							
Africa south of the Sahara	2130	2240	95	58	9	63	91
Central Africa	2010	2220	91	41	9	60	68
East Africa	2110	2270	93	63	11	63	99
West Africa	2170	2230	97	60	7	64	93

Table 1. *Continued*

	Calories			Proteins			
	Supplies	Requirements	Supplies as percentages of requirements	Supplies in total proteins	of animal proteins	Requirements (practical allowances)	Supplies as percentages of requirements
	Per caput per day			Grams per caput per day			
Zone C							
Near East and North Africa	2140	2340	91	64	13	64	100
Near East	2155	2330	92	65	14	62	105
North Africa	2081	2360	88	59	9	70	84
Zone C							
Asia and Far East	1990	2210	90	51	7	58	88
India	1980	2200	90	52	5	60	86
Pakistan	1940	2280	85	47	9	53	89
Other countries	2115	2200	96	51	11	56	91

SOURCE: Food and Agriculture Organization. *Provisional Indicative World Plan for Agricultural Development: A Synthesis and Analysis* (Rome: FAO, 1970), vol. 2, p. 491.

Table 2. *Existing Recommendations for Dietary Allowances*

	Age (years)	Weight kg.	Weight (lb.)	Height cm.	Height (in.)	Calories	Protein gm.
Men	25	65	(143)	170	(67)	3,200	65
	45	65	(143)	170	(67)	2,900	65
	65	65	(143)	170	(67)	2,600	65
Women	25	55	(121)	157	(62)	2,300	55
	45	55	(121)	157	(62)	2,100	55
	65	55	(121)	157	(62)	1,800	55
	Pregnant (3rd trimester)					Add 400	80
	Lactating (850 ml. daily)					Add 1,000	100
Infants‡	months 0–1§						
	1–3	6	(13)	60	(24)	kg. × 120	kg. × 3·5‡
	4–9	9	(20)	70	(28)	kg. × 110	kg. × 3·5‡
	10–12	10	(22)	75	(30)	kg. × 100	kg. × 3·5‡
Children	years						
	1–3	12	(27)	87	(34)	1,200	40
	4–6	18	(40)	109	(43)	1,600	50
	7–9	27	(59)	129	(51)	2,000	60
Boys	10–12	35	(78)	144	(57)	2,500	70
	13–15	49	(108)	163	(64)	3,200	85
	16–20	63	(139)	175	(69)	3,800	100
Girls	10–12	36	(79)	144	(57)	2,300	70
	13–15	49	(108)	160	(63)	2,500	80
	16–20	54	(120)	162	(64)	2,400	75

NOTE: *Food and Nutrition Board, National Research Council, Recommended Daily Dietary Allowances,* Revised 1953. Designed for the maintenance of good nutrition of healthy persons in the U.S.A. Allowances are considered to apply to persons normally vigorous and living in temperate climate.

SOURCE: Food and Agricultural Organization, *Human Protein Requirements* (Bristol. Eng.: John Wright, 1957), p. 182.

billion people, one billion, two hundred million have diets deficient in protein—from minor deficiency up to the 25 grams a day deficiency.

Production Costs

What might be the production costs involved in providing the desirable quantity of protein? Greatly increased quantities of protein can be obtained from fish protein concentrate, oilseeds (cottonseed soy beans, and peanuts), synthetic amino acids, assorted leaves and grasses, and even from chickens.[8] Apparently, for two cents or less. fishmeal concentrate can meet the daily protein supplement needs of a person. Protein from soy beans may cost one-half to one-fifth as much. Cottonseed (also inexpensive) has the advantage that it "comes from a plant that is indigenous to protein-poor tropical areas of Asia, Africa, and Latin America."

Don Fabun says with regard to some of the various protein production possibilities:

> Probably the most efficient use of a greatly increased fish harvest would be in the form of Fish Protein Concentrate, which may be defined as "any inexpensive, stable, wholesome product of high nutritive quality, hygienically produced from fish." The fish, in its entirety, is ground up, reduced to eliminate the water and fish oil, and the resulting product emerges as a powder-like concentrate that is about 80 per cent protein. One hundred metric tons of fish yields 15 metric tons of concentrate, equivalent to 12 tons of 100 per cent protein. The concentrate can be used as a food additive to traditional foods, although some problems of taste and consumer acceptance remain. About 25 grams of Fish Protein Concentrate, used as an additive to already available foods, provides sufficient protein intake per day for an adult.
>
> Costs are high, but not prohibitive. A 90,000-ton capacity plant, capable of producing enough protein for one million people per year, would require a capital investment of about $2.5 million, plus two fishing vessels of 120 feet in length, costing about $3 million, plus dock, handling facilities and distribution. Some $7 million overall would meet the protein supplement needs of a million persons per year, at a cost of less than two cents per person per day.[9]

Fabun points out some other possibilities. Chickens are very efficient as producers of protein, which suggests uses for curassow fowl in the tropics. With regard to inland fisheries, Fabun says: "When ponds are enriched with grains and seed meals, the yield is from 1,000 to 16,000 pounds per acre. These gains are important; the yield is not only high in protein content, but where ponds are fertilized, one pound of fertilizer yields from five to eight pounds of fish. In many areas of the world, these rich potential sources of protein [rice paddies used to raise fish as well as rice, and salt water estuaries] are not being exploited at the present time. Unfortunately it doesn't appear that much is likely to be done about them either, although the costs are minimal and the results significant."

Two cents per person per day (or perhaps much less, but let us use that figure and also disregard inflation) can provide enough protein to make up the "maximum" deficiency (25 grams). It has been estimated above that one billion, two hundred million people are deficient. If, on the average, they are deficient by 12.5 grams (half of the maximum), then the average deficiency could be met for one cent a day. That is $12 million a day, or about $4.4 billion a year. It averages about $3.65 per needy person per year.

Given the magnitude of these figures, a significant but not impossible effort virtually could solve the world's protein problem if governments simply would make the effort. The production capabilities are available; we do not have to await new scientific advances. The problem is one of almost pure institutional adjustment, with only a minor aspect involving the need for new technical knowledge.

What would happen if the United States were to address a letter to the governments of North Vietnam, the Soviet Union, and the People's Republic of China (with copies to all other governments and to Kurt Waldheim) saying:

> The United States understands that the poor of the world need about 15 billion grams a day more protein than they are receiving. This amount can be provided for about $4.4 billion a year. The United States stands ready to donate either this amount of protein or this amount of money to a committee to be constituted jointly by the governments of North Vietnam, the Soviet Union, and the People's Republic of China, with the understanding that the committee will supervise the distribution of the protein to the hungry people of the world in an equitable fashion.
>
> The United States stands ready to begin the program the day the Vietnam War ends. It hopes that on that day meaningful negotiations on disarmament (such as do not seem to have occurred in Moscow in May 1972) may begin.

Put the monkey on someone else's back for a change. Perhaps the United States also should state that in the future this is the only unilateral foreign aid to which it will be a party—no more military aid, no more tractors, no more "nothing else."

The suggestion is serious, but one should not put all of his eggs in one basket. Even if by some stretch of the imagination the United States and the other three parties should agree on such a procedure, there would be other difficulties. There are the problems of identifying the needy poor, of delivering the protein or of making it available to them, and of their eating it.

The Distribution Problem

First, the problem of delivering the protein. Should commercial marketing processes be used or some kind of gift dispensing? Should processes differ in cities, villages, and in the countryside? Should a distinction be made between the very poor and those who consume almost enough protein and can "afford" to buy the necessary additional amounts if they were only aware of the importance of protein? This latter situation may be more a result of strictures, customs, and ignorance than of the sheer inability to finance the consumption of more protein. Let us look at the possibilities in the cities and then in the villages and countryside.

The Cities

The distribution problem in the cities is of rising importance relative to the problem in the countryside because urban population is rising relative to country population.[10] Among the methods used to distribute protein supplements in urban areas has been the effort to foster its commercial but subsidized sale in pure form. The buyer would add the supplement to appropriate foods, thus ensuring adequate protein ingestion.[11] Experiments of this sort have been made involving heavy subsidies to permit very low pricing, and there have been substantial propaganda efforts to explain the usefulness of the product. This method has failed primarily because brief explanations of the need to the needy (in the expectation that the individual then would do the appropriate things to meet the need) is a process that has not worked very well.

There is an implication that the circumstances under which people are told about the protein supplements and the circumstances under which they are made available to people do make a difference. Some of these programs were aimed at the fairly poor rather than at the extremely poor. The psychological reaction frequently was: "If it is almost free, it cannot be worth much."

Perhaps governments should require that protein supplement be added to a variety of products sold commercially—perhaps bread, flour, or the equivalent of potato chips in the country in question. In the United States, one could reach some people by fortifying catsup. This procedure might deal with the problem of those of modest income who are consuming slightly less protein than is desirable, where the chief problem is one of ignorance of the need for additional protein, or ignorance as to an easy means for meeting the need, or unwillingness to eat unappetizing food merely because it is good for one. Also, there is a certain "inconvenience" involved if one has to add the supplement himself.

Certainly some types of fortification of some foods result in tastes that people find unpleasant for cultural or other reasons. But many reasonably likable foods can be produced by various known fortification procedures involving moderate costs.[12] Sugar may be fortified with Vitamin A. The protein content of macaroni may be increased with soy flour. A clorine bioxide can improve the efficacy of pasteurization in removing salmonella and staphylococcus from milk. Amino acids may be added to cereals. "Thus each of the major cereals may be made adequate as the sole source of food for man at any stage of his development by proper fortification at costs of 23 to 92 cents per child per *year*. The cost per adult would be approximately twice this figure." [13]

There is a somewhat more controversial proposal for dealing with the nutritional problem of the urban poor. Public markets and selected stores in the poorer areas should make soy beans (or the most inexpensive high protein content food obtainable locally) available free to their customers. Perhaps a protein fortified staple such as rice, manioc, or wheat flour also might be added. The basic idea is that one or two staples should be made available gratis. The number should be small to keep the process simple.

The government would provide the staples free to the stores and markets. The latter would cooperate in the program because the free distribution of the staples would attract customers, many of whom would buy other items. Such a procedure would no more destroy the value of other commodities or the viability of the market system than does the fact that air is available free destroy the value of perfume.

To prevent a sudden massive drainage of the supply of free staples because of the whims of isolated customers, there might be a provision that only limited quantities of the free staples could be acquired at one time by one person. Also, there well might be a major effort to discipline people who waste their free staples. Stated positively, a major propaganda program could attempt to indoctrinate people with the idea that they have an obligation to use their free staples effectively. However, this might be a difficult aspect of the procedure.

Incidentally, the wealthy United States might do worse than use such a program itself in lieu of the present complicated and unsatisfactory procedures such as food stamps. The basic staples would be free to all, rich and poor alike.

As to the government's difficulty in acquiring stocks of the free staples, what can be said? Most governments are up to their ears in costly price-support programs, many of which probably involve spending more money to curtail production than would be involved in this plan. Perhaps Brazil should spend more money on the production and distribution of rice and beans and less in trying to keep coffee off the market.

The Countryside

These are possible schemes for handling the distribution of protein in the cities, but what of the rural areas and the villages? One could maintain that in the thickly populated agricultural areas farmers are in close enough contact with villages (and villages with larger towns) that the same procedure could be used. Only relatively isolated rural areas would be left unattended, and they represent only a small percentage of the total population of underdeveloped countries. For example, much of highland Bolivia and Ecuador is in surprisingly intimate contact with cities such as La Paz and Quito.

But the isolated areas should not be entirely disregarded. Furthermore, the fact remains that in densely populated areas much of the food consumption has involved home-grown, nonenriched grain, rice, manioc, potatoes, and so forth. As already discussed, this problem involves the institutional changes necessary to induce the population to take positive steps to use protein additives in their home-grown food.

Perhaps an appropriate policy in remote areas and in more accessible areas with subsistence agriculture would be to encourage the planting and domestic consumption of soy beans, or other pulses, and other crops (peanuts, for example) that are high in protein. Changing cropping patterns and changing consumption patterns would become part of the same procedure. Does that make the problem twice as difficult or simplify it somewhat?

(I might say, parenthetically, that I am by-passing the land tenure problem. It may be that the institutional reorganization that would effect the results discussed here would involve land tenure changes or major shifts in the production practices of large landowners. Large-scale agriculture needs to become a business-like operation subject to the social security and wages and hours laws rather than remain a social status institution shielding archaic production practices.)

Consumption Mores

People do resist changing their diets even if they are told that a different diet will be better for them.[14] Thus, in the case of protein there is the difficulty involved in the willingness of the needy population to consume it, even when they have it. The protein, especially if it comes from fishmeal, may carry a slight odor which people will decide they simply will not tolerate, even if they drop dead in consequence. Or people may rebel against the mere knowledge that there is an ingredient in the food to which they are not accustomed, whether or not they can identify its presence.

Muzafer Sherif has cited an example involving Mohammedans and pork: "Present freshly broiled pork chops to two hungry men. One of our hungry men is a Mohammedan whose religion tells him that anything connected with pigs is disgusting—this is an established taboo, a norm. The other person is a Christian. He will seize the chops and eat them with gusto. The first person will not only not touch the chops, he will be filled with disgust both for them and for the person who eats such filthy things."[15] Then there are Hindus and cows.

A Spanish-language news magazine called *Visión* reports that an Argentine expert on nutrition working with the World Health Organization, Dr. Jaime Atlas, is skeptical about fostering the consumption of soy beans as a solution to the protein deficiency problem. Dr. Atlas is quoted as saying: "The problem invariably has been rejection. The consumers will not accept them."[16] He cited examples involving the effort to implement the commercial sale of *incaparina* in Colombia and Central America: "In Guatemala, where first class experiments have been made along this line, and in spite of intensive propaganda and ridiculously low prices, the effort has been a fiasco. It is very difficult to change the eating habits of people."

Since World War II the United States has made considerable effort to provide condensed and powdered milk to the poor and the protein deficient in the underdeveloped countries. Certainly this has been one of the more praiseworthy of the foreign aid activities, but the effort often has run afoul of difficulties. (1) It has not been of respectable magnitude; (2) much of the milk (how much, who knows) has been stolen and blackmarketed; and (3) frequently the people who need the milk most, and are entitled to it, have rejected it. "Pet" milk out of a can does not smell quite like what they are used to. (Canned milk also is a rather expensive way to meet the protein need.)

Perhaps one can conclude that a procedure which simply makes cheap (subsidized) protein available and advertizes the advantages is not likely to be a sufficient program. Or perhaps whether it is an adequate program depends a great deal on the nature of the advertising, the style and persistence of the appeal.

The Institutional Adjustment Problem

The institutional adjustment problem frequently is viewed as an almost insuperable barrier to the implementation of appropriate policies for fostering economic development. For example, raising the rate of saving or the consumption of new forms of protein are impossible tasks. The implication is that the planner should turn to other policies (such as foreign aid in lieu of higher domestic saving) if development is to be implemented. Some such critics seem proud to raise these objections, which imply their understanding of anthropology and the role of institutional barriers to development. If the truth were told, this attitude (combined with the typical economic development planner's propensity for Harrod-Domar growth models and their constant capital-output ratios) probably explains in large part why there has not been more development in the underdeveloped countries in the post-World War II period.

Changing the institutionalized behavior patterns that need changing (and leaving undisturbed those that do not) should have been the essence of development planning in the postwar period. A large measure of such an art would involve inducing the institutional change in a manner that makes the person who is changing believe that it is his own idea, or that he heartily endorses the change.

Dr. Jaime Atlas was cited earlier as emphasizing the difficulties in changing consumption habits. Yet, in the same article in *Visión*, a successful effort to feed a soy bean additive to school children in the province of San Juan, Argentina, was reported. A controlled experiment involved giving the supplement to some students and not others. There were no major difficulties in persuading the children to eat the additive, and there were significant gains in height, weight, and vitality for those consuming it. The report of the Instituto de Technología Agropecuaria, which conducted the experiment, "expressed satisfaction with the results obtained and concluded that the low cost, easy preparation, and high nutritive value of the soy beans 'indicate the desirability of using soy beans in school cafeterias as well as in the family diet.'"[17]

For those who buy their flour or bread commercially, there seems to be a relatively straightforward solution to the institutional resistance problem: Add tasteless and odorless protein to the flour or bread. Some of the proteins obtained from oilseeds and grasses do not affect taste or odor perceptibly. Surely national laws requiring bakers and/or millers to add the appropriate amount of protein to their product would avoid the consumer rejection problem. Perhaps such a program could be implemented without subsidization. The price of bread or flour would merely rise appropriately, and appropriately should be very little. Since there undoubtedly would be protests from the bakers or millers, some subsidization might abate the complaints.

The general predilection of people in the middle classes to imitate their "betters" and to experiment with foreign restaurants and exotic cooking (à la the emulation or demonstration effect) should mean that the institutional resistance hurdle in this area should not be a major one, especially if a few shahs and pashahs can be induced to allow themselves to be photographed eating the enriched bread with gusto. Julian Simon and David Gardner recommend this approach.[18] Sell the prestigious market first and count on the emulation effect to attract a large segment of the underprivileged. With regard to marketing ProNutro protein in South Africa they say: "Sell the white market first and the nonwhites will then imitate the white purchasing pattern."[19] Such an approach allegedly worked for Hind Brothers, promoters of ProNutro: Sales to blacks became a rising share of total sales with the passage of time.

But the relatively well-to-do are the least important part of the problem. We know that incomes in very poor countries vary from an average of $50 to $60 a year to $400 or $500 a year, but this tells us nothing about who actually can afford the $7.30 a year for protein. Even if incomes are better allocated, how many desperately may need income supplement to help with obtaining the protein? The psychology of the Simon and Gardner approach is good, but they are not addressing the most needy audience. The very poor are the important problem and a different kind of problem. The issue is: How is protein to be gotten to the undernourished infants of poverty-stricken parents in very poor countries?

Perhaps the initial, specific solution must be worked out within each culture. Obviously, it is extremely important that there be meaningful and understandable communication back and forth between the agents trying to implement change and the people who are supposed to benefit from the change.[20] A workable and specific format in some instances would be to have the protein provided through the church and eaten during the ritual. Each communicant could be influenced to take home an appropriate amount of the protein to be eaten promptly by all the backsliding members of the family. Village leaders should be at the front of the church, cooperating in the activity. Word could be spread that those who went to church received something special for their pains. Obtaining the cooperation of churches in this activity might not be easy in all cases, but it is a pretty sorry church that does not provide these blessings to its communicants. This suggestion is not made as a general solution to the problem, but it is an example of "a reasonably feasible institutional change" in some situations. Perhaps more difficult is the chore of convincing governments to organize the programs, to obtain and provide the protein, and to arrange for the necessary financing. But that problem was discussed, if not solved, earlier.

Effecting Institutional Change: Alternatives

In the preceding section it was indicated that the use of the emulation effect might be a possibility in inducing people to change their habits. It may be helpful at this point to offer a catalog of possible approaches available to would-be policy makers or planners. As they try to expedite the acceptance of a new behavior pattern by a group of people they should tread lightly so that, essentially, people will be making the appropriate changes because they want to do so.[21]

The basic pattern, as suggested by institutional theory, is that the accumulation of technical knowledge (an inherently dynamic process in which the unearthing of one bit of new knowledge naturally leads to the unearthing of another) occurs with a speed regulated by the effectiveness with which the institutional order resists the assimilation of the new knowledge. The assimilation of the new knowledge or technology is a rational act as people (and institutions) become aware of the implications and usefulness of it. The institutional changes needed then will happen more or less as an automatic by-product of the assimilation process—no fuss, no feathers. People eat food that contains the protein supplement because they have come to understand that is the best thing to do. Through their understanding of the implications of the technology they have played a role in development. An institutionalized pattern of behavior is changed almost without protest (and certainly without regret after the change is a *fait accompli*). That is the natural evolution of the process, a process more or less inevitable if it is given time.

Matters are more difficult and sensitive when an effort is made to expedite the process. In this context the least dangerous policy tool, the one which is least likely to backfire, is the emulation effect. If the group whose habits are to be changed sees other people whom they respect or envy engaged in the behavior pattern, they may well change their behavior norm readily. If the former maharajah would sit in the town square, eat a little protein, and lick his fingers afterward (or even kill a cow and barbecue it), the effect might be electric. (Perhaps the barbecue had best be approached by easy stages. It certainly should not be performed suddenly on a Monday morning by a foreign economic development adviser or a foreign tourist.) That the Catholic church has proved capable of modifying its Friday meat rules indicates that such changes are possible.

Another tool is an appeal to the profit motive or the desire for gain (over and above the natural role of the profit motive in inducing rational men to make intelligent use of new technology). An all-day sucker could be offered to each child who would eat his protein like a good little boy or girl. Bribing or subsidizing the adults to cooperate may be a bit more difficult, but certainly bribery, subsidization, and appeal to the desire for gain are possible policy tools in urging people to change consumption habits in particular and behavior patterns in general. Of course, this method will work better in a society where one of the respected, institutionalized behavior patterns is a desire for gain or wealth. A closely related approach might be to state that a person will be stronger or smarter, or some such, if he eats more protein. This procedure will appeal to those who admire strength, or intelligence, and so forth.

Then there is repetitious cajoling, arguing, and demonstrating. In the United States the county agricultural agent and visiting nurse programs frequently have worked wonders in showing people how to do things better, demonstrating that things can be done better, and by repeatedly making the same points finally inducing people to do things differently. This is prosaic, hard work that requires a permanent organization and conscientious, continuing day-to-day activity. The one-shot visit by an expert does not often get the job done—especially if it is a one-shot visit by a foreign expert. However, film of some popular star (like Jane Fonda or María Felix) downing *incaparina* might work wonders.

There are other, not so polite, procedures for changing behavior patterns. One such is shock. A nineteen-year-old will change a lot of behavior patterns within a few days of being inducted into the army. Mother's home cooking is something he will learn to do without quickly. During World War II, South Sea Islanders, Arabs, and Italian bambini who chanced to find themselves in the neighborhood of military action and U.S. Army installations changed many behavior patterns rapidly. After the war or after removal of the installations, things were never quite the same again. Things certainly will never be the same again among the Vietnamese. Another possibility is imposition of change by a dictator. Anyone who doubts the method should recall Joseph Goebbels. Whether much use should be made of such shock treatment or coercion in effecting institutional change seems doubtful, yet this is the approach of many Marxist revolutionaries.

In summary, possibilities for effecting the assimilation of new technical knowledge include: (1) adaptation as a result of the natural, rational working out of the impact of new technology upon the prevailing institutions; (2) the emulation effect; (3) appeals to the desire for gain or the implementation of some other prized goal; (4) cajoling, arguing, and demonstrating; (5) shock; and/or (6) coercion. Many of the nuances involved in these procedures are yet to be understood, and there well may be other procedures which it would be helpful to identify and discuss.

In the protein case these various alternatives might be used. In the first instance the planner has no role. Technical knowledge about the importance of protein and about production processes may or may not lead to the consumption of adequate amounts of protein in the near or distant future. The emulation effect and some of the implications of the desire for gain and other prized goals already have been discussed. The emulation effect and cajoling, arguing, and demonstrating would seem to be the most respectable alternatives. Dictatorial coercion surely must be ruled out. Are these possibilities adequate for the job? I believe they are, but not before there has been a lot of difficult experimentation.

Conclusion

In addition to the protein problem there are other important consumption problems such as adequate supplies of calories and vitamins, and adequate clothing and housing. All of these have their special features and complications, many of which differ greatly from the protein problem. Nevertheless, the manner in which the protein question is approached may indicate how problems connected with other consumption needs might be handled.

I am tempted to summarily state that the solution to the problem of adequate total quantities of basic consumption items involves opting for large-scale commercial agriculture and for enforcing the social security laws, minimum wage laws, and so on, in agriculture. There also should be provision for the forfeiture by the landowner of land he is not using effectively. Then the government should deal with the unemployment problem with a job guarantee program. Many such jobs can be and should be in rural areas involving road maintenance, irrigation, garbage disposal, and sanitation generally, plus the provision of entertainment by those with skills along that line. On the other hand, I do not want to declare that one unique solution formula should be applied everywhere, or that a given solution will continue to be effective with the passage of time.

The possibilities for providing decent food, clothing, and shelter for all, at modest cost, are there if the planners simply will come down to earth. There is another powerful "if." Some firmly entrenched domestic institutional resistance must be overcome. The answers given so often by underdeveloped countries, that we cannot pass that tax law because of the resistance of business, or we must have that tariff because the industry demands it, or we cannot change the land tenure system because of landlord resistance, no longer will suffice. The underdeveloped countries simply must change major aspects of their own social and economic systems or, in the vernacular, shut up. Grants in foreign aid, it was proven long ago for numerous reasons, cannot step into this breach and provide welfare by magic. Major amounts of responsibly supervised self-help are the crux of the matter. Economic development planners need to leave their desks and computers and start working in the projects.

There are some consumption issues that are not of overshadowing importance to a poverty-stricken country but which will be of somewhat more relevance as the country begins to get its head above water. One of the real contributions of Keynesian theory was its demonstration that prior personal monetary saving is not necessary to set moving the wheels of investment, production, rising income, and rising welfare. In fact, a relatively high marginal propensity to consume (the same as a relatively low marginal propensity to save) well may mean that a given amount of new investment will increase income and welfare more than would be the case if people were trying to save relatively more.

Deborah Freedman writes with regard to Taiwan: "The consumption of modern objects appears to make a positive contribution to economic development in Taiwan. The characteristics and economic behavior of the families who buy modern durables in Taiwan is inconsistent with the idea that such consumption necessarily decreases savings and capital formation and, thus, impedes development efforts. Instead, the families who are modern in consumption are characterized by a complex of characteristics, attitudes, and behavior which, on the whole, are likely to be beneficial to the development process. . . . The desire to own modern objects is a motivational force."[22] This would seem to be another example of Duesenberry's demonstration or emulation effect, and it is one more bit of evidence that conning people into saving rather than spending may not be the best way to "get ahead."

Actually, the problem of changing consumption patterns may not be as difficult as it seems. For example, among the young the word gets around that things may be done differently than their fathers have done them. It becomes the vogue, or even a mania, to do things differently, and there is a new sort of institutionalized procedure.

But now the effective social pressure is by youth upon youth not to be "square," rather than pressure by parents on children to behave like their parents. Youth between ages fifteen and twenty-five can be fantastically adaptable in both developed and underdeveloped countries. With the aid of films and the emulation effect, it is possible that changes may occur faster than is desirable.

The conventional wisdom regarding consumption habits is that it is difficult if not impossible to change them because of cultural mores. Development should be planned in such a way that it does not butt heads unnecessarily with these sacrosanct institutions. Frequently, these habits are exactly what does need to be changed. The problem is how, not whether, or "we cannot." All too much of the economic development planning since World War II has assumed that certain cultural traits could not be changed and, consequently, has tried to implant desired change by oblique and frequently futile methods, such as heavy reliance on tariffs, or foreign investment, or grants-in-aid. People are quite capable of changing ostensibly deep-rooted cultural traits quickly and dramatically if they are forced to do so. In fact, they may be quite proud of themselves afterward, although they balked like mules beforehand.

Most of the argument of this article is fairly trite and obvious. It hardly can appeal to the economist who wants his models sophisticated and mathematized. Returning to propositions like these after thirty years of development planning involving capital-output ratios and complete planning for whole economies, with interrelations in multiequation models checked out for consistency, hardly can appeal to those who have been perfecting these sophisticated methods during that time. These proposals, being trite and obvious, are not easily implemented. They require hard work and difficult interpersonal contact among people, which probably explains why so little of this sort of thing has been done in the underdeveloped countries. Let me hedge a little. More has been done than I am recognizing, but a lot more needs to be done.

There is nothing really innovative in this article. It chiefly involves the preachment that a lot of things should be done more effectively, energetically, conscientiously, and understandingly by more people, when in fact a lot of conscientious people have been trying to do something for a long time. But the frustrations involved in effective institutional resistance to the making of appropriate changes have been an inhibiting influence, and the methodology of modern economics has not helped much.

286 Wendell Gordon

Notes

1. David Hamilton, *The Consumer in Our Economy* (Boston: Houghton Mifflin, 1962), pp. 64, 65, 76.
2. Muzafer Sherif, *The Psychology of Social Norms* (New York: Harper and Row, 1966 [1st ed. 1936]), p. 1.
3. Pedro Belli, "The Economic Implications of Malnutrition: The Dismal Science Revisted," *Economic Development and Cultural Change* 20 (October 1971): 1-23.
4. Donella H. Meadows et al., *The Limits to Growth* (New York: Universe Books, for Potomac Associates, 1972), p. 49.
5. United Nations, Department of Economic and Social Affairs (Panel of Experts on the Protein Problem Confronting Developing Countries), *Strategy Statement on Action to Avert the Protein Crisis in the Developing Countries* (New York: United Nations, 1971), p. 5.
6. Food and Agriculture Organization, *Provisional Indicative World Plan for Agricultural Development: A Synthesis and Analysis of Factors Relevant to World, Regional, and National Development*, 2 vols. (Rome: FAO, 1970), vol. 2, p. 491; and FAO, *Provisional Indicative World Plan for Agricultural Development: Summary and Main Conclusions* (Rome: FAO, 1970).
7. Meadows et al., *Limits*, p. 46; and David Turnham, *The Employment Problem in Less Developed Countries* (Paris: Organisation for Economic Co-operation and Development, 1971), pp. 80-92.
8. Don Fabun, "The Protein Path: Hunger Begins with a Hungry Plant," in Donald P. Lauda and Robert D. Ryan, eds., *Advancing Technology: Its Impact on Society* (Dubuque, Iowa: Wm. C. Brown Co., 1971), pp. 351-59, especially p. 353.
9. Ibid., pp. 351-59, especially pp. 352-53.
10. FAO, *Provisional Indicative World Plan . . . A Synthesis*, vol. 1, p. 8.
11. The protein supplements involved have been called *incaparina* in Colombia and Central America, *fafa* in Ethiopia, *supro* in various other African countries, and *argentinina* in Argentina. *Visión*, 17 June 1971, p. 52.
12. *New York Times*, 15 October 1972, p. 24; *New York Times*, 13 September 1972, first page, second section; and *Visión*, 4 November 1972, p. 15.
13. President's Science Advisory Committee, *The World Food Problem* (Washington, D.C.: U.S. Government Printing Office, 1967), vol. 2, p. 325.
14. The headline of a *New York Times* article in the 31 October 1972 issue read: "If People Won't Eat the Healthful Foods, What Can Be Done?" Serious studies of these matters include: National Research Council, Committee on Food Habits, *The Problem of Changing Food Habits* (Washington, D.C.: U.S. Government Printing Office, 1943) and *Manual for the Study of Food Habits* (Washington, D.C.: U.S. Government Printing Office, 1945); and Margaret Mead, *Food Habits Research: Problems of the 1960's* (Washington, D.C.: National Academy of Science-National Research Council, 1964).
15. Sherif, *Psychology*, p. 28.
16. *Visión*, 17 June 1972, p. 52.

17. Ibid.
18. Julian L. Simon and David M. Gardner, "World Food Needs and 'New Proteins,' " *Economic Development and Cultural Change* 17 (July 1969): 520-26.
19. Ibid., p. 522.
20. Arthur H. Niehoff, ed., *A Casebook of Social Change* (Chicago: Aldine, 1966), *passim*; and Conrad Arensberg, *Introducing Social Change* (Chicago: Aldine, 1964).
21. Niehoff, *Casebook*; and Arensberg, *Social Change*. George Zollschan has addressed himself to these questions also, but his results do not seem very helpful in the present context. See George K. Zollschan and Robert Perrucci, "Social Stability and Social Progress: An Initial Presentation of Relevant Categories," in George K. Zollschan and Walter Hirsch, eds., *Explorations in Social Change* (Boston: Houghton Mifflin, 1964), pp. 99-124, especially pp. 116-20.
22. Deborah S. Freedman, "the Role of the Consumption of Modern Durables in Economic Development," *Economic Development and Cultural Change* 19 (October 1970): 25-28, especially p. 47.

16

Jei *JOURNAL OF ECONOMIC ISSUES*
Vol. VIII   No. 4   December 1974

Beyond Capitalism: A Role for Markets?

David Dale Martin

Clarence E. Ayres's last published work called for the abandonment of the "market system." He ended his new introduction to a reissue of two of his earliest works with the following words that are very much relevant to the topic of this symposium in his honor:

> Surely the species that has found its way from savagery to husbandry, and from husbandry to automation can do better than what Karl Marx called capitalism. The market system was a product of the industrial revolution of the eighteenth century. But we are now approaching the twenty-first century and a world-wide economy. Like the first stone hand-ax, the first fire brand and articulate speech itself, computerized automation is a manifestation of the technological process. Human life and well-being depends upon the furtherance of that process now no less than it did a thousand years ago when (as we have lately discovered) the foundations of the industrial economy was [*sic*] being laid, or a million years ago when mankind was first embarking upon its technological adventure. The values we seek are those of human life and well-being. The process by which we seek them is an experimental process, as it has always been. By pursuing this process we will go beyond capitalism, as our forebears went beyond the systems into which they were born.
>
> This is the message of institutionalism.[1]

The experimental, technological, process through which mankind seeks the values of human life and well-being is inhibited by the

---

The author is Professor of Business Economics and Public Policy, School of Business, Indiana University, Bloomington.

tendency to fetter itself with ceremonies, myths, folklore, and other "institutional" constraints. That message of institutionalism came through to this student of Ayres so strongly that no aspect of human behavior could ever again be viewed without asking whether it stemmed from the technological process or the institutional side of the dichotomy. The market, itself, must be scrutinized from this point of view to ascertain whether it is a system of institutional arrangements that inhibit the technological process and thwart the search for human values and well-being, or whether it can be made to play a positive role in that search for something better than "what Karl Marx called capitalism."

This article will attempt to explain why at least one "Ayresian" economist has concluded that decentralized, competitive markets are not exclusively characteristic of the sort of market system conceived of by Adam Smith and deplored by Ayres, but are also characteristic of the technological process itself, through which we seek the values of human life and well-being. Furthermore, and most important, policies designed to achieve decentralized, competitive market processes of decision making can be the most effective instrument for moving society "beyond capitalism" because the technological process is experimental, and market mechanisms, if truly competitive, are more conducive to that process than the centralized, bureaucratic, hierarchical alternatives most likely to emerge whether they be Galbraithian or Demsetzian.

Ayres's Rejection of the Market System

Both Galbraithians and Chicagoans have abandoned advocacy of Henry Simon's type of competitive market system in which government plays a crucial role in maintaining a structure on control of property conducive to decentralized decision-making processes. Conventional wisdom all across the spectrum today seems to recognize a technological imperative for centralized planning of very large sectors of economic activity. Whether democratic government should play a role in that planning or leave it to the corporate governments called the "private" sector is now widely debated by economists. Ayres's institutionalism does not necessarily support either side of that debate, which takes place very much within the classical conception of the economy, although he shared the view of both Galbraithians and modern-day Chicagoans that antitrust policy offers little to a progressive society eager to make good use of modern technology.

The classical conception of the economy against which Ayres struggled throughout his career was challenged at those very foundations held in common, although implicitly, by orthodox economists for two centuries. The alternative he offered in the institutional conception of the economy was a consciousness of cultural processes embodying the imperfect human search for a better life. About the classical conception, Ayres's last work said:

> [It] assumed the prevalence of private property and organized markets. Thus the economy so conceived is commonly identified as a market economy, an identification which glosses over the predominance of private property as well as the whole complex of cultural processes through which the present (and very recent) state of affairs has eventuated.
>
> The founders of this system believed that the universe, including man, had been endowed at the Creation with a harmony of forces which needed only to be left alone to work to optimum effect. It was of course this belief which prompted Adam Smith to remark in his most famous passage that a man who seeks only the best bargain he can find "is led by a guiding hand to promote an end which is no part of his intention"—meaning, of course, the general welfare. Present day apologists no longer invoke "pre-established harmony." They argue only that, lacking any absolute truth or value, the market (for which read "the *status quo*") is the only alternative to chaos. Such negativism is less inspiring than Adam Smith's Deism, and its effect is no less stultifying.[2]

Ayres's essential message to this writer was that the economic system does not necessarily result in a socially optimal allocation of resources whether or not income is equitably distributed and competition prevails in all markets. With John Dewey's epistemology underpinning his study of human history, Ayres was able to reject the "stultifying" classical conception without needing to put in its place an alternative conception that included a clear statement of the necessary and sufficient conditions for social welfare.[3] Be it enough that we recognize that human beings are creative, curious, and intelligent animals who behave "technologically" in ways that tend to move them toward a better life if they can escape from the inhibitions on technological progress that stem from the human tendency to cling to outmoded ceremonial patterns of behavior.

Ayres, I think rightly, viewed the logical positivist philosophy of science and the orthodox economic doctrines based on it as part of the inhibiting institutional side of the dichotomy in human culture. The "market system" is a concept used, on the grounds of welfare optimization, to justify preserving aspects of the status quo that do, indeed, inhibit technological progress and the seeking of the values of human life and well-being. We need to distinguish, however, between the "market system" as a stultifying conception of the economy and the actual use of markets in the organization of society's economic activity. Markets can be judged instrumentally in terms of their usefulness in achieving proximate ends in precisely the same way that technological alternatives are judged.

Just as the market as an organizing mechanism can be placed on the technological side of the "technology-institutions dichotomy," so also can much of orthodox economic theory. Although the theory gives little assurance that mankind is optimizing even when governments stand aside and leave those with power free to behave "efficiently," orthodox theory does provide valuable insights into the causes and consequences of much of human economic behavior. The theory can even lend support to the judgment that public policies aimed at promoting more use of markets as well as more competitive markets are consistent with Ayres's vision of a better society "beyond capitalism."

The Alleged Autonomy of Corporations

The structure of control of the world's economic activity includes centers of power in the form of organizations of human beings whose relations to each other differ significantly from their relations to "outsiders." Some persons are members of organizations with more power to control economic activity than others. Within any one organization some persons exercise more power than others. Most persons are part of more than one economic organization, and individuals may move in and out to some extent. Economic organizations persist through time and have a life of their own apart from the life of their individual members.

The study of the structure of control of economic activity can be as broad as human ecology, cultural anthropology, or the whole of the social sciences; or it can be restricted by premises that delimit the scope of analysis either by delimiting the concept of economic activity or by simplifying the assumptions about the nature of human beings and their relations to each other. Little is accomplished by so realistic an approach that one is left merely with an assertion that the world is one big organization about which we know very little. Nevertheless, without rejecting the process of reasoning in which the real world is simplified for purposes of analysis, one can suggest some of the consequences of particular sets of simplifying assumptions that affect ways of looking at the observable facts.

Economic theory has made much progress in developing the implications of a particular set of assumptions about the nature of human beings and the essential characteristics of their organizations. Crucial to that development has been the assumption that both households and firms are maximizing entities. With that premise it is possible to analyze all relations between insiders and outsiders as market transactions. An alternative assumption is that firms are not independent entities but parts of larger and more complex organizations.

Less abstractly, let us consider the possibility that the structure of the U.S. economy still resembles that depicted by the National Resources Committee in 1939.[4] A large number of the largest corporations were found to be part of eight "interest groups." These intercorporate, nonmarket relationships were further studied by the Temporary National Economic Committee.[5] A more recent study of one of those eight "interest groups" has set forth much evidence, albeit largely circumstantial, that a Rockefeller financial interest group exists and includes within its sphere of influence, or domain, a very large part of the world's economic activity.[6]

Corporations are linked not only by common directors and a community of interest in ownership of stock, but also through joint ventures, particularly in the control of mineral inputs.[7] Such facts about nonmarket relations among corporations raise serious questions about the consequences of treating corporations as maximizing entities.

Joint ventures in the form of corporations of which most or all the stock is owned by two or more customer corporations present the obvious question of whether the owning corporations are independent of each other. That question can be answered only by examining in detail the effect of ownership of stock on the control of the jointly owned corporation and the degree to which the contractual arrangements with the participating corporations constrain their autonomy. The effect of the joint venture arrangement on the economic structure may be quite different if one or more of the participants is a government or a government controlled corporation, but the distinction between governments and corporations as centers of economic power is becoming increasingly less meaningful.

One way to recognize the fact of joint ventures and still retain the simplifying assumption that firms are entities that relate to outsiders through markets is to group participating corporations together as a single firm. In view of the large number of joint ventures and the overlapping nature of participation in them, solving the theoretical problem by such grouping would radically change our perception of the number of "firms" in the economy. In iron ore, for example, the result would not be merely to reduce the number of firms and increase the degree of perceived concentration in that market, but the perception of a market itself would disappear. A similar effect would result in crude petroleum production.

One basic problem in all attempts to identify the corporations to be included within a "financial interest group" is the fact that "joint ventures" may exist on that level as well as on the level of industrial corporation joint ownership of mineral ventures. For example, for many years the General Motors Corporation was closely related by stock ownership and interlocking directorates with both the Morgan and the duPont interests.[8] When United States Steel Corporation was created in 1901, several powerful interests participated. Not only was the Morgan group involved, but also John D. Rockefeller became one of the largest single stockholders in exchange for his iron ore properties.[9] If James Knowles were to use the method of analysis with which he attempted to identify the Rockefeller group to attempt to identify a Morgan group, he would very likely find that his lists of controlled corporations were not mutually exclusive.

Here again the problem could be solved by lumping together all interest groups that are linked by such joint control. Indeed, careful examination of community of interest through stock ownership and interlocking directorates among the combined groups and with other corporations probably would result in the perception of still other corporations as part of the enlarged group.

If economic power is concentrated to the degree suggested here, then our perception of the economic system as a market system is, indeed, called into question. John Kenneth Galbraith, of course, has called to attention the "charade" of antitrust and the "planned" nature of a large part of the economy.[10] Our ability to analyze and forecast the functioning of the economic system might be improved if we looked at the system with a better awareness of the degree to which it is in fact centralized and bureaucratically controlled—that is, awareness that transactions perceived as market transactions are in large part intragroup transfers.

The picture of the economy painted here is by no means a new one. It seems, however, that each generation must rediscover for itself the distinction between the actual structure of economic power and the "market system" as a conception of the reality. Adolf Berle and Gardiner Means in 1932 showed clearly the degree to which industrial corporations are not independent entities.[11] Means went on to head the National Resources Committee study that first identified eight "interest groups." Ironically, the Berle and Means work laid the basis for the myth that each corporation is a completely autonomous entity! The message of Berle and Means was that the corporate revolution had separated ownership from control, as indeed it had if one looks only at the universe of property owners. Just as with the trusts in the 1880s, many owners of common stock found themselves by 1932 with no voice in management. That owners in general no longer control their property, however, does not mean that those who exercise power make no use of ownership interest to retain their power. Nor does separation of ownership from control necessarily imply that each corporation is autonomous.[12]

In his preface to the 1932 work, Berle said: "The translation of perhaps two-thirds of the industrial ownership to ownership by the large, publicly financed corporations vitally changes the lives of property owners, the lives of workers, and the methods of property tenure. The divorce of ownership from control consequent on that process almost necessarily involves a new form of economic organization of society."[13]

That new form of economic organization requires more change in economic analysis than appears in the literature of industrial organization of the past four decades. Empirical research in recent years has focused on four-firm–four-digit industry concentration ratios. As important as that literature is, most of it is based on data that are grounded on the assumption that each corporation is an autonomous decision-making entity unless more than half of its voting stock is known to be owned by an acknowledged parent corporation.[14] Theoretical work on industrial organization has focused on the theory of markets.[15] But if the "financial interest group" hypothesis holds, then we must focus on the group's internal organization simply because of the magnitude of economic activity that takes place intragroup.

Ayres was quite correct, it seems to me, in his perception that the classical, including the Chicagoan, conception of the system "glosses over the predominance of private property" when it identifies the system as a market economy. The Berle and Means idea of separation of ownership from control contributed to conventional wisdom with which "present day apologists" defend the status quo by defending a mythical competitive market system.[16] Neither Berle nor Means interpreted their own findings in 1932 or later as supporting that myth, and both have made substantial contributions to the development of an institutionalist alternative to the classical conception of the system.[17] And like Ayres, neither Berle nor Means mourned the disappearance of the decentralized structure of control which all supposed to be incompatible with modern technology.

778   David D. Martin

Interest Groups, Markets, and Technology

Technological progress has proceeded at an accelerating pace within
the "new industrial states" that have emerged during the past century.
That fact, however, does not prove that a less centralized structure
of control would have inhibited technological change. Indeed, we
have much evidence to indicate the contrary.[18] The consequences
of the centralization of control within a small number of financial
interest groups would be, if true, far greater than the consequences
of oligopoly or monopoly in most of the markets of an economy
that retained the essential characteristics of a market system. The
theory of the firm rather than the theory of markets affords some
insight into some of these consequences. If financial interest groups
behave as maximizing entities, then orthodox economic theory can
tell us much about the way their decisions on investment and technical
innovation would differ from those of automonous corporations with
or without some measure of monopoly power in markets.

Much has been written in recent years on the question of what
constitutes rational investment behavior for a "firm" operating within
a market system.[19] The traditional short-run theory of the firm is
based on the assumption that the firm seeks to maximize its net
revenue per unit of time. With a fixed amount of investment in plant
and equipment the firm simultaneously would maximize net revenue
per dollar of capital invested. If a firm's investments in new capital
equipment always took the form of immediate lump-sum outlays that
result in a constant flow of net revenue in perpetuity, then the long-run
concept of profit maximization would be essentially the same as the
short-run concept. Under these simple assumptions the rational firm
would rank alternative investment projects by comparing either internal
rates of return or discounted present values of estimated future net
cash flows and invest in *all* projects whose return is above the interest
rate or whose present value is positive using the interest rate as
the discount rate.

The macroeconomic theory on which contemporary monetary and
fiscal policies are based rests essentially on this simple analysis of
investment behavior of firms. Managerial economics and the theory
of the firm have explored a large number of more complex sets of
assumptions since Armen Alchian's pathbreaking article in 1955.[20]
Franco Modigliani and M. H. Miller recognized that the taking into
account of uncertainty raises serious questions about the use of the
"rate of interest" as well as the meaning of profit maximization for
a corporation with many stockholders with disparate utility functions.[21]

To avoid the theoretical indeterminancy that stems from basing investment theory on a criterion that depends upon "who happens to be the owners of the firm at the moment," they chose to assume that a corporation's investment (and technological) decisions are based on maximization of the market value of the owners' stock, whoever the owners may be. That means, of course, that their theory of investment tells us very little about the behavior of a corporation the top management of which is subservient to the objectives of a larger organization.

If it be true that many of the large industrial corporations are, as Knowles alleges, controlled by an informal coalition of persons acting through official positions on boards of directors of financial institutions and nonprofit corporations, all of which have substantial portfolio interests in the industrial corporations, then the orthodox theory of investment is crucially affected. Each industrial corporation not only would be maximizing something other than the market value of its common stock, but also would not be dealing at arms' length with the suppliers of its capital.

If several corporations are under the common control of a larger interest group, then the interests of "outside" stockholders will enter into the investment decision as constraints rather than as part of the goal being maximized. If the group is organized so as to move investment decisions up toward the top levels of management for approval or veto, it seems reasonable to assume that at some level the effect of each corporation's investment proposals would be evaluated in terms of their probable effects on the performance of all other corporations in the group.

Perhaps an interest group reasonably could be assumed to have a well-defined objective of maximizing a weighted aggregate of market values of its interests in all the corporations in the group. On the other hand, it may be more reasonable to assume that control of the group rests in the hands of a small number of natural persons whose utility functions are maximized. In either case investments that tend to spoil markets in any industry in which the group has an interest would be inhibited.

Investment behavior of industrial corporations is intimately related to technological development and innovation. Particularly relevant is the effect of investment in new technology on the value of assets that embody alternative technology. Joseph Schumpeter's notion of creative destruction raises questions about the incidence of the costs and benefits of the processes of technical change. If our institutional structure is better characterized by a few large interest groups than by a decentralized market system, then we should not judge the efficacy of markets in terms of that centralized system just because the defenders of the status quo label it a market system.

Interest Groups and Stabilization Policy

The viability of capitalism was most seriously threatened by the Great Depression almost a half century ago. The "new economics" of J. M. Keynes provided a new lease on life for "liberal" governments in the Western industrialized part of the world. The system seems to be threatened again in the mid-1970s by similar internal stresses. Despite continued economic development and growing affluence, the governments of most capitalist nations have been unable to cope adequately with inflation without risk of precipitating economic collapse. The unemployment-inflation dilemma has grown worse at an accelerating pace in the United States in the past decade. If economists persist in their conception of the system as a market one rather than a highly centralized but poorly planned system, they risk dismissing as unfeasible the alternative of introducing competitive markets.

Stabilization policy has rested primarily on control of aggregate demand with monetary and fiscal policy measures. As the incompatibility of full employment with price level stability became apparent in the 1950s, the employment objective was sacrificed. In the 1960s more expansive fiscal policies were adopted, and "incomes policies" were developed to cope with inflation, culminating in direct price and wage controls beginning in 1971. The failure of controls to solve the dilemma was evident by 1974. Clearly, markets had to be allowed to clear to avoid the chaos of shortages and bottlenecks. Put another way, the "planned" sector of the U.S. economy was even more poorly planned with direct controls.

The problem of achieving truly full employment of the labor force is more than a problem of adequate aggregate demand. Ever rising aggregate demand somehow must induce adequate investment to provide jobs and adequate output to hold average prices stable. Holding the prices down by Presidential admonition, guideposts, price controls, or any other incomes policy merely will postpone the inflation if it discourages investment in new plant and equipment. Tight money and the acceptance of a higher level of unemployment as "full employment" also discourages investment. Investment spending has been viewed primarily from the standpoint of its short-run contribution to aggregate demand rather than from its longer run effect on the supply of goods and thereby on employment and price levels.

Given the present centralized structure of control of the economy prices rising at increasing rates may be necessary to induce investment at sufficient rates to provide jobs for all who wish to work. Likewise, the centralized character of decision making with respect to technological innovations may inhibit the processes of creative destruction that would otherwise lessen scarcity and thereby reduce inflationary pressure from full employment macroeconomic policies.

The Industrial Reorganization Alternative

In recent years several serious proposals have been made for restructuring the economy to reduce concentration and increase competition.[22] The most powerful argument against such proposals is that concentration is no greater than that required by economies of scale. If that be the case, then whatever is to evolve "beyond capitalism" must be a planning mechanism at least as centralized as the existing structure. The problem of industrial reorganization then would be not how to break up giant corporations and interest groups, but how better to plan the economy.

Before accepting the inevitability of a centralized planning mechanism, would we not be well advised to find out whether competitive markets could be given a larger role without inhibiting the use of the best available technology? At stake is not only the use of the best technology of the past, but also the encouragement of continued technical development and innovation uninhibited by the tendency of those with power to use it to protect asset values rooted inevitably in continued scarcity.

The customary concept of the plant in economic theory is very fuzzily defined, if indeed it is defined at all. The Bureau of the Census operational definition of an *establishment* is quite arbitrarily defined in terms of contiguity of site of diverse equipment under the same ownership. But both uniformity of ownership and contiguity are really quite irrelevant to the *technical* questions of plant design and location of equipment except insofar as they might affect transportation costs and the location of sources of inputs and destination of outputs. Whether goods in process or workers are transported inside the bounds of a chain-link fence or over great distances is not particularly important to analysis. It is not unreasonable to conceive of all establishments in the United States with railroad sidings to be part of a single plant that includes the railroad lines and equipment.

By attributing to the twenty-first century a "worldwide economy," Ayres, it seems to me, was recognizing the fact that transport and communication technology have developed to the point that economic activity anywhere on the planet can be coordinated with activity

782   David D. Martin

anywhere else on the planet and made interdependent with all economic activity of all the human species.

One can view the question of how humans might order their economic activity in terms of the concept of the single plant–multiple product worldwide economy. If the world were starting from scratch, it would face the technical problems of plant design and layout that any firm faces when it undertakes investment in a new plant. Technical questions can be answered by technicians, but managers or planners must give the technicians the parameters within which to solve such technical problems. The "system," be it the market system or some as yet to be evolved successor to industrial capitalism, must provide such parameters.

That the values of human life and well-being are not adequately served by the system that now exists for ordering the human species's economic activity was indeed the message of Clarence Ayres's institutionalism. He recognized particularly the evolutionary, experimental nature of the process by which we seek these values. The problem is one of designing a worldwide plant and control system conducive to continued technological change. We are not starting from scratch. We must seek ways to move from what we have to something better.

Decentralization in the structure of control does not need to interfere with appropriate plant design. If one abandons the classical welfare proposition that prices are the appropriate measures of value to use in making technological choices, then the quest for certainty about the "right" plant design can be abandoned as well. Instead, we seek an iterative process in technical change that holds open options and encourages enlargement of the set of technical alternatives. Decentralization of control of investment decisions seems more likely to yield continued technical change than bureaucratic, centralized control.

Viewing the world economy as one plant requires that we recognize the possibility of market interfaces among the many parts of that whole. Physical integration of two stages in production processes controlled by two corporations is certainly not uncommon in the economy today. Corporations locate production activities close to one another to facilitate the flow of goods in process. For Alcoa to supply General Motors with molten aluminum does not require merger of the two corporations.

If society wishes to restructure the economy by moving toward more use of competitive markets, then the chief problem is not economies of scale but the identification of appropriate points within the economy at which to interpose markets with arms'-length bargaining to replace bureaucratic administration. Particularly important is the question of vertical integration. Only by creating markets for inputs in which autonomous firms can buy on equal terms can we encourage autonomous decisions on investment and technical change.

Notes

1. Clarence E. Ayres, *Science: the False Messiah (1927) and Holier than Thou: the Way of the Righteous (1929)* in one volume with a new introduction: *Prolegomenon to Institutionalism* (Clifton: Augustus M. Kelley, Publishers, 1973), pp. xi-xii.
2. Ibid., p. xi.
3. John Dewey, "Theory of Valuation," *International Encyclopedia of the Unified Sciences*, vol. 11, no. 4 (Chicago: University of Chicago Press, 1939).
4. National Resources Committee, *The Structure of the American Economy, Part I, Basic Characteristics*. A Report Prepared by the Industrial Section under the Direction of Gardiner C. Means (Washington, D.C.: 1939).
5. *The Ownership of the 200 Largest Non-Financial Corporations*, Monograph No. 29, Temporary National Economic Committee (Washington, D.C.: U.S. Government Printing Office, 1941). For a review of more recent literature on the question of the extent of autonomy of corporations, see John M. Blair, *Economic Concentration* (New York: Harcourt Brace Jovanovich, Inc., 1972), pp. 75–81.
6. James C. Knowles, "The Rockefeller Financial Group," in *Superconcentration/Supercorporation*, Ralph L. Andreano, ed. (Andover: Warner Modular Publications, Inc., 1973).
7. Gordon Bava, "The Concentrated Control of Iron Ore by Major Steel Companies as an Unfair Method of Competition," *Southern California Law Review* 46(1973): 1116–67; and John R. Munkirs, "Joint Ventures in the International Petroleum Industry: Production and Pipelines." unpubl. Ph.D. diss., University of Oklahoma, 1973.
8. National Resources Committee, *The Structure of the American Economy*, chart II, facing p. 162, and letter from Pierre S. duPont to Irénée duPont dated 26 November 1920, printed in Alfred P. Sloan, Jr., *My Years with General Motors* (Garden City, N.Y.: Doubleday & Company, Inc., 1964), pp. 32–38.
9. "Rockefeller, John Davison," in *The National Cyclopaedia of American Biography* 29(1941): 1–6.
10. John K. Galbraith, *The New Industrial State* (Boston: Houghton Mifflin, 1967).
11. Adolf A. Berle, Jr., and Gardiner C. Means, *The Modern Corporation and Private Property* (New York: The Macmillan Company, 1932), pp. 80–84.
12. Adolf A. Berle, Jr., *Power Without Property: A New Development in American Political Economy* (New York: Harcourt, Brace and Company, 1959).
13. Berle and Means, *Modern Corporation*, pp. vii–viii.
14. Blair, *Concentration*; and *Studies by the Staff of the Cabinet Committee*

784   David D. Martin

on Price Stability (Washington, D.C.: U.S. Government Printing Office, 1969).

15. Joe S. Bain, *Industrial Organization,* 2d. ed. (New York: John Wiley & Sons, Inc.).

16. See testimony of J. Fred Weston, Harold Demsetz, and George Hilton in *The Industrial Reorganization Act,* Hearings before the Subcommittee on Antitrust and Monopoly of the Committee on the Judiciary, United States Senate, 93rd Congress, 2d sess., on S.1167, Parts 1 and 3A (1973 and 1974).

17. Gardiner C. Means, "Beware Phase III," *Washington Post,* 18 February 1973, reprinted in Hearings on S.1167, Part 1, pp. 35-43.

18. *Studies by the Staff of the Cabinet Committee on Price Stability,* Study Paper Number 2; and Blair, *Concentration,* Part 2, pp. 85-254.

19. Irvin M. Grossack and David D. Martin, *Managerial Economics: Microtheory and the Firm's Decisions* (Boston: Little, Brown and Company, 1973), pp. 189-218.

20. A. A. Alchian, "The Rate of Interest, Fisher's Date of Return over Cost, and Keynes' Internal Rate of Return," *American Economic Review* 45 (1955), reprinted in *The Management of Corporate Capital,* Ezra Solomon, ed. (Glencoe: The Free Press of Glencoe, 1959), pp. 67-71.

21. Franco Modigliani and M. H. Miller, "The Cost of Capital, Corporation Finance, and the Theory of Investment," *American Economic Review* 49 (1959), reprinted in *Corporate Capital,* Solomon, ed., pp. 150-81.

22. The "White House Task Force Report on Antitrust Policy, for President Johnson, July 5, 1968," released 21 May 1969, reprinted in *Economic Concentration,* Hearings before the Subcommittee on Antitrust and Monopoly of the Committee on the Judiciary, United States Senate, 91st Congress, 2d sess. (1970). Part 8, pp. 5053-82, known as the "Neal Commission," proposed legislation to break up corporations in concentrated industries. A much more comprehensive proposal was introduced by Senator Philip A. Hart as S.3427 in 1972 and again as S.1167 in 1973. See Hearings on S.1167 cited above.

[17]

Jei *JOURNAL OF ECONOMIC ISSUES*
Vol. XVII   No. 3   September 1983

Externalities, Property Rights, and Power

Andrew K. Dragun

This article explores the economic problem of externalities in a conceptual framework focusing on the issues of property rights and power. Externalities in an economy are pervasive as a function of the nature of individual interdependence. There are always two or more sides to an externality issue, with the problem of externalities a question of which interests are to be exposed (to bear the costs). An unavoidable issue of income distribution is essential to all externality situations.

Underlying the consideration of externalities is the explicit nature of the economy "as a system of mutual coercion." The recognition of individual *powers to coerce* is a cornerstone of present and future economic activity. Such individual power, as an ability to exercise choice, is a function of income and wealth distribution. But the economic system is interrelated in that income and wealth distribution are a function of the law, while the use of government to influence the law is ultimately a product of the power structure.

Ultimately, where the ubiquity of choice according to the interrelation of legal and economic processes is recognized, an analytical theme is developed to consider the question, *Whose interests are to count?* as well as the role of government in the resolution of specific externality situations.

The author is Research Fellow, Center for Resource and Environmental Studies, Australian National University. He has benefited from valuable comments from Warren Samuels and David Anderson. The editor and two anonymous reviewers also provided useful suggestions.

Individual Choice, Coercion, and Power

The traditional perspective of individual choice exists within a framework of a restricted opportunity set and an existing vector of market prices; the rational economic individual acts to maximize the relevant objective function. Within the realm of society, individual economic choices are interdependent.

With individual economic choice defined within given opportunity sets, the conceptual precursor is clearly the need to specify the economic and social criteria that determine each individual's opportunity set: what are the factors and forces that govern the available alternatives and their respective costs? To be more explicit, individual choice is a direct function of the individual's opportunity sets; the question then is to determine how specific opportunity sets determine individual choice.

Warren Samuels delineates two categories of individual choice based on notions of the opportunity set.[1] Choice may be delineated according to the degree of autonomy of individual action, firstly *as voluntary*, where individuals have complete autonomy or freedom in choice of behavior, or *volitional*, where individual choice is restricted to a particular range of given alternatives and their respective prices.

The crux here is that "voluntary" choice, as usually construed in the market context, is analogous to volitional choice in that available alternatives are always limited and determined by existing price vectors. Individual choice in such a setting is only voluntary given that significant restrictions have already been imposed to limit possible choice.

Particular actions as a consequence of volitional choice affect the actions and choices of others. In this context *coercion* is the "impact of the behavior and choices of others upon the structure or array of one's opportunity set, that is, upon the scope of one's volitional choice."[2] Ultimately, the economy becomes a "system of mutual coercion," where the choices of each individual affect the opportunity sets and volitional choices of other individuals. Subsequently, *injury* becomes the product of coercion in terms of explicit losses and reductions of volitional choice by the restriction of available alternatives or the increase in their costs.[3] *Benefits*, on the other hand, are the opposite of injury, and may be expressed as the gain of an increased range of alternatives available as a result of specific coercion.[4]

Within the framework of mutual coercion, the final link in the choice paradigm is the individual power of choice. Individual *power* is the ability to assert particular choices and to participate in certain decisions. Individual power is directly a function of the individual opportunity set, but it is more in that it is explicitly related to the general economic system of mutual coercion. Power is the ability to coerce, but it does need to be weighed as to the coercion and injury of others in return. Power, then, is determined by the individual's relative position in both formal and informal organizations; hence government is ultimately a function of individual power, as well as the relative rights structure and the existing law.

Having established a foundation, it is now possible to consider the dynamics and processes of volitional choice. Fundamentally, the individual's opportunity set determines volitional choice. Volitional choice relates directly to the individual's ability to coerce, to conduce benefits for self and injury for others. The ability to coerce is a function of the individual's (relative) power, this power in turn being a function of the law. Subsequently, income and wealth distribution being derived from the opportunity set, both are a direct function of individual powers and the law.

But ultimately the use of government is a function of individual powers, with the law being determined by existing income and wealth distribution. Hence, individual opportunity sets, and inevitably individual choice, are a direct function of individual power and income and wealth distribution. The circle is complete: volitional choice determines the law, and is itself determined by the law.[5] The question of individual choice then transcends "given" opportunity sets to focus on how individual power and the law determine individual volitional choice, and conversely, how individual choice gives rise to individual power and does determine the law.

Choice and the Economic System

Individual power, the law, and government, as well as market prices, determine individual choice in a market transaction. To be more explicit, individual opportunity sets are not given; rather they are under continual dynamic pressure from the effects of individual power, the law, and government, factors that in turn are determined by those same opportunity sets.

Depending on existing opportunity sets, certain individuals may be better situated to express and utilize their powers to influence government and direct the law in their favor. Subsequently, in later periods, such individuals may enhance their opportunity sets together with their range of volitional choice and their prospects for exercising power and invoking coercion. Fundamentally, economic choice, derived from existing opportunity sets, is related to the power to influence government politically, thereby determining the range of economic choice in the future. The position of large organizations and corporations, considered to be legal individuals, is especially relevant in this context. The power of large corporations, as a function of assets, employment, and output, places them in an advantageous position not only to influence the rules under which they operate, but also to be instrumental in determining economic choices by individual citizens.

In the institutional setting of the market, price, output, and efficiency are related to existing individual opportunity sets. The *status quo* definition of opportunity sets, the existing power structure, and the related income and wealth distributions determines prices derived from existing markets. Subsequently, it follows that market prices, as a measure of social choice, must necessarily reinforce both the existing power structure as well as the established income and wealth distributions. Market prices are then a specific expression of a certain structure of opportunity sets and power, with the implication that social choice based on such prices must necessarily be normative sentiment on whose interests and choices are to count.

Similarly, output and production in an economy are products of the established legal system and the existing power structure. While production in an economy is a function of particular technologies as well as output, output itself is defined according to specific opportunity sets and relative individual interests in the demand context. Efficiency, on the other hand, is a product of circumstances. Efficiency is a function of individual interests or rights, and not vice versa. Given a particular structure of law, it is possible to determine a specific individual rights scheme and subsequently a relative efficiency. Efficiency is rights-structure specific and since there is no unique structure of rights, it cannot be said that there is a unique efficient social solution.

Where the Paretian criterion is applied to practical policy, its conservative bias or re-enforcement renders explicit the arbitrariness of efficiency in the traditional sense. At the policy level the welfare significance of Paretian improvements is dubious where the multitude of social changes inevitably render some individuals worse off while rendering certain others better off. Consequently, while the notion of Pareto optimality assumes institutional criteria, it is impossible to utilize the Pareto criteria to determine "better" institutional situations.[6]

Given such assumptions underlying Pareto optimality, the pursuit of Pareto improvements becomes a way of fine-tuning a specific and very well-defined institutional structure. As S. V. Ciriacy-Wantrup observes, the procedure thus attenuated is essentially technical engineering.[7]

In a broader institutional perspective, such as in externality circumstances where the economic problem can be defined according to the non-existence of a property rights structure, no unique Pareto optimum will exist as a function of the range of potential property rights structures. For each conceivable institutional structure it follows that there does exist a unique Pareto optimum, whose efficiency cannot be compared to other Pareto optima. Consequently, the ultimate issue of externality is reduced to a direct choice of the respective institutional alternatives themselves: Which property rights structure is to be given standing?

Beyond the consideration of efficiency, to which the Pareto criterion is addressed legitimately within a well-defined institutional structure, the criteria originally assumed as given in the initial Paretian framework now emerge as variables for comparison. Hence, when the comparison is between two different institutional structures, income distribution, the distribution of wealth, the existing legal and moral systems, and the distribution of power all become criteria of comparison along with efficiency. Where efficiency *is* defined according to a particular institutional structure, it becomes clear that comparing different institutions according to the criteria of efficiency is conceptually erroneous.

Finally, within a dynamic social environment where opportunity sets and individual interdependencies are always in a state of flux, the utility of pursuing a Paretian search for efficient optima is futile because of the continually changing institutional conditions. Fundamentally, society is always confronted with the need to choose between competing interests, it being inevitable that some individuals will be rendered worse off and others better off, with direct implications for income distribution and the structure of power.

The Pareto criterion must be reappraised further in relation to the Public Choice "fundamentalist developments" of Paretian principles.[8] Within the notion of volitional choice considered above, the Wicksellian unanimity rule, fundamental to individual decisions in the Public Choice context, emerges as arbitrary as a consequence of the existing individual opportunity sets.[9] Individual choice and subsequent economic transactions and agreements are necessarily a function of an existing structure of power, the existing law and rights system, and the established income and wealth distributions. Consequently, individual choice and resultant transactions emerge as the product of the general system of mutual coercion; the questions then are, What choice do particular individuals have? And, What coercion is inflicted on them by the choice of others?

Hence, the voluntary and unanimous agreements envisaged in the Wicksellian context are the product of coercive circumstances. The agreements may be voluntary given that certain individuals have no other volitional choice; however, to assert a degree of "rightness" in such agreements is to effect an implicit normative judgment that the existing individual opportunity sets are in some manner more preferable than others. In this context, as W. J. Samuels notes, "the Pareto criterion functions conservatively to reinforce the *status quo* decision making process."[10]

Property Rights—Externalities

Issues of property rights are at the core of the theory of externalities. Where specific externality situations are characterized by an indeterminate property rights structure, subsequent externality solutions rest on decisions concerning which individual's opportunity sets are to be enhanced by the assignment of a particular beneficial right, as well as whose opportunity sets are restricted by the resulting exposure. Externalities are reciprocal by nature and any subsequent "solution" must explicitly account the beneficial rights assignment, together with the inevitable costs of exposure. The pervading issue is, Who is to benefit and who is to bear the costs?

The relationship of power to property rights is a central distinction in property rights theory. On one hand, the existence of power is a crucial factor in the emergence of property rights as an element in Western society, and on the other, power is an essential determinant in the delineation of specific property rights. In the analysis of J. R. Commons, property is distinct from power. As Don Kanel observes, "Property in the sense of physical security in possession of things emerges as a result of containing arbitrary physical violence and converting it into 'constitutionally' restrained monopoly of physical power vested in the state."[11] In this context, property rights are a countervailing and stabilizing force to the raw physical power that was intially the prerogative of the autocracy.

Beyond the restraining of raw physical power, recognition of property rights is a significant development in the economic sphere where the emergence of economic power is now of primary concern. As delineated above, economic power is the means or capacity by which individuals exercise economic choices. Within the context of mutual coercion, the relative economic opportunity sets of respective individuals determines economic choice recognized as volitional. However, economic power is also instrumental in delineating specific opportunity sets and hence future volitional choices.

Within the institutional structure of the competitive market, the potential for the economically powerless to be subjected to the arbitrary and uncontrolled activities of the economically powerful generates "property-like devices," where the economically weak attempt to "convert the arbitrary power of the strong into constitutionally regulated power."[12]

As Kanel notes, the conversion of arbitrary to responsible power requires that all involved parties participate in the making and changing of specific social rules governing the relationships between them, with the necessary provision of third party quasi-judicial and quasi-political institutions at various levels of social organization.[13]

While property rights have emerged to control arbitrary power in society, it is implicit that those property rights are a direct function of existing regimes of power in society. In this context Jeremy Bentham's work on positive rights provides useful insights. Developing the notion of positive rights as a critique of the established natural rights tradition, as exemplified by Sir William Blackstone—and as a cornerstone in his utilitarian theory of society—Bentham introduces the notion of the power of individuals and of the state into the social determination of rights and duties.[14] According to Bentham, the essence of all rights assignments is normative, on one hand, in that every rights description inevitably confronts one person's wishes and interests against another's. On the other hand, actual rights declarations are positive in that they are a direct function of the existing power structure of individuals and of government.[15] Inevitably, however, it is the ultimate threat of physical violence vested in government that does determine how particular rights are assigned and who is exposed to injury.

The crucial issue of rights assignment is implicitly normative. The central question of property rights assignment is, Whose interests are to be favored and whose relatively restricted? The question of income distribution is an essential and irremovable component here; rights assignment will change the existing distribution of income. Subsequently, where government does act to delineate and assign property rights, the final distribution of rights and hence income is a function of the structure of economic power, since the actual use of government is a function of the power structure. As Samuels observes, "The power structure is a function of the law *and* the use of government is a function of the power structure, and income and wealth distribution."[16]

The issue of government is then one of the government for whom rather than big government as against small government. Where the *status quo* is the explicit product of past government activities and regulations, a claim to curtail government involvement relative to the *status quo* becomes a normative claim that the governmentally assigned and protected rights in the *status quo* are somehow better than a potential rights assignment in another scheme. The traditional justification for the "non-interventionist" view is of course founded in the classic liberal philosophy of individual freedom—where freedom is defined as a function of established rights and hence of the existing power structure.[17] Subsequently, the result of government non-involvement in the matter of property rights assignment, unavoidable in any externality resolution process, is that the "freedom" and power structure inherent in the *status quo* are given precedence to other interests. The question of government then is whether the ideals of liberalism or some other justification are to be given standing; or more generally, "Whose interests are to count?"

Consequently, governmental decisions are ubiquitous and an inescapable part of all individual activity. The dilemma becomes more significant when one recognizes that such choice will be profound in terms of income distribution, since income distribution is an inevitable outcome where institutional change is an issue. It follows that a governmental choice between the interests of different individuals is inevitable in resolving an externality. Government will determine who has the right to act and accrue specific benefits and who is to be exposed to bear the costs.

The important point here is the explicit recognition of *duality* in rights assignment. The assignment of a particular right involves a clear and normative social and governmental choice between the interests of different individuals; the choice is unavoidable. The interests of certain individuals may be enhanced by the assigning of a beneficial right, but the interests of others will be relatively restricted by exposure to those rights. The explicit question is, Whose interests are to be enhanced and whose to be exposed and injured?

Subsequently, legal and institutional criteria beyond the competitive market are clearly pertinent in addressing the value of specific rights. Besides the exchange considerations developed from the market, the actual legal identification of rights, the relative use of rights, the limits of physical and legal definition of rights, and the prospects of both legal and non-legal change will all influence the relative valuation of specific property rights. Fundamentally, given the continually changing pattern of interrelationships between respective individuals, rights definition and value will always be in a state of flux.

As alluded to above, externalities are reciprocal as a consequence of the duality of property rights. Externalities are pervasive in all individual activity. To solve one specific externality creates another. The enhancement and restriction of respective opportunity sets is unavoidable.[18] Essentially, the focus of externalities here transgresses the usual limits of economic efficiency, to emphasize the consequences for income distribution of particular individual activity. Hence externalities are not irrelevant because they do not conduce to Pareto-better bargaining arrangements, or because they don't generate specific cases of resource misallocation.

The basis for contemplating externality situations in this setting is the indeterminate rights structure within which the externality is recognized, with particular emphasis on the actual *rights* existent in the *status quo*. As Samuels and A. A. Schmid observe, individuals acting in the real-world *status-quo* of external diseconomies may or may not have an explicit legal right to act.[19] The usual impetus of external diseconomy is the initiation of some activity as a matter of course in the use of certain physical property, without any legal sanction by court precedent or statute.[20] The crux of the externality solution then is that the legislature or the courts will have to act either to affirm a right to the generator of the externality or to deny the generator the presumed use. For the legislature or the courts not to act would render the "presumed" right to generate the externality of *de jure* consequences.

Within this framework of presumed rights and indeterminate inter-relationships, externality solutions inevitably involve a process of delineating and assigning rights, where presumed rights are made explicit with legal sanction and force. In the traditional diseconomies example of pollution, the polluter's "presumed" right to generate effluent will be made explicit and sanctioned or the pollutee's presumed right not to be exposed will be affirmed. In either case there is a clear question of income distribution; in the former, the polluter obtains use of the environment as an assimilator of produced wastes, thus enabling the polluters to realize greater than normal profits, while in the latter case, the erstwhile pollutee obtains an unspoiled and much valued increment to personal satisfaction. It is basic that the actual rights assignment that will overcome the previously existing externality occurs as a non-compensated loss to the restricted party, in that the restricted individual is not recognized as having a legitimate right to lose.[21]

Subsequently the delineation of externalities is ubiquitous within the existing system of mutual coercion. As Samuels notes, "The *existence* of any externality and the total pattern of externalities both are a function of the structure of mutual coercion, ultimately of the structure of power."[22] Hence, externalities are the product of the interaction and exercise of relative power, since externalities, being the substance of mutual coercion, are the direct result of the impact of the choices of respective opportunity sets and power is the means to realizing choice.

The essence of externalities and their resulting solutions is that the individual interdependence at the heart of a given externality will not disappear in the normal realm of economic activity. The process of externality

676   Andrew K. Dragun

solution, or internalization, is part of a process whereby asserted legal rules and sanctions institutionalize certain activity once existent in an indeterminant rights system. Consequently, activity once thought of as initiating general external diseconomies can subsequently be established, with legal rules, as legitimate economic enterprise. While this process of internalization is clear, the crucial question remains: Which externality activity is to be given legitimacy and sanction so that it may appear as a normal component in the structure of mutual economic coercion?[23]

A general scheme of human interdependence and externality can be observed in the accompanying figure.

Beyond the fact that externalities are ubiquitous in the general system of mutual coercion, it is apparent that the underlying structure of individual interdependence is in a continual state of flux and development as a consequence of technological innovation, changing individual tastes, changing resource availability, increasing population, and varying market and institutional structures. Consequently, we observe over time a continually emerging system of externalities with new legal action inevitably needed to assign a new structure of relative rights and hence a new system of mutual coercion. As additional information becomes available on established interrelationships, new conflicts will emerge which may change the established pattern of rights resulting in the implementation of a new rights structure.[24]

In another dimension, the complexity and interdependence of the general system of individual behavior is expected to provide no basis for clear and absolute distinctions of property. As J. L. Sax observes, the inevitable characteristic of property is the *interconnectedness* of various aspects of property use; property cannot be delineated in a vacuum independent of all other property and individual activities.[25] Subsequently, to emphasize the claims inherent in one class of property is to neglect the claims associated with a second class of property; the question again is, Whose property is to be favorably considered?

Conclusions

The theme of this article has been that externalities are a ubiquitous part of social institutional choice. The interdependent forces that characterize externalities are the same interdependent forces observed in legitimate economic and social intercourse. The difference between the two classes of interdependent forces is that society, through government, has acted to render certain relationships explicit with legislative statute or court decree. However, this sanctioning process does not eliminate the

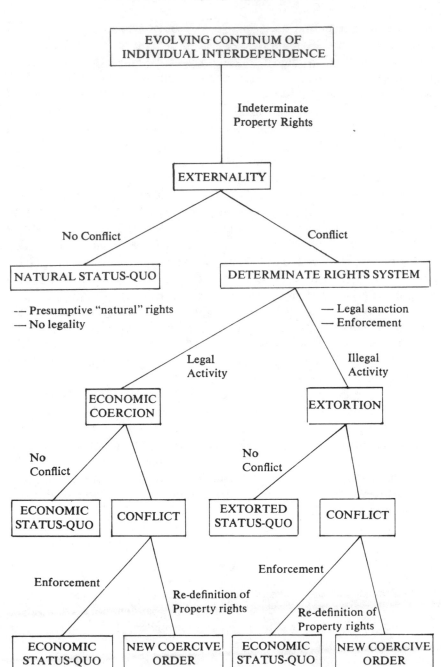

Figure 1. *Taxonomy of Individual Interdependence*

interpersonal distribution of benefits and costs, nor does it imply any degree of rightness of particular activities.

Benefits and costs are inevitable in externality situations, just as they are inevitable in the realm of legitimate economic and social activity. The crucial question is, Who is to benefit and who is to be injured? The significance of externality situations here is not that they are legal or illegal; they are non-legal. For society and government to refrain from making specific choices and decisions on particular externality questions is to *de facto* sanction economic forces best able to take advantage of the *status quo* structure of power.

Notes

1. W. J. Samuels, "Welfare Economics, Power, and Property," in *Perspectives of Property*, ed. G. Wunderlich and W. L. Gibson (University Park, Penn.: Penn State University Press, 1972), p. 7. The citations are from the draft manuscript.
2. Ibid., p. 8.
3. Ibid., p. 9.
4. Samuels summarizes the general paradigm of choice and coercion thus: (1) The economy is a decision making process, and a decision making structure; (2) as such the economy is a structure and process of mutual coercion and mutual opportunity; (3) the acting individual exercises volitional choice from an opportunity set that is both a dependent and independent variable in relation to the structure of mutual coercion: the individual's choices visit injury through coercion upon others, and others' choices visit injury through coercion in reverse; similarly with benefits; (4) the allocation of resources and the distribution of income are a function of the structure of mutual coercion, the structure of opportunity sets, the structure of volitional choice, and the actual choices made. Ibid., p. 9.
5. J. M. Buchanan and W. J. Samuels, "On Some Fundamental Issues in Political Economy: An Exchange of Correspondence," *Journal of Economic Issues* 9 (March 1975): 15-38.
6. Samuels delineates the institutional assumptions of Pareto optimality as follows: (1) The distribution of *income* is assumed, as either the *status quo* distribution or indifference to any distribution; (2) the existing distribution of *wealth* and endowments of property rights is given; (3) the existing system of *legal and moral rules* is assumed; including the rights of access to and use of private property—income and wealth in general—and the operation of social control; (4) the existing distribution of *power*, or power structure in society, is assumed; (5) existing *technology, resources,* and *tastes* are assumed; (6) the existence of a *market* for exchange is assumed; (7) all individuals are assumed to have a bounded consumption set (individuals are assumed to be able to participate in market activities—beyond mere survival); (8) the existing distribution of capacity to derive utility from consumption, and the social value

structure in general, are assumed; (9) efficiency is comprehended in terms of maximization; (10) the economy is assumed to be competitive; (11) it is assumed that externalities and public goods do not exist; (12) it is assumed that sufficent knowledge exists to produce intertemporal optimality; (13) second order optimality or stability conditions such as convexity and perfect divisibility are assumed; (14) assumes the price-cost structure that emerges as a consequence of demand-supply interaction, given the other assumptions; (15) assumes that individual preferences are to count, given the other assumptions, as well as scarcity; (16) assumes that a local rather than the largest maximum is acceptable as an optimum; (17) assumes that second-best considerations, to the extent not excluded by earlier assumptions, are either nonexistent or acceptable. From Samuels, *Welfare Economics*, Section 3, pp. 16–18. Also, for background on Paretian Economics see W. J. Samuels, *Pareto on Policy* (New York: Elsevier, 1974).

7. S. V. Ciriacy-Wantrup, "The Economics of Environmental Policy," *Land Economics* 47 (February 1971): 36–45.

8. See C. K. Rowley and A. T. Peacock, *Welfare Economics: A Liberal Restatement* (New York: Halsted Press, 1976), for useful background on the fundamentalist view of Public Choice Theory.

9. On the notion of Wicksellian unanimity, see J. M. Buchanan, "Politics, Property and the Law: An Alternative Interpretation of Miller et al. v. Schoene," *Journal of Law and Economics* 15 (October 1972): 439–452.

10. Samuels, *Welfare Economics*, p. 45.

11. Don Kanel, "Property and Economic Power as Issues in Institutional Economics," *Journal of Economic Issues* 8 (December 1974): 827–40.

12. Ibid., p. 829.

13. Ibid., p. 833.

14. See J. R. Commons, *Institutional Economics* (Madison: University of Wisconsin Press, 1959), p. 219–21.

15. Ibid.

16. See Buchanan and Samuels, "On Some Fundamental Issues," p. 17.

17. On the liberal concept of freedom, see Gerald MacCallum, "Negative and Positive Freedom," *Philosophical Review* 76 (July 1967): 312–34; and also A. Levine, "Foundations of Unfreedom," *Ethics* 88 (January 1978): 162–72.

18. Both Samuels, *Welfare Economics*, and R. R. Coase, in "The Problem of Social Cost," *Journal of Law and Economics* 3 (October 1960): 368–91, come somewhat close to this recognition.

19. See W. J. Samuels and A. A. Schmid, "Polluters' Profits and Political Response: The Dynamics of Rights Creation," *Public Choice* 28 (Winter 1978): 99–106.

20. Ibid.

21. See especially W. J. Samuels "Interrelations Between Legal and Economic Processes," *Journal of Law and Economics* 14 (October 1971): 435–50.

22. Samuels, *Welfare Economics*, p. 73.

23. On externality solutions, Samuels delineates four criteria with institutional import: (1) Externality solutions impose externalities of their own; (2) externality solutions involve the use of power, the restructuring of the use of power, and the redirection of the use of power; (3) externality solutions involve the restructuring of opportunity sets and the redistribution of costs and benefits; (4) externality solutions create a new decision making structure, giving effect to hitherto excluded interests and/or participants. Samuels, *Welfare Economics*, p. 73.

24. Ibid., p. 68.

25. See J. L. Sax, "Takings, Private Property and Public Rights," *Yale Law Journal* (December 1971): 149–86.

[18]

Jei *JOURNAL OF ECONOMIC ISSUES*
Vol. XII   No. 1   March 1978

Property Institutions and
Economic Behavior

Alan Randall

It is the purpose of this essay to identify and evaluate the contributions of neoinstitutionalist-heterodox economists to the elucidation of the complex interrelationships between property institutions and economic performance. As the term *neoinstitutionalist-heterodox* suggests, this is a somewhat ill-defined group, the product of diverse intellectual influences. In order to place these economists and their contributions in perspective, it is necessary, first, to consider how concepts of property have been handled by earlier schools of economic thought and by contemporary non-institutional economists.

John Locke, Adam Smith, and the classical economists, the neoclassical economists, and the Chicagoans developed and sharpened an economic theory which found social virtue in the outcome of myriad independent decisions, each based on individual self-interest.[1] While self-interest was the motivating force behind individual decisions, individual ownership and control of resources were essential in order to permit the decentralization of allocative decisions. The competitive, laissez-faire, free enterprise system, which has served generations of mainstream economists as both a subject for study and a utopian ideal, requires the existence and wide distribution of private property.

Not only does the laissez-faire system guarantee all manner of desirable

The author is Professor of Agricultural Economics, University of Kentucky, Lexington.

1

economic outcomes (its adherents tell us), but also it is compatible with the highest conceivable degree of human freedom to do what one wants with one's self and one's property within a framework of minimal restrictions essential for the common good.[2]

Private property has been the keystone of mainstream classical, neoclassical, and Chicagoan economic theory and ideology for more than two centuries. Yet, curiously, neither the classical nor neoclassical schools undertook a detailed analysis of the intricacies of existing property institutions, or the development of property institutions over time. It seemed that these economists were satisfied with a highly idealized concept of property; provided that property was in some broad sense privately owned and transferable, they were not especially curious about how existing property institutions might differ from that idealized concept.

The Institutionalists

By the end of the nineteenth century, the marginalists, Austrian and neoclassical, had set mainstream microeconomics on a path from which it has deviated little through the present century. Its methods had become deductive, relying on abstraction to permit the drawing of conclusions from highly simplified models of the economic system, assuming that human motivations can be adequately represented as a unidimensional, hedonistic self-interest. These models were adaptable not only to verbal logic but also to that form of symbolic logic called mathematics; and mathematical economics flourished, providing precise answers to questions which were necessarily framed with more cognizance of the needs of mathematical analysis than the complexity of the real world.

This methodology was productive, both of precise theorems with respect to abstract and simplified models of the real world and of hypotheses which could be tested empirically. However, it was inevitable that some would be dissatisfied, since it seemed more an exercise of considerable abstract beauty than a study of the economic problems of Western man struggling to survive in the economic system in which he found himself. Not only were marginalist methods systematically unrealistic, but also they seemed to have a systematic conservative bias. Hard questions about the structure of the economic system and the way in which it generates economic opportunity were not asked, or were asked in such a way as to guarantee answers, such as the marginal factor productivity theory of distribution, which seemed too close to saying: Whatever is, is right.

Toward the end of the nineteenth century several writers, later to be identified as institutionalists, began to question neoclassical methodologies in the most fundamental ways.[3] The early institutionalists were identified with the following: a contempt for abstract theorizing;[4] a concern that institutional realities be addressed rather than assumed away, and treated as variables rather than givens; a concern with human purposes of economic activity, that is, with ends rather than means alone; an evolutionary rather than static approach, which viewed the economic-institutional system as highly complex, interactive, and always in a state of adjustment to changing conditions; and an interventionalist-reformist approach to policy and institutional design. Where the neoclassicals saw a harmony of interests arising through voluntary exchange from the interactions of independent and entirely selfish individuals, the institutionalists, working from a much more complex concept of human motivation and social organization, saw conflict as the predominant economic phenomenon.

The institutionalist approach was very fruitful of insights, but less fruitful of testable hypotheses. Its diversity resisted systematization,[5] and its lack of systematization was a major reason for its relatively meager influence on twentieth-century economics.

However, this is not the place for a detailed evaluation of the institutionalist contribution.[6] Rather, we must focus on property institutions and economic analysis. We pass over Thorstein Veblen's devastating critique of neoclassical economics, and the tireless data collection and naïve empiricism of Wesley C. Mitchell, to concentrate on the legal economic tradition of John R. Commons. Our focus is on Commons's contributions to institutional economics and his influence on land economics.[7]

Commons's legal economics, which he viewed as a branch of sociology in which the theories of law and economics were to be coordinated,[8] is basic to an understanding of how the institutionalists and land economists viewed property. In the face of material scarcity, as Commons saw it, self-interest breeds conflict and disorder. Men insist on private ownership, which is a person-to-person relationship with respect to property and is based on coercion. Social classes arise as men with similar ownership patterns perceive their common interests. But private ownership does not stifle conflicts of interest; class conflicts replace some person-to-person conflicts. Then, organized and unorganized institutions emerge to permit conflict resolutions and to provide security for some claims and aspirations.[9]

Institutions are defined as collective action in control, liberation, and expansion of individual action; institutional forms are unorganized customs and organized going concerns.[10] For Commons, the basic unit of analysis is the transaction, which involves alienation and aquisition of the rights of property and liberty created by society and which therefore must be negotiated between the parties concerned before production, exchange, and consumption can take place.[11] The institutional framework makes the transaction feasible by providing the parties with reasonably sure expectations of performance. By establishing and enforcing working rules, the institutional framework reduces the complexity of daily life by making many conceivable kinds of transactions unnecessary.[12]

While the institutional framework limits and controls man in his pursuit of his selfish ends, it liberates him in at least two ways: by relieving him from the need endlessly to make and enforce specific agreements about everything with everyone, and by providing him with some secure rights and placing some limitations on the actions of others which might impinge upon him.

Commons rejected the Lockean concept of natural rights. To him, rights are relative, evolutionary, and subject to change as power relationships and societal needs change. The process of evolution of working rules is not, however, subject to a Darwinian natural selection and survival of the fittest. Rather, they evolve as a result of what Commons called "artificial selection," the outcome of deliberate collective action. Thus, the responsible social scientist should be not only an observer but also a reformer, identifying and consciously working for institutional changes which would redress imbalances in power relationships and correct injustices.

Commons's concept of working rules was a major contribution to legal analysis. Working from ideas attributable to Wesley N. Hohfeld, he developed a schema which allowed the analysis of working rules as a general structure of authority relationships.[13] The *right* of party A (to act) imposes a *duty* on party B to act in accordance with the right being asserted. But rights are subject to limits. The limit of A's right is his *exposure,* which provides a *liberty* for B. Officialdom has *powers* which place *liabilities* on citizens. The limit of liability is *immunity,* and the immunity of a citizen provides a *disability* for the official by limiting his power. None of these (right, duty, and so forth) is absolute or infinite. Each has its limits as well as its correlatives.

Institutions, while themselves the creation of man, tend to shape man by influencing his patterns of thought, behavior, and expectations. In aggregate, working rules establish a social framework specifying how economic, social, and spiritual life is organized. Thus, man shapes institutions and is shaped by them. Commons's model, then, while pregnant with profound insights, was fundamentally insoluble, since everything was both endogenous and variable. For this reason, it resisted systematization and was not especially productive of testable hypotheses. Its weakest attributes were precisely those qualities most highly prized by twentieth-century mainstream economists. Commons insisted that his legal economics was in no way an alternative to mainstream economics, but a complement intended to round it out and permit the achievement of its fullest potential.[14] However, he failed to integrate his own and mainstream economics, and no subsequent scholar has managed to complete the task.[15]

While mainstream economic theorists did not seem to know quite what to do with Commons, his ideas were influential among certain applied groups, including land, labor, and international development economists, and those marketing economists who work with the structure-conduct-performance paradigm. The land economics which flourished from the late nineteenth century until the 1950s combined four major influences: (1) a Jeffersonian rural fundamentalism, (2) Ricardian and Marshallian doctrines which identified land as the uniquely fixed resource, (3) history as a methodological orientation, and (4) empiricism as a method.[16] The latter two influences are unadulterated institutionalism. In addition, while some of the earlier land economists had been criticized for an overly disinvolved descriptive approach,[17] the later land economists (as did Commons[18]) gravitated toward an instrumentalist philosophy of science not unlike that of John Dewey.

It is instructive to compare the land economics approach to the mainstream neoclassical approach as they stood, say, around 1950. Some major differences may be noted.

First, the land economist (L) viewed the economic system as a vast interactive whole, in a continuous state of evolution. He resisted the neoclassical (N) economist's deductive methodology and its emphasis on abstraction. L's approach was historical and descriptive; he attempted, unsuccessfully, to achieve systematization through classification.

Second, L was conscious of existing institutions and their powers of self-preservation. N had little patience with institutions, assuming away the existence of those he (sometimes mistakenly) thought insignificant. He was apparently confident in his expectations that the collective common sense would do away with inefficient public sector institutions when their inefficiency was revealed, all the while maintaining a remarkable equanimity in the face of private sector organizations which departed from his beloved competitive model.

Third, L viewed the planning horizon as long term and saw the need for proper resource management for the benefit of future generations. N rejected the idea of public sector planning and seemed confident that the power of bequest gave private decision makers a sufficient stake in the future. N was suspicious of theories of conservation,[19] and he was thor-

6   Alan Randall

oughly repulsed by concepts of trusteeship.[20]

Fourth, while the concept of interdependency was basic to L, it was N who defined and analyzed the nature of externality.

Fifth, L was preoccupied with land tenure institutions. To the extent that he was a reformer, he was a land reformer, seeking to open up economic opportunity to the masses. N was inclined to believe that the marginal factor productivity theory of distribution ensured that each was already getting about what he deserved.

Sixth, when the existing institutional structure was clearly promoting inefficiency, or other undesirable consequences. N's instinct was to clean up the institutional structure, simplify it, and bring it into closer correspondence with the competitive ideal. L, on the other hand, was inclined to propose the imposition of yet another layer of decision making to solve the problem.[21]

Just as the institutionalists, being basically out of step with twentieth-century fashions in scientific methodology, lost the academic contest so badly to the neoclassical microeconomists that they barely avoided extinction, surviving only in a few embattled enclaves, the land economists came under increasing attack among agriculture and natural resource oriented economists.[22] Not only institutionalism, but also the study of institutions, fell under disrepute.

The Property Rights Approach

Considering the fundamental importance of institutions to economic systems, it would have been surprising if the economics discipline could have maintained forever its insouciance toward institutions. And, considering the dominance of neoclassical methods (in all but the macroeconomic area), it was not surprising that the next major attack on institutional questions came from neoclassical economists. This time, it was taken seriously by the economics profession.

The seminal article is usually considered that of Ronald Coase [1960], although it was less of a clean break with the past than its enthusiasts suggest.[23] A voluminous literature on what came to be called the property rights approach sprang up. Since this literature has been reviewed extensively,[24] a brief summary of some of its major characteristics is presented here.

The property rights (PR, or sometimes PR-PC to signify property rights–public choice) approach is entirely consistent with neoclassical microeconomics and represents an extension of price theory, Chicago style, to an awesome range of concerns: history and cultural anthropology;[25]

private and public civil law;[26] criminal law,[27] comparative economic systems;[28] management of complex corporations, not-for-profit firms, and bureaucracies;[29] regulation of business;[30] the theory of clubs and organizations;[31] the behavior of legislative bodies; [32] and economic justice, constitutional choice, and the theory of the state.[33] It assumes a unidimensional, hedonistic model of human motivation, determines the most advantageous action for each participant, and assumes each will behave that way. This, of course, is entirely consistent with the microeconomic theories of production, consumption, and exchange and with the welfare concept of Pareto-efficiency.[34]

The PR-PC approach is militantly individualistic and opposed, in principle, to the notion of a social welfare function. Thus, it tends to see Pareto-efficiency and Pareto-safety as the only acceptable welfare criteria.

Not surprisingly, the practitioners of this approach see virtue in the classical capitalist firm, the laissez-faire system, and the minimal state. If there is one normative statement which sums up their position it is this: The opportunity for trades, of all types, should be maximized. I am convinced that much of the early success of this group in attracting attention can be attributed to the combination of their neoclassical orthodoxy with their fascinating and somewhat heretical habit of visualizing potential trades in situations where trading is illicit or, at least, not customary.

Accordingly, PR-PC practitioners prescribe the establishment of non-attenuated property rights,[35] which maximize the opportunities for trade and ensure that trading outcomes are Pareto-efficient, as the solution to any and all perceived economic and/or institutional problems. Institutional changes which encourage efficiency and minimize transaction costs (the costs, broadly conceived, of making and enforcing decisions) are viewed with favor, while changes which redistribute rights are viewed with suspicion.

The PR-PC school is hostile to regulation, in general and in particular, and seems over time to be growing bolder in the expression of that hostility.[36]

It has developed its own (untestable) hypothesis about the evolution of institutions, of the Darwinian natural selection type, called the "induced institutional innovations" hypothesis.[37]

While the PR-PC approach has been used to generate a multitude of tautological propositions, it has, on occasion, been used to generate empirically testable hypotheses.[38]

The property rights approach represented a major neoclassical attack on institutional questions and generated substantial interest among economists in these questions. While institutional economics remained in dis-

8   Alan Randall

repute, the study of institutions using a price theory approach became not only respectable but also quite fashionable.

The Neoinstitutionalists

Since 1960, many economists who would reject the labels of "thoroughly unreconstructed institutionalist" and "totally committed Chicagoan" have been active in the study of property institutions and economic behavior. A number of these could be loosely classified as neoinstitutionalist-heterodox, a title as unsatisfying as it is unpronounceable. Given the difficulty of defining this group, Figure 1 offers a diagramatic representation of my view of the place of neoinstitutionalism in the history of economic thought about property.[39] Briefly, I see neoinstitutional economics as having antecedents in institutionalist thought, but as having internalized most of the theory and methodology of neoclassical economics.[40] Perhaps the major difference in the thinking of the neoinstitutionalists and the Chicagoans of today is that the former are more acutely aware than the latter of the limitations of neoclassical economics as an analytical framework and its inadequacy as a theology.[41] Neoinstitutional economists are quite comfortable with at least some elements of the PR-PC way of thinking, while they find themselves in direct conflict with some of the more directly Chicago-derived elements of that approach.

I suspect that several whom I have defined as neoinstitutionalists might be surprised to find themselves thus classified. Many of the younger members of the group had a typical modern graduate training with little or no exposure to institutionalism and were startled to find that some of the doubts they felt with respect to received theory had antecedents in institutionalist thought (some may not yet have found out). It is also possible that some committed institutionalists may be offended that I have used a definition of neoinstitutionalist-heterodox which is so broad as to include almost anyone to the left of Chicago.

The Neoinstitutionalist Critique

The neoinstitutionalist critique of the Chicagoan PR-PC approach takes many directions. Some major elements of this critique are discussed below, moving from the fairly specific to the quite general.

Coase's 1960 article was an attack not on institutionalism but on Pigovian externality theory (one of the few remaining areas of neoclassical microeconomics which allowed a legitimate role for government intervention). It attracted the immediate attention of natural resource economists,

Property Institutions   9

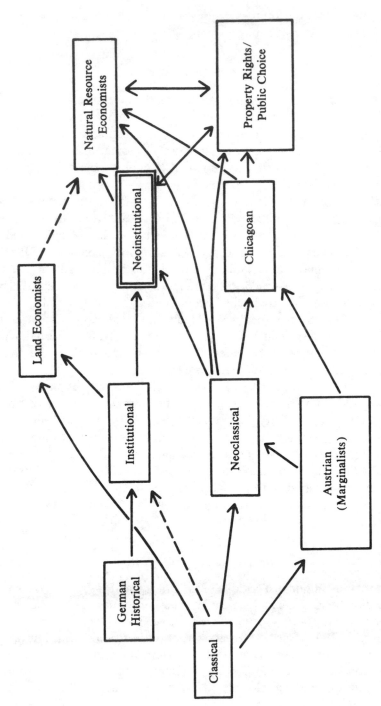

Figure 1. *Interrelationships among some Schools of Economic Thought with Respect to Property*

environmental economists, and the heirs to the Pigovian theoretical tradition. The Coase theorem seemed to imply, and was interpreted by many
to imply,[42] that environmental quality would be provided at the unique optimal level in the market, if only the market were permitted to function
within a structure, any structure, of rights conducive to such outcomes.
Where externality was observed to exist, uncorrected, that must be because the transaction costs of making the correction exceed the net benefits, and therefore the correction itself would be inefficient. Attempts to use
the regulatory or taxation powers of government to intervene in externality situations were misguided.

The environmental economists pointed out the unreality of this approach to large-scale externalities of the type that become social concerns. Where environmental resources are nonexclusive and environmental amenities and disamenities are indivisible (and exhibit public goods
properties), numerous parties must be involved in any potential internaliz-
ing trade. Given the problems created by nonexclusiveness, indivisibility,
and massive transaction costs, the strong possibility exists that some form
of regulation, either direct or via manipulation of prices, would result in
greater social product than the laissez-faire solution.[43] Where indivisibility
is pervasive, Pigovian solutions are, in fact, efficient.[44]

The Coase theorem in its findings of allocative neutrality of liability
rules ignored income effects or failed to see that alternative distributions of
rights directly imply alternative distributions of income and wealth. Different assignments of rights place the responsibility for payment, in the event
of trade, on different parties, and thus the possibility of trade under different rights assignments is strictly limited by different sets of budget constraints.[45] Externalities which are Pareto-irrelevant under one set of rights
may be internalized under another.[46] This finding, together with those reported in the previous paragraph, reduces proponents of a strict Coase
theorem of allocative neutrality to statements such as "assuming zero
transactions costs and no income effects, the assignment of rights is al-
locatively neutral"; these have a distinct "if pigs could fly" character.[47]
Furthermore, E. J. Mishan [1971] and others have found an intolerable
moral and ethical insensitivity in an approach which sees no economic
distinction between rules which place the burden of the costs of pollution
control on polluters and receptors.

These rather specific concerns about the Coase theorem and environmental policy are capable of generalization to the whole corpus of the PR-
PC literature.

The PR-PC analysis is, like most of neoclassical economics, value laden
and in ways which tend to be implicit rather than explicit. Since it addresses

itself to institutions, those devices through which a society gives effect to its values as working rules, the value laden nature of this analysis takes on added importance.

The PR-PC school claims to have developed a positive approach to institutional analysis, deliberately avoiding the kind of "playing god" inherent in social welfare function formulations.[48] Such claims have an element of self-delusion. For example, it is clear from the lengthy interchange between James Buchanan and Warren Samuels that Buchanan had a tendency to see positivism in value laden analyses which led to normative conclusions congenial to him, whereas he saw normativism in (relatively) value free analyses which may give aid and comfort to readers holding normative positions uncongenial to him.[49]

Let us consider, first, the value elements inextricably embedded in the so-called positive PR-PC analysis and, then, the values applied to admittedly normative PR-PC analyses. The PR-PC analysis maximizes product, within the confines of existing opportunity sets. Income, wealth, and the distribution of power, rights, and entitlements are held constant. The needs of those with insufficient endowments are Pareto-irrelevant, and the failure to meet those needs casts no shadow on Pareto-efficiency. Slavery must have been efficient; if not, the slave could have mortgaged his expected lifetime earnings and bought his freedom (or, more precisely, some small residual thereof after the banker had been paid off). Such presumptive efficiency analyses, which maximize that which is itself a function of the status quo, must inevitably tend to strengthen and entrench that status quo, an effect which has been called conservative reinforcement.[50] For such analyses to have any prescriptive power, the endowments of income, wealth, and rights, which are held constant, must be assumed proper and just.

As Allan Schmid [1975] says, the PR-PC inquiry is not addressed to the broader questions of the original and subsequent vestures of rights among people. It speaks only to the secondary question of carying out the logic of the costs implicit in a given rights distribution.

The Chicagoan PR-PC approach is, its proponents claim, aimed at maximizing human freedom.[51] Yet, it relies on a peculiarly atrophied concept of freedom. The poor man whose endowment effectively keeps him out of the market is nevertheless free *because* the market is free. Warren Samuels, working with a paradigm inspired in part by Commons, shows that freedom is defined by the opportunity set, and an income, wealth, or (unattenuated) rights constraint restricts the individual as much as any other constraint.[52] A poor man, and his children, are less free than the rich.

The admittedly normative applications of the PR-PC analysis are aimed

12   Alan Randall

at avoiding coercion and replacing it with a consensual, contractual approach to life within the rights structure and the (occasional) redefinition
of that structure. The analysis avoids the coercion of the social welfare
function approach, but replaces it with the coercion of the status quo distribution. Pareto-safety is proposed as the pervasive social rule, but we
know that Pareto-safety constrains future distribution of a set of possibilities which can be reached by consensual agreement (voluntary exchange)
starting from the status quo. Buchanan opts, he says [1975, p. 27], for the
status quo because "we start from here not from somewhere else." Yet,
even this is unclear since, in a complex dynamic society, the status quo is
not subject to precise definition.[53]

Samuels makes it quite clear that a generally applied rule of Pareto-
safety, if it were desirable (and it is not), would be unworkable since injury, defined as nonconsensual realignment of the opportunity set, is
ubiquitous and is caused by many factors in addition to institutional
change.[54] This argument effectively denies the possibility of universal
Pareto-safe compensation for injury and necessitates determination of the
compensation issue, case by case, on a basis explicitly incorporating ethical and moral judgments.

A somewhat different and even more general neoinstitutional attack on
the PR-PC school claims that the latter does not really understand the
nature of institutions.[55] These are not all *property* and not all *rights*.[56]
Failure to understand the complex nature of institutions is directly responsible for some of the simplistic analyses and naïve recommendations
emanating from the PR-PC school. Perhaps, these scholars are only a little
less guilty than their neoclassical forebears of abstracting away from institutional reality, even in the study of institutions.

The amorality of much PR-PC scholarship is not viewed by critics as a
welcome escape from normative methodological traps, but as symptom of
failure to understand the fundamental nature of institutions. As Commons
knew, institutions express a society's value system and give it effect in the
form of working rules. As such they tend to shape the individual's habits of
thought and action and his expectations. However, in order to be reasonably stable, institutions must be broadly consistent with the ethical values
of the society. Man responds positively to institutions he sees as ethically
right and openly or surreptitiously undermines those he sees as wrong.
When institutions are in harmony with a broad social consensus about
what is right and wrong, the day-to-day transactions of individuals and
groups will proceed smoothly; when that is not the case, defiance and perhaps social upheaval and insurrection will result. The failure of the PR-PC
scholars to understand this seriously undermines their analysis.[57]

The PR-PC concept of property rights emphasizes the role of these rights in providing a structure of incentives and facilitating trade. Yet, the social purposes of property rights in securing expectations and protecting the right holder from arbitrary actions of the sovereign,[58] and from any need to consider the claims of the dispossessed,[59] are at least equally important to a complete understanding of institutions. Thus, the neoclassical preoccupation with means rather than ends limits the ability of its adherents to understand working rules which institutionalize both means and ends.[60] In this context, Commons's model of institutional evolution by deliberate social selection is so very much less naïve than the Darwinian models of induced institutional innovations.[61]

Finally, one must note that the PR-PC analysis, in the hands of many of its practitioners, has a palpable air of unreality about it. Institutions are divided into two sets: attenuated and nonattenuated. In our increasingly regulated mixed economy, the nonattenuated set is empty or nearly so. Yet, that so often is where the analysis rests. With a smugness which arises from a sense of being one of the chosen few sheep in a world populated with goats, they admonish society to go unattenuate its institutions.[62] I, along with H. L. Mencken, am suspicious of simple solutions. But, regardless of that, the tendency of the PR-PC scholars to concentrate on the empty set has the result of excluding them from much of the action in real world policy analysis.

A Neoinstitutional Alternative?

It is clear that the neoinstitutionalists have a critique of the PR-PC approach, and the best of it is a wide-ranging, relevant, and fundamentally sound critique. At the very least, the economist considering application of the PR-PC approach to any real world problem must be familiar with that criticism, for the caveats it provides should save him from numerous pitfalls.

But do the neoinstitutionalists have a coherent alternative to the PR-PC formulation? Joseph Spengler [1974] notes that the institutionalists failed to develop a recognizable and widely accepted definition and a delimitation, both intellectually satisfying and persuasive, of institutional economics. Surely that applies, and to an even greater degree, to the neoinstitutionalists we have been discussing. However, is it essential that institutionalism, or neoinstitutionalism, define itself as something clearly separate and apart from mainstream economics? Commons did not seem to think so; instead, his dream seemed to be an institutionalism which would complement and complete mainstream economics.[63] The resulting prod-

14   Alan Randall

uct would be distinguishable from, and superior to, existing neoclassical formulations.

Perhaps the more appropriate question is: What creative contributions have the neoinstitutionalists made toward such a distinct alternative formulation of economics? Much of the critique has been creative. The environmental economists' response to the Coase theorem has improved environmental economics and policy. Samuels's analysis of property rights as part of the system of power has facilitated understanding of property rights and permitted analysis (albeit nonquantitative) of diverse questions ranging from the appropriate policies with respect to compensation to the proper allocation of public sector intellectual resources among research topics. [64]

Neoinstitutionalists have drawn attention to important, but perhaps unnoticed, manifestations of property,[65] and they have developed new, different, and equally testable alternatives to PR-PC hypotheses.[66] This activity is to be encouraged, since institutionalists (neo, or otherwise) need to elude their twin albatrosses: the charges that their methods are not "scientific" and that their forte is criticism and dissent, but not creativity.

A recent article points the way to a major potential contribution by showing conclusively that alternatives exist between the poles of exclusive private property and *res nullius,* no one's property.[67] There are numerous possible arrangements, all in the attenuated set and thus ignored by many PR-PC scholars, which are workable and not terribly inefficient. Some of these arrangements, given the societies in which they exist and the resources to which they are applied, are more nearly in accord with social customs, accepted ethical norms, and the needs for intergenerational equity in resource conservation than exclusive, private property institutions would be. There is a definite need for economists, using rigorously formulated models and the most powerful quantitative methods, to examine systematically these viable and socially acceptable institutional alternatives which have been unceremoniously cast into the attenuated set and dismissed by the PR-PC school. The unattainable (but Pareto-efficient) "best" must not be permitted to divert attention from the attainable good.

A Neoinstitutional-Mainstream Synthesis?

A neoinstitutional-mainstream synthesis seems a more appropriate goal than a neoinstitutional alternative. The function of neoinstitutionalism must be to inform, humanize, and thus improve mainstream economics, rather than to supplant it. While the creative contributors mentioned above do not provide even a beginning to a distinguishable alternative formulation of economics, they do suggest possibilities for a neoinstitutional-mainstream synthesis. More generally, several writers in the symposium on Commons and J. M. Clark which appeared in this journal,[68] including R. A. Gonce and Victor Goldberg, see opportunities for a synthesis of Commons's ideas with the PR-PC analysis. In particular, a leavening of Commons would liberate the PR-PC school from its excessively restrictive view of institutions as property rights, with no clear distinctions among types of working rules and no clear concept of the limits imposed on individual prerogatives by the structure of authority relationships.

Vincent Ostrom [1976] optimistically envisions a productive new generation of work which will array theoretical arguments, reach conclusions, and, through the chain of logical inference, formulate testable hypotheses. If competing theories can be used to derive contradictory conclusions, then the stage is set for empirical research to test multiple alternative hypotheses. Ostrom sees the possibility that Commons's structure can be used either directly to derive testable hypotheses different from those emanating from pure PR-PC analyses, or to inform and modify current PR-PC analyses in order to derive alternative hypotheses. Through the careful derivation and testing of such hypotheses, a neoinstitutional-mainstream synthesis may develop, to the general benefit of economic science and public policy.

Joseph Spengler [1974] suggests a paradigm which he believes will permit the development of a systematic approach to the analysis of institutions, while retaining the desirable features of institutionalism. He looks at the total social system, S, and considers interactions within and between its subsets: the allocative system, a; the institutional matrix, m; the political system, p; and a nondescript subset of residual systems, r. Given that Spengler's analysis of this system is intended only to suggest starting points, it is successful. However, it is not clear how we will proceed from there.

One likely possibility, perhaps, is via the analytical methods for the rigorous study of resource allocation mechanisms, which have been reviewed by Leonid Hurwicz [1973]. These methods are in an early stage of development, but show promise. They rely on a sophisticated mathematics to study, for example, the information networks and incentive systems which guide interactions within and between organizations. The irony is that, if this approach is ultimately successful, it will render the PR-PC approach as exemplified by the work of, say, Harold Demsetz technologically obsolete in much the same way that rigorous microtheory and mathematical economics overwhelmed institutionalism earlier in this century.

16   Alan Randall

Notes

1. See the Chicago School symposium, *Journal of Economic Issues* 9 (December 1975) and 10 (March 1976).
2. See, for example, F. A. Hayek [1948], Frank Knight [1960], and Milton Friedman [1962].
3. The institutionalists, of course, were not the first. The German historical school, which was antecedent to the institutional school, was based on a profound distaste for abstract theorizing and a preference for historical-empirical methods.
4. As H. H. Liebhafsky [1976b] points out, and as J. J. Spengler [1974] suggests, the early institutionalists exhibited not only a contempt for abstract theory but also a failure to understand the more intricate elements of the neoclassical theory which dominated mainstream thought. This limited the institutionalist analysis and generated an almost insurmountable communications gap with those they were trying to reform.
5. See Spengler [1974, p. 887].
6. For such an evaluation, brief but comprehensive and insightful, one could scarcely do better than read Spengler [1974].
7. In this context, we must acknowledge the seminal contribution of Richard T. Ely, who has been called the father of both institutionalism and land economics.
8. John R. Commons [1934].
9. See R. A. Gonce [1971].
10. Commons [1931].
11. Ibid.
12. Without effective institutions, economic transactions would be limited to physical exchanges in instantaneous time.
13. See Vincent Ostrom [1976] for an excellent exposition.
14. See, for example, Commons [1931, p. 648].
15. Commons's "theoretical structure remains exactly where he left it: a tangled jungle of profound insights" (Boulding [1957, p. 8]).
16. See Walter E. Chryst and W. B. Back, in W. L. Gibson, R. J. Hildreth, and Gene Wunderlich [1966].
17. Leonard E. Salter [1948].
18. See Liebhafsky [1976b].
19. For example, see S. V. Ciriacy-Wantrup [1952].
20. For example, see John F. Timmons and John M. Cormack [1970].
21. Parenthetically, one cannot help but observe that while N may have won the battle for the hearts and minds of his fellow economists, L and the institutionalists were victorious in postdepression U.S. politics.
22. For example, see Gibson, Hildreth, and Wunderlich [1966], a compendium of essays designed to hasten the reconstruction of the land economists. According to the various authors, the land economists were to be purged of the habits of tedious description and exhaustive classification. The instrumentalist approach of Dewey was to be exorcised and replaced by Karl Popper's [1957] scientific method, bolstered by the latest computerized techniques of quantitative analysis.
23. Ronald Coase, as early as 1937, had laid part of the foundation for his

1960 argument. Frank Knight, in many of his writings, had developed most of the essential structure of what came to be called the Coasian approach. Commons [1924] and J. M. Clark [1926] anticipated major parts of the Coasian argument. See Goldberg [1976b].

24. For a quick sampler, see the panegyric by Eirik Furubotn and Svetozar Pejovich [1972], the vehement attack by Liebhafsky [1976a], and the gentler critiques by Goldberg [1974] and this author [1975].
25. See, for example, Douglas North [1973] and Harold Demsetz [1967].
26. For example, Coase [1960].
27. For example, Gordon Tullock [1971] and Richard Posner [1972].
28. For example, the articles by Furubotn and Pejovich, individually and jointly, referenced in Furubotn and Pejovich [1972].
29. For example, Armen Alchian and Harold Demsetz[1972] and Roland McKean in Wunderlich and Gibson [1972].
30. For example, Posner [1975].
31. For example, Mancur Olson [1965].
32. For example, Tullock [1959] and James Buchanan and Tullock [1962].
33. For example, Buchanan and Tullock [1962] and Buchanan [1973].
34. "Microeconomic theory properly developed is the property rights approach" (Furubotn and Pejovich [1972, p. 1157]).
35. See Steven Cheung [1970], Furubotn and Pejovich [1972], and this author [1975].
36. Witness the progress of Coase from [1960] to [1974].
37. See Yujiro Hayami and Vernon W. Ruttan [1971].
38. The *Journal of Law and Economics* has published a number of articles testing such hypotheses.
39. Figure 1 is specialized in its focus on property and economic thought. Thus, it includes the categories land economists and natural resource economists and excludes Keynesians. The double border of the neo-institutional box does not denote either importance or impermeability, but functions only to draw attention to the primary subject of this essay.
40. This is consistent with Allan Gruchy's [1969] definition of neoinstitutional economics.
41. Liebhafsky [1976a] emphasizes this last point.
42. For example, Demsetz [1964].
43. See Allen Kneese [1971], E. J. Mishan [1971], and this author [1974b].
44. William J. Baumol and Wallace E. Oates [1975].
45. Mishan [1971] and this author [1971].
46. This term is attributable to Buchanan and W. C. Stubblebine [1962].
47. Nevertheless, some valuable insights in the Coase [1960] article have stood the test of time: the view of rights as factors of production; the reciprocal nature of costs; that efficient correction of externality will not, in general, involve its elimination. Notwithstanding Goldberg's [1976b] argument that few of these insights are original to Coase, it remains true that the article served a major educational role within the economics profession.
48. See Robert D. Tollison, in Buchanan and Tollison [1972].
49. See Buchanan [1972], Samuels [1972], and Buchanan and Samuels [1975].

18   Alan Randall

50. Samuels [1974a].
51. Compare Milton Friedman [1962].
52. In Wunderlich and Gibson [1972].
53. Samuels [1974a].
54. Ibid.
55. Although the property rights scholars often discuss institutions, and William Breit [1976] called a number of them "institutionalists," Spengler [1974] makes it clear that institutional economics needs to be distinguished from mere economic discussion of institutions.
56. See Gonce [1976], Goldberg [1976a], Leibhafsky [1976b], and Lowry [1976]. Commons's analysis of working rules, discussed above, is clearly superior to the PR-PC specification.
57. For example, Tullock [1971] and William Landes and Richard Posner [1975].
58. See Don Kanel [1975].
59. See Allan Schmid [1975].
60. See Gruchy [1969].
61. Compare Hayami and Ruttan [1971].
62. Instead of repairing the model to conform to the real world, the burden of conformity is placed on the real world (Samuels [1975]).
63. Commons [1934].
64. See Samuels, in Wunderlich and Gibson [1972], Samuels [1974b], and Randall [1974a].
65. For example, Bruce Yandle [1975].
66. For example, Philip R. Coelho's [1976] equally plausible, but quite different, alternative to the Alchian-Demsetz [1972] analysis of tenure in the not-for-profit firm and the Buchanan-Devletoglou [1970] analysis of the university.
67. S. V. Ciriacy-Wantrup and Richard Bishop [1975].
68. *Journal of Economic Issues* 10 (December 1976).

References

Alchian, Armen, and Harold Demsetz. 1972. "Production, Information Costs, and Economic Organization." *American Economic Review* 62 (December): 777–95.
Baumol, W. J., and Wallace Oates. 1975. *The Theory of Environmental Policy*. Engelwood Cliffs: Prentice-Hall.
Boulding, Kenneth. 1957. "A New Look at Institutionalism." *American Economic Review* 47 (May): 1–12.
Breit, William. In Four reviews of David Seckler: *Thorstein Veblen and the Institutionalists*. *Journal of Economic Issues* 10 (December): 943–58.
Buchanan, James. 1972. "Politics, Property, and the Law: An Alternative Interpretation of Miller et al. v. Schoene." *Journal of Law and Economics* 15(October): 437–52.
Buchanan, James. 1973. "The Coase Theorem and the Theory of the State." *Natural Resources Journal* 13 (October): 579.

Buchanan, James, and Nicos E. Devletoglou. 1970. *Academia in Anarchy: An Economic Diagnosis.* New York: Basic Books.

Buchanan, James, and Warren Samuels. 1975. "On Some Fundamental Issues in Political Economy: An Exchange of Correspondence." *Journal of Economic Issues* 9 (March): 15–38.

Buchanan, James, and W. C. Stubblebine. 1962. "Externality." *Economica* 29 (November): 371–84.

Buchanan, James, and Robert Tollison, eds. 1972. *Theory of Public Choice.* Ann Arbor: University of Michigan Press.

Buchanan, James, and Gordon Tullock. 1962. *The Calculus of Consent.* Ann Arbor: University of Michigan Press.

Cheung, Steven. 1970. "The Structure of a Contract and the Theory of a Nonexclusive Resource." *Journal of Law and Economics* 13 (April): 49–70.

Ciriacy-Wantrup, S. V. 1952. *Resource Conservation Economics and Policies.* Berkeley: University of California Press.

Ciriacy-Wantrup, S. V., and Richard Bishop. 1975. " 'Common Property' as a Concept in Natural Resources Policy." *Natural Resources Journal* 15 (October): 713–28.

Clark, J. M. 1926. *Social Control of Business.* Chicago: University of Chicago Press.

Coase, Ronald. 1937. "The Nature of the Firm." *Economica* 4 (November): 386–405.

Coase, Ronald. 1960. "The Problem of Social Cost." *Journal of Law and Economics* 3 (October): 1–44.

Coase, Ronald. 1974. "The Choice of the Institutional Framework: A Comment." *Journal of Law and Economics* 17 (October): 493–96.

Coelho, Philip. 1976. "Rules, Authorities, and the Design of Not-for-Profit Firms." *Journal of Economic Issues* 10 (June): 416–28.

Commons, John R. 1924. *Legal Foundations of Capitalism.* New York: Macmillan.

Commons, John R. 1931. "Institutional Economics." *American Economic Review* 21 (December): 649–57.

Commons, John R. 1934. *Institutional Economics.* New York: Macmillan.

Demsetz, Harold. 1964. "The Exchange and Enforcement of Property Rights." *Journal of Law and Economics* 7 (October): 11–26.

Demsetz, Harold. 1967. "Toward a Theory of Property Rights." *American Economic Review* 57 (May): 347–73.

Friedman, Milton. 1962. *Capitalism and Freedom.* Chicago: University of Chicago Press.

Furubotn, Eirik, and Svetozar Pejovich. 1972. "Property Rights and Economic Theory: A Survey of Recent Literature." *Journal of Economic Literature* 10 (December): 1137–62.

Gibson, W. L., R. J. Hildreth, and Gene Wunderlich, eds. 1966. *Methods for Land Economics Research.* Lincoln: University of Nebraska Press.

Goldberg, Victor. 1974. "Public Choice—Property Rights." *Journal of Economic Issues* 8 (September): 555–80.

Goldberg, Victor. 1976a. "Toward an Expanded Economic Theory of Contract." *Journal of Economic Issues* 10 (March): 45–61.

Goldberg, Victor. 1976b. "Commons, Clark and the Emerging Post-Coasian

20   Alan Randall

Law and Economics." *Journal of Economic Issues* 10 (December): 877–93.

Gonce, R. A. 1971. "John R. Commons's Legal Economic Theory." *Journal of Economic Issues* 5 (September): 80–95.

Gonce, R. A. 1976. "The New Property Rights Approach and Commons's 'Legal Foundations of Capitalism.' " *Journal of Economic Issues* 10 (December): 765–97.

Gruchy, Allan. 1969. "Neoinstitutionalism and the Economics of Dissent." *Journal of Economic Issues* 3 (March): 3–17.

Hayami, Yujiro, and Vernon W. Ruttan. 1971. *Agricultural Development: An International Perspective*. Baltimore: The Johns Hopkins Press.

Hayek, Friedrich. 1948. *Individualism and Economic Order*. Chicago: University of Chicago Press.

Hurwicz, Leonid. 1973. "The Design of Mechanisms for Resource Allocation." *American Economic Review* 63 (May): 1–30.

Kanel, Don. 1974. "Property and Economic Power as Issues in Institutional Economics." *Journal of Economic Issues* 8 (December): 827–40.

Kneese, Allen. 1971. "Environmental Pollution: Economics and Policy." *American Economic Review* 61 (May): 153–66.

Knight, Frank. 1960. *Intelligence and Democratic Action*. Cambridge, Mass.: Harvard University Press.

Landes, William, and Richard Posner. 1975. "The Private Enforcement of Law." *Journal of Legal Studies* 4 (January): 1–46.

Leibhafsky, H. H. 1976a. "Price Theory as Jurisprudence: Law and Economics, Chicago Style." *Journal of Economic Issues* 10 (March): 23–43.

Leibhafsky, H. H. 1976b. "Commons and Clark on Law and Economics." *Journal of Economic Issues* 10 (December): 751–64.

Lowry, S. Todd. 1976. "Bargain and Contract Theory in Law and Economics." *Journal of Economic Issues* 10 (March): 1–22.

Mishan, Ezra. 1971. "The Post War Literature on Externalities: An Interpretive Essay." *Journal of Economic Literature* 9 (March): 1–26.

North, Douglas. 1973. *The Rise of the Western World*. London: Cambridge University Press.

Olson, Mancur. 1965. *The Logic of Collective Action*. Cambridge, Mass.: Harvard University Press.

Ostrom, Vincent. 1976. "John R. Commons's Foundations for Policy Analysis." *Journal of Economic Issues* 10 (December): 839–57.

Popper, Karl. 1957. "Philosophy of Science: A Personal Report." In *British Philosophy in Mid-Century*, edited by C. H. Mace. London: George Allen and Unwin.

Posner, Richard. 1972. *Economic Analysis of Law*. Boston: Little, Brown.

Posner, Richard. 1975. "Antitrust Policy and the Supreme Court: An Analysis of Restricted Distribution, Horizontal Merger and Potential Competitive Decisions." *Columbia Law Review* 75 (March): 282–327.

Randall, Alan. 1971. "Market Solutions to Externality Problems: Theory and Practice." *American Journal of Agricultural Economics* 54 (May): 175–83.

Randall, Alan. 1974a. "Information, Power and Academic Responsibility." *American Journal of Agricultural Economics* 56 (May): 227–34.

Randall, Alan. 1974b. "Coasian Externality Theory in a Policy Context." *Natural Resources Journal* 14 (January): 35–54.

Randall, Alan. 1975. "Property Rights and Social Microeconomics." *Natural Resources Journal* 15 (October): 729–48.

Salter, Leonard. 1948. *A Critical Review of Research in Land Economics.* St. Paul: University of Minnesota Press.

Samuels, Warren. 1972. "In Defense of a Positive Approach to Government as an Economic Variable." *Journal of Law and Economics* 15 (October): 453–59.

Samuels, Warren. 1974a. "The Coase Theorem and the Study of Law and Economics." *Natural Resources Journal* 14 (January): 1–34.

Samuels, Warren. 1974b. "Commentary: An Economic Perspective on the Compensation Problem." *Wayne Law Review* 21 (November): 113–34.

Samuels, Warren. 1975. "Introduction: The Chicago School of Political Economy." *Journal of Economic Issues* 9 (December): 585–604.

Schmid, Allan. 1976. "The Economics of Property Rights: A Review Article." *Journal of Economic Issues* 10 (March): 159–68.

Timmons, John F., and John M. Cormack. 1970. "Role of Land Tenure in Use of Land Resources." Journal Paper No. J-6659. Ames: Iowa Agricultural Experiment Station.

Tullock, Gordon. 1959. "Problems in Majority Voting." *Journal of Political Economy* 67 (December): 571.

Tullock, Gordon. 1971. *The Logic of the Law.* New York: Basic Books.

Wunderlich, Gene, and W. L. Gibson, eds. 1972. *Perspectives of Property.* State College: Institute for Research on Land and Water Resources, Pennsylvania State University.

Yandle, Bruce. 1975. "Property in Price." *Journal of Economic Issues* 9 (September): 501–14.

[19]

Jei JOURNAL OF ECONOMIC ISSUES
Vol. VIII No. 4 December 1974

Property and Economic Power as Issues in Institutional Economics

Don Kanel

One of the central themes in John R. Commons's *Legal Foundations of Capitalism* is the distinction between power and property.[1] He makes two key assertions about property. First, it is something taken from the state and vested in individuals: "Taxes are not something taken from private property by the sovereign, but property is sovereignty taken collectively from the King by his tenants" (1, p. 221). Second, property is a protection of the weak against the strong.

Control of material goods (wealth) and other advantages by power is distinct from control by property rights. One who is rich and commands others by power and influence does not need property rights to protect him. The emergence and enforcement of property

The author is Professor of Agricultural Economics and the Land Tenure Center, University of Wisconsin, Madison. He would like to dedicate this article to his two teachers at the University of Wisconsin, Kenneth H. Parsons, who opened to him the ideas of John R. Commons, and Carl M. Boegholt, who introduced him to the ideas of John Dewey. Walter C. Neale at the University of Tennessee, who interested him in the writing of Karl Polanyi, shares many intellectual interests, and their discussions and disagreements have been stimulating and enlightening. In particular, this work was influenced by Neale's article, "Land Is to Rule." The author owes much to his students in the course on institutional economics, particularly to Franco Lombardi of the Institute of Philosophy of Law, University of Genoa, Italy. To his wife, Bettina, he is indebted for her encouragement and for giving him confidence to publish ideas that seemed incomplete.

rights provide the weak with secure possession of home, harvest of fields, and so forth.

In *Legal Foundations* the story of the emergence of property rights begins with English history subsequent to the Norman Conquest in 1066. The initial examples refer to struggles between the barons and the king which attempt to convert royal favors (land grants, tolls, franchises) into secure property rights protected by orderly procedures (court and legislative action with respect to taxation, changes of property rules, taking of property for public purposes, and so forth) (1, pp. 100–108 and chapter 6). The historical setting is a violent age where control over land and subject people is by raw physical power: the ability of a lord and his armed retainers to retain control, to repulse neighboring lords by clash of arms. In such situations possession depends on stalemate between equal power of arms always subject to test by renewed struggles, shifting alliances between lords, revolts from below, and so forth. In Commons's terminology this is a control over physical resources by power and not by property.

In this setting the struggle for property is at first one for secure physical possession. For the humble it is the security of possession of home, fields, and harvest of the fields against armed social superiors. For the powerful it is the security of possessions against the king. In both cases it is a matter of limiting the arbitrary decisions of the powerful (not by equal countervailing physical power, but by orderly procedures of courts and legislative assemblies). In the language of John R. Commons, the transformation is one from unlimited prerogative of kings to sovereignty (constitutional government), property, and liberty (citizenship). Arbitrary physical power of kings is converted into limited power of sovereigns, and rights of property owners and citizens are created by this conversion of arbitrary into constitutional power.

There is a background to these developments that is only implied by Commons. The original raw physical power of the monarchy had to be met and stalemated either by countervailing physical power or by other forces: revolts of subjects; decreased tax revenue; inability to mobilize military force; and increased power of neighboring monarchies which became more powerful by organizing their societies on a different, more stable, and less physically coercive basis. For these reasons a system of social relations and conflicts based on encounters of raw power gave way to institutionalized rules which created sovereignty, property, and citizenship, and the rules of the game shifted from encounters of raw power (warfare and violence) to royal court intrigue, political processes, judicial court cases, and legislation.

While Commons uses historical examples, the accuracy of historical details is not important for his argument. The issue is theoretical rather than historical. The theoretical assertion is twofold: (1) Property, in the sense of physical security in possession of things, emerges as a result of containing arbitrary physical violence and converting it into "constitutionally" restrained monopoly of physical power vested in the state, and (2) property is distinct from power.

In a more generalized sense these relations between diminution of arbitrary power and emergence of property or property-like devices continually reappear in new arenas as social change proceeds. While the original illustrations in Commons dealt with evolution from the unlimited prerogative of kings (raw physical power) to orderly political processes and property as a device for security of physical possessions, this was but a prelude to a discussion to the emergence of economic power and secure property in an economic sense.

Schematically, in an age of raw physical violence, arbitrary physical power is all, property does not exist, and conflict takes the form of threats and fears of war and actual warfare. As a stronger state emerges that monopolizes physical violence, eliminates private physical violence, and institutionalizes legal rules, property emerges as secure possession, and conflict between private parties and between them and the state takes primarily a political and judicial form (although resort to physical violence always lurks as a possibility). In these new forms of conflict there are those who are politically powerful and those who are politically weak (just as earlier there were those who were physically strong or weak). New struggles take place to limit the arbitrary power of the politically strong: court favorites, semi-independent feudatories in earlier times, or political bosses in modern history. These are struggles for democracy, universal suffrage, civil service, control of corruption, party rules, and so forth, and they take three forms. One is directly parallel to confrontations of physical power: Countervailing political power is created to confront and stalemate original political power in order to control it; these struggles use the existing political rules to build new coalitions in order to change political rules. Another form of struggle occurs when the political process fails and there is resort to "older" forms of physical violence (riots, revolts, civil wars) to create the stalemate which may bring changes in political institutions and rules. The third type of struggle is among political contenders when new aspirants attempt to oust others from seats of power without any change in rules; this would be analogous to armed conflict between neighboring lords which changes the fortunes of individuals without changing the system.

The economic evolution of both property and power parallels the above. Commons traces the evolution of the economic dimensions of property through various stages. Initially, property protected only the physical safety and possession of the owner against violent trespass, theft, arbitrary taking by government officials, and so forth (1, pp. 238-39). Then practices of merchants were given court protection by enforcement of promises and negotiability of debt so that owners were protected in their rights to receive the *value* of property in transactions creating or transferring debts (1, pp. 238-40; 246-52). Finally, in the nineteenth century in the United States the meaning of property was further enlarged to protect the taking of the value of property by state regulation. (Owners subject to physical taking of property by the state under eminent domain long have been protected by requirements for just compensation and by the test of public purpose in the uses to which the taken property was to be put, both subject to court review.) In the case of regulation which involved no physical taking but which affected property values, the owners were to be protected by court review of the public purpose of the regulations and reasonableness of the rates (zoning cases; regulation of rates of railroads, warehouses, and other public utilities; maximum hours and minimum wages; and so forth) (1, pp. 11-21).

The emergence of modern fee simple property is a matter of evolution in two sets of relations: the relation between those who become owners and their former superiors, and between those who become owners and their former inferiors. Commons deals primarily with the evolution of the first relation between property owners and those who threatened them from above with arbitrary power. When one looks at the "premodern" relations between latent owners and their inferiors, one sees classes differentiated by status with relations governed by custom. or even relatively equalitarian groups which may become subject to processes of differentiation which enable some members of the group to emerge as property owners. Before the emergence of fee simple property the relation between superior and inferior is one of patron and client, with mutual obligations between each arising out of their status in society. After the emergence of fee simple property, the relation becomes one of landlord and tenant or employer and worker entered into by contract, and the transition from patron to property owner involves the shedding of patronal obligations to clients. The owner assumes only those obligations that he contracts.[2]

We can shift our point of view and analyze social systems in terms of access to livelihood: who controls that access and how it is distributed among classes and families. Before the emergence of fee simple property, controls over access to livelihood are diffused; after the emergence they are vested in clearly defined property owners. In equalitarian systems all members of the group have access to livelihood; in differentiated systems access depends upon power, status, and custom, but again with some access to all. Thus in European manorial (feudal) agriculture the lord as well as the serfs had access to a share of the produce, and the access of the serfs was not by consent of the lord but by virtue of their status; he was not free to dispense with their services. The lord was powerful in relation to the serfs and, if inclined to be arbitrary, was not easily opposed by either the court or the king. Yet his dominance over the serfs and his limited freedom to do with his land as he wished (dispense with the serfs) was controlled more by legitimized and routinized custom than by either raw power or property. Thus the Commons terminology may need to be enlarged beyond the power-property dichotomy because it neglects the stability of relations in legitimized social systems, which do not run primarily by raw power at the same time that they do not have clear fee simple property rights. (Commons recognizes this tangentially by writing of the powerful as juridically unlimited although psychologically limited [1, pp. 100–102], or more properly as culturally limited.) These omissions by Commons would seem grossly deficient to anthropologists, but they are not crucial to his central theme.

The above conception of the emergence of property as the limitation of arbitrary power of superiors and the shedding of obligations to inferiors implies that any of the previously existing classes can emerge as fee simple owners after the transition. Thus the English enclosures vested land ownership in the landed aristocracy, while the French Revolution vested it in the peasants.

Commons's main argument is concerned with the emergence of economic power. The taming of physical power and establishment of orderly political and judicial procedures, the recognition and protection of the economic value of property, all created a basis for preeminence of economic relations between persons. Access to livelihood came to depend upon being hired. There emerged the economically strong and the economically weak. The former are those who control opportunities for jobs and markets and who survive and grow by success in organizing production, adopting new technology, aggregating financial capital, and so forth. By analogy to physical warfare, survival by stalemate, and growth by conquest of feudal lords, one now can speak of economic competition and adaptability, survival and growth of firms, and control of opportunities by successful firms. To the economically weak the problem becomes the unlimited prerogative (arbitrary action) of the economically strong. In the typical relation this is the dependence of the worker on his bosses, from foremen to top management.

Orthodox economic theory misses the issue of economic power because it asks different questions. It views members of society as consumers and asks whether the economic system delivers efficiently what consumers want, given available resources, technology, and consumer wants. The only power question that arises is whether markets are imperfect (monopolistic, oligopolistic, or imperfectly competitive) because this deprives consumers of potentially available output. But a different perspective emerges if members of society are viewed not as consumers, but primarily as weaker and stronger members of the system. The weak are threatened both by the arbitrariness of the strong and by their vulnerability to economic change. The flexibility of a competitive market system, which is seen as good by the insights of orthodox theory (because it efficiently incorporates technological change to enrich members of society as consumers), now can be seen also to contain threats as storms of economic change and uncontrolled decisions of the economically strong force the weaker members of society into unemployment, occupational obsolescence, and so forth. This might be clearer if several analogies are developed between physical violence and economic competition and change. The loss of a job due to the whim of a foreman is analogous to the helplessness of a serf to the exactions of a lord or his bailiff; the loss of crops and livestock to marauding warriors of a neighboring lord is analogous to the situation of employees of a firm which is loosing out to competitors because of poor management: losses suffered at the hands of foreign invaders who adopt a superior military technology are analogous to those suffered by employees of a firm which fails to adopt new technology or adjust to new market conditions.

Selig Perlman, a colleague of Commons's, attempted a distinction between the scarcity-conscious and the opportunity-conscious (4, pp. 239–45). This is a distinction between the weak, who want security and livelihood (and who hope that the system may improve their opportunities), and the strong, who are ambitious for power. He does not imply a neat dichotomized classification of people. Rather, he makes a useful distinction between what people expect of the social systems in which they live. At one extreme are those who need an income from a job so that they can tend their own garden and who seek dignity and respect for themselves on the job. If they live in a system with expanding levels of consumption, they expect to participate in such increases. Their efforts and interests are concer trated on their personal life, their own specific work skills, working conditions, and fellow workers and superiors with whom they have personal dealings. They may have little interest or knowledge in how the system as a whole works, or in the relation of their own little world to the larger units of which they are a part. This does not imply uniformity or lack of intelligence. Some may be very skillful, dependable, knowledgeable, and outspoken and possessed of a great deal of initiative with respect to work skills and interpersonal relations.

At the other extreme are those who either for personal advancement, by virtue of capacity for leadership, or for reasons of ideology concentrate upon opportunities for advancing within the social system or upon modifying the system (looking for loopholes, creating new arrangements, pushing, corrupting, inspiring, agitating, and so forth). These are very much concerned with how the system works; they may be incorrect in their analysis, but they actively probe for weaknesses and opportunities for change. They are engaged in conflict—economic, political, bureaucratic, public opinion—for positions of power.

Acceptance of the system by the weak depends upon its ability to satisfy their needs for security and dignity and to give a reasonably equal chance (compared to other groups) to participate in increasing opportunities. Acceptance of the system by the strong depends upon its ability to satisfy their ambitions and upon their feeling that the struggles for power are conducted according to legitimate rules, that frustrated ambitions in one area can be satisfied by opportunities in other areas or at a later point in time. Not everyone can be satisfied, but what is important for a system is how much erosion of legitimacy occurs as a result of dissatisfaction (leading either to cynical attempts to corrupt or ideological attempts to overthrow).

Commons and Perlman view the rise and objectives of the labor movement as directly parelleling the political struggles for democracy: the weak attempting to convert the arbitrary power of the strong into responsible and constitutionally regulated power. What emerges are property-like devices; Commons and Perlman even use the term "property right in a job." The main devices are seniority and grievance procedures (tenure in academia, civil service procedures in government) whereby the arbitrary right to fire employees is limited by seniority and subject to review by grievance procedures (4, pp. 262-79). Some unions have gone further and gained some control over introduction of technological change by requiring that resulting employment decreases be limited to a rate consistent with normal attrition due to retirements and voluntary changes of employment, with additional provision for large severance payments when workers must be laid off.

In general, conversion of arbitrary into responsible power requires that those adversely affected can ask for reasons, that reasons can be reviewed by third parties, and that all affected, the weak and the strong, can participate in making and changing rules which govern the relations between them. This requires the creation of quasi-judicial and quasi-political institutions in industry and other organizations.

In parallel to other struggles reviewed above, the creation of orderly procedures in labor-management relations required stalemating the unlimited economic powers of management. In struggling against employers, workers resorted to devices available to them: physical violence, strikes, and political activity.

The devices of collective bargaining, seniority, and grievance procedures share out property rights more widely and vest them in groups. In a sense this is a reversal of the movement toward fee simple property which concentrated economic rights in property owners, destroyed or eroded the role of groups in economic affairs (the feudal manor; the Indian village community and its castes; kin, clan, and tribal communities in most parts of the world), and created a property-less working class exposed as *vulnerable individuals* to changing economic conditions. But the unions as groups are much better adapted to an economy of changing technology and changing occupational opportunities. They create some security in the jobs people already have but do not prevent the more ambitious from moving to better opportunities; they leave workers open to pull factors while decreasing their exposure to push factors.

The discussion so far has been about arbitrary and responsible power. But is power necessary? As the discussion above brings out, each kind of social system generates characteristic kinds of power: In an age of violence the powerful were war leaders and armed men, in orderly political systems feudal lords and court favorites, later capable key bureaucrats, still later party bosses and charismatic party leaders and ideologues, in economic affairs merchant princes, captains of industry and finance, union leaders, and so forth. Power is necessary to make each kind of system run; it is a combination of responsibility and the capacity to coordinate and concentrate resources and foresee dangers and opportunities. The European feudal age emerged out of barbarian invasions and the dissolution of the Roman Empire; the situation created opportunities for strong men in the vacuum opened by the disappearance of central authority, but at the same time these strong men were needed to give the peasants some security of life and production. In the university setting, for example, the faculty needs the administration to construct buildings, equip laboratories, ensure that classrooms are cleaned and supplied with chalk, announce class schedules to students, and obtain funds from legislatures, alumni, and foundations. The entrepreneurial function in industry often has been described. So not only do social systems create opportunities which the ambitious can use better than the weaker and less ambitious, but also these opportunities exist because the survival and continuation of a system require powerful roles to be performed.

However, the problem with power is that its wielders are free to use it for their personal purposes. In government, the conceptualization of the separation of public and private functions of government officials has been well developed; the general rule is that office is a public trust and not to be used for private purposes. While this is never fully achieved and new remedies have to be developed as ingenious people find new tempting misuses of public power, the general principle is clear. Similar distinctions apply to any position of power: in industry, in unions, in political parties. In each of these there is a function relevant to what the position holder needs to do for the system, and there are opportunities for the position holder to benefit privately and to act arbitrarily simply because he is powerful. The latter attributes are abuses of power, and in no way are they capacities required to make the system operate successfully. As employers have learned throughout the Western developed world, they can operate successfully with unions, high taxes on income, regulations over issues of stock, and controls on their political activity and without arrogance and vulgar display of great wealth. (This does not mean corporate managers unilaterally will forego exploring opportunities for enrichment under tax and other provisions based, for example, on the capital gains tax.) On the other hand, countries have learned that managerial roles, whether performed by private or public managers (including the managers in socialist economies), are different from those of civil service bureaucrats or political leaders. The former require an aggressiveness, a degree of freedom of action and a kind of leadership distinct from qualities required for the latter roles.

This way of conceiving of power implies that a frequent social problem is abuse of power. Furthermore, likely remedies are those which preserve the necessary power but limit its capacity to act arbitrarily toward those dependant upon the power wielder and to restrain the latter's ability to use power for his personal purposes. A general characteristic of the remedies discussed above is to "consti-tutionalize" power. At the same time it should be realized that such solutions are not for all time. The institutions which constitutionalize one kind of power bring forth new rules of conduct and new powerful roles, whose abuses in turn will need attention.

This conception that power is necessary but prone to abuses contrasts with the ideas of Marx. To him the crucial aspect of capitalist society is the relation between capital and wage labor, the extraction of surplus value from labor, and the alienation of the worker. The latter two phenomena seem to be the major consequences of economic power, in contrast to the argument above that economic power is needed to organize production and that what is problematic are its abuses. Marx argues as follows:

> Nothing can be more foolish than to conceive the *original formation* of capital as if it meant the accumulation and creation of the *objective conditions of production*—food, raw materials, instruments—which were then offered to the *dispossessed* workers. What happened was rather that monetary wealth partly helped to detach the labour power of the individuals capable of work from these conditions. The rest of this process of separation proceeded without the intervention of monetary wealth. Once the original formation of capital had reached a certain level, monetary wealth could insert itself as an intermediary between the objective conditions of life, now "liberated" and the equally liberated, but now also *unfettered and footloose*, living labour powers, buying the one with the other (2, p. 113).
>
> Production based on exchange-value . . . presuppose and produce the separation of labour from its objective conditions. . . . The exchange of equivalents occurs [but it is merely] the surface layer of a production which rests on the appropriation of other people's labour *without exchange*, but under the *guise of exchange*. . . . For the rule of exchange-values . . . presupposes the separation of living labour power from its objective conditions; a relationship to these . . . as someone else's property (2, p. 114).
>
> If labour is once again to be related to its objective conditions as to its property, another system must replace 'hat of private exchange, for as we have seen private exchange assumes the exchange of labour transformed into objects against labour-power, and thereby the appropriation of living labour without exchange (2, p. 115).

"Labour transformed into objects" or "objective conditions of labour" is machinery or capital in general. The "separation of labour from its objective conditions" is essentially consistent with my own brief account of the emergence of fee simple property by the shedding of the patronal obligations to the former social inferiors of the eventual property owners. That this was a despoiling of inferior social classes is also true. But Marx proceeds beyond with the following key assertions: Capital already existed and was not created by monetary wealth; monetary wealth merely inserted itself to reunite, in the production process, the now separated capital and labor; and it thereby appropriated part of the product of labor without an exchange (extraction of surplus value from the worker).

It seems to me that Marx implies that power is unnecessary, at least in the sense that eventually, in a socialist society, labor and capital can be reunited without the need for direction by powerful managers. Again it is a matter of what questions are being asked. The way that Marxist analysis is formulated, major problems in modern society appear to be the economic exploitation of workers, and the power problem is expected to disappear in a classless socialist society with the withering away of the state. Against this I am arguing that the major problem in Western societies, especially in the period of rampant and uncontrolled capitalism of the nineteenth century, was the power of big business. In the modified post-World War II developed welfare states, the powerful and the major problems are somewhat different. The problem of power and its abuses is very much present in the socialist societies that have been created since 1917, with abuses greatest under Stalin and attempts to deal with abuses probably carried farthest in Yugoslavia and in the aborted 1968 attempt at "socialism with a human face" in Czechoslovakia. China seems to be making the most serious attempts to organize a modern society without permanent power holders and without the crystalization of powerful groups and separation of experts and workers. On the basis of my argument this seems an impossible and misdirected task, but the seriousness and magnitude of the Chinese effort makes it a most interesting experiment for confronting the ideas presented here.

The above presentation concludes the main argument. Before closing I want to consider two related areas, the relevance of which I recognize, but which I have not had time or have not been able to work out.

I do not mean to assert that eliminating abuses of power is the only way of reforming social ills, although I think that it is the policy issue more often than is assumed in more radical analyses. One way to classify social problems is to distinguish three kinds of struggles for power: (1) competition for power roles which determines who shall occupy them; (2) conflicts to limit arbitrariness of power by confronting existing with countervailing power in order to modify the rules; and (3) revolutionary power struggles induced by changes in the nature of the social system. This article has been concerned primarily with the second type of change, and, as indicated above, in this kind of change power is constitutionalized without eliminating the crucial roles which power needs to perform for the system. Thus implicit in this is the assumption that the social system itself remains essentially unchanged. But a further implication is a tentative conclusion that there has been no basic system change between nineteenth-century capitalism and modern models of Western welfare states and that basic system changes in this century have occurred only with transformation to socialism. I am not ready to accept fully the last conclusion.

In any case, a distinction should be made concerning the kinds of social changes or needs for change which cannot be cured by limiting abuses of power. Technological change is a powerful force in causing political, social, and economic transformation. I am tempted to use Marxist terminology of base (technological) and superstructure (economic, political, and social) and to distinguish revolutionary struggles for power as arising from a change in the base. Also I am tempted to think of changes in the base as less deliberate, in the sense that many deliberate, separately taken decisions are involved in incorporating new technology, but there is little overall deliberate choice to achieve the changed social system that emerges out of the interactions of separate decisions. An example of this is the transformation brought about by the automobile. While the decisions of a Henry Ford, a state highway commission, and a car purchaser are deliberate, the world that the automobile has created (mobility, the changing role of small towns, large cities and suburbs, change in courting patterns, decline of railroads, highway accidents, and pollution) was unknown and largely unforeseen. Perhaps changes in the base proceed largely in an uncontrolled manner, and the superstructure needs to evolve so as to enable the successful use and adaptation to changing technology. Perhaps different social systems (superstructures) are experiments, more or less successful, competing with each other (in a pattern possibly analogous to biological evolution). The less developed world in particular is an example of many experiments to cope with poverty, population growth, rural-urban migration, technological change, powerful influences of developed countries, tribal and group conflicts, and rapid and uneven social change. There is a casting about for models and modification by local experience. Perhaps there is an initial and somewhat separate task of first groping for a superstructure that works and one which, when established, needs certain key roles to be performed and affords major opportunities to those who successfully can occupy these roles, and subsequently the abuses of this power will need to be corrected.

Another related area is that power can be tamed not only by constitutionalizing it but also by balancing it by creating alternatives for those who depend upon the power wielder. In economics we deal with this by the importance we place on competitive and smoothly functioning markets; in political theory we talk of checks and balances and pluralistic societies. There are many social problems which do not lend themselves to solution by constitutionalizing someone's power; examples of this are pollution, traffic congestion, and so forth. On the other hand, the presence or creation of alternatives still leaves individuals facing an impersonal and faceless world and provides no obvious channels for asking for explanations and for redress.

Notes

1. This article is largely dependent on the ideas of John R. Commons and inspired by them, but is in no sense an exposition or summary of *Legal Foundations of Capitalism* (1924) (Madison: University of Wisconsin Press, 1957). Commons does not really use a dichotomy of property and power. He is, however, the direct source of my presentation describing how the solution of abuses and inequalities of one kind of power sets the stage for the emergence of new kinds of power.

   In general the ideas presented here are the result of reading Commons, selecting some of his ideas, and developing them further in my course on institutional economics. I am aware of interrelations of this material to economic anthropology, other social sciences, and law, but have only limited knowledge of related concepts and studies in those fields. Since I have based this article on my reading of only a few books, this work is incomplete and is primarily a matter of pushing somewhat further the logic of ideas in Commons and a few other works. Yet I believe (or hope) that this presentation contains some ideas which have not been developed in other literature, that it may be useful to some, and that in combination with other ideas it can be developed further by others.

2. While I have not used directly the material from Karl Polanyi, I have been very much influenced by his ideas in developing the argument on the dissolution of patron-client relations between eventual property owners and their social inferiors. Polanyi discusses these issues as the emergence of a market economy; his discussion of the emergence of markets in labor and land is analogous to my discussion of the emergence of fee simple property. See Karl Polanyi, *The Great Transformation* (Boston: Beacon Press, 1957), chapters 3, 4, 5, and 6 and pp. 156–61, 163–65.

   It seems to me that my discussion at this point is also consistent with Marx's statements on the emergence of capital and wage labor as "liberated" from each other. Karl Marx, *Pre-Capitalist Economic Formations* (New York: International Publishers, 1965). See the quotations from him and my discussion of them below.

840   Don Kanel

References

(1) Commons, John R. *Legal Foundations of Capitalism.* 1924. Madison: University of Wisconsin Press, 1957.
(2) Marx, Karl. *Pre-Capitalist Economic Formations.* New York: International Publishers, 1965.
(3) Neale, Walter C. "Land Is to Rule." In *Land Control and Social Structure in Indian History,* Robert Eric Frykenberg, ed. Madison: University of Wisconsin Press, 1969. Pp. 3-15.
(4) Perlman, Selig. *A Theory of the Labor Movement.* 1928. New York: Augustus M. Kelley, 1966.
(5) Polanyi, Karl. *The Great Transformation.* 1944. Boston: Beacon Press, 1957.

Name Index